THE CHANGING AUSTRIAN VOTER

Contemporary Austrian Studies

Sponsored by the University of New Orleans and Universitiit Innsbruck

Editors
Günter Bischof, CenterAustria, University of New Orleans
Anton Pelinka, University of Innsbruck

Production Editor Ellen Palli
Copy Editor Jennifer Shimek
Assistant Editor Josef Kostlbauer
Executive Editors Franz Mathis, UNO Coordinator, University of Innsbruck
Robert L. Dupont, Dean, Metropolitan College

Advisory Board

Ingrid Bauer
University of Salzburg
Siegfried Beer
University of Graz
Evan Bukey
University of Arkansas, Fayetteville
Mario Caciagli
University of Florence
Gary Cohen
Center for Austrian Studies
University of Minnesota
Christine Day
University of New Orleans
Wilhelm Kohler
Tübingen University
Jacques Le Rider
University of Paris VIII
Kurt Richard Luther
University of Keele
Andrei S. Markovits
University of Michigan, Ann Arbor

Margareta Mommsen
University of Munich
Hanspeter Neuhold
University of Vienna
Max Preglau
University of Innsbruck
Sonja Puntscher Riekmann
University of Salzburg
Peter Pulzer
Oxford University
Oliver Rathkolb
University of Vienna
Sieglinde Rosenberger
University of Vienna
Dieter Stiefel
University of Vienna
Franz Szabo
Center for Austrian Studies,
University of Albel1a
Ruth Wodak
University of Lancaster

Publication of this volume has been made possible through one time generous post-Hurricane KaIrina grants by the Austrian Ministry of Science and Research as well as the Austrian Ministry of Foreign Affairs through the Austrian Cultural Forum in New York. The Austrian Marshall Plan Anniversary Foundation in Vienna has also supponed the production of this volume. Metropolitan College al the University of New Orleans and the AlIslalldsaml of the University oflnnsbruck have provided additional financial support. The University of Chicago Press has gramed pennission to reprint David Luft's lead essay.

THE CHANGING AUSTRIAN VOTER

CONTEMPORARY AUSTRIAN STUDIES
VOLUME 16

GÜNTER BISCHOF
FRITZ PLASSER
EDITORS

TRANSACTION PUBLISHERS
NEW BRUNSWICK (U.S.A.) AND LONDON (U.K.)

Copyright © 2008 by Transaction Publishers, New Brunswick, New Jersey.

All rights reserved under International and Pan-American Copyright Conventions. No part of this book may be reproduced or transmitted in any form or by any means, electronic or mechanical, including photocopy, recording, or any information storage and retrieval system, without prior permission in writing from the publisher. All inquiries should be addressed to Transaction Publishers, Rutgers—The State University, 35 Berrue Circle, Piscataway, New Jersey 08854-8042. www.transactionpub.com

This book is printed on acid-free paper that meets the American National Standard for Permanence of Paper for Printed Library Materials.

Library of Congress Catalog Number: 2007051037
ISBN: 978-1-4128-0751-7
Printed in the United States of America

Library of Congress Cataloging-in-Publication Data

Bischof, Günter, 1953-
The changing Austrian voter / Gunter Bischof and Fritz Plasser.
    p. cm.—(Contemporary Austrian studies, vol. 16)
  Includes bibliographical references and index.
  ISBN 978-1-4128-0751-7
    1. Elections—Austria—History—20th century. 2. Elections—Austria—History—21st century. I. Plasser, Fritz, 1948- II. Title.

JN2029.B57 2008
324.9436—dc22   2007051037

Table of Contents

INTRODUCTION   1

TOPICAL ESSAYS

Oliver Rathkolb, *The Austrian Voter in Historical Perspective*   12

Fritz Plasser and Peter A. Ulram, *Electoral Change in Austria*   54

Christoph Hofinger, Günther Ogris, and Eva Zeglovits,   79
   It Ain't Over 'til It's Over: Electoral Volatility in Austria
   from the 1970s through 2006

Herbert Dachs, *Regional Elections in Austria from 1986 to 2006*   91

Kurt Richard Luther, *Electoral Strategies and Performance*   104
   of Austrian Right-Wing Populism, 1986-2006

Günther Lengauer, *Framing Campaigns: The Media*   123
   and Austrian Elections

Fritz Plasser and Gilg Seeber, *Austrian Electoral Behavior*   150
   in International Comparison

FORUM
Austrian Experts Interpret the National Elections
of October 1, 2006

Rudolf Bretschneider, *Political Discontent, Negative*   179
   Campaigning and an Overrated Monster: A Short
   Comment on the Austrian Parliamentary Elections of 2006

Peter Gerlich, *Europeanization in Disguise*   182

Imma Palme, *Did the ÖVP Lose, or Did the SPÖ Win the 2006 National Parliamentary Election?* — 186

Anton Pelinka, *Who Is the Winner?: The Strategic Dilemma of "the People's Choice"* — 189

Manfred Prisching, *The Conservative Turn to Socialism* — 193

NON-TOPICAL ESSAYS

Peter Ruggenthaler, *A New Perspective from Moscow Archives: Austria and the Stalin Notes of 1952* — 199

Thomas Fischer, *The Birth of the N+NA: Austrian and Swiss Foreign Policy in the CSCE* — 228

REVIEW ESSAYS

Matthew Paul Berg, *Refocusing the Critical Gaze from Sixty Years' Distance: Austrians' Experiences of the Nazi Past in Recent Historical Studies* — 259

Peter Berger, *György's Machine Gun, Ildikós New Car: The Controversial Hungarian Revolution of 1956 Revisited* — 277

Alexander Lassner, *New Scholarship on Austria, Germany, and Italy in the International Area during the 1930s* — 287

BOOK REVIEWS

Thomas Nowotny: Michael Gehler, *Österreichs Aussenpolitik der Zweiten Republik – von der alliierten Besatzung bis zum Europa des 21. Jahrhunderts* — 307

Günter Bischof: Fritz Fellner and Doris A. Corradini, eds., *Österreichische Geschichtswissenschaft im 20. Jahrhundert: Ein biographisch-bibliographisches Lexikon* — 318

ANNUAL REVIEW

Reinhold Gärtner, *Austria 2006* — 328

LIST OF AUTHORS — 337

INTRODUCTION

The Changing Austrian Voter

Fritz Plasser and Günter Bischof

Structural changes in voting behavior are an indicator for social change and societal modernization. In fact, in the course of the last thirty years, with regard to educational and occupational structures, the Austrian electorate developed from a primarily industrially-oriented electorate toward a post-industrial information- and service-oriented one.[1] During the same period, the relations of voters to political parties also changed substantially. While thirty years ago more than 60 percent of the electorate always voted for the same party at national and regional elections, only about every third voter can be classified as a party loyalist in 2006. At the same time, the number of loyal members of political parties was cut in half. Thirty years ago, 25 percent were registered members of a political party; in 2006 only 12 percent were members of political parties. The result is a dramatic erosion of stable party affiliations which clearly shows in Austrian voting behavior. In the National Election of 1975, 95 percent of the voters knew the party for whom they would vote prior to the start of the election campaign; in the 2006 election, a mere 24 percent of the voters had already decided on the party of their choice during the last week of the campaign. Never before had such a high share of "late deciders" existed in the history of Austrian elections.[2]

In the National Election of 1975, only 3 percent voted for another party than they had voted for in the previous election; in 2006 there was a whopping 26 percent of party changers. This was the highest change rate in Austrian elections to date. It shows how much Austrian voting behavior has approached the European mainstream. For example, 28 percent of the voters changed their party at the German parliamentary election of 2005. During the Swedish parliamentary election of 2006, there were 30 percent party changers. Within thirty years, a segmented, party-loyal, *Lager* electorate turned into a highly mobile, issue-driven electorate. In Austria as in the rest of Europe, no longer do *traditional party loyalties* but *competence of parties on issue* count first and foremost.

The erosion of stable party affiliations has simultaneously affected the rate of voting participation. While thirty years ago voter turnout rates still remained constantly above 90 percent, Austria—third behind Italy and Belgium—was, comparatively speaking, among the countries with the highest rates of voter turnout; however, in the 1980s voting participation progressively declined.[3] In 2006, only 78.5 percent participated in the national elections—the lowest voter turnout at national elections so far. In voter participation rates, Austria clearly is approaching the European average, too. In neighboring Germany, with only 77.7 percent of the population voting, the turnout rate at the Parliamentary Elections of 2005 also reached an historical low. Similar declines of voter turnout could also be observed at the recent parliamentary elections in Italy, the United Kingdom, and Sweden. In all of these countries, participation in elections—especially among the younger generation of voters—is not seen as a civic duty anymore. Reasons for declining voter turnout, however, are not only found in traditional political participation repertoires, but also in an increased readiness of politically disappointed and/or annoyed voters to express their protest by demonstrative voting abstinence.

To abstain from casting ballots is only one of several options for angry voters. Angry voters can be directly approached and mobilized by protest parties. Besides the *exit*-option, then, there is also the *voice*-option. This option was realized for the first time in the 1986 National Elections with Jörg Haider. After seizing the leadership of the FPÖ, Haider turned his party into a right-wing, populist party within the short period of ten weeks by directly appealing to voters frustrated with the traditional parties (the SPÖ and ÖVP). The National Elections of 1986 launched a spectacular series of successful elections for the FPÖ under Haider, culminating in the National Elections of 1999, when the FPÖ surpassed the ÖVP with a share of 26.9 percent of the votes. Leading by only several hundred votes, the victory was marginal, but the FPÖ for the first time became the second strongest parliamentary party in Austria. This development in the *right populist movement* in Austrian electoral history left a deep imprint on voting behavior. For instance, the share of blue collar workers voting for Haider and the FPÖ quadrupled between 1986 and 1999. With a share of 47 percent of blue collar voters, the FPÖ became the strongest party among workers in 1999, overtaking the Socialist Party, Austria's traditional labor party.

But the voting behavior of labor was not alone in being gravely impacted by Haider's right-wing populism. Haider's management of fickle emotions and perfunctory impressions increasingly attracted younger generations of voters, too. In the National Elections of 1999, the FPÖ garnered a majority of votes from the electorate below the age of thirty.[4]

The National Elections of 1986, then, marked the beginning of the electoral ascendancy of Haider and the FPÖ. Yet the immediate backlash of this election was the return to a grand coalition between the SPÖ and ÖVP for the first time in twenty years; grand coalitions had governed Austria after World War II from 1945 to 1966. Facing a serious threat from the upstart, right, populist, opposition course of the FPÖ, the traditional, increasingly centrist parties governing Austria were looking for salvation in defensive cooperation and agreed to form a grand coalition under Socialist Chancellors Franz Vranitzky and Victor Klima. The electoral strength of the grand coalition parties—originally with a solid two-thirds majority in parliament—eroded further in the following years in a series of electoral defeats revealing diminishing voter confidence in their can-do spirit.[5] In the National Elections of 1999, the SPÖ and ÖVP again faced severe electoral losses. It marked both the end of the defensive cooperation and of grand coalition governments (1987-1999).

Although the ÖVP only found itself in third position behind the SPÖ and FPÖ in 1999, it agreed to form a coalition government with the FPÖ, with ÖVP leader Wolfgang Schüssel heading the government as chancellor. Haider, the governor of Carinthia, steered clear of taking any cabinet position in Vienna. In 2000, he handed the FPÖ party chairmanship to Susanne Riess-Passer who became vice-chancellor. The rest of the members of the European Union ("the EU-14") levied sanctions against the Schüssel government, which strongly polarized the Austrian electorate. Yet the governing ability of the FPÖ and ÖVP coalition seemed guaranteed at first. However, FPÖ dissatisfaction with the specific policies of the coalition government was growing steadily. Internal tensions within the FPÖ culminated in the summer of 2002 and led to early elections in the fall, resulting in a fatal defeat of the FPÖ at the polls. About 700,000 voters switched their allegiance from the FPÖ to the ÖVP, which became the strongest party, ahead by about 17 percent of the vote for the first time since 1966, when it governed alone.[6] In spite of the basic willingness of both the SPÖ and the Green Party to form a coalition government with the ÖVP, Chancellor Schüssel decided to continue his coalition with a now gravely weakened FPÖ.

The renewed ÖVP/FPÖ government launched a series of drastic reform measures shortly after its entry into office. It set into motion basic reforms of the pension system—which large parts of the population found to be too painful. Numerous voters were turned off by both coalition parties, who consequently suffered considerable losses in regional elections. The ÖVP lost its majority in Salzburg and Styria, two traditional regions of strength where it had governed since 1945. The FPÖ approached a low point of voter confidence with only 5 percent support in the weekly tracking polls. Responding to this precipitate decline in the polls, the FPÖ ruptured and split into two factions in 2005. Haider launched a new party, "The Coalition for the Future of Austria" (*Bündnis für die Zukunft Österreichs*, or BZÖ), hanging onto the coalition government. The FPÖ came under the new party chairmanship of Heinz Christian Strache from Vienna, who repositioned the party as an oppositional protest party. Regarding its favorite issues and appeals, Strache revisited the right populist mode of the successful years 1986 to 1999.

The National Elections of the fall of 2006 spawned similar profound repercussions as the National Elections of 1999 had. The SPÖ—in spite of the looming shadows of a major scandal involving the near-bankrupt, union-owned bank BAWAG—succeeded by a tiny margin to become the strongest party once again. But the common share of SPÖ and Green Party votes was not sufficient to form a center-left coalition government. This was equally true for the ÖVP and BZÖ—their combined votes could not top 50 percent to continue the existing coalition. The SPÖ and the ÖVP therefore reluctantly agreed in January 2007, after three months of intense negotiations, to return to the combination of the grand coalition government. The Greens and Haider's BZÖ were forced to accept opposition roles. Strache's FPÖ had determined before the election to continue with its opposition role.

The results of the Austrian National Elections of 2006 demonstrate that elections have become a referendum regarding the performance and policies of the governing parties. Just as in Germany in 2005, Italy in 2006, and Sweden in 2006, Austrian voters expressed their dissatisfaction with the course of government in no uncertain terms. Political changes and switches of coalition partners were the result in all four countries as long-term governing parties and government coalitions had to face considerable losses.

On the one hand, voters demonstrated that they agreed with their chosen party's policies—as stated by two-thirds of the voters. Yet on the other hand, one-third of the voters cast *negative* votes and based their decision on dissatisfaction with their parties and annoyance with the political process. It does not come as a surprise and highlights the protest character of the vote in 2006 that 60 percent of the party changers were tracked as angry voters. Those voting for the ÖVP and the Greens were largely positive voters placing the acceptance of the policies of those parties in the foreground. Among SPÖ supporters, every third voter was an angry voter. The FPÖ and the BZÖ attracted the highest share of angry voters with their populist messages. Half of the voters for these right-wing, populist parties were primarily driven by negative emotions and attitudes in the casting of their votes.[7]

Increasingly, both volatility in voting behavior and declining party loyalty seem to be the principal trends. Declining turnout and the growing importance of issue- and performance-oriented evaluations for influencing voting decisions are indicators of the modernization of Austrian electoral behavior, clearly now approaching European mainstream voting behavior.

The topical essays in this volume analyze these trends in considerable detail. *Oliver Rathkolb* examines the long-term historical context of access to the polls and changing electoral outcomes. He goes back to the final decades of the Habsburg Monarchy when a small proportion of the propertied populace had access to the polls. On the eve of World War I, all males gained access. After the break-up of the Habsburg Monarchy at the end of the war and the founding of the First Austrian Republic, universal suffrage was declared, and women became a vital part of the electorate. In the interwar years, the principal political camps (conservative Christian Socials, Socialists, and German Nationalists) increasingly "pillarized." The give and take of seemingly chaotic democratic governance did not have broad appeal and descended into civil conflict between armed party camps. It ended in the seizure of government by the authoritarian Dollfuss and Schuschnigg regimes and the ultimate invasion of the country and takeover by the German Nazis. After World War II—and with the guidance of occupation powers—the more stable democratic regime of the post-World War II Austrian Republic emerged. Half a million Nazi party members were readmitted to the polls in 1949. Voters demonstrated great loyalty to the political camps, and the "pillarization" of Austrian politics intensified. Austrian politics stabilized in grand coalition governments and the "*Alleinregierungen*" Josef Klaus and Bruno Kreisky. Rathkolb also shows that an authoritarian mindset continued in the subterranean mentality of Austrian voters even as female voters became increasingly independent.

Trends and patterns in Austrian voting behavior based on data gathered from representative post-election surveys and exit polls covering the period from 1970 to 2006 are at the core of the contribution by *Fritz Plasser* and *Peter A. Ulram*. Starting with a retrospective view of the *Lager* culture and its impact on the extraordinary stability of Austrian voting behavior until the early 1970s, the authors deal with the consequences of accelerated socioeconomic and sociocultural changes that have gained momentum since the 1970s. They focus on the decline of party affiliations and the resulting increased voter volatility. Since the 1970s, both party affiliations and loyalties among the Austrian electorate weakened, so did traditional determinants of voting behavior such as church affiliation and proximity to trade unions.[8] *Plasser* and *Ulram* also deal with the erosion of voting according to class in Austria and sketch a temporary blue collar realignment that culminated in the National Election of 1999, when the traditional Social Democratic party lost its sway of labor voters to Haider's populist FPÖ. Recent social change in the electorate and the development of a cleavage structure also has led to progressive gender-specific differentiation in Austrian voting behavior, resulting in a widened gender gap reinforced by generational and educational factors. These changes produced a gender-generation realignment of Austrian voting behavior and the ongoing polarization of values as well as a new value cleavage between authoritarian orientations and predominantly post-materialist/libertarian orientations.

Substantial increases of electoral volatility since the 1970s are the topic of the contribution by *Christoph Hofinger, Günther Ogris*, and *Eva Zeglovits*. Based on data from voter transition analyses, they analyze both the permanent increase of swing voters and changing voters and the permanent reservoir of a growing group of non-voters, evident since the 1980s. Structural factors such as the generational and social changes in Austrian society as well as the success and failure of the FPÖ to attract available protest voters from other parties contributed to this increasing volatility. An analysis of the National Election of 2006 demonstrates that all parties suffered from heavy losses to non-voters, a behavior that, in part, was also caused by negative campaign strategies that seemingly had a more demobilizing effect in 2006 than in the previous elections.

The dynamics of regional elections and their relation to the electoral behavior on the federal level are at the core of the contribution by *Herbert Dachs*. Starting with an informative analysis of the specific framework

for party competition on the sub-national level, *Dachs* differentiates between *three* phases of party majorities in regional elections: the phase of clear majorities and extraordinary stability until the 1980s; the boost of voter-mobility in the mid-1980s; and the mixed pattern of stable absolute majorities in select regions, and changing majorities in two regions, both previous strongholds of the conservative ÖVP ever since 1945.

Electoral strategies and the performance of Austrian right wing populism from 1986 to 2006 are the focus of *Kurt Richard Luther*'s essay. After an examination of the electoral performance of the FPÖ and more recently of the BZÖ, *Luther* focuses particularly upon the extent to which changes of their strategic goals were reflected in the composition and motivations of their electoral vote. Based on extensive interviews with leading representatives of the FPÖ and the BZÖ, as well as additional data from a series of Austrian Election Studies, the author differentiates between *four* phases of electoral strategies: the shift of policy-seeking to office-seeking between the 1960s and 1986; populist vote-maximization under Haider, 1986-1999; office-seeking and increasing internal disunity as a party in the ruling governing coalition, 2000-2005; and starting in 2005, a step-by-step return to populist vote maximization. Overall, the FPÖ vote was highest during its period of sustained populist vote-maximization and lowest when the party members were merely engaged in office-seeking within the coalition government; the internal polarization about strategic visions for the party did not help either. Considering the FPÖ's dismal electoral record since 2002 and its fracturing into two camps in 2005, as well as the personal animosities between the leadership of the two groups, the author comes to cautious conclusions regarding the future of Austrian right-wing populism. Clearly, a remarkably stable potential for populist electoral appeals does exist in Austria, so right-wing populism is likely to persist due to a demand for it in the electorate as a result of the enduring mobilizing capacity of polarizing issues like immigration, crime, and xenophobia.

The crucial role of the media in framing Austrian election campaign discourse is at the heart of *Günter Lengauer*'s essay, based on findings of content analysis of campaign coverage in the electronic and print media during the period from 1999 to 2006. After providing an overview about characteristic features of the Austrian media system, political information habits, and the specific relationship between political and journalistic elites, the author focuses on long-term trends in journalistic campaign coverage such as the increased personalization of campaign reports, the growing journalist-centeredness of campaign coverage, the increasingly negative tone of journalists' evaluations of candidates and parties, and the predominant horse-race character of media reporting.[9] Almost half of the political stories in the Austrian media during the 2006 campaign focused on personalities rather than policy issues. A mere one-third of all political news stories predominantly focused on policies and substantially issue-oriented information. Contrasting his findings with comparable data from international studies, the author concludes that the Austrian style of campaign coverage resembles patterns and trends that have recently been identified for U.S., British, and German election campaign coverage.

Putting long-term trends and patterns of Austrian electoral behavior in a comparative European and global context is the goal of *Fritz Plasser* and *Gilg Seeber*'s ambitious essay. They base their findings on comparable data sets from recent National Election Studies in Germany, Italy, France, the United Kingdom, and the United States.[10] After comparing central determinants of Austrian electoral behavior, the authors conclude that national deviations from international trends in electoral behavior are smaller than similarities and concordance. While Austrian voting behavior—at the height of the right populist moment in the National Election of 1999—had briefly deviated from European electoral trends, it again is approximating Western European standards since that election. Patterns of recent electoral behavior in Austria conform to mainstream trends observable in advanced Western democracies.[11]

The concluding FORUM on the National Elections of October 2006 brings this analysis of changing Austrian voting behavior up to the present. Prominent Austrian political scientists and survey researchers discuss old and new trends in the election of 2006 and speculate about its impact upon the future direction of Austrian party and governmental politics.

The two non-topical essays in this volume by two young historians deal with important moments in post-World War II European Cold War history. Together they can be read as an archaeology of efforts for an early détente in Europe. Graz-based Peter Ruggenthaler has mined new records in the Molotov files of the Russian State Archive of Social and Political History. He analyzes the interaction of the Soviet initiative on German unification and neutralization ("Stalin notes") presented to the West on 10 March 1952 with the "short treaty" initiative on the Austrian State Treaty of 13 March 1952, by the Anglo-American powers. Both initiatives were propaganda initiatives of sorts rather than serious diplomatic efforts. While Stalin ignored the Western short-treaty initiative, the West fought Stalin's scheme for Germany tooth and nail. Due to a spy in the French Foreign Ministry, the Kremlin was exceedingly well informed about the West's short treaty plans. Stalin had no plans for a division of Austria, but did not want to conclude an Austrian treaty and make it a "model" for the solution of the German question. The Austrian treaty would not be signed before the division of Germany was completed. Hopes for an early détente in the Cold War in Central Europe were, thus, dashed.

The young Swiss historian Thomas Fischer analyzes a signal moment in the arrival of détente in Europe, namely the genesis of the Conference of Security and Cooperation in Europe, culminating in the Helsinki Final Act of 1975 in which the group of "Neutral and Non-Aligned" countries ("N & NA") played an important role. Switzerland, worried about neutrality being written into the treaty, and Austria, less worried about neutrality entering the conference documents, cooperated very closely from the beginning in 1969 to launch the CSCE and détente in Europe. Together with the Dutch, they pioneered the idea of organizing the conference agenda in "baskets," of which "Basket 3" on the admittance of human rights as a subject for international dialogue was particularly important. During the second stage of the conference in the Geneva preparatory meetings in 1973/74, the new caucus of "N + NA" (Austria, Switzerland, Sweden, Finland, and Yugoslavia, with Malta, San Marino, and Liechtenstein joining later) emerged through proposal of confidence-building measures between East and West. Their "moment of glory" and recognition of increased N + NA power came when they combined the principles of non-intervention in internal affairs as advocated by the Soviets with respect for human rights and fundamental freedoms as demanded by the West in "Basket 3." They kept the CSCE idea and the "Helsinki process" alive in the successor conferences of Belgrade (1977-1978) and Madrid (1980-1983) against all odds and, thus, made a vital contribution to the peaceful end of the Cold War in the late 1980s.

Extensive review essays, book reviews, and the annual review of Austrian politics complete the volume. Peter Berger's review essay on recent literature published on the occasion of the 50th anniversary of the Hungarian Revolution of 1956 is a particularly poignant piece written from a very personal angle. Berger's essay shows that after half a century the historical memory of "Hungary 1956" is still highly contested terrain, especially in the contentious Hungarian political camps. No consensus about the meaning of this turning point in Hungarian history has yet emerged. With the tens of thousands of refugees and the security crisis on Austria's eastern border, the events in Hungary in the fall of 1956 have always been a "site" of Austrian memory, too, and the memory of Hungarian refugees turned Austrians is equally contested. Matthew Berg's review essay on recent literature on Austrian memory of World War II treads a similarly contentious terrain as does Alexander Lassner's discussion of the still partisan meanings and memories of the *Ständestaat* in Austrian consciousness.

Finally, we treasure the opportunity to thank the people who have made this volume possible, first and foremost our contributors with the timely submission of their manuscripts and their good cheer in suffering the extensive copy-editing process with us. With Fritz Plasser as the new co-editor on the Innsbruck side, the new team is clicking as efficiently as ever. The topical essays and the FORUM are largely his initiative, and he has hit the road running with great enthusiasm and commitment to continuing the fifteen year-old tradition of *Contemporary Austrian Studies*.

In New Orleans and at UNO, Sigrid Harrer, the 2006/7 Austrian Ministry of Science dissertation fellow at CenterAustria from the University of Graz, accompanied the daily tracking of manuscripts with wonderful efficiency and aplomb. We hope her own dissertation research on aid abuse by Hurricane Katrina victims did not suffer too much from the demands of her job as assistant to the editors. Jennifer Shimek at Loyola University of New Orleans performed the demanding work of copy-editing the essays and streamlining them to conform to our style-sheet in a timely fashion and with her usual superb skill and good cheer. Gertraud Griessner was pinch-hitting when needed. It is with great regret that we noted Robert Dupont's resignation as Dean of Metropolitan College. He has helped shepherd *CAS* from the very beginning towards financial viability against all odds. Over the past half dozen years, he also served as one of the executive editors of *CAS*. We would like to thank him for his trust and emotional support and wish him well in his new role as professor of history at UNO. We will sorely miss him. In Innsbruck, Ellen Palli has produced photo-ready copy of the final manuscripts with her usual professional skill in spite of the numerous tables in the topical essays. Franz Mathis has supported our endeavors when and wherever needed. At Transaction Publishers, Irving Louis Horowitz, Mary Curtis, and our editor Cheryl Orson have helped bring the manuscript to publication.

Funding for the publication of this volume has come from the Universities of New Orleans and Innsbruck through their partnership agreement, as well as from the Austrian Foreign Ministry through the Austrian Cultural Forum in New York and the Marshall Plan Anniversary Foundation in Vienna which is a generous institutional supporter of CenterAustria. Ernst Aichinger has returned to the headquarters in Vienna from his post at the Cultural Forum in New York. Like Bobby Dupont at UNO, he has always been the most kind and enthusiastic of supporters for *CAS*. We wish him well and look forward to cooperating in the same beneficial manner with his successor, Mr. Rauchbauer.

Larose / Innsbruck May 2007

Notes

1. Consequences of the structural modernization of Austrian society for sociocultural and political values and beliefs are documented in Wolfgang Schulz, Max Haller, and Alfred Grausgruber, eds., *Österreich zur Jahrhundertwende: Gesellschaftliche Werthaltungen und Lebensqualität 1986-2004* (Wiesbaden: VS Verlag, 2005).

2. See Fritz Plasser, Peter A. Ulram, and Gilg Seeber, "Was Wähler(innen) bewegt: Parteien-, Themen- und Kandidatenorientierungen 2006," in *Wechselwahlen. Analysen zur Nationalratswahl 2006*, ed. Fritz Plasser and Peter A. Ulram (Vienna: WUV Verlag, 2007), esp. 166-74.

3. See Mark N. Franklin, *Voter Turnout and the Dynamics of Electoral Competition in Established Democracies Since 1945* (Cambridge: Cambridge UP, 2004).

4. See Fritz Plasser, Gilg Seeber, and Peter A. Ulram, "Breaking the Mold: Politische Wettbewerbsräume und Wahlverhalten Ende der neunziger Jahre," in Fritz Plasser, Peter A. Ulram and Franz Sommer, eds., *Das österreichische Wahlverhalten* (Wien, WUV Verlag, 2000), 55-116.

5. See Fritz Plasser and Peter A. Ulram, "Trends and Ruptures: Stability and Change in Austrian Voting Behavior 1986-1996," in *The Vranitzky Era in Austria*, vol. 7, *Contemporary Austrian Studies*, ed. Günter Bischof, Anton Pelinka, and Ferdinand Karlhofer (New Brunswick, NJ: Transaction, 1999), 30-55.

6. See Fritz Plasser and Peter A. Ulram, eds., *Wahlverhalten in Bewegung: Analysen zur Nationalratswahl 2002* (Vienna: WUV Verlag, 2003).

7. See Plasser et al., "Was Wähler(innen) bewegt," esp. 185-87.

8. See also Günter Bischof, Anton Pelinka, and Hermann Denz, eds., *Religion in Austria*, vol. 13, *Contemporary Austrian Studies* (New Brunswick, NJ: Transaction, 2005).

9. For an analysis of political communication practices in Austria, see also Fritz Plasser, ed., *Politische Kommunikation in Österreich: Ein praxisnahes Handbuch* (Vienna: WUV Verlag, 2004).

10. A modified German language version of this article has been published synchronously in Fritz Plasser and Peter A. Ulram, eds. *Wechselwahlen: Analysen zur Nationalratswahl 2006* (Vienna: WUV Verlag, 2007), 255-86.

11. See Jacques Thomassen, ed., *The European Voter: A Comparative Study of Modern Democracies* (Oxford: Oxford UP, 2005).

TOPICAL ESSAYS

The Austrian Voter in Historical Perspective[1]

Oliver Rathkolb

The following article attempts to sketch an historical typology of voters in Austria, including the female part of the population who entered the picture when they were granted suffrage in 1919. What hampers such an attempt is the absence of reliable data on the basis of opinion polls, voter transition analyses, and exit polls until well into the 1960s. Therefore the article concentrated on analyzing the historical context of the public election campaigns in tandem with the election results. On the basis of numerous historical studies[2] and a few social-historical analyses—particularly of NSDAP voters before 1933—it appears possible to identify a number of trends.

Elite Suffrage for the Few in Habsburg Cisleithania (1867-1873-1906)

Because the Parliament building in Vienna, which was first opened in 1883, continues to serve as the central memory site for the will of the voters in the terms of Austrian parliamentarism and is, therefore, also part of the official politics of history, it is necessary to cast a brief glance at suffrage in the era before 1919. This will also enable us to raise the important question as to the extent continuities and discontinuities in voting patterns are discernible in the First and Second Republics.

On the territory of modern Austria, the revolution of 1848 did not, as is well-known, achieve any major breakthrough, nor were parliamentary democracy and suffrage the results of any single fiat; rather, they evolved through a long series of social compromises. The first—if highly unbalanced—step forward on the road that would ultimately lead to universal and general suffrage was the *Reichsratswahlordnung*, the law governing elections to the Imperial Assembly, in 1873. The lack of balance is evident from the fact that for men (or women) to be eligible for voting, they had to be owners of large estates and at least twenty-four years old; fifty-nine votes from this privileged curia were all that was required to dispatch a male representative—women being barred from candidacy—to the Imperial Assembly:[3] In this system, 4,931 big landowners elected a total of eighty-five representatives; the second and third curiae were reserved to the Chambers of Trade and Commerce (499 voters and twenty-one representatives) and to towns and marketplaces (186,323 voters, 118 representatives) respectively. The fourth and most disadvantaged curia was brought up by the rural districts (1,062,259 voters, 129 representatives); here as well as in the second and third curiae, women were excluded from voting. In the fourth curia, the right to vote was tied to open balloting; secret balloting was not available to its members. Because suffrage was also tied to the payment of taxes, only 17 percent of citizens of legal voting age were eligible to vote. In 1882, there was an increase in the number of urban voters owing to a change in the census (*Fünfgulden-Männer*, that is, men who paid an annual tax of five *gulden*, the currency of the time)—from approximately 186,000 to 299,000.

Faux General Suffrage (1907) and the Decline in Importance of the Imperial Assembly

Pressure in favor of general suffrage increased, and after the Unification Congress at Hainfeld in 1881, where the labor movement patched up its ideological differences, the Social Democrats stepped up their demands for general and equal suffrage, which was to be granted to men as well as to women. The climax of this particular strand of development was a demonstration in Vienna on 29 November 1905 with around 250,000 workers demanding this expansion of suffrage.

As early as 1903, Victor Adler, the leader of the Social-Democratic Party (SDAP) had advised the feminists in his party to waive their justified demands temporarily in order not to furnish the other side with a pretext for refusing to grant general manhood suffrage. Parliament itself ultimately resorted to formal considerations in order to explain its rejection of women's suffrage:

> The majority of the committee was swayed by the argument that to this day women's suffrage has not been adopted by any of the countries that have already introduced general suffrage and that it would be highly dubious to make the at-

tempt to draw women into political life at a time when Austria is going through a decisive phase of its evolution.[4]

Yet the women's movement stayed on course in their political work in the direction of equal rights.

The reform did not mean that universal manhood suffrage had been granted on the city council level. In Vienna, for example, the "curiate" system remained in force until 1918, and the propertied and the educated classes and the Liberals maintained the upper hand. In 1896, the petty-bourgeois Christian Socialists succeeded through a reform of the electoral system to supersede the Liberals as the majority party. It was not until the elections of 4 May 1919 that radically new majorities formed in Vienna: 100 Social Democratic members as opposed to fifty Christian Socialists, eight members of the Czech Party, three each from the German Nationalists and the Jewish Nationalists, and one from the Democratic Party; on the level of the Viennese districts, 339 out of 630 district representatives belonged to the Social Democrats.[5]

The Imperial Assembly and its workings remained marginalized. The government was nominated by the *Kaiser*, who had an extensive repertoire of emergency measures to resort to in case the Imperial Assembly was unable to come up with the desired laws. The German population segment was given preferential treatment through gerrymandering; others, most notably the Ruthenians, were discriminated against. The anti-Semitism that surfaced, particularly in the election campaigns of the Christian Socialists and the German Nationalists, further exacerbated a tendency for exclusion.[6] Members of the armed forces were not eligible to vote, either.

A careful analysis of the distribution of seats shows that in spite of their smaller numbers, German-speaking voters were able, through the inclusion of the direct payment of taxes, to command a greater number of seats than the Czechs, Ruthenians, southern Slavs, Italians, or Romanians.[7] All in all, votes carried a different weight in a number of ways, and the German-speaking population segment clearly benefited from this dispensation.

While the outcome of the elections of 1907 and 1911 was reflected in the composition of the House of Deputies, the House's influence on the actual political decision-making process was extremely limited. At a time when parliament succumbed more and more to paralysis owing to smoldering ethnic conflicts, the government tried, first under Freiherr von Bienerth, then, as of November 1911, under Graf Stürgkh, to deprive parliament of its *raison d'être* through a regime of bureaucratic absolutism.[8] The government's objective was to undo the damage inflicted by electoral reform. The Imperial Assembly degenerated more and more to become merely a stage of ethnic conflict.

The dominant role of the two mass parties, which was to become a characteristic feature of Austria's First and Second Republics, was already taking shape. Both parties developed their organizational structures and many of their specific affinity groups before 1918. The result was analogous to the Netherlands with their Protestant, Catholic, and Socialist "pillars" (plus a liberal pillar that critiqued the process of *verzuiling*,[9] or pillarization). This was already clearly in evidence in the elections in Vienna, when the Christian Socialists, who dominated the City Council, received 49 percent of the popular vote and were followed by the Social Democrats, who had already won 39 percent.[10]

In Cisleithania, too, the two big mass parties began to develop their subcultures, their *Lager* (or camps), each with its own papers and its own, separate cultural clubs (mostly choirs or choral societies) and sports clubs. In the period between the first two elections in 1907 and 1911, 60 percent of all newspapers were in open ideological alignment with one of the two parties.[11] In 1907, the Christian Socialists won the majority in the House of Deputies[12]; in 1911, the Social Democrats succeeded them in that role.

The contingent of 102 German Nationalist and German Liberal deputies was too heterogeneous and much too fixated on the elites to be able to form a mass party.

Voters in 1907 and 1911 had to meet the requirements specified in Beck's reform of the electoral law: at least twenty-four years of age, with Austrian citizenship for at least three years, and domiciled in their constituency for at least one year. Eligibility was tied to a minimum age of thirty.

The fault lines dividing the parties already followed those of ethnic exclusion/inclusion as well as those indicated by competing political models for the solution of the problems caused by social and economic developments; these developments had brought about major social changes as the result of the first wave of globalization and industrialization. Anti-Semitism and ethnic hatred were used openly to transmit enemy stereotypes. In this way, it was above all Social Democratic politicians such as Victor Adler and Otto Bauer who became targets of anti-Semitic agitation while at the same time the Social Democrats increasingly defined themselves as Austro-Germans. The twenty-four Czech Social

Democrats elected in 1911 acted as "autonomists" refusing to take orders from "Germans and Jews."[13] Therefore, the numerical superiority of the Social Democrats vis-à-vis the Christian Socialists (eighty-one versus seventy-six) was a purely theoretical one. The Christian Socialists in their turn had suffered losses through conflicts with a nationalistic, aggressively anti-Semitic faction.

While Christian Socialist voters tended to be found mainly outside urban areas and in certain districts of Vienna, the Social Democrats were successful above all in those districts of Vienna with a great deal of industry and in industrialized pockets in rural areas.

The statements referring to *Lagerbildung* (or camp formation) made by the Social Democrats, who had been the protagonists in the struggle for the franchise, were not lacking in clarity, either. Victor Adler, for instance, had this to say in a speech on 20 December 1906:

Today we are justified in saying that electoral reform is complete and that the basis of Austria's Constitution is general, equal and direct suffrage. This achievement is owed above all to the working class, to its skill and to its energy. If the working class has, on the one hand, added a new weapon to its arsenal for the class struggle, the new nature of the conflict will impose on it new duties and ever more difficult tasks. It will only be able to discharge those duties if it remains committed to that path in future which has perforce led to this day: loyalty to the principles of Social Democracy, a sense of purpose and an unswerving commitment to the pursuit of our goals.[14]

Yet the Social Democrats were no more immune than anyone else against the socio-economic and geopolitical crises of the Habsburg monarchy and lost seats in 1911, even though they emerged as the victorious party (eighty-one Social Democratic seats as against seventy-six Christian Socialist ones). Otto Bauer, who was to succeed Victor Adler as the leader of the Social Democrats, summed up the mood of crisis, which had an adverse effect on the political culture of the time before World War I, in the following apposite words:

The total collapse of domestic and foreign policy has had a paralyzing effect on people; the workers have come to the conclusion that things in Austria are past cure and slide back into a political indifference that weakens the development of our party. This is compounded by the severity of the economic crisis, which weakens our organization and our press, and by the reformist education of the workers, whose frustration at the failure of the hoped-for successes to materialize turns them against the party. All in all, a rather dispiriting situation[. . .][15]

The signals that the pre-democratic structures were also going to be dominated by politically motivated violence multiplied, not least when the leading Social Democratic functionary of Wien-Ottakring was murdered on 12 February 1913 by the brother of Leopold Kunschak, the

Christian Socialist politician. In March 1914, the Imperial Assembly was adjourned by the Emperor and was not called again until 30 May 1917 so that World War I was begun without a debate in the Assembly.

Gender Equality of Voters from 1919 Onward

World War I had reinforced the sense of crisis through traumatic experiences on a large scale and had created from the start an atmosphere that aided and abetted militancy and an inclination towards violent solutions also among male (and to a much lesser extent among female) voters. Fully 75 percent of the male population of the Austro-Hungarian Monarchy had been called up for military service. The population of the *Hinterland*, also in Cisleithania, notably women, was plagued by famine due to the lack of supplies and a flourishing black market. The bare outline offered by an encyclopedia entry is sufficient to indicate the extent of the damage:

> WWI, which lasted 1,563 days for the Austro-Hungarian Empire, cost its armed forces more than 1 million dead and permanently missing (of whom approximately 400,000 died as POWs in Russia, 50,000 in Serbia and more than 30,000 in Italy), 1,943,000 injured and 1.2 million POWs, many of whom did not return until years after the cessation of hostilities. The war is said to have cost approximately 90 billion *kronen*, the public debt rose from 13 to 72 billion *kronen* between July 1914 and November 1918, and inflation spiraled to 1,400% between 1914 and 1924.[16]

Otto Bauer addressed the psychological effects that the war had also on future voters when he conceded that "the years in the trenches had instilled in them a belief in violence [. . .]."[17] At home, they found a state of unmitigated crisis with a galloping rate of inflation and high unemployment. In addition to this, the old system of the authority of the monarchy, as well as its legal system, had been destroyed, as Alexander Spitzmüller, one of the finance ministers of the empire, rightly noted in his memoirs: "The most serious crime during the war was the destruction of the legal order, which made itself felt in numerous court-martials."[18]

In spite of their international peace initiatives during World War I, the Social Democrats had also been unable to distance themselves in an appropriate symbolic form from violence as a means to further a domestic political agenda. This is demonstrated by the assassination of Karl Reichsgraf von Stürgkh, then the prime minister of the Austro-Hungarian Empire, by Victor Adler's son, Friedrich Adler. In the public's perception, this was little more than a desperate measure to demand the convening of the Imperial Assembly, which Stürghk had refused to grant.

Approximately 1.04 million men from the territory that became modern Austria had served as soldiers; 180,000 of them had been killed. Moreover, 60,000 civilians, men and women, were also killed. A further consequence of the war, 90,000 widows and 270,000 orphans were part of the ruinous social structure, and more than 760,000 refugees and displaced persons were stranded within the borders of the republic of *Deutsch-Österreich*.

The very foundation of the new state on 12 November 1918, when Franz Ringhofer, one of the German Nationalist deputies of the Provisional National Assembly, proclaimed the Republic of *Deutsch-Österreich*, led to mass panic and a violent brawl, which left forty people injured and a man and a boy trampled to death in the stampede following a shooting.

Nevertheless, it was possible within a very short time, owing to the possibility of recourse to the body of administrative expertise of the monarchy, to establish a framework for elections and for the passing of social-political laws in the National Assembly such as those on the eight-hour work day, child labor, and outwork. Priority went to general suffrage for women, the lowering of the voting age to twenty, and the introduction of closed-list *proporz* with joint lists. Initially, the Ministers of Parliament (MPs) had proceeded on the assumption that German Bohemia (forty-five MPs) and the Sudetenland (fifteen MPs) would be included; that is, they assumed the total number of voters would be 10,299,000—so there would have been 48,000 voters for any one MP.[19] Another five seats were reserved for the German-speaking minorities in Brno, Olomouc, and Jihlava pending the necessary contractual agreements with Czechoslovakia. Allied *Realpolitik* as well as the integration of the German-speaking territories into Czechoslovakia put an end to these pie-in-the-sky games in the same way in which the St Germain peace treaty ended all speculations about *Anschluss* to Germany in 1920.

In spite of all this the first truly free and democratic elections were held on 16 February 1919 with a relatively high turnout (82.10% women and 86.97% men). The Christian Socialists managed to establish themselves as the party for women, whereas the Social Democrats held even less appeal for female voters than the pan-German People's Party.[20]

In a campaign that was short and intense, the Social Democrats took the offensive and advocated in radical language the switch to a new social model and the beginning of the "class struggle,"[21] that is, a continuation of the ideological development that had been interrupted by the outbreak of the war in 1914. The Catholic Church, on the other hand, lent its support openly to the Christian Socialists; in one case in the Waldviertel parish of Oberndorf near Zwettl, this escalated into the threat not to hear the confessions of those who did not vote Christian Socialist. Wilhelm Miklas, a Christian Socialist member of the State Council (and a federal president-to-be), was attacked and manhandled during an election meeting in another Waldviertel parish, St. Leonhard near Horn.[22]

In 1919 the Christian Socialists, addressing their canvassing mainly to "farmers and artisans," focused on the need to ward off a "socialist republic" and on the metaphor of a "Christian people." Time and again, the bogeyman of a communist putsch was invoked.[23] The Social Democrats, on the other hand, plied the antagonism of the people against the rich through such concrete demands as the nationalization of the big corporations and the taxation of "unearned super incomes" and pinned the blame for widespread destitution squarely on capitalism. In addition to this, they tried to position themselves as the exemplary peace party that could be trusted to oppose another war. The German Nationalists played the xenophobic card and appealed covertly—and in diverse newspapers overtly—to anti-Semitism and the need to bring about the Anschluß to Germany.

It is remarkable that the election platform of the first "German National Socialist Labor Party," which put up candidates in some electoral districts, was already complete and remained fundamentally unchanged in its basic messages throughout the 1920s and 1930s in spite of the party's change of leadership: "... democratic, libertarian, nationalistic and therefore strictly anti-Semitic in the sense of being opposed to rampant Jewish influence in all walks of economic, public and cultural life." "What distinguishes the party from the Social Democracy," the platform continues, "is its emphasis on the concept of the nation (*ihre streng völkische Gesinnung*), its rejection of the rule of any one party and of other forms of tyranny and of revolutionary movements and its endorsement in principle of private property [...]." The element that was lacking to translate this into electoral success was an appropriate political context and the possibility of latching onto the rise of Hitler's NSDAP in Germany.

Even though the German Nationalists suffered heavy losses compared to its results in 1911, twenty-six of its candidates did get elected, and on 7/8 August 1920, they founded the Pan-German People's Party (*Großdeutsche Volkspartei*), a relatively staid affair, in which the tone was set by senior civil servants and teachers. The dominant themes apart from the stock-in-trade *Anschluß* to Germany were anticlericalism and anti-Semitism. However, as coalition partners of the Christian Socialists, they were part of a number of governments between 1921 and 1932.

Voter mobilization had brought the Social Democrats initial electoral success; however, mobilization resulted also, as the ensuing coalitions and election results were to show, in a long-term majority right of the center, which had profound consequences for Austria's political culture. The Social Democrats also got stuck at around 40 percent of the vote throughout the First and in the early Second Republic. It was not until the party benefited in 1971 from Bruno Kreisky's electoral platform and strategic skills that a temporary improvement materialized, which resulted in a narrow 50+ percent majority until 1983.

In 1919 however, the social, economic, and, above all, unresolved geopolitical problems in the phase before the conclusion of the peace treaty were so daunting that only a grand coalition—the only one in the First Republic—under a Social Democratic chancellor, Karl Renner, seemed to offer a way out.

Social Democratic electoral success remained focused on Vienna, which was both a strength and a source of controversy. In 1920, Vienna was set up as a political entity independent of Lower Austria; ever since, the Social Democrats have been in a majority in the capital, whereas the Christian Socialists tended to predominate in the other eight provinces.

The Erosion of the Political Culture of the First Republic: "Pillarization," the Militarization of Voters 1920-1932 until the Dissolution of Parliament, Government by Dictatorship, and the Anschluß to Hitler's Germany in 1938

Electoral Results in Comparison

One of the facts to emerge from a comparison of historical Austrian election results—in spite of problems with vote weighting and the exclusion of women and members of the armed forces from the 1907 and 1911 elections—is the trebling of the numbers of citizens entitled to vote in the period between 1907 (1.25 million excluding Burgenland) and 1930 (3.959 million, again excluding Burgenland).

This did not prevent the same political parties from being dominant both in 1907 and in 1930, particularly as regards the coalition potential right of the center. While the Social Democrats' share of the vote had increased substantially by 1930 to 41.15 percent of the vote, which translated into seventy-two seats, compared to the Christian Socialists' 35.65 percent and sixty-six seats, it was the Christian Socialists who had a potential coalition partner close at hand in the form of a new electoral alliance between the Pan-German People's Party and the *Landbund*, which had received 11.52 percent of the vote and nineteen seats.

In 1927 a joint list of the right-of-center coalition consisting of Christian Socialists and Pan-Germans had received 49 percent of the vote. That was slightly less than in 1930, but if the votes of the *Landbund* (9 percent of the vote, nine seats) are added, it turns out that the center-right bloc was stronger in 1927 than in 1930. In contrast, the Social Democrats, at 42 percent of the vote and seventy-one seats in 1927, achieved roughly the same result in both elections.

A comparison of verified data of the general elections of 1920 and 1923 yields the following results relevant to the (male and female) electorate:[24]

1) The prevalence of women entitled to vote remained the same (52.8 percent), whereas the total number of eligible voters rose slightly from 3.75 million in 1920 to 3.849 million in 1923.
2) Voter mobilization measures boosted turnout from 80 percent in 1920 (including the by-elections in Carinthia and in Burgenland after the settlement of Yugoslav and Hungarian territorial claims) to 87 percent in 1923.
3) Men still had the edge over women in turnout; they were also the focus of strategic voter mobilization measures. Male voter turnout rose from 73 percent in 1920 to 90 percent in 1923; female turnout increased only slightly in the same period (from 83 percent to 85 percent). There were, however, substantial regional differences: in Vienna, 90 percent of eligible female voters cast their vote (compared to 92.56 percent of the men); in the Tyrol, 91.49 percent (92.85 percent), and in Vorarlberg as many as 93.8 percent (94.44 percent).

In 1920 and 1923, election advertising became much more professional. Text-only posters disappeared to make room for posters with color-printed visual elements. The central political codes and metaphors, which were designed to appeal to the voters' value and anxiety systems, remained basically the same. Yet they became much more focused, clearer, and emotionally charged in the pictorial language; they were, in fact, designed to serve as "meaning formulae" capable of triggering the desired voter behavior. An aggressive coding became a pervasive feature of election posters. The 1920 working-class giant of Mihály Birós,[25] a graphic artist who had fled to Vienna after the suppression of the Republic of People's Councils in Hungary, swept away "papists and capitalists and the military" wielding a huge broom or attacks the "unified front of capitalism" with his hammer.[26] In 1930, Victor Slama, a graphic artist and organizer of political mass events,[27] designed another working-class giant along similar lines, a creature of light vengefully waiting in the dark of the night for *Hahnen-schwanzler*, members of the paramilitary *Heimwehr*.

Christian Socialist graphic artists in their turn depicted Social Democracy in the guise of a snake strangling the eagle, the Austrian national emblem, and urged German Christians to "save Austria."[28] Frequently, the myth of Karl Lueger, a popular Christian Socialist lord mayor of Vienna, was invoked, preferably hovering above the town hall in a cloud, to "save" Vienna, as in 1923.

Ernestine Bennerstorfer[29] has analyzed 500 election posters from the period between 1920 and 1930 and comes to the conclusion that "[a]ll posters are based on the simple recipe of polarization; they construct a stereotype of the political enemy. Each party envisaged the others in terms of the 'enemy' and made this their chief contribution to the political culture of the period between the two wars."[30]

Polarization, however, did nothing to alter the fact that until the rise of the NSDAP, the Social Democrats remained in a state of stagnation; they achieved no more than relative electoral successes and were unable to prevent center-right coalitions, mostly under the aegis of the Christian Socialists, from obtaining the required parliamentary and government majorities.

At the same time, pillarization, in the sense of the formation of political camps, received powerful boosts. This is evidenced, for example, by "Red Vienna's" model attempt to create a new culture embracing all aspects of life, ranging from kindergarten and novel, non-religious forms of interment to comprehensive new educational policies and by the fact that in Vienna, too, the universities were dominated by professors with pan-German and conservative leanings and that anti-Semitism was getting more and more virulent and aggressive.

Way back in the 1860s, the first Workers' Educational Associations were established as well as Workers' Choral Societies; around 1900, the latter were given an organizational framework in the *Reichsverband der Arbeitergesangsvereine Österreichs*. In November 1919, the Social Democratic party created its own *Kunststelle* to coordinate its cultural activities; its first leader was David Josef Bach, the cultural editor of the *Arbeiter-Zeitung*. The realization of the increasing importance of sports as a social phenomenon had already led to the foundation of the *Allgemeiner Turnverein in Wien* before the war. In 1919, centralization spread to this area as well in the form of the

Verband der Arbeiter- und Soldatensportvereinigungen (VAS), which was relaunched in 1924 as *Arbeiterbund für Sport und Körperkultur in Österreich* (ASKÖ).

The organization of sports provides an accurate reflection of pillarization in Austria, whose beginnings date back to the closing phase of the monarchy. The *Turnerbewegung*, a broad movement aimed at popularizing exercise to promote physical and mental well-being, with its strong German nationalistic component, had already introduced the so-called *Arierparagraph*, which aimed at excluding Jews from membership, prior to 1900. One of the consequences was the foundation in 1897 of the *Erster Wiener jüdischer Turnverein*, which was followed by the *Turnverein Zion* in Graz.[31] As the *Deutscher Turnerbund*, in addition to pursuing anti-Semitic, anticlerical, anti-Socialist, and antidemocratic goals, was also in favor of "Anschluß" to Germany, the Christian Socialists founded their own sports organization, the *Christlich Deutsche Turnerschaft Österreichs*.

Rudolf Müllner's[32] graph below reflects the athletic aspect of the pillarization that has been repeatedly mentioned; the Jewish associations, however, are missing:

The totality of organization of all areas of life shaped the outlook of voters between the two wars. Yet it must be pointed out that the trend towards social segmentation with its political consequences dates back to the times of the Monarchy, in particular to the phase of "internationalization" and the global economic crisis in the nineteenth century.

Alpinism too had already been subject to differentiation along ideological lines prior to 1914 and to subsequent massive politicization.[33] The Social Democrats' foundation of the *Naturfreunde* dates back as far as 1895.

Pillarization, which was only briefly checked by a grand coalition in 1918/1919-1920, reached its high-water mark in the foundation of paramilitary organizations. In the time immediately following the proclamation of the republic in 1918, small militias and loose groups of demobilized soldiers played an important direct and indirect role. The *Volkswehr* under Social Democratic leadership had 15,000 men under arms, and in the provinces, home guards and columns of local self-defense irregulars were active, for instance, in Southern Carinthia, where they repelled the territorial claims of the Kingdom of the Serbs, Croats, and Slovenes.

The *Heimwehren*, a rightist conservative militia, were particularly in evidence in the provinces, for example, in the Tyrol and in Styria.

Table 1
Sports and Gymnastics Associations (*Turnorganisationen*) in Austria's First Republic

Sports and Gymnastics Associations	Membership	Ideology
Deutscher Turnerbund (1919) DTB	In 1932, approx. 115,000 members, of whom 45,000 were children or adolescents	• German Nationalistic • anti-Marxist • anti-Semitic • anticlerical
Christlich Deutsche Turnerschaft (CDTÖ)	In 1930, approx. 40,000 members 1937 c. 58,000	• German-Christian • anti-Marxist • anti-Semitic • antidemocratic • authoritarian Ständestaat
Arbeitersport (ASKÖ)	In 1932, approx. 240,200 members	• social political • mass sports • opposed to competitive sports
Österreichischer Haupverband für Körpersport (ÖHK)	Approx. 80,000 members	• apolitical • in favor of competitive sports • individual sports

Source: Müllner, "Sportgeschichte Österreich 1918-1938," 36.

Between 1924 and 1926 in a period of relative economic stability, these militias kept a low profile. Yet from 1927 onward, militant anti-parliamentarian activities were on the rise again owing to socioeconomic crises. A clash between members of the rightist Association of Front-Line Fighters and members of the *Republikanischer Schutzbund in Schattendorf* left two dead, a man and a child, as in 1918. When the trial of the men who had fired the fatal shots ended, in a clear miscarriage of justice, with an acquittal, the Palace of Justice was stormed and set on fire by an angry crowd. Austria was the brink of civil war.

In 1923, the Social Democrats had combined their former factory and workers' brigades and the association of their party stewards to form the *Republikanischer Schutzbund* as a counterweight to the *Heimwehr* and the rightist Federal Army.

Gerhard Botz[34] has analyzed the profiles of the 305 men and the one woman involved in politically motivated violent crimes between 1923 and 1933. His findings include that 25 percent of the perpetrators were between sixteen and nineteen years of age (compared to 21 percent of the victims and 42 percent of the witnesses in this age category). Most of the perpetrators (63 percent) were between twenty and twenty-nine years old; there were hardly any in the age group of forty years of age or older, where this kind of radicalization was negligible.

There is a significant correlation between violence and high rates of unemployment, as has been empirically documented by new regional studies.[35] The increasing militarization and radicalization of political conflict, of which the fire at the Palace of Justice in 1927 is the most notorious example, seemed inevitable against the backdrop of perpetual social and economic crises. The authoritarian policies of Engelbert Dollfuss, the Christian Socialist federal chancellor who suspended parliament after a standing orders crisis on 4 March 1933, did not make it easier for the model of the small state as a viable political entity to be endorsed by a broad majority.

Finally, it was these authoritarian policies that led to civil war in February 1934 and to the *Sozialdemokratische Arbeiterpartei* (SDAP) being banned. The attempt to hold National Socialism, in power in Germany since 1933, at bay through the establishment of an authoritarian government failed. The terror attacks of the Nazis continued, and Dollfuss was murdered in July 1934 during an abortive Nazi putsch. His successor, Kurt Schuschnigg, opted for an agreement with Hitler's Germany (the July Agreement of 1936) and a continuation of authoritarian government. The cautious opening towards the banned "left" and the trade unions at the end of 1937 came too late and was no more successful than the referendum called for 9 March (but subsequently banned by Hitler): "For Austria, free and German, independent and just, Christian and united!" When the German *Wehrmacht* marched into Austria on 12 March 1938, the Austrians offered no resistance. In the context of the time, this marked the end of the idea of Austria surviving as a small, independent political entity. Approximately 250,000 people welcomed Hitler as the "liberator", while at the same time the first series of arrests were taking place that targeted 50,000 Austrian men and women, political opponents and Jews. This also served to stake out the arena in which Hitler's referendum about the *Anschluß* was going to take place on 10 April 1938, which ended with almost unanimous approval (99.6 percent), the result of opportunism, ideological conviction, the exertion of massive pressure, perfect propaganda, and occasional vote rigging.

The NSDAP in Austria and its Attraction for Voters

Because the NSDAP was not successful as a party in the parliamentary elections of 1930—the political and, later on, also the personal proximity to the *Heimwehr*, which obtained 6.26 percent of the votes and eight seats, are disregarded in the present context—there are no data on which to base a comparison on parliamentary elections level in Austria. It is, however, possible to discern a clear trend on the basis of the provincial elections in the most populous provinces (Vienna and Lower Austria) as well as in Salzburg (24 April 1932) and Vorarlberg (6 November 1932) and of the local council elections in Carinthia on the same day.

At the Vienna provincial elections (*Landtagswahlen*), the National Socialists quintupled their share of the votes[36] (336,000 compared to 66,000 in the general elections of 1930), and the Social Democrats lost marginally (984,000 compared to 1,032,000 in 1930). The Christian Socialists lost the same number of votes (640,000 compared to 695,000 in 1930); the Pan-Germans, the *Landbund* and the *Heimatblock*, lost massively to the NSDAP (53,000 compared to 304,000).

In a pioneering move in Austria, Gerhard Botz has sketched an outline of the social structure of the NSDAP membership based on the analysis of random samples drawn from the party member files at the Berlin Document Center, which are stored today at the Bundesarchiv Berlin[37]:

> The Austrian NSDAP was, from the moment it achieved its massive breakthrough, successful—if erratically—as a protest reservoir, in which, while it attracted people from all social classes, workers and farmers were underrepresented, whereas white-collar employees and civil servants were heavily, and the self-employed somewhat overrepresented; it was an "asymmetrical people's party." Compared to other parties, it was one with a disproportionate appeal to male voters with relatively youthful activists. The generation of those born between 1894 and 1913 was typically particularly prominent. It received a special boost since the 30s from high unemployment and the permanent socio-economic crises in industrial areas as well as in rural ones. It benefited increasingly from the rise of the NSDAP under the leadership of Adolf Hitler, an Austrian, in the Weimar Republic. Even though the unemployed tended either towards apathy or spontaneous violence, no trend is discernible for that group to attach itself preferably to the NSDAP. However, groups potentially threatened by unemployment or those whose social standing had been eroded by modernization or the members of former elites were ideal fodder for the NSDAP.

The latent potential of sympathy for the NSDAP would presumably be seen to have been much bigger also among the working classes from 1933 onward, if those applications for party membership that were put on hold because no more members were accepted for the time being were fed into a social structure analysis. A total of 536,660 Austrian men and women were registered as former NSDAP members in 1946. Having been confiscated by U.S. troops, the applications for membership are today stored in the Austrian State Archive and—in the form of microfiches—in the U.S. National Archives; they would yield a somewhat different social profile, as random samples have shown.

A Democratic Relaunch in 1945 under Allied Supervision[38]

It was an issue of overriding importance for the Allies, who had liberated Austria in 1945, and for the political elites of the Second Republic how loyal to the Second Republic the former National Socialists were going to prove as voters. Another issue unique to Austria was the integration into a parliamentary system of the elites and functionaries of the Dollfuss-Schuschnigg dictatorship of the years 1933/34-38. A number of Allied experts pointed out that Austrian voters had had little experience with a live democracy and that the monarchy had been an authoritarian system. Whatever traces of democratic attitudes had developed were sure to have been swept away by National Socialism. In 1945 the Allies noted with surprise how quickly the reconstitution of state authority and the organization of elections were implemented by Karl Renner's provisional government, a government moreover that had been installed freehandedly by the Soviet Union without the consent of the Western Allies. For the United States it was apparently unthinkable in their forward planning during the final stages of the war that an Austrian government could be functional without a solid military administration, possibly under the umbrella of the United Nations, to prop it up. In mid-1944, the planners at the Office of Strategic Services (OSS) came forward with the pessimistic conclusion that an independent Austria was going to lack ingredients essential for the survival as a state or as a nation: there was no army, no police force, no independent economy; the population was heterogeneous also owing to the presence of a large number of people of German origin (*Reichsdeutsche*), and there was still no sense of national identity.

The confrontation with their authoritarian *Ständestaat* past, which U.S. planners expected the Austrians to engage in as part of the reconstruction effort, was avoided after 1945 and remained subordinated to the state doctrine of pooling the best efforts of all sides to establish a sovereign state and to bring about the withdrawal of the four allies (the United States, the USSR, Great Britain, and France). The suffering caused by National Socialism was used to justify this course and the "spirit of the camp street" was invoked again and again. This was understood as referring to the traumatic times that functionaries of the ÖVP and SPÖ had spent together in Nazi concentration camps, the implication being that shared suffering could serve as a basis on which to overcome the massive differences of the past. There had, in fact, been isolated contacts between representatives of different parties in concentration camps. However, the majority of the SPÖ elite of 1945 (Karl Renner, Adolf Schärf, Oskar Helmer) had not been incarcerated in concentration camps, and a number of ÖVP politicians (such as Leopold Figl, Felix Hurdes, Heinrich Gleissner, and Lois Weinberger) who had been subjected to this ordeal used this fact in order to justify indirectly why they had no wish to address themselves now to the topic of the 1933/1934-1938 era. The "camp street" myth was meant to draw a line under the past in the same way in which the mythological construct of the "victim" doctrine was meant to reduce Austrian collaboration with the Nazi extermination and conquest machinery to a few guilty individuals.

In spite of a clear absolute majority of the ÖVP, Leopold Figl (ÖVP) formed a coalition with the SPÖ, included one KPÖ minister, and announced his cabinet on 8 December 1945. The challenges posed by the task of reconstruction, the Allied administration, and the onset of the Cold War made cooperation possible in spite of the ideological differences and conflicts. The electoral success of the ÖVP was partly due to a reorganization of the party system along the lines of its existence until 1933. In a move that reflected the Nazi terror and extermination regime and the involvement of many supporters and functionaries of these parties in Nazi crimes, the pan-Germans and the NSDAP were banned, and the *Landbund* was swallowed by the ÖVP.

It is remarkable that in 1945, in spite of dictatorship, National Socialism, World War II and the Holocaust, Austrian voters continued to tend towards the center right. The rejection of the Communists, who received a meager 5.41 percent of the vote, was obvious. At the same time, the Social Democrats, who had been picked to win the elections, were also considered to be too radical and got only 44.6 percent of the votes cast; even as the votes were being counted, many old hands still took a Social Democratic victory for granted. Yet a brief glance at historical precedent would have suggested a different outcome. The tendency that had been evident in the First Republic was still at work: women tended not to vote for either the SPÖ or the KPÖ; this was in itself enough to significantly affect the outcome in elections that were dominated by the female vote—3.5 million were eligible overall, of whom an extraordinary 63 percent were women because former members of the NSDAP were barred from voting. Women tended also to feel frustrated at the debate that ensued, occasionally with radical overtones, among SPÖ functionaries about the "Nazi issue"; this debate reflected the infighting in the Social Democratic camp between the party left around Scharf, Krones and Hackenberg, who wanted to keep contact with the Communists, and the "party establishment" around Schärf, Renner, and Helmer.

Josef Schöner, a diplomat, young at the time and from a Christian Socialist background, describes in his diaries the mood of the electorate as follows:

> It's election day today and it's been fifteen years in coming. I cannot help feeling elated to a certain extent, in spite of my old skepticism as regards the so-called will of the people [. . .] People's interest in politics is beyond doubt; what they don't want is mass gatherings and demonstration marches. This development [...] favors the so-called "bourgeois" ideologies, which appeal more directly to the voters *qua* persons because they're more individualistic in character [...] It's remarkable how little the ÖVP has done by way of public relations compared to the other two parties [...] It all amounts to a choice between the center and the left [...]"[39]

After the general elections of November 1945 when the new government under Leopold Figl was already in office, it became apparent that it was the pragmatic right wing of the SPÖ that was calling the shots in the party. To what extent this radical position with regard to the Nazi issue had had an influence on the outcome of the elections (and, therefore, on the ÖVP's electoral success) is a moot question awaiting further research. The repercussions of the SPÖ's infighting have been remarkably long-lived, as can be seen from Franz Olah's memoirs, in which he mistakenly blames Erwin Scharf, the SPÖ central secretary of the day, for having commissioned a *Nazi-Austauschplakat*, a poster demanding the exchange of POWs in Allied captivity for notorious Nazis. The truth is that Scharf was responsible for the first radical poster addressing the Nazi issue including its design, whereas the *Austauschplakat*, which caused much more of a stir than Scharf's text-only poster, was the brainchild of Vienna's Socialist youth movement. It was quite obvious that this radical ideological position of the SPÖ, which was limited to the Vienna branch of the party and to a number of members of the party's leadership without affecting the government level, had failed to "deliver" at the 1945 general elections.

In the *Proklamation der Vorstände der antifaschistischen Parteien Österreichs*, a statement of the leaders of Austria's antifascist parties issued as early as 27 April 1945, which was, in fact, the first programmatic declaration of the provisional government, the idea of a kind of "retribution law" was included. It was to have been applied as a kind of emergency law to those former members of the NSDAP, "who, out of contempt for democracy and democratic rights, established and upheld a regime in Austria based on violence, denunciation, persecution and repression and who had recklessly plunged the country into a disastrous war and laid it open to devastation." The plan provided for "fellow travelers" to be reintegrated into society as quickly as possible. Order No 1 issued by the Representatives of the Red Army's High Command signaled likewise that ordinary NSDAP members were not to be incriminated by the Red Army simply on the basis of their "party membership [. . .] provided they show themselves to be loyal to the Red Army." Ideas initially supported by Karl Renner, the chancellor of the provisional government, of "barring all fascists (members of the *Heimwehren* and clerical and nationalistic fascists) who were not simply taking orders from their superiors [. .] from exercising their democratic rights for a ten-year probation period"—ideas, incidentally, that coincided with recommendations advanced by U.S. experts—were dropped after being voiced in political discussions. Renner's proposal of getting *Zensurkommissionen* (review committees) to draw up complete lists of the former NSDAP members was taken up and realized.

The *Verbotsgesetz*, a constitutional law dated 8 May 1945 concerning the banning of the NSDAP, and the War Criminals Act dated 26 June 1945 created the basis for the legal processing of ordinary ex-members and of the ex-functionaries of the *Nationalsozialistische Deutsche Arbeiterpartei* in legal and administrative terms instead of in political and revolutionary ones. This act became immediately valid in Vienna and in the territory occupied by the Red Army (Lower Austria, the Mühlviertel part of Upper Austria, and Burgenland); in the remaining provinces of Austria (those administrated by the Western Allies), it did not become valid until 5 February 1946. All persons who had been formally in contact with the NSDAP (as members, candidates for membership, members of paramilitary formations, members of the SS or candidates for SS membership) between 19 June 1933, the date of the NSDAP being banned as a party in Austria, and the date of the declaration of independence, 27 April 1945, had to register with the authorities.

Registration was followed in a number of cases by *Sühnefolgen* (retribution measures) which were aimed above all at former illegal Nazis, those who had belonged to the NSDAP between the banning of the party in 1933 and 13 March 1938, party functionaries, and members of the SS. The *Sühnefolgen* could take the form of a temporary loss of civic rights, a temporary employment ban, internment in an *Anhaltelager* (in Glasenbach, Wolfsberg, Tulln, and Korneuburg; as of 15 September 1946, a mere 258 individuals were interned in the Soviet zone compared to 11,234 in the U.S. zone, 7,186 in the British zone, and 1,871 in the French zone), confiscation of property, or the imposition of a fine. Registered individuals were banned from voting in the general elections in November 1945. Until the beginning of 1946, the Austrian authorities as well as the Allies actively pursued an agenda of getting heavily incriminated people discharged from their jobs, making arrests, and organizing trials of war criminals; initially, the Americans and the British were particularly active as regards employment bans and discharges. With the onset of the Cold War, they started toning down their de-Nazification efforts in favor of an inclusive anti-communist movement and leaving the whole business of de-Nazification to the Austrian authorities and parties. The Soviet Union, in turn, seized on de-Nazification to argue the need for the continued administration of Austria by the Allies.

The tendency to want to draw a line of demarcation in the past was increasingly in evidence from 1947/48 onwards. Even in the field of penal justice, the People's Courts stepped up the number of acquittals to 52 percent (compared to 26 percent in the period 1945-1947). At the same time, the two big parties, the ÖVP and SPÖ, openly discussed an issue that had direct bearing on election strategy: a large number of former NSDAP members were again going to be entitled to vote in the 1949 general elections. As a result of the amnesty for less incriminated former NSDAP members, an influx of 500,000 new voters was bound to have a significant impact on the political landscape. In Lower Austria alone this meant 74,000 additional votes. The two political protagonists tried in different ways to secure the votes of the "formers" for themselves—even if this involved giving up on de-Nazification altogether; de-Nazification was scheduled by the grand coalition to be phased out by 1947, but had to be kept going owing to pressure from the Allies. The amnesty of 1948 and the election campaign of 1949 put an end to de-Nazification in all its forms, even though the People's Courts remained in session until 1955 and a number of government agencies continued to use the instrument of the *Sühnefolgen*.

The *Verbotsgesetz* in its 1947 version was repealed almost entirely by the 1957 amnesty for Nazis; the War Criminals Act was repealed in its entirety. The consequence was that from 1957 onward, Nazi crimes were adjudicated according to the Austrian penal code and the code of criminal procedure.

There is no doubt that there had been a desire on all levels of Austrian society to adapt to the Nazi regime, which was offset to an extent by a resistance that was above all a reaction to German domination and to the negative consequences of the *Wehrmacht*'s expansionist campaigns in Europe. However, after the liberation by the Allies, with the Red Army bearing the brunt in the east and the U.S. armed forces doing the same in the west, public debate in Austria did not focus on Austria's responsibility and its contribution to the Holocaust and the war, but on the role of the Austrians as victims: as POWs, as the victims of the bombing campaigns, and as the persecuted in the Nazis' repressive system. Even the suffering of the Jewish victims—approximately 150,000 people had been driven into exile and 65,000 people in Austria had fallen victim to the Nazi terror and to their extermination machinery—was pushed aside to make room for the suffering and the blows of fate that the Austrians had had to endure.

Austria's central national memory was shaped by the shock when the *Ostmark* and its inhabitants were integrated into the National Socialist German Reich not as an elite group, but as a provincial society with limited appeal. Having been denied the self-devised role of the "superior German civilization," the Austrians began to harbor tendencies of emotional emancipation from Germany, which were quickly reinforced by the series of military setbacks after the battle for Stalingrad in 1941. By 1945, hardly anyone would have questioned the need for Germany and Austria to go their separate ways, but this did not mean that Austria had already developed a mature, independent identity as a small nation in its own right.

Austrian consensual democracy, which has often been called a democracy of *proporz* (proportional representation), was the result, as these examples have shown, both of necessities active within the country itself and of geo-strategic necessities. After all, the last free elections to be held had taken place in 1932, and in 1945 the country was confronted with the gigantic tasks of separating itself from Germany, of building the structures appropriate to a small state, and of establishing a republican system along the lines of its pre-1933 former self.

The idea of *proporz* was quite an old control tool. As early as 1914, Renner had pleaded in favor of its introduction within a wider proportional voting system instead of a first-past-the-post system in spite of its tendency to produce no clear majorities and a fragmentation of the parties. As he saw it, *proporz* was "[a] system that enables the majority to rule while ensuring at the same time that the minority is adequately represented." There was a first step towards a transparent "proportionately weighted" cabinet in 1920, yet it took until 1945 for the system to be implemented in full. In Renner's provisional government, the KPÖ, too, was made part of this complex mechanism of power and control sharing. In practice, this meant that every secretary of state had at least two undersecretaries at his side for control and communication purposes. *Proporz* was introduced throughout the various elites of civil servants. It should be noted that this was the only possibility for the Social Democrats to gain a foothold in the almost exclusively Christian Socialist or Conservative German Nationalistic elites.

Proporz functioned as a kind of buffer system for the aggressive "pillars" that continued to characterize Austrian society, whose potential for conflict it channeled and neutralized. It was, therefore, a major stabilizing factor for a time. However, when the system had degenerated by the 1960s into a mechanism for allotting jobs and flats to co-religionists and had more or less exhausted its political know-how and reformist élan, first grumblings became audible. Opposition was particularly strong in the field of the media, where increasingly rigid ossification along *proporz* lines had set in from the mid-1950s. Every radio program of RAVAG, the Austrian broadcasting corporation, was monitored by two party journalists; on one occasion, tempers flared into a fist fight when a news program was aired which appeared one-sided to one of the two gentlemen. The advent of television widened the scope of *proporz*; the "Black Wave," the continued radio dominance of the ÖVP, was now complemented by the "Red Screen," for the heads of TV were nominated by the SPÖ. The so-called "Radio Referendum," initiated mainly by one of the dailies, the *Kurier*, and its editor-in-chief, Hugo Portisch, was a first attempt to alert the public to the cozy and ubiquitous power sharing arrangements in state-owned radio and TV.

Federal Chancellor Josef Klaus used plain language to describe the abstruse ends *proporz* was used for in the first grand coalition: "*Proporz* meant the continuation of a practice through which the coalition parties secured their share of power in the state for themselves; posts, subsidies, even government and civil service delegations who were sent abroad had to be split between the parties strictly on a one-to-one basis."

The upside of *proporz* was that it prevented one social political model from steamrolling the other—as had been the case with the Catholic conservative model in the First Republic; while the nationalized industries remained an ideological bone of contention, they were accepted as a fact of political life by the ÖVP. The leading positions in the nationalized industries and in the nationalized big banks with their extensive industrial holdings were the subject of detailed negotiations that preceded the signing of the coalition pacts, which meant that after a period in the mid-1950s during which the ÖVP had enjoyed a clear advantage, the SPÖ pulled level; this situation changed slightly when a couple of FPÖ protégés were installed at the expense of the SPÖ. A new and growing trend was appointing people from outside the party hierarchies to top positions as CEOs and as members of boards of directors.

The Long Haul of the Grand Coalition under ÖVP Leadership (1946-1966) and the First Cracks in Postwar Pillarization (1966 and 1970)

Even in the outwardly successful re-democratization experiment of 1945, latent dictatorial patterns continued to exist. When the U.S. occupation authority conducted a poll in Vienna, Linz, and Salzburg[40] to ascertain the relative public support for Communism and National Socialism, 26.4 percent of those polled openly endorsed National Socialism in Linz, more than 43.2 percent did so in Salzburg, and 35.6 percent in Vienna. Both in Vienna and in Salzburg, almost 50 percent opted for "neither … nor"; in Linz the rejection of authoritarian ideologies was even more pronounced at 62.8 percent. In another poll, 39.3 percent opted for a democracy, 23.7 percent for a socialist republic (a term that most of the people in the poll understood to refer to an anti-communist republic with a social democratic government, whereas U.S. pollsters took it to refer to a communist regime), 3.3 percent endorsed a dictatorship, a sizeable 15.9 percent a monarchy, and 17.8 percent did not commit themselves. A latent authoritarian potential was indisputably present, and in the 1950s outside observers such as the political scientist Hans J. Morgenthau drew attention to authoritarian structures at Austrian universities. In view of massive evidence of "clericalism and corporatist traditions as relics of the 'Ständestaat'" and of ÖVP "solidarism" in economic and social policies, the very fact that a grand coalition had been put into place following a "shotgun marriage" and the pressure exerted by the Allied administration minimized the danger of an authoritarian course being resuscitated.

In the 1950s, political analysts left no doubt that in their judgment Austrian postwar structures fell short of the requirements of a classical liberal democratic system. Hans J. Morgenthau, who had emigrated from Germany to become one of America's most renowned political scientists, drew the sober conclusion from his fact-finding mission to Austria in October 1951 that it was precisely these specific authoritarian structures and the grand coalition that made sure that radical communism and radical neo-Nazism were kept on a short leash without these parties being deserted by their voters altogether.[41] In 1952, a confidential report critiqued the un-American decision-making structures and processes in the Austrian economy. The report, "The Restraint of Competition in the Austrian Economy," written by a junior employee of the Economics Division of the U.S. embassy in Vienna, was to have highlighted the extent to which competition was distorted by structural deficiencies, whose removal appeared crucial to obtaining further funds under the Marshall Plan.[42] In terms of *realpolitik*, the report was simply another academic exercise without genuine understanding of the Austrian situation, for aid under the Marshall Plan sought above all economic stabilization and by no means economic restructuring. Stabilization had top priority in Austria at the time, for it was thought that it was going to ensure the country's integration into the Western bloc; it was pursued even if it meant an acceptance of the concentration of economic power in the nationalized big banks, in nationalized industries and in the corporatist state, all of which were called into question in the report. It was no coincidence that it was Julius Raab, the most influential ÖVP politician of the day, who was most vociferous in utterly rejecting this critique.

One of the reasons why the voting blocks that dated from the First Republic remained so stable was the tightly knit organization of the parties which had various kinds of rewards in store for their supporters: their voters could count on the system for such goodies as de-Nazification certificates (for which a small donation for the party became due) and for jobs and apartments.

This behavior was reinforced through the remarkable continuity of the different political socializations. "Obedience" and "subordination" were not phenomena Austria owed to National Socialism, even though they reached their abysmal low point in the perverseness of that period. A glance at the educational traditions of the Monarchy will reveal their emphasis on obedience and coercion. The more liberal educational ideas of the times between the wars, which in any case, like the reforms of Otto Gloeckel, remained confined for the most part to Vienna, produced a tiny counter elite, but did not otherwise change the basic situation. The authoritarian Dollfuss-Schuschnigg regime blocked this alternative approach to educational issues, which appears as downright progressive in retrospect, and National Socialism finished the job. A replay of the "obedient decades" seemed inevitable after 1945, when absolute priority was given to political and especially economic reconstruction. It took until the late 1950s for resistance to stir, particularly in youth culture, and to become articulate in political terms without ever getting anywhere near the explosive dynamics of the youth and protest movements in France or in the Federal Republic of Germany.

Judging from their voting patterns, the Austrians seem to have taken grand coalitions for granted. This impression is confirmed if one takes a look at the coalition debates since 1945. Until 1955, the presence of the Allies was an additional guarantee for the continuation of the regulatory framework of two-party rule. In 1949, it only took a period of thirty days after the elections for a grand coalition to be sworn in; both parties had lost votes and seats in the elections to the VdU, the predecessor party of FPÖ/BZÖ, whose revisionist electoral platform was attractive for many ex-members of the NSDAP. The VdU gained sixteen seats. In 1953, more time was needed for the formation of a new government; the ÖVP replaced Leopold Figl, their chancellor, with Julius Raab. Their plan of involving the VdU in the government in order to neutralize the SPÖ, who had in the meantime drawn almost level with the ÖVP in terms of seats, failed when Theodor Körner, the federal president, and the SPÖ refused to accept the political program that had been all but agreed between the ÖVP and the VdU; in a matter of thirteen days this "threesome" was already a thing of the past.

In 1956, the ÖVP did not have the courage to end the grand coalition in spite of clear gains—it was only one seat away from an absolute majority—but it managed to increase its clout within the government through tough negotiations. In 1959, the SPÖ had a majority of votes, but ended up trailing the ÖVP by one seat because of the vagaries of electoral law. Raab was left out on a limb by his own party when he wanted to make Bruno Kreisky, the SPÖ's shooting star, his finance minister; this was presumably to Kreisky's advantage since the success he was later to have as foreign minister gave him the opportunity to distinguish himself sufficiently to be considered a candidate for the chancellorship. In 1959, the formation of a government proved for the first time extremely time demanding and was only surpassed in that respect by the 129 days in 1962.

In 1962, the ÖVP gained two additional seats and expected to be handed both the Foreign Ministry and the Ministry of Justice. In addition, it also wanted more influence in the field of nationalized industries. Even though it became clear from the very first negotiations immediately after the elections that the positions of the two parties were very far apart, it took more than four and a half months, until 27 March 1963, to resolve the differences and launch another edition of the grand coalition. The ÖVP's absolute majority of seats (with 48.35 percent of the votes) in 1966 put an end to the grand coalition, which had already been on the ropes in the negotiations of 1962/1963; these negotiations had been opposed by a part of the ÖVP under the leadership of Josef Klaus. In 1966 it was clear to the SPÖ after forty-four days that in spite of its almost complete renunciation of power it would not be able to accept the ÖVP offer of participation in the new government, and the Second Republic's first period of one-party rule under Josef Klaus got under way.

The crucial problem with *proporz* in the 1950s and 1960s was the gradual substitution of power sharing for the original principle of mutual control. This is the background against which the election results of 1966 should be interpreted: they show a preference of the ÖVP among first-time voters and women because the party had signaled more believably that it wanted to break the traditional mold in that respect. From 1970 onward, Bruno Kreisky showed he was willing to reduce party-political dominance in crucial areas of power by co-opting nonparty ministers and personalities (such as Rudolf Kirchschläger as foreign minister and federal president and Erich Bielka as foreign minister).

The Long Kreisky Era (1971-1983): Voters Prepared to Travel Part of the Way Together and the Heyday of Social Partnership

That this kind of pragmatism had suddenly turned the SPÖ into a "liberal popular party" is in no way borne out by the facts. In 1969, it was obvious that the SPÖ had succeeded under Kreisky's leadership in focusing on its potential of attracting the working-class vote; it put this focus to good effect after the secession caused by Olah. Strikingly, 59 percent of the workers in a poll at the time said they felt close to the SPÖ.[43] As of 1970, a trend became noticeable among the educated classes (university graduates and GCE) to vote for the SPÖ (1969: 18 percent; 1972: 29 percent; 1977: 30 percent). At the same time, women increasingly began to vote for the SPÖ in general elections (1969: 39 percent; 1972: 45 percent). Among young voters, the SPÖ already had an absolute majority in 1970.

The SPÖ reformist electoral platform, which had been supplemented shortly before the general elections by a slogan about the duration of national military service ("Six months is enough"), was particularly well received in small rural districts that had hitherto been dominated by the ÖVP and went down particularly well also with the upper middle class, women, employees, and young voters. Altogether, 158,000 votes were directly transferred from the ÖVP to the SPÖ.[44] The core areas where the SPÖ gained votes were, moreover, particularly affected by primary structural change. Peter Ulram has summed up the results of general elections between 1970 and 1979 as follows: "The SPÖ managed to transform the socialist-liberal coalition of interests and values into an electoral coalition that lasted for more than a decade and became the dominant force in the Austrian party system."[45]

Kreisky had a knack like no other Second Republic politician of addressing the conservative basic convictions of the voters that had been clearly in evidence in elections results since the days of the Monarchy, of adding carefully measured doses of innovation and of sweetening the pill through strengthening social partnership. In the volume of his memoirs entitled *Links und Frei. Mein Weg 1930–1950*, Willy Brandt, the former German chancellor, described Bruno Kreisky as possessing a "double nature": he was kindly and grumpy, he was a Socialist dyed in the wool with a considerable admixture of liberalism, who had a way of leaving both workers and university professors spellbound through his addresses. In a way that is without parallel in the case of any of the other chancellors of the Second Republic, all the traditional structural facts of domestic politics seemed to have conspired against him, all the social and international trends for him. Bruno Kreisky had left the *Israelitische Kultusgemeinde* in 1931, yet his Jewish descent was no secret in the Socialist youth movement, in the time when the Social Democrats had been banned as a party and after 1945. Since latent but virulent anti-Semitism had marked the time when Kreisky was a university student, had escalated further after 1938, and was still active below the surface after 1945, Kreisky never believed that he was going to make it to the very top in politics. He often used the dictum of the "best man one step from the top." On the other hand, politics had been his clear goal from grammar school onwards: his classmates at Vienna's Radetzkygymnasium envisioned him as a city councilor, for Vienna's city council was the only place that still boasted Social Democratic politicians of Jewish descent as government members.

This situation, which was exacerbated through the upward mobility of his family (and his mother's family ties to the upper middle-class Felix clan in Znojmo), put Kreisky into a minority position twice over. As a Jew and an intellectual, he had problems being accepted on equal terms by the Socialist Workers' Youth movement. Kreisky made no secret of his bourgeois origins, yet he was also unwilling to become active in the *Verband Sozialistischer Mittelschüler/Studenten*, a sizeable proportion of whose members were Jewish. He wanted to be close to the rank and file, to working-class children and adolescents and was not to be deterred by implicit (and, during the time of the ban on the party, very much explicit) anti-Semitism. Even when he was ousted from his position in a putsch in Wien-Wieden, his district organization, and sent into the "desert" of Tullnerfeld where the Christian Socialists were in an almost unassailable position of strength, he regarded this not as a defeat, but as a challenge. There was no question for him that the SPÖ was where he belonged.

What his indefatigable optimism, his unerring instinct for the right moment, and his inside knowledge of life in a minority group had taught him was how to turn an indisputable handicap into an advantage. Part of this was his strategy of addressing groups of voters who, in view of the traditions of pillarization, did not appear to hold out any hope to him. During election campaigns, he loved to travel to the Tyrol, for instance, where he initially was met with complete rejection, and he speeded up the granting of subsidies to mountain farmers and the transfer of resources to the "black" provinces in western Austria.

There is no doubt that the new medium of television was instrumental in reaching new groups of voters. Between 1965 and 1970, the number of private owners of TV sets rose from 30 to 67 percent of the population. This enabled a considerably more individualistic style of opinion forming than the mostly *Lager*-influenced communal TV consumption in the pub or in a gathering of neighbors. The reform of ORF, the Austrian radio and TV corporation, which had been initiated by the ÖVP and FPÖ on the basis of the "Radio Referendum," had resulted in TV being professionalized under Gerd Bacher, a conservative journalist. Because some of these changes were patterned on American models, they created new challenges and new possibilities for politicians. In his direct confrontation with Josef Klaus, the then-chancellor Bruno Kreisky was obviously much more adept at handling the new medium than his opponent. He had had much more common ground both with Julius Raab and Alfons Gorbach than with Josef Klaus. In addition to this, he cultivated a much more relaxed style of contact with journalists than was the rule in Austria in the 1950s and 1960s, a consequence, perhaps, of Kreisky's experiences as a journalist in Sweden and of his secret longing for a career in journalism. Time and again, Kreisky provided the stuff of which stories—and headlines—are made. His experiences as secretary of state and as foreign minister had also contributed to the open style with which he communicated political content.

Kreisky tried to sweep taboo topics that had the potential of being politically damaging to him under the carpet. Prominent among these topics was a principled confrontation with the Nazi past of roughly one million Austrian men and women and Austria's contribution to the preparation and execution of the Shoah.

Above all, he was determined to avoid anything that could be interpreted as a partisan attitude arising from this Jewishness. He therefore left the negotiations concerning the so-called *Wiedergutmachung*, (indemnification) to others for a long time. His emotional overreaction in 1970 is no doubt connected to Simon Wiesenthal (whom Kreisky not unreasonably also suspected of following a party-political agenda) broke an Austrian taboo: during the time of the grand coalition under ÖVP leadership, Wiesenthal had refrained from criticizing members of the government because of their former NSDAP membership, as is evidenced by Reinhard Kamitz, the renowned ÖVP finance minister, whose Nazi past was an open secret. However, in 1975 Wiesenthal wanted to prevent a replay of the SPÖ relying on the support of the FPÖ under the leadership of Friedrich Peter and informed Rudolf Kirchschläger, the federal president, of the fact that Peter (as is borne out also by the most recent evidence) belonged to an SS unit that was involved in liquidations. Wiesenthal had already been in possession of the information at the time of the election campaign, but had chosen not to pass it on. Kreisky's reaction was extreme and disproportionate, particularly when he indirectly accused Wiesenthal of collaboration with the Nazi regime. Kreisky's overreaction is often linked to his presumed intention to use the incident in order to win over the "formers" as voters. In this case, however, it was a personal taboo that Wiesenthal had hit upon knowingly or unknowingly. Bruno Kreisky did not want to be played off as a Jew against that stable bloc in society that advocated the reintegration of ex-members of the NSDAP and of former soldiers of the *Wehrmacht* in the 1970s. The reaction he showed was an emotional reflex from the gut. A politician with an excellent grounding in history, he was familiar with the taboo subjects of the Austrian electorate like few others.

A case in point was the first comprehensive poll in 1978 centering on authoritarianism, which focused on average voters rather than on radicalized ex-Nazi functionaries in order to analyze the reception conditions for anti-democratic, authoritarian codes and propaganda. Authoritarian leanings were in evidence in SPÖ voters concerning areas that touched on conventionalism, irrationalism, and latent aggressive potentials against marginalized groups and minorities.[46] Here SPÖ core voters displayed considerably more elaborated authoritarian attitudes than supporters of the FPÖ. The latter had a tremendous lead over SPÖ and ÖVP voters as far as the rationalization and glorification of the Nazi past and anti-Semitism were concerned.

This stock-taking—one year before the greatest Social Democratic electoral victory for Bruno Kreisky's one-party government in 1979— surely signals an extremely high authoritarian potential, which was obviously kept at bay by means of the socioeconomic guarantees of the welfare state with its policies of safeguarding jobs at all costs. It was above all the contingent of authoritarian SPÖ voters that remained loyal to Kreisky, for his model of the welfare state appeared to them more important than the sweeping reform of the judicial system or the democratization of other areas of life including the liberalization of the arts. Bruno Kreisky—and that appears to be another key element—was accepted in the role of leader; indeed, he was revered by many. Kreisky himself was probably more aware of these authoritarian continuities than anyone else; he had experienced them himself as a prisoner in the times of Austro-Fascism and in extreme situations during the Nazi era; he was, therefore, very careful never to overstep the limits of acceptability in sociopolitical discourse.

How easy it was to make this authoritarian potential boil over was demonstrated in 1972, when most of the bilingual place-name signs that had been put up in mixed-language areas in pursuance of Austria's obligations outlined in Article 7 of the 1955 State Treaty were torn down in a show of violence. Kreisky himself met with downright hostile reactions even from members of the SPÖ when he attempted to give political comfort to Hans Sima, the governor of Carinthia. In 1976 the Ethnic Minorities Act was passed with the votes of all the three parties, but failed to gain the support of the two most representative organizations of Slovenians, who did not nominate their representatives for the planned ethnic minorities advisory committee until 1989. Kreisky, too, took a back seat on an issue in which he had originally been deeply interested, thereby finally sealing Sima's fate. Even in 1999 the media went into overdrive, when Franz Vranitzky, the former chancellor, intervened by phone in a live TV interview of Jörg Haider, the governor of Carinthia, to critique one of Haider's statements on Austria's cooperation in the organization of the Olympics with one of the country's former enemies (that is, Slovenia). A flood of comments evoked a replay of the instrumentalization of the

Carinthian *Abwehrkampf* based on German nationalistic publications of the 1930s and 1940s. One of Carinthia's central myths seemed to be in acute danger. Factually correct and unemotional historiography might be practiced elsewhere; here latent Slovenophobic smears seemed to be *de rigueur*, at least in 1999, even though much had changed for the better in Carinthia's treatment of its minority. In the meantime, Jörg Haider has fulfilled some long-term Slovenian requests, for Austria's own minorities appear so much more acceptable these days than the "hostile" hordes of migrants from abroad. It was, moreover, an expedient move to show tolerance in this political field, for it ensured a new wave of attention for this kind of austrocentrism. Vis-à-vis Slovenia, it appears opportune from time to time to revive the old propaganda saga.

Contradictions and cracks in Austria's democratic identity are a central constant, yet they also demonstrate the importance that attaches to social partnership—however discredited it may seem today—that has been used as an additional element of control in outbreaks of right-wing populist prejudices since 1945. This political "containment" has been all the more effective owing to a widespread acceptance of political authorities even though numerous prejudices have managed time and again to at least partly discredit political goals or persons (for example, Bruno Kreisky as a "Jew," or the "communist" Christian Broda). These elements were reinforced through one of the central taboos of Austrian postwar society: to address anti-Semitism or the "Jewish question" in a context of Austrian political co-responsibility.

Return to the Grand Coalition (1987) under SPÖ Chancellorship after the Failure of the First "Small" SPÖ-FPÖ Coalition

Kreisky's coalition talks with the FPÖ under Norbert Steger in 1983 were short and conclusive: thirteen days after the elections, it was clear that the option of the "small" coalition was going to be realized. Kreisky had repeatedly justified his contacts with the FPÖ not only with party strategic arguments, but also with the attempt to bring about a transformation of the FPÖ into a genuinely liberal party along the lines of the once right-wing FDP in the Federal Republic of Germany. What he had not included in his equations was, first, the debate on the wartime past of Kurt Waldheim, which was to give Austria's victim doctrine a last gasp at life, and, second, the firebrand Jörg Haider, who succeeded in fashioning the FPÖ in the mold of the VdU with even greater electoral successes than those of 1949.

Franz Vranitzky put an end to the coalition of the SPÖ and FPÖ after Jörg Haider had assumed power amid unmistakably right-wing, nationalistic background noises. In spite of opinion poll results that held out little promise for the SPÖ, Vranitzky moved the general elections forward to the fall of 1986; the loss of ten seats (with an overall share of valid votes at 43.12 percent) still left a clear margin between the Socialists and the ÖVP. The conservative leader, Alois Mock, who professed himself disappointed with the 41.29 percent that the ÖVP had received, was temperamentally disinclined to grand coalitions, yet he could not but agree to enter into one in the end. The FPÖ, in the meantime an openly radicalized party, had doubled its vote by means of a cleverly populist campaign, in which criticism of the grand coalition played the most important role; it received 9.73 percent of the votes.

Mock's attempts to enter into a coalition with the FPÖ was reputedly blocked by opposition to that project from the majority of the party's leadership; many of the party's leading lights and most notably representatives of big business realized that a number of reforms were overdue in the Second Republic, such as the country's re-positioning with regard to the process of European integration, the transformation of the nationalized industries, and a new perspective on Austria's role with regard to National Socialism.

Jörg Haider took aim with his radical rhetoric at the two big parties, particularly at the SPÖ and Franz Vranitzky, the chancellor, and used the increasingly emotional debate on migration to garner votes on a massive scale also from groups of voters who were traditionally part of the Social Democrats' core electorate. The probability for a xenophobic election campaign to be rewarded with electoral success can be calculated on the basis of the xenophobia statistics of Günther Rathner, the Innsbruck psychologist and sociologist. In 1998, the screening of a sample of 2,000 Austrians of both sexes between fifteen and seventy-five years of age revealed that "a quarter of the Austrian population are clearly not xenophobic, another quarter is 'neutral' and almost half the population is highly (22 percent) or very highly (26 percent) xenophobic. If one adds the 'neutral' quarter to the 'xenophiles', one gets the picture of a society split down the middle: one half is xenophile to moderate, the other half is xenophobic."[47] Even though it may be inadvisable automatically to classify the "neutrals" as xenophiles, as Rathner has done, the high potential on the negative side—48 percent of xenophobes— nevertheless underscores the amount of political gunpowder stored up in Austrian society in 1998.

This topic demonstrates the importance of the political and social conditions that may further authoritarian prejudices and encourage them to break cover. The authoritarianism poll of 1978 referred to above revealed massive prejudices against "aliens," yet this potential remained politically deactivated at the time owing to Bruno Kreisky's social and labor market policies. First indications that this strategy had not resulted in a sweeping change in attitudes toward migrants became visible in 1981, when a wave of refugees swept over Austria in the wake of the introduction of martial law in Poland.

An area where changes in attitudes do become visible when compared to the 1978 authoritarianism poll is Rathner's 1998 analysis of anti-Semitism. Asked whether, "In view of the way they behaved, Jews were entirely without blame as regards their persecution," survey results revealed that 14 percent declared themselves as highly and 6 percent as very highly anti-Semitic. Almost 50 percent were classified as not anti-Semitic or as slightly anti-Semitic.

What remains disconcerting about the society in which the Austrian electorate is embedded is its general tendency to perpetuate through its educational strategies an automatic, unthinking subordination to authority. Reflections on the authoritarian potential should not be limited to taking a mere inventory of people's prejudicial universes but should seek to understand these patterns of attitudes as products and results of socio-political conditions and long-term historical processes. The cross-fertilizations that can be observed in this context are charged emotionally and historically with debates and stereotypes from the past and create complex developments and climaxes. Political discourse about the most provocative topics of the authoritarian potential is gaining in importance as is the tendency to use populist discourse strategies to bring about the translation of existing attitudes into concrete voting behavior.

ÖVP-FPÖ 2000: A Coalition against the Will of the Voters Sanctioned *ex post* in 2002

"Homo Austriacus" had been confronted with the need to make another policy decision since 3 February 2000. The road that Austria had relied on for its progress and whose chief characteristics had been an element of control and a socio-economically successful consensual democracy with a strong component of social partnership appeared to be no longer viable. Two alternatives were available in the reservoir of democratic ideologies: a rightist, identitary or a leftist, participatory type, with the simultaneous availability of the classical types of representative democracy (à la Hans Kelsen) or the ideological expansion of that concept into "social democracy" as well as of a type of conservative democracy stressing the role of free competition in the democratic process (à la Alois Schumpeter).

Under a purely party ideological perspective, Austria has had a center-right majority since 1983, which was not translated into governmental executive terms until 2000 owing to the impact of Austria's accession to the European Union and to forces opposing right-wing populism. The erosion of *Lager*-formation was already fully operational, and *Lager*-inspired loyalty tied only older voters to their original political socialization.

After the elections of October 1999 with their disastrous result for the ÖVP—for the first time ever they trailed not only the SPÖ, but also the FPÖ and, with only 26.91 percent of the vote, slipped to third place—the chancellor, Viktor Klima, tried to steer negotiations once more towards a grand coalition. Yet several years earlier Wolfgang Schüssel had already taken to regarding Klima as his junior partner, and in the new situation, he devised a strategically perfect plan: the formation of a coalition government with Haider's FPÖ.

Schüssel was not to be deflected from this plan by Thomas Klestil's strong opposition to it or by the humiliating treatment he received at the federal president's hands, and the coalition took office accompanied by demonstrations at home and the so-called "sanctions" imposed by the fourteen EU partners. In retrospect, it becomes obvious that it was those very reactions that ultimately caused the unequal partnership to jell even if the thin supply of qualified candidates on the part of the FPÖ called for an almost monthly replacement of ministers. The extent to which this was anticipated and used for a master plan by Schüssel, the perfect strategist, who managed to paint the clear electoral victors, the Social Democrats, as the losers, is unknown. The fact remains that Schüssel had learned the ropes of domestic politics in the Waldheim controversy.

All things considered, it seems that Schüssel, in a way, turned the clock back to the First Republic, where it was the order of the day for the runner-up in the elections to secure a government majority through a coalition with a right-wing partner; he, of course, went one better and achieved the same result from third position.

Even though the "sanctions" were only symbolic ones against the country's diplomatic and political representatives while the normal channels remained intact, the tabloids and the ÖVP-FPÖ coalition enthusiastically jumped onto this particular bandwagon. Rising to his top form, Haider started to pander to Austrian feelings of inferiority. Viktor Klima, new to the role of leader of the opposition, was showered with tokens of appreciation on the international stage and contacted such senior EU politicians as Tony Blair to register his protest against the new coalition; in the meantime, the SPÖ initially left the field of the "Save Austria" movement completely to the ÖVP and was stigmatized once again as treasonous. Less than half a year later, an EU report exonerated the new government and rehabilitated—with a number of critical footnotes—the coalition *ex post.*

Schüssel's real qualities were in evidence in the way he relatively calmly and stoically stuck to his course, refusing to let himself be dismayed by the inferiority of his coalition partner. His electoral victory in 2002, which came as a surprise to some, must be seen in connection with that inferior coalition partner, whose electoral support kept dwindling on all levels outside Carinthia. By keeping aloof from most conflicts and intervening only sporadically and then with rhetorical panache, he gave the impression of being in the eye of the storm even in the turbulent phases his government passed through. He was also able to create considerable elbow room for himself in his everyday work routines.

When Haider realized that his FPÖ was only being instrumentalized by the ÖVP, the only course left to him was another swerve to the right, which provoked new elections. The electorate had already made their peace with this provisional coalition. Schüssel managed, moreover, to draw the glitzy ex-FPÖ finance minister over to his side and to rid himself completely of the sins of his past in the eyes of the voters. The FPÖ lost the most votes in those elections of any Austrian party ever.

It was not the putsch-like installation of the then-youthful Jörg Haider as the leader of the FPÖ as much as his successful strategies against the social partnership and the grand coalition that served as further indicators for the voters' willingness to venture outside their traditional political camps. In this transformation phase, authoritarian codes were also welcome provided they surfaced in a context that had the right mix of right-wing populism, Zeitgeist, and cool youthfulness.

This Janus-faced development—a gradual disappearance on the one hand of the authoritarian undercurrent in society, on the other, a rising tide of new authoritarian codes directed against aliens, migrants, criminals, and so forth—was a characteristic of the late 1980s and of the 1990s.

A poll commissioned by the author at the end of 2004 to repeat the one on authoritarian attitudes from 1978 provided clear evidence of

Austria's continued evolution in democratic political terms.[48] In the survey, 1,420 persons above fifteen years of age, who had been selected on the basis of "stratified multistage clustered random sampling" were interviewed in person (there were no telephone interviews) by IFES, who had been entrusted with the project by its initiator, in August and September 2004. It is quite clear that the relatively strong continuity as regards reactions to the introductory statement, "Obedience and respect for those in authority are important virtues that children should acquire" (2004: 68 percent agreement as against 74 percent in 1978) is offset by a pronounced decline in the acceptability of such authoritarian codes as the reintroduction of the death penalty, the unwillingness to take responsibility, or an emphasis on society being split into strong and weak individuals.

Among statements concerning the Nazi past, the claim, "There are worse things than the emergence of another Hitler" met with significantly reduced approval (84 percent disagree as against 62 percent in 1978; in 1978, 19 percent signaled agreement, which had shrunk to 4 percent in 2004). The same applies to the "glorification of the Nazi past": the statement, "Obviously there were aberrations in the Third Reich, but it's out of the question that six million Jews were killed" met with 61 percent disagreement as against a mere 5 percent who agreed (compared to 35 percent who disagreed and 21 percent who agreed in 1978).

That there is still a certain amount of leeway for revisionism in this area is shown by the response to the statement, "In view of the way they behaved, Jews are not entirely without blame as regards their persecution": in 2004, 52 percent signaled total disagreement and 12 percent total agreement compared to 29 percent of total disagreement and 25 percent of total agreement in 1978.

The reintroduction of the death penalty "to put an end to terrorism" would have been welcomed by 60 percent without ifs, and, or buts in 1978, at a time, in other words, when the reform of the judicial system was in full swing. In 2004, the approval rate had shrunk (despite 9/11) to a mere 12 percent; 66 percent disapproved completely compared to a meager 19 percent in 1978.

That the context of migration continued to be beset by prejudices is borne out by the fact that approval rates had remained roughly the same with reference to the question whether vagabond foreign youths should be barred from entering the country: in 2004, 45 percent were unequivocally in favor, and only 21 percent were totally opposed. In 1978, the corresponding ratio was 68 percent versus 16 percent. Sex with juveniles below the age of consent was still up for severe punishment: in 2004, 42 percent agreed, in 1978, 67 percent; the figure of those totally opposed remained almost the same: 13 percent in 2004 as against 12 percent in 1978. The topics involved—migration, crime rate, and sex with juveniles below the age of consent—had been at the focus of media and political attention in the period between the two pollings.

A clear breakthrough was achieved as regards the status of women. In 1978, 51 percent came out in favor of the "nature-given role of housewife and mother," which holds out for women the only hope of "real fulfillment"; in 2004, this had shrunk to 13 percent. Disagreement rose from 16 percent to 65 percent.

The Smallest Common Voter Consensus:
The Third Grand Coalition (SPÖ-ÖVP) 2007

In a development that came as a surprise to most pollsters, the victor of the elections in 2002, Wolfgang Schüssel, was narrowly voted out of office in 2006, perhaps because he made the same mistakes as Viktor Klima, who was actually very popular: he had no clear messages for the voters, he avoided direct confrontations in his function as chancellor, and he tended to claim that everything was alright anyway. The two major parties were again traditionally equal in strength, even though the level differed drastically from what it had been in the 1950s and 1960s. The FPÖ (Phase 2) was roughly comparable to Haider's FPÖ in 1986; the Greens were the third strongest party as far as the votes were concerned. Another novelty of the election results was that the majority for the center-right was again a thing of the past for the first time since 1983, a majority that incidentally existed—in a way similar to the First Republic—also between 1949 and 1970.

The fact that the Greens are beginning to be defined as an also-ran party is another indication for the slow decline of authoritarianism, for they have consistently identified with anti-authoritarian positions vis-à-vis all issues related to authoritarian potential. The defeat of the SPÖ under Bruno Kreisky in the 1978 referendum on Zwentendorf, the nuclear power station, was an indication of the onset of that decline, but even more than that was result of the ÖVP's political wheeling and dealing and of intransigence on the part of Kreisky, the SPÖ, and the social partnership. In the last resort, the Greens remain an urban party with a youthful electorate who came close to accepting governmental responsibility in 2002. The failure of a genuinely liberal party, which had looked like a real option when Heide Schmidt broke away from the FPÖ, has to do with the center-right value system that has had such a stranglehold on Austrian voters since the days of the monarchy. Whoever wants to push through reforms and to have electoral success cannot afford to ignore that system. Majority voters have pronounced value-based conservative attitude patterns that continue to decide elections in spite of an indisputable rise in democratic consciousness.

Notes

1. I appreciate very much the advice and work of Prof. Otmar Binder, who translated the article from German into English.

2. An early study on the basis of sociological research and public opinion polls is Karl Blecha, Rupert Gmoser and Heinz Kienzl, *Der durchleuchtete Wähler* (Vienna: Europa Verlag, 1964), based on research by the Sozialwissenschaftliche Studiengesellschaft (founded in 1960) and using a sample of 30,000 voters and 35,000 trade union mem-

Table 2
General Elections Results, 1945-2006, in Percent

Date	Eligible Voters	ÖVP	SPÖ	KPÖ	FPÖ	Greens	LIF
25 Nov. 1945	3,449,606	49.8	44.6	5.4 (4 seats)	–	–	–
9 Oct. 1949	4,391,815	44.0	38.7	5.1 (5 seats)	11.7	–	–
22 Feb. 1953	4,586,870	41.3	42.1	5.3 (4 seats)	10.9	–	–
13 May 1956	4,614,464	46.0	43.0	4.4 (3 seats)	6.5	–	–
10 May 1959	4,696,603	44.2	44.8	3.3 (no seats) 7.7		–	–
18 Nov. 1962	4,805,351	45.4	44.0	36	7.0	–	–
6 March 1966	4,886,818	48.4	42.6	0.41	5.4	–	–
1 May 1970	5,045,841	44.7	48.4	1.0	5.5	–	–
10 Oct. 1971	4,984,448	43.1	50.0	1.4	5.5	–	–
5 Oct. 1975	5,019,277	42.9	50.4	1.2	5.4	–	–
6 May 1979	5,186,735	41.9	51.0	1.0	6.1	–	–
24 April 1983	5,316,436	43.2	47.6	0.7	5.0	–	–
23 Nov. 1986	5,461,414	41.3	43.1	0.7	9.7	4.8	–
7 Oct. 1990	5,628,912	32.1	42.8	0.6	16.6	4.8	–
9 Oct. 1994	5,774,000	27.7	34.9	0.3	22.9	7.3	–
17 Dec. 1995	5,768,039	28.3	38.1	0.3	22.0	4.8	–
3 Oct. 1999	5,838,373	26.9	33.2	0.5	26.9	74 (no seats)	3.7
24 Nov. 2002	5,912,592	42.3	36.5	0.56	10.0	9.5	–
1 Oct. 2006	6,107,686	34.33	35.34	1.01	11.04	11.05	–

Source: Bundesministerium für Inneres.

bers. All authors have been influenced by the studies of Paul Lazarsfeld. In the 1980s the focus, however, was on an analysis of the political culture including the voters, as is well summarized in Peter A. Ulram, *Hegemonie und Erosion: politische Kultur und politischer Wandel in Österreich* (Vienna: Böhlau, 1990); in the 1990s the perspective shifted towards "voting behavior." This trend is well documented in *Das österreichische Wahlverhalten*, ed. Fritz Plasser et al. (Vienna: Signum Verlag, 2000).

3. Karl Ucakar, *Demokratie und Wahlrecht in Österreich: Zur Entwicklung von politischer Partizipation und staatlicher Legitimationspolitik* (Vienna: Verlag für Gesellschaftskritik 1985), 154.

4. Quoted from "1900 bis 1907 – Frauen wird das Wahlrecht verwehrt," *85 Jahre allgemeines Frauenwahlrecht in Österreich* <http://www.onb.ac.at/ariadne/projekte/frauen_waehlet/Raum04.html>.

5. Karl Ucakar and Mare Seliger, *Wahlrecht und Wählerverhalten in Wien. Privilegien, Partizipationsdruck und Sozialstruktur*, Kommentare zum Historischen Atlas von Wien 3 (Vienna: Verlag für Jugend und Volk, 1984).

6. Anton Pelinka, "Demokratie: Österreich 1900—Österreich 2000," *Demokratiezentrum Wien* <http://www.demokratiezentrum.org/media/pdf/pelinka.pdf >.

7. See also the relevant statistics in Wolfdieter Bihl, *Von der Donaumonarchie zur Zweiten Republik: Daten zur österreichischen Geschichte seit 1867* (Vienna: Böhlau, 1989), 59. With reference to the countries represented in the Imperial Assembly, 36 percent were German speakers with 63 percent of direct tax payments which commanded forty-five deputies; 23 were Czech speakers with 20 percent of direct tax payments which commanded twenty-one deputies; 16 percent were Polish speakers who commanded sixteen deputies (with 7 percent of direct tax payments); 13 percent were Ruthenians with only 6.8 percent of direct tax payments, while southern Slavs were at 7.3 percent, Italians were at 4.1 percent, and Romanians had 1 percent—yet each of the four groups contributed 10 percent each in tax payments.

8. Ottokar Czernin, who rose to be foreign minister and advisor to Franz Ferdinand, the first in line to the throne, wrote to him in June 1910: "Above all the monarch must rely on a united nobility and even if feudalism and absolutism unfortunately belong to the past, the nobility, with the monarch at its head, must nevertheless play the leading role and must shape the decisions in all matters concerning the Empire. This will prevent such dreadful times as those of Koerber, Gautsch, and Beck, which rocked the Monarchy to its foundations, from ever occurring again" (qtd. in Julius Braunthal, *Victor und Friedrich Adler: Zwei Generationen Arbeiterbewegung* (Vienna: Wiener Volksbuchhandlung, 1965).

9. Arend Lijphart, *The Politics of Accommodation/Pluralism and Democracy in the Netherlands* (English version of *Verzuiling, pacificatie en kentering in de Nederlandse politiek*, 1968), (Berkeley: U of California P, 1975).

10. John W. Boyer, *Culture and Political Crisis in Vienna: Christian Socialism in Power*, 1897-1918 (Chicago: U of Chicago P, 1995).

11. Josef Seethaler, "Die Presse in der Habsburgermonarchie um 1900: Probleme und Chancen in einem multinationalen Raum," Beitrag zum Kolloquium "Europäische Kulturzeitschriften um 1900 als Medien transnationaler und transdisziplinärer Wahrnemung," Göttingen 2004, *Österreichische Akademie der Wissenschaften* <http://www.oeaw.ac.at/cmc/data/Seethaler%20-%20Vortrag%20G%F6ttingen %202004.pdf>.

12. In June, the sixty-six Christian Socialists amalgamated with the thirty deputies of the Catholic People's Party to form the *Christlichsoziale Reichspartei*. The eighty-six

Social Democrats consisted of fifty Germans, twenty-three Czechs, seven Poles, four Romanians, and two Ruthenians.

13. Bihl, *Von der Donaumonarchie*, 65.

14. Original sound recording from "100 Jahre Wahlrecht: Historische Stimmen auf CD," *ORF on Science* <http://science.orf.at/science/news/146843>.

15. Quoted from Braunthal, "Victor und Friedrich Adler," 173.

16. "Weltkrieg, Erster," *Österreich Lexicon*, AEIOU <http://aeiou.iicm.tugraz.at/aeiou. encyclop.w/w438953.htm>.

17. Otto Bauer, *Die Österreichische Revolution* (Vienna: Volksbuchhandlung, 1923), 120.

18. Alexander Spitzmüller, *... und hat auch Ursach," es zu lieben* (Vienna: Frick Verlag, 1955), 378.

19. Christine Klusacek and Kurt Stimmer, eds., *Dokumentation zur österreichischen Zeitgeschichte 1918-1928* (Vienna: Verlag Jugend und Volk, 1971), 52.

20. Reliable data are available as of 1920. In the Christian Socialist electorate, there were 1,315 female voters per 1,000 men; for the Pan-German People's Party, the ratio is 945 female voters per 1,000 men and for the Social Democrats it is 888: 1,000. Data obtained from the exhibition *Frauenwahlrecht und Parlament Vertretung der Frauen in Österreich*, Vienna 2005 <http://www.parlinkom.gv.at/portal/pls/portal/docs/page/SK/VLESESAAL/AKAT/2005_VOLKSVERTRETERIN.PDF>.

21. *Neues Wiener Tagblatt*, 15 Jan. 1919.

22. Klusacek and Stimmer, eds., *Dokumentation 1918-1928,* 54.

23. See also Marianne Jobst-Rieder, "Politische Plakate in Österreich im 20. Jahrhundert", Koop-Poster Projekt, *Österreichische Nationalbibliothek* <http://www. onb. ac.at/koop-poster/projekte/Oesterr_Plakatgeschichte.pdf>.

24. See also "Die Wahlen in den Nationalrat im Jahre 1923," Bundesministeririem für Inneres <http://www.bmi.gv.at/wahlen/wahldownloads/NRW_1923.pdf>.

25. "Graphic Design in Vienna," Österreichische Nationalbibliothek <http://www. onb. ac.at/sammlungen/plakate/archiv/ausstellungen/gdv/biro_ptxt.htm>.

26. Jobst-Rieder, *Politische Plakate*, 7.

27. For his biography, see "Slama, Victor Th.," *Wiener Stadt- und Landesbibliothek* <http://www.wienbibliothek.at/sammlungen/handschriften/nachlass-verzeichnis/s/slamavictor-th-de.htm>.

28. Jobst-Rieder, "Politische Plakate," 8.

29. Ernestine Bennersdorfer, "Kampf der Symbole. Plakate zu den Nationalratswahlen Erste Republik Österreich," Ph.D. diss., Universität für angewandte Kunst Wien, 2002 <http://www.uni-ak.ac.at/culture/diss-abs/bennersd-2002.html>.

30. Ibid.

31. Heimo Halbrainer, "Hoppauf Hakoah—oder: Als Hakoah Graz noch Sturm Graz und G.A.K. besiegte," *DAVID Jüdische Kulturzeitschrifte* <http://www.david.juden.at/kulturzeitschrift/50-54/Main%20frame_Artikel53_Halbrainer.htm>.

32. Rudolf Müllner, "Sportgeschichte Österreich 1918-1938," Universität Wien <http://www.univie.ac.at/Sportwissenschaft/geschichte/VO%20VIII%20%D6sterreic h%201918%20-%201934.pdf>.

52 The Changing Austrian Voter

33. See also Rainer Amstädter, "Antisemitismus in den alpinen Vereinen Wiens von ihren Anfängen bis zum Ende des Ersten Weltkrieges: die politische Dimension des Alpinismus im Spiegelbild der Vereinsgeschichte der 'großen Fünf' von Wien: Sektion Austria des Deutschen und Österreichischen Alpenvereins, Österreichischer Touristenklub, Österreichischer Alpenklub, Österreichischer Gebirgsverein, Touristenverein 'Die Naturfreunde,' sowie der Akademischen Sektion Wien des DÖAV, der Sektion Wien des DÖAV und der alpinen Gesellschaft 'd' Reichensteiner'," M.A., thesis, University of Vienna, 1992.

34. Gerhard Botz, *Gewalt in der Politik: Attentate, Zusammenstöße, Putschversuche, Unruhen in Österreich 1918 bis 1938*, 2nd ed. (Munich: Fink, 1983).

35. Kurt Bauer, "Struktur und Dynamik des illegalen Nationalsozialismus in der obersteirischen Industrieregion 1933/34," M.A. thesis, University of Vienna, 1998, 20 <http://www.kurt-bauer-geschichte.at/PDF_Texte%20&%20 Themen/Diplomarbeit_ Kurt_Bauer.pdf>.

36. All figures below according to Bihl, *Von der Donaumonarchie*, 174, and Emmerich Tálos et al., eds., *Handbuch des politischen System Österreichs* (Vienna: Manz, 1995).

37. See also his latest contribution to the topic: Gerhard Botz, "Arbeiter und andere Lohnabhängige," paper delivered at the International Conference of Labour and Social History 42, Linzer Konferenz, 14-16 September 2006, <http://www.lbihs.at/Botz ArbeiterNS.pdf.4>.

38. The following chapters concerning the period 1945-2005 are based on my book *Die Paradoxe Republik. Österreich 1945-2005* (Vienna: Paul Zsolnay Verlag, 2005), which will appear in an English version in 2007 from Berghahn.

39. Josef Schöner, "Wiener Tagebuch 1944/1945," in *Vom Geachteten zum Gea(chteten: Erinnerungen des k. und k. Diplomaten und k. ungarischen Aussenministers Emerich Csa'ky (1882-1961)*, ed. Eva-Marie Csaky et al. (Vienna: Böhlau, 1992), 425.

40. Oliver Rathkolb, "N.S.-Problem und politische Restauration: Vorgeschichte und Etablierung des VdU" in *Verdrängte Schuld - Verfehlte Sühne. Entnazifizierung in Österreich 1945-1955*, ed. Sebastian Meissl et al. (Vienna: Verlag für Geschichte und Politik, 1986), 73-99.

41. Oliver Rathkolb, "Hans J. Morgenthau und das Österreich-Problem in der letzten Phase der Truman-Administration 1951/1952," *Geschichte zwischen Freiheit und Ordnung. Gerald Stourzh zum 60. Geburtstag*, ed. E. Brix et al. (Graz: Verlag Styria, 1991) 277-98.

42. Johnstone to ambassador, 5 May 1952. NA, RG 84, Vienna Legation Files, Box 3178, Folder as 350.

43. Quoted in Christian Haerpfner, "Die Sozialstruktur der SPÖ: Gesellschaftliche Einflussfaktoren der sozialdemokratischen Parteibindung in Österreich 1969-1988," *Österreichische Zeitschrift für Politikwissenschaft* 4 (1989): 375.

44. Peter A. Ulram, *Hegemonie und Erosion: Politische Kultur und politischer Wandel in Österreich* (Vienna: Boëhlau, 1990), 238.

45. Ibid., 240.

46. Oliver Rathkolb, "Autoritäres Potential und demokratische Werte in Österreich 1978 und 2004," in *Österreichisches Jahrbuch für Politik 2005*, ed. Anreas Kohl et al. (Munich: R. Oldenbourg, 2006), 113-22.

47. Rathner, Günter, "Autoritarismus als notwendige Bedingung von Fremdenfeindlich keit in Österreich," *Bundesministerium für Bildung, Wissenschaft, und Kultur* <http://

archiv.bmbwk.gv.at/medienpool/4291/ff_29d.pdf>. According to this scale, xenophobic attitudes in 1998 were very low for 11 percent of the persons in the poll and low for 15 percent; 26 percent declared themselves neutral; 22 percent displayed strong and 26 percent very strong xenophobic attitudes. Rathner was not aware of the 1978 poll, and he was, therefore, unable to take it into account. Nevertheless, he is wrong in thinking that his was the first such poll to be carried out in Austria. "Österreicher: Halb fremdenfreundlich halb fremdenfeindlich," *ORF ON* <http://vgarchiv.orf.at/austria/de/archiv02/01_11_02_de/oesterreicher_auslaenderfeindlich.htm>.

48. For the following figures, see Rathkolb, "Autoritäres Potential und demokratische Werte," 113-22.

Electoral Change in Austria

Fritz Plasser and Peter A. Ulram

Twenty-five years ago when more than 92 percent of Austrian citizens frequented the polling booths and more than nine out of ten voters cast their votes for the SPÖ or ÖVP, the authors of this article published a book with the title Unbehagen im Parteienstaat (Discontent in the Party State).[1] It goes without saying that the then still tentative predictions about electoral dealignment, party-weariness, the rise of populism, and new political movements were met with little enthusiasm if not outright rejection by leading figures of the dominant parties. In the following decades, several key developments occurred. First, the Austrian Freedom Party (FPÖ) which during the SPÖ-FPÖ coalition (1983-1986) had lost most of its meager electoral support rose to the position of the second largest party in the national elections of 1999, reducing the two former major parties to the status of only medium sized parties. As a consequence, the grand coalition broke down, and an ÖVP-FPÖ coalition government was formed in 2000 which provoked overreactions by the other EU members[2] without much impact on domestic politics. As a governing party, the FPÖ then saw a considerable electoral decline which culminated in the loss of about 60 percent of its former voters in the elections of 2002.[3] The ÖVP gained a landslide victory in 2002,[4] but suffered a sound defeat in the national elections of 2006, making the SPÖ the leading political party albeit by a small margin and with reduced electoral support.

Party competition and electoral behavior in Austria thus underwent unprecedented changes. The following article gives an overview of trends and patterns in Austrian voting behavior based on data gathered from representative post elections polls and/or exit polls covering the period from 1970 to 2006.[5]

The Traditional Sphere of Austrian Party Competition

Until the early 1970s, Austrian voting patterns could be described along the concepts of *"Lager* culture" and *"Lager* affiliation."[6] Embedded in specific subcultural social milieus which were characterized by a relative stability of distinct structural features such as socio-cultural orientation, emotional attachment, and disciplined partisanship the *Lager* shaped the political behavior of the regular voter and the party's group of core voters. The extraordinary stability of deeply rooted party affiliation was based on a conflict pattern that structured Austrian society and which was composed of three main cleavages in the 1950s and 1960s, namely the denominational cleavage (active Catholic milieu or denominationally affiliated milieu versus laicistic, non-denominational milieu), the welfare state cleavage (expectation that the state should provide and regulate social welfare versus stronger orientation towards the free market based on individual initiative and risk) as well as an—albeit weakened—German national versus Austrian national cleavage. These three main cleavages, complemented by traditional tensions between urban and rural areas as well as central and peripheral areas, defined the logics of conflict in post-war Austria as well as the boundaries of the dominant political *Lager*.

It was along the first two cleavages that the dominant political camps formed, representing subcultures with strong emotional, ideological, and organizational ties. The SPÖ and ÖVP were both the political expression of the political *Lager* and their organizers; the party colonization of the administration, public economy, and education sector expanded the reach of camp-oriented relations and mentalities, which were then duly stabilized through the award of material benefits. The other relevant parties, namely the Communist Party (KPÖ) and the Freedom Party (FPÖ, and its predecessor VdU and WdU), lacked either this linkage with the state apparatus and/or an adequate organizational network, resulting in a lack of the internal and external stabilization factors needed to retain voters' loyalty, even in difficult situations. In fact, during the late 1950s and 1960s, these parties lost a considerable share of their vote, which had been quite significant in the first years of the Second Republic. While small parties were still capable of capturing some 17 percent of the vote in the elections of 1949 and 1953, this percentage dropped to just above 10 percent in the elections from 1956 to 1966. Conversely, the SPÖ and ÖVP succeeded in increasing their combined share of the vote to almost 90 percent. During this phase, party competition was limited. "Mobile" voter groups comprised:

- younger voters who were not yet completely integrated into a particular political *Lager*;
- a small group of politically disinterested and poorly informed voters whom Heinz Kienzl[7] pithily described as "political drifting sand";
- supporters of the small parties;
- various political splinter groups that had broken away from the SPÖ and ÖVP, to be seen, for instance, in the parliamentary elections of 1966.

Accordingly, with the exception of the parliamentary elections of 1970, electoral volatility was by international standards quite low.[8] The two traditional parties, in particular, concentrated on mobilizing their core voters rather than on intensifying competition between each other. Over time, however, this cleavage structure underwent a number of major changes. As the Austrian nation was built up, the national cleavage disappeared or at least became irrelevant as German national orientations dwindled to leave an ever smaller and noticeably aged group of voters.[9] At first, this constituted a crucial problem for the Freedom Party (FPÖ) because a central element of its ideological self-image no longer produced any positive political response in terms of electoral result. Moreover, the remaining German national sentiments among functionaries even triggered conflicts within the party, thus creating barriers to appealing to new voter groups. It was only by greatly eliminating this "burden of history," by replacing the old cadres and manipulating ethnocentric (then, however, Austro-chauvinist) orientations in the 1990s, that this strategic handicap could partly be overcome. In a similar, though less dramatic way, it was also the religious secularization process that undermined the secular-Catholic cleavage. Though the latter retains a structuring function,[10] it lost a great deal of political significance in terms of electoral impact due to the strong fall in church affiliation. At first, this development weakened the competitive position of the ÖVP. The old conflict configuration "employee versus employer and farmer" was eventually transformed into a conflict between welfare (and state interventionist) orientations on the one hand and market-related and individualistic orientations on the other. Originally, this was a considerable challenge for the SPÖ, although the problem was mitigated by the fact that its main opponent along the socio-economic cleavage, the ÖVP, was not able to position itself clearly at the free-market pole for a long time due to the interests of a broad clientele, and, more particularly, due to its integration into the social partnership and its strong presence in the public sector of the economy, which was highly oversized up to the 1980s.[11]

The consequences of the socioeconomic and sociocultural changes that have gained momentum since the 1970s are equally grave. The core social groups of the traditional parties are shrinking in number, and the traditional social milieus are breaking up, which in turn has led to the disintegration of the old networks of social contacts and personal relationships that once guaranteed the social homogeneity of political attitudes. Ideological interpretation patterns are fading or are no longer adequate to take into account an ever more differentiated social reality. The ÖVP and SPÖ are losing some of their subcultural anchorage just as the ever-diminishing subcultures are losing the power to integrate and to influence politics. The consequence is an affective and organizational destructuring of the electorate, accelerated by the rise of the mass media to the role of key player in the political communication process. All in all, this means a fundamental change in the basic parameters of party competition.[12]

Decline of Party Affiliation and Increased Volatility

The decline of traditional party affiliation and the fiercer competition resulting from this for the political parties have, in the meantime, become standard diagnoses in Western European party studies. In contrast to the situation in the 1980s, controversies are not stirred up by the question of whether dealignment is taking place, but to what extent the ties of traditional party affiliation have already been loosened. Firstly, sociological literature defines dealignment as an uncoupling of social class features and voting behavior. In this context, dealignment means the loosening of the structural anchorage of the parties in traditional social cleavage configurations. Secondly, dealignment is defined as the erosion of more long-term, affective identification with one particular political party. In this context, party identification as measured in representative opinion polls is a prominent indicator.

The "Golden Age of Parties"[13] was characterized by large shares of regular voters, a marked sense of party loyalty, stable—and in most respects—predictable voting behavior, intact organizational structures, and working communication between the parties and their voters. Far-reaching changes of the electorate and the terms of competition made the environment of parties much more complex.[14] As early as the 1950s and 1960s, the continual industrialization and modernization of production structures led to a decline of the industrial and agricultural sectors. Parties whose main support came from these milieus were forced to aim at broadening their appeal to new groups of voters. While at first it was the ÖVP that was affected by this development, from the late 1960s onward the socioeconomic structural change also threatened the SPÖ, which mainly relied on groups of voters from the industrial sector. The decline of the share of industrial workers, decreasing class awareness, and the erosion of class-specific milieus posed a threat to the SPÖ's future electoral success. However, the ÖVP, too, was forced on the defensive by this social transformation. The progressing secularization of society—the decline in church affiliation, the dwindling number of regular churchgoers, and the undermining of denominational networks and milieus—reduced the influence of religious affiliations on election results.

Since the early 1970s, new issues and conflicts as well as changed attitudes towards values and expectations of postmodern, cognitively mobilized groups of voters have reinforced the competitive pressure on parties.[15] Newly formed Green and libertarian parties intensified the competitive situation and, as a first step, threatened the monopoly of the traditional parties in representing the public. Since the 1980s, Austria's political parties have had to face an electorate that is increasingly critical and periods of increased political disenchantment and fluctuating groups of protest voters. The right-wing populist FPÖ has underwent radical change since 1986. It has been injecting polarizing topics into public discussion, pooling emotional protest attitudes and anti-party reflexes ever since Jörg Haider's accession to the chairmanship in 1986. As a consequence, the FPÖ has been penetrating deeply into the core voter groups of the traditional parties. Behind the electoral success of the FPÖ during the 1990s, lay not only pent-up criticism and the discontent of weary voters, but also conflicts between those who are benefiting from modernization and those who are losing out, as well as conflicts between those who belong to the sheltered, public sector and those who find themselves in the unsheltered, private sector. Problems which result from the business cycle coupled with increasing economic rationalization and competitive pressure in the 1990s only intensified these conflicts.[16]

It was only when the FPÖ entered government in 2000 and failed to reconcile populist politics with governing responsibilities that this process came to an (at least temporary) end. The party lost the subsequent elections and later split in two (FPÖ and BZÖ). However, the elections of 2006 showed an electoral upswing of right-wing populist voters albeit on a reduced level.[17]

Finally, the most recent challenge to political parties has been the far-reaching changes in political communication. On the one hand, this affects internal organizational communications between party head-quarters and party members, and, on the other, the party elite's ability to communicate externally in media-oriented democracies.[18] Ensuring appropriate media presentation of the respective issues, personalizing the party image, devising a marketing strategy for successful positioning vis-à-vis one's opponents, segmentation of the electorate, and precise targeting ensure short-term success in mobilizing voters, but at the same time weaken long-term party affiliations based on sentiment and interests.

The time series presented in Table 1 reflect the degree of erosion of traditional party affiliations. While about three quarters of the Austrian electorate still had a stable affiliation with a political party in the 1960s, only half of the country's voters showed a long-term emotional inclination towards a certain party at the end of the century. Similarly, the proportion of registered party members has almost halved as the

Table 1
Indicators of Party Loyalty, 1969–2006

Year	Party Identification	Strong Identification	Strong Party Affiliation	Straight Ticket Voters	Waverers	Party Members
	(a)	(b)	(c)	(d)	(e)	(poll data)
1954	73		71			
1969	75		65			24
1972			61	76	8	23
1975	65	30	61			
1979	63		56	66	16	22
1983	61	27	47			
1986	60	21	39			23
1990	49	19	34	58	26	18
1994	44	12	31			15
1995	49	13	28	44	44	
1999	51	16	26	43	46	
2002	55	22	25	41	53	15
2006	53	26	29	35	60	12

(a) Percentage of respondents with party identification.

(b) Percentage of respondents with strong party identification.

(c) Percentage of respondents stating that they would always vote for the same party, even if not totally satisfied.

(d) Percentage of respondents stating that they always voted for the same party.

(e) Percentage of respondents stating that they occasionally change their voting behavior.

Source: FESSEL-GfK, Representative Surveys.

Table 2
Share of Non-Voters and Party Changers, 1979-2006, in Percent

	1979	1983	1986	1990	1994	1995	1999	2002	2006
Non-Voters	7.8	7.4	9.5	13.9	18.1	14.0	19.6	15.7	21.5
Party Changers	7	10	16	17	19	20	18	24	26

Source: FESSEL-GfK, representative post-election polls, 1979-1983, or exit polls, 1986-2006, respectively.

general capability of Austria's traditional parties to mobilize voters and to campaign efficiently has in some cases dramatically decreased. Demotivation, a lack of incentives, and an electorate that has become far more critical of political parties in general since the 1980s have all demobilized the party supporters.

As the Austrian parties' body of core support waned, so the proportion of non-affiliated floating voters has steadily increased. While, for instance, only 8 percent of the electorate could be classified as "mobile voters" in 1972, this figure had risen to as high as 60 percent in 2006. More than one in two voters supported different parties in the parliamentary and *Land* elections. Only 35 percent of those eligible to vote in Austria may be called consistent voters, constantly voting for the same party in all elections in which they take part. The share of floating voters has also steadily increased with regard to parliamentary elections. During the parliamentary election of 1979, only 7 percent voted for a party other than the party they had voted for in the parliamentary election of 1975, yet the proportion of swing voters in the 2006 parliamentary election was 26 percent. Over the same period, Austria's traditionally high electoral turnout also declined. Just as party affiliation has waned, so has electoral participation, with abstention as a form of protest becoming an option for dissatisfied voters and those who have become disenchanted with politics in general.

At the same time, the share of voters who did not decide whom to support until the final phase of the election campaign has increased. While only 9 percent belonged to the group of late deciders back in 1979, the equivalent figure was as much as 24 percent in the parliamentary election of 2006. The increasing share of late deciders logically raises the mass media's power to influence voters in their coverage, such as of crucial events during the election campaigns and appearances of candidates in TV interviews and studio confrontations and/or their interpretation and evaluation by the mass media.[19]

Table 3
Timing of Final Voting Decision, 1979-2006, in Percent

Voters Who Made a Final Decision	Year								
	1979	1983	1986	1990	1994	1995	1999	2002	2006
Late Deciders (shortly before the election)	9	8	16	14	18	21	20	23	24
Early Deciders (at an early stage)	91	92	84	86	82	79	80	77	76

Source: FESSEL-GfK, representative post-election polls, 1979-1983, or exit polls, 1986-2006, respectively.

Exit poll data from 1999 and 2002 show that party-shifters frequently reported that they were strongly influenced in their personal decision by the mass media's political coverage of the campaign. Twenty-two percent of this group said that statements made by the top candidates on radio and television had strongly influenced their personal voting decision; 30 percent said that the televised debates between the top politicians had done so. However, talking to friends and family as well as reading commentaries and analysis in the print media had also strongly influenced a large share of shifters (22 percent and 14 percent respectively). After all, 4 percent of the party changers interviewed considered that they had been strongly influenced by the opinion polls published in the media. Taking into account the "third person effect"—according to which people consider third persons to be much more susceptible than themselves—and the fact that interviewees in general tend to play down the impact of the media on their own behavior, this percentage is quite remarkable.

Finally, voting motives underwent a change. The reasons to cast a vote for a party or to abstain from voting are multidimensional bundles of motives which do not allow for a unidimensional explanation of voting behavior.[20] Nevertheless, a long-term analysis of voting motives which abstracts from special electoral contexts, actual political issues, and party positions as well as political constellations (for example which parties are in government and which ones in opposition) indicates a trend. Political tradition and party affiliation, ideology and the representation of interest of social and professional groups are in decline; these were of decisive importance for about 40 percent of the electorate in the parliamentary elections of 1986 and 1990, but only for less than one third of voters in all elections since 1995. At the same time, one finds a concomitant increase of motives related to party performance and competition, issues, and candidates, as well as negative voting.[21] Not surprisingly, the latter show considerable variations over time and between the parties. A marked difference can be found, however, in voting motives for the SPÖ and the ÖVP on the one hand and for the new (Greens, LIF, BZÖ, Martin Party) or newly positioned (FPÖ) parties on the other: while traditional reasons still represent a relevant share of motives in the first case, they are nearly absent in the second.

Table 4
Classifications of Voting Motives,* 1986-2006

Classification of Motive	By Year, in Percent of the Total Electorate						
	1986	1990	1994	1995	1999	2002	2006
Tradition, ideology, representation of social groups and interests	38	42	35	30	32	28	31
Performance/competition, issues, candidates, negative voting	62	58	66	70	68	72	68

Classification of Motive	By Party, in Percent of Voters in the 2006 Election			
	SPÖ	ÖVP	GREEN	FPÖ
Tradition, ideology, representation of social groups and interests	49	30	15	12
Performance/competition, issues, candidates, negative voting	51	70	85	88

* Motives that can be classified according to the model, only parties represented in parliament.
Source: FESSEL-GfK AUSTRIA, exit polls, 1986-2006.

Traditional Determinants of Voting Behavior

Church affiliation and proximity to trade unions used to be two of the traditional determinants in Austrians' voting behavior. In the past few decades, both have contributed to the extraordinary stability in Austrians' voting behavior. The vast majority of voters with a strong church affiliation, defined as regular church attendance, support the ÖVP, whereas the majority of trade union members vote for the SPÖ. The social modernization process, however, has not only undermined the social and subcultural ties of the traditional parties (SPÖ and ÖVP), but—due to ongoing pluralization and individualization—has also weakened formerly binding collective values and interpretation patterns. This development has also had its effect on traditional determinants of Austrian voting behavior such as denominational church affiliation and trade union membership. Over the past few decades, ties with the church have been loosened, the frequency of church attendance has decreased, and in particular, the strong foothold of the ÖVP in denominational milieus has become increasingly more fragile. While the Catholic milieu is still largely intact in rural regions and villages, it is losing its cohesion in the urbanized centers, its networks are becoming more and more fragile, and its socio-political relevance is diminishing.[22]

While in the early 1970s 35 percent of the voters still belonged to the core group of regular Catholic churchgoers, this percentage had dropped to a mere 20 percent by the late 1990s. Despite this trend, integration into a church still has considerable significance for voting behavior:

> [T]his applies to Austria more than to West Germany for—as opposed to the CDU/CSU—the ÖVP did not succeed in gaining as strong a foothold among the non-denominational and those with no church affiliation. This is the very reason why Austrians who are close to the church and those who are not differ so strongly in their voting behavior and this is also precisely why the frequency of church attendance determines voting behavior to a much higher degree in Austria than in the Federal Republic of Germany.[23]

In 2006, 42 percent of ÖVP voters belonged to the Catholic core. In 1990, this figure was 49 percent, but at the beginning of the 1960s more than two-thirds of ÖVP voters had belonged to the group of Catholics who regularly attended church. The religious cleavage can still be seen at the end of the 1990s in Austrian voting behavior and shows only marginal changes over time. The Lijphart index of "religious voting" has been at around 40 points in Austria since the 1980s. While 57 percent of those who regularly attend Catholic churches voted for ÖVP, 15 percent of the non-denominational did so. On the other hand,

Table 5
**Voting Behavior of Voters with Strong Denominational Affiliation,
1990-2006, in Percent**

Year	Party					
	SPÖ	ÖVP	FPÖ	BZÖ	GREENS	LIF
1990	22	60	10	-	5	-
1994	20	59	14	-	5	1
1995	20	59	12	-	2	2
1999	20	59	13	-	4	1
2002	22	69	3	-	3	-
2006	22	57	8	1	7	-

Source: FESSEL-GfK, exit polls, 1990-2006.

the SPÖ captured 40 percent of the votes of the non-denominational, and only 22 percent of the votes of the regular Catholic churchgoers. A similar pattern applies to the other parties. Thus the frequency of church attendance continues to be a stable predictor for voting behavior in favor of the ÖVP.

The second traditional determinant of Austrian voting behavior, trade union membership, has been subject to stronger changes. In line with church affiliation, trade union affiliation has also weakened. The membership statistics of the ÖGB (Austrian Trade Union Federation) show a persistent decrease in membership. For the Social Democratic Party, however, affiliation with the trade unions has a similarly stabilizing function as an intact church affiliation has for the ÖVP. Sixty-one percent of SPÖ voters in the parliamentary elections of 1990 were trade union members. Sixteen years later, it was still 55 percent. The "trade union affiliation" predictor, however, has lost much of its ability to shape voting behavior in the course of the 1990s.

While in 1990, 62 percent of the trade union members still voted for the SPÖ, this figure dropped to about 50 percent in the following years. In 1999, the FPÖ was able to double its share of voters among trade union members as compared to the 1990 election. But even when the FPÖ suffered a strong electoral setback in 2002 and only a relative stabilization in 2006, the SPÖ was no longer capable of reaching its former high preference among trade union members, due to a scandal involving a union owned bank, which caused widespread discontent and demobilization among social democratic union members.

Table 6
Voting Behavior of Trade Union Members, 1990-2006, in Percent

Year	Party			
	SPÖ	ÖVP	FPÖ/BZÖ	GREENS
1990	62	19	11	4
1994	50	19	19	7
1995	55	16	18	3
1999	49	19	21	6
2002	55	29	8	7
2006	51	21	9	10

Source: FESSEL-GfK, exit polls, 1990-2006.

Erosion of Class Voting and New Sectoral Cleavages

Up to the early 1980s, social and occupational circumstances did well as predictors of Austrian voting behavior. In particular, the professional status and, in this context, the dividing line between mainly manual and non-manual activities, shaped voting behavior and led to the comparably stable pattern of class voting. Since the 1980s, socioeconomic and generational changes in conjunction with progressive individualization and social differentiation contributed to a substantial weakening of class voting. The most prominent indicator for measuring class voting is the Alford index which is calculated on the basis of the difference between the percentage of blue-collar workers and white-collar workers who vote for a left-of-center party. While the Alford index for Austrian voting behavior was still constantly above the average value of Western industrialized democracies in the 1970s, the same index has decreased since the 1980s and reached a *negative* value in the parliamentary elections of 1999 for the first time. In the meantime, the index recovered slightly in 2002 and increased to 12 points at the parliamentary election in 2006 (see Table 7).

However, it was not only the strong erosion of class voting—a *"class voting dealignment"*[24]—that was characteristic of the Austrian electorate, but also the simultaneous re-orientation of the voting behavior of Austria's working class during the 1990s. It was no exaggeration to speak of *blue-collar realignment* in this respect. Back in 1979, 65 percent of Austria's blue-collar workers were still voting for the SPÖ, but this figure had fallen to a mere 35 percent by 1999. Within twenty years, the SPÖ's share of the vote among the working class had fallen by half; the FPÖ's share, however, has increased tenfold.

Table 7
Alford Index of Class Voting, 1961-2006

Period	Mean Index Value
1961-1970	27.4
1971-1980	28.9
1981-1990	18.3
1990-1999	8.7
1999	-1.0
2002	4.0
2006	12.0

Source: Paul Nieuwbeerta and Van Dirk De Graaf, "Traditional Class Voting in Twenty Postwar Societies," 32;[25] FESSEL-GfK, exit polls, 1994-2006.

Table 8
Voting Behavior of Blue-Collar Workers, 1979-2006, in Percent

Year	Party		
	SPÖ	ÖVP	FPÖ
1979	65	29	4
1983	61	28	3
1986	57	26	10
1990	53	22	21
1994	47	15	29
1995	41	13	34
1999	35	12	47
2002	41	34	16
2006	47	25	18

Source: FESSEL-GfK, representative post-election polls, 1979-1983, and exit polls, 1986-2006.

In 1999, the FPÖ has become the predominant blue-collar workers' party by far with a share of 47 percent of the working class vote. Only 35 percent of the blue-collar workers voted for the SPÖ, and a mere 12 percent for the ÖVP. In the late 1990s, the voting behavior of the Austrian working class differed considerably from the blue-collar vote in other Western European democracies.[26] Interesting attempts to explain this temporary blue-collar realignment are provided by Scott C. Flanagan[27] and Herbert Kitschelt[28] who deal with the effects of the changes of societal cleavages on voting behavior.

In Flanagan's model, advanced industrial societies are characterized by *three* main cleavages. The first conflict axis represents the traditional cleavage between redistributive welfare policies and free market policies with the lowest possible degree of state intervention. This conflict has been a constitutive element of party competition in elections for decades. The second conflict axis is the cleavage between a policy of economic and technological growth and a policy that is focused on ecology and environmental protection. This cleavage contains a sub-dimension which relates to the conflict between groups with values of duty and acceptance (who basically share materialist values) and groups oriented towards values of personal freedom and development (who have post-materialist life styles).[29] Flanagan goes further and adds a third conflict axis to the two-dimensional conflict pattern of advanced industrial societies, namely the cleavage between a libertarian *New Left* and an authoritarian *New Right*, which is stirred up by polarizing controversial issues such as immigration or the integration of immigrants. According to Flanagan, parts of the traditional blue-collar voters' segment in particular get caught up in a cross-pressure situation, which may result in members of the working-class left voting for a party of the New Right.

While Flanagan's model concentrates on the new socio-cultural cleavages, Kitschelt deals with the shift in the main axes of political competition as a consequence of market and work experience in advanced industrial societies. The central issue is the drifting apart of occupational experience in highly interactive, skilled white-collar jobs that entail responsibility from that of blue-collar jobs, which are less interactive, and often require only minor qualifications, but which are subjected to the much higher pressure of international competition and technological rationalization. However, this conflict is not only based on different occupational experiences and the interests linked to them, but also on different attitudes. Accordingly, individuals in highly interactive, skilled occupations tend to have liberal to libertarian attitudes, while persons who are involved in mechanical working processes more often show right-wing authoritarian attitudes. Thus, different market and occupational experiences combined with different attitudes may prompt blue-collar workers to break with the traditional left workers' party and—provided these parties put up candidates—to turn to a right-wing populist party, which they think articulates their life and occupational experiences more accurately. However, it took concrete market and occupational experiences as well as the pressure of international competition, which has become stiffer and fiercer of late, alienating a large proportion of industrial workers from the representatives of their traditional interest groups to allow the rise of the right-wing populist FPÖ to become temporarily the new workers' party in the late 1990s.

Compared with the spectacular reorientation of the voting behavior of the Austrian working class during the 1990s—in the meantime reversed to traditional patterns due to the collapse of the right-wing populist movement and the electoral defeat of the Freedom Party at the parliamentary elections 2002—the changes in the voting behavior of white-collar employees have been moderate. To a large extent, the SPÖ has managed to stabilize its vote share among white-collar workers. While 40 percent of the white-collar workers voted for the SPÖ in 1986, 35 percent did so in 2006. The ÖVP suffered comparable losses among the new white-collar middle class. In 1986, 13 percent of white-collar workers voted for the FPÖ, compared with 11 percent in 2006. The post-materialist Greens made similarly high gains in the segment of white-collar voters. In 1986, 7 percent of white-collar workers voted for the Greens. Twenty years later, the respective percentage doubled to 16 percent.

In contrast to the situation in the working class segment, the SPÖ was able to maintain its lead among white-collar workers. The attractiveness of the ÖVP among the members of the white-collar middle class, however, diminished considerably during the 1990s, recovering only recently. Also the voting behavior of civil servants and those working in the public sector is now much more volatile. Public-sector employees tend to vote for the SPÖ or ÖVP depending on the respective budgetary policies and any controversial reform plans proposed during parliamentary elections. The FPÖ's share of this voter segment is below average, while that of the Greens is, unsurprisingly, above average.

Table 9
Changes in the Voting Behavior of White-Collar Workers, 1986-2006, in Percent

Year	Party			
	SPÖ	ÖVP	FPÖ	Greens
1986	40	36	13	7
1990	38	27	16	7
1994	29	25	22	12
1995	32	28	22	7
1999	36	23	22	10
2002	37	37	11	12
2006	35	31	11	16

Source: FESSEL-GfK, exit polls, 1986-2006.

Table 10
Changes in the Voting Behavior of Civil Servants and
Public-Sector Employees, 1986-2006, in Percent

Year	Party			
	SPÖ	ÖVP	FPÖ	Greens
1986	49	33	8	6
1990	40	30	14	8
1994	35	23	14	18
1995	48	20	17	6
1999	33	30	20	12
2002	39	41	7	12
2006	36	36	7	20

Source: FESSEL-GfK, exit polls, 1986-2006.

The voting behavior of civil servants and those who work in the public sector relates to a cleavage that has also influenced Austrian voting behavior since the 1980s: the welfare state cleavage, as Patrick Dunleavy and Christopher Husbands call this new *sectoral cleavage*.[30] In essence, this cleavage model deals with the fact that those belonging to the *public* and *private* sector are drifting apart in terms of voting behavior and there is indeed potential for conflicts between the sheltered and the unsheltered production sectors. The first signs of this sectoral cleavage have been visible in Austria since the mid-1980s, and they have become more evident due to the collapse of the nationalized industries, the privatization of state-owned enterprises, and the de-monopolization of sheltered service and utility companies resulting from Austria's accession to the European Union. In the long run, this affected the SPÖ, but even more the ÖVP, which fell behind the FPÖ in private sector employees' electoral support as early as 1994. While in 1986 there was a gap of 19 percentage points between the SPÖ and the FPÖ in the group of private sector employees, the SPÖ was only 5 percent ahead of the FPÖ in 1999. The FPÖ clearly and consistently tapped the potential for tension and conflict inherent in the cleavage of public versus private sector. The SPÖ and ÖVP have suffered above-average losses among voters of the private sector since 1986. During the 1990s, it was the FPÖ which benefited from this development, capturing an above-average share of the vote in the private sector.

The cleavage of public versus private sector deepened during the 1990s in Austria. This can be seen from an above-average share of the vote for the FPÖ in the private sector and, conversely, in the tendency towards above-average shares of the vote for the Greens among public-sector employees (particularly in the fields of public services, education, and administration). Thus, occupation and sector-specific trends in Austrian voting behavior can be interpreted only to a limited extent by means of traditional micro-sociological explanations. New cleavage theories such as the "radical model" of Dunleavy and Husbands or Kitschelt's model of the social positions offer realistic perspectives to explain the class dealignment in Austrian voting behavior.[31]

Gender and Generation Realignment

Since the 1980s, it has been possible to observe a gender-specific differentiation in Austrian voting behavior. In the course of the 1990s, this gender gap widened so that by the late 1990s it was perfectly legitimate to speak of the existence of two gender-specific party systems in Austria.[32] This *gender gap* was reinforced by a clear distancing on the part of women from right-wing populist protest parties, whose polarizing issues as well as conflict-oriented management aimed at arousing negative emotions is particularly strongly disliked by younger women. The widening of the gender gap was caused, firstly, by increased educational and qualification opportunities for the younger generation of women, as well as an active and more self-confident role definition with regard to equal rights in personal relationships and at the workplace, and secondly, by specific issue preferences and general outlooks with women placing special emphasis on humanitarian and liberal development values such as ecological and social considerations.

The alignment of the voting behavior of men and women, which took place in the 1970s still resulted in minor gender-specific deviations in voting behavior in the early 1980s. If the gender gap is calculated as the sum of the percentage differences in the votes cast by men and by women for the parties represented in parliament, the difference in percentage points was only 2 percent in 1979. In 1983, this gender difference rose to 5 percentage points. It was only in the 1986 parliamentary elections, with the beginning of the strategic and stylistic reformation of the right-wing populist FPÖ, that the gender gap began to widen. With a gender difference of 24 percentage points, the 1994 parliamentary elections mark the peak of gender-specific differences in Austrian voting behavior to date. The gender gap of 21 percentage points in the subsequent 1995 and 1999 elections again pointed to striking differences in the voting behavior of

Table 11
Gender-Specific Voting Behavior, 1986-2006, in Percent

Year	Gender	Party			
		SPÖ	ÖVP	FPÖ	Greens
1986	Men	42	38	13	4
	Women	43	43	7	5
1990	Men	39	29	20	4
	Women	44	33	12	5
1994	Men	34	25	29	6
	Women	36	30	18	9
1995	Men	35	26	27	4
	Women	40	29	16	5
1999	Men	31	25	32	5
	Women	35	27	21	9
2002	Men	32	44	12	7
	Women	40	40	8	10
2006	Men	34	35	13	9
	Women	38	35	9	10

Source: FESSEL-GfK, exit polls, 1986-2006.

men and women as compared to those found in other Western European democracies. While the gender gap at the parliamentary election in 2002 held at 19 percentage points, the difference between the voting behavior of men and women narrowed in 2006 and declined to 12 points.

Behind the gender-specific differences in voting behavior, however, there are complex patterns correlating with factors such as age and educational and professional status. A highly concentrated duopoly of the two traditional parties (SPÖ and ÖVP) among female pensioners contrasts with a wide-ranging multi-party system among younger women with higher education qualifications, in which it is no longer possible to identify a predominant party. The voting behavior of women under thirty is particularly remarkable. About 25 percent of younger women, however, voted either for the Greens or for the Liberal Forum. In 2006, 24 percent of young women and about one-third of younger women with a university degree supported the Greens.

When examined in a more differentiated way, the gender gap in Austria actually resembles a branched canyon. The ÖVP's and, to a lesser degree, the SPÖ's lack of attractiveness to younger, more qualified women contrasts with the above-average share of the female vote held by post-materialist and libertarian parties. A disproportionately high number of SPÖ voters among female pensioners contrasts with above-average support for the Greens among women under thirty. The emergence of differentiated voting behavior by the younger generation of female voters is described as "gender realignment" in international electoral studies, thus focusing on the reorientation of younger women's voting behavior.

However, during the 1990s the voting behavior of younger men also showed a gender-generation realignment, albeit a one-directional reorientation towards the FPÖ. With a share of 41 percent in the parliamentary election in 1999, the FPÖ became by far the preferred party in the segment of younger, male voters. But in the following election, the FPÖ could mobilize only 14 percent of the younger male voting block; recently, only 10 percent of male voters under thirty voted for the FPÖ.

Long-term trends in the voting behavior of the younger generation of voters illustrate the steady increase in generation realignment in Austrian voting behavior to the detriment of the two traditional parties, the SPÖ and ÖVP. The steady decline in attractiveness of the traditional parties among the voters of the younger, up-and-coming generation is clearly confirmed by the trend in the voting behavior of first-time voters, both male and female. While the SPÖ and ÖVP managed to attract 97 percent of first-time voters in the 1979 parliamentary elections, this figure dropped to a mere 42 percent twenty years later and recovered slightly reaching 60 percent in the parliamentary election in 2006.

An assessment of long-term trends and patterns in Austrian voting behavior defines the key determinants of electoral competition:

1. a *gender-generation realignment*, that is, a re-orientation in the voting behavior of the younger generation of voters, in which gender combined with age and education have led to new voter coalitions;
2. a temporary, in the meantime reversed, *realignment* of the voting behavior of the Austrian working class to a degree unprecedented in Western Europe;
3. the emergence of new sectoral cleavages, with the *public* versus *private* sector cleavage being of particular relevance to Austrian voting behavior;
4. a polarization of values or a new *value cleavage* between a New Right with authoritarian emphasis and the New Left with a predominantly post-materialist/libertarian orientation;
5. the persistent pattern of *negative voting*, that is, a form of voting behavior that is primarily motivated by diffuse protest attitudes and generalized discontent, and which is particularly susceptible to the right-wing populist affect management;
6. signs of an *issue polarization*, as has become apparent in the issues of immigration and integration versus exclusion and xenophobic sentiment;
7. a *demobilization*—albeit moderate by international standards—as can be seen in the decline of electoral turnout; and last not least

8. an ongoing *dealignment* of traditional party attachments resulting in increased electoral mobility and fluctuating voting patterns.

Voters on the Move

General trends in Austrian voting behavior as well as voting patterns of specific groups must be seen against the background of changes in the mood of the electorate and in the format of party competition. In the early 1990s, the political landscape in Austria changed: immigration and its consequences for the labor market, education and the housing situation in urban areas, economic restructuring and resulting unemployment, the costs and distributive effects of welfare policies, and questions of national independence versus European integration made their way onto the public agenda. Among the lower social and educational groups of the population, these changes were often met with diffuse fears of worsening social conditions and economic prospects, as well as with preoccupations about a loss of traditional sociocultural identities. The FPÖ then redirected its oppositional impetus from political renewal to *"politics of resentment,"* mixing up fears and preoccupations with an ever more aggressive attack against the political class.

The FPÖ's rise to become the most successful right-wing populist party in Western Europe at that time was inseparably linked to structural

Table 12
Austrian Parliamentary Elections, 1986-2006, in Percent of Valid Votes

Party	Year						
	1986	1990	1994	1995	1999	2002	2006
SPÖ	43.1	42.8	34.9	38.1	33.2	36.5	35.3
ÖVP	41.3	32.1	27.7	28.3	26.9	42.3	34.3
FPÖ	9.7	16.6	22.5	21.9	26.9	10.0	11.0
BZÖ	-	-	-	-	-	-	4.1
Greens	4.8	4.8	7.3	4.8	7.4	9.5	11.0
LIF	-	-	6.0	5.5	3.7	1.0	-
Others	1.1	3.7	1.6	1.4	1.9	0.7	4.3

SPÖ (Social Democratic Party).
ÖVP (Austrian People's Party).
FPÖ (Freedom Party).
BZÖ (Alliance Future Austria). Founded as an offspring of the FPÖ by Haider in 2005.
Greens (Green Party).
LIF (Liberal Forum). Founded in 2003 as a liberal, libertarian offspring of the FPÖ in opposition to the xenophobic appeals of the FPÖ under Haider.

Source: Austrian Departments of the Interior, Electoral Commission.

changes in and the symptoms of a breakdown of Austria's traditional party system. Essential preconditions for the FPÖ's electoral success were the erosion of traditional party alignment, the dissolution of socio-cultural milieus and the orientations linked to them, and the diminishing capability of the major parties of old to integrate and mobilize. The activation of latent anti-party sentiments, a diffuse party weariness, and anti-institutional effects as a reaction to an ever increasing confidence gap prepared the way for populist arguments and attacks.[33]

At the same time, the erosion of the foundations of the traditional party system and the installment of a grand coalition government offered a wide field of opportunities for oppositional and populist politics. The FPÖ, a party extremely focused on its leader, was very successful in presenting itself as a "TV or media party," a symbolic mobilization agency which tried to capitalize on latent protest attitudes, resentment, and deeply rooted frustration.[34]

The elections of 1999 represented the culmination of successful populist politics. The formation of an ÖVP-FPÖ government in February 2000, however, marked the beginning of a new era. Both the changing political opportunity structure and the behavior of the FPÖ turned former points of strength to new factors of weakness. The replacement of the Grand Coalition which had been held responsible for political stagnation and its tendency to prevent meaningful political competition ("whatever the electoral result the political outcome is an SPÖ-ÖVP-coalition") led to resurgence of competition (between a center-right government and a center-left opposition) and lowered the level of overall political dissatisfaction.[35] Even more important, the participation of the FPÖ in the government brought its internal differences to light and caused an increase of political stress for the FPÖ electorate. Budgetary consolidation cuts in social expenditures and the need for compromise and accommodation conflicted with election promises and the impetus on straight and simple solutions which had played an important role in the FPÖ's campaign rhetoric. In addition, in terms of qualified personnel and concrete programs the FPÖ was ill prepared for governmental politics and became an easy target for media criticism. Various scandals, failures and the daily bickering not least with the coalition partner undermined the party's image as a political actor "different from all the others." Fourth, Haider was no longer the sole and undisputed leading figure of the party. At first, he did not fill an office in the government but maintained the party leadership. Later, he passed this position to Vice Chancellor Riess-Passer, but remained the dominating figure in the party. Various FPÖ ministers, especially the Vice Chancellor, became the focus of media interest and developed their positions not always in accordance with those of Haider and members of the rank-and-file. As a consequence, the overall party image worsened considerably, and the FPÖ's loosely tied voter coalition began to dissolve. Defeats at regional elections increased the internal strife: the party was continuously torn between its "populist mood" and the requirements of professional and responsible government politics. Here, its deinstitutionalized structure and strong leadership-orientation—once a strength contributing to strategic flexibility and public performance—proved to be a fatal weakness.

At the elections of 2002, the majority of former FPÖ voters had to look for a new point of reference. Although the SPÖ managed to gain more than 100,000 voters from this group,[36] the main bulk (more than 500,000) of dissatisfied FPÖ adherents cast their vote for the ÖVP which offered a continuation of reform politics albeit in a reliable version and with credible leadership.

Although the FPÖ reentered government in 2003, the problems continued leading to a split of the party.[37] In the following regional elections as well as in the national elections of 2006, the newly founded BZÖ did rather poorly while the "old FPÖ" under its chairman Heinz-Christian Strache secured the main bulk of former FPÖ voters also winning back some voters the parties had lost to the SPÖ and ÖVP in previous years.

Both parliamentary elections of 2002 and 2006 saw a high degree of electoral volatility. While the 2002 results indicated a clear preference of the majority of voters for a continuation of conservative-liberal reform politics (as opposed to a social democratic or green alternative), the 2006 results showed voters' considerable dissatisfaction with governmental politics without pointing to a clear new direction. Electoral turnout declined, and nearly one-third of the electorate said they voted against other parties rather than in favor of the chosen parties. Furthermore, party-changers distributed their preferences rather equally among the various competitors.

A volatile electorate without a stable alignment to old and new parties as well as open party competition has been characteristic of Austrian voters for the last two decades and probably will remain so for the next future. Traditional explanations of electoral behavior, either in terms of ideological orientations or deeply rooted social cleavages, are only relevant for an ever diminishing minority and are, therefore, unlikely to capture the moods or reasons of voters.

Table 13
Spontaneous Voting Motives of Party Shifters to the ÖVP in the 2002 Elections

Motive for Shift	Percentage
Economic and budgetary politics	14
Satisfaction with governmental politics, reform politics	13
Top candidate Schüssel	10
Dissatisfaction with FPÖ	10
Prevention of SPÖ-Green coalition, dissatisfaction with SPÖ	9

Source: FESSEL-GfK, exit poll, 2002.

Table 14
Spontaneous Voting Motives of Party Shifters from the ÖVP in the 2006 Election

Motive for Shift	Percentage
Dissatisfaction with governmental politics	14
Protest	14
Dissatisfaction with pension reform, social politics	14
Dissatisfaction with immigration politics	13
Dissatisfaction with political personnel	12

Source: FESSEL-GfK, exit poll, 2006.

Notes

1. Fritz Plasser and Peter A. Ulram, *Unbehagen im Parteienstaat* (Vienna: Böhlau, 1982).

2. Erhard Busek and Martin Schauer, eds., *Eine Europäische Erregung: Die "Sanktionen" der Vierzehn gegen Österreich im Jahr 2000* (Vienna: Böhlau, 2003).

3. Fritz Plasser and Peter A. Ulram, "Die Erdrutschwahlen 2002 in Österreich," in *Wahlen und Wähler*, ed. Jürgen W. Falter et al. (Wiesbaden: VS Verlag für Sozialwissenschaften, 2005), 572-94.

4. Fritz Plasser and Peter A. Ulram, eds., *Wahlverhalten in Bewegung: Analysen zur Nationalratswahl 2002* (Vienna: WUV-Universitätsverlag, 2003).

5. These are nationwide sample surveys of randomly selected voters having taken part in parliamentary elections. The polls were carried out by FESSEL-GfK AUSTRIA with a sample size of about 2,000 voters for each election.

6. Fritz Plasser, Peter A. Ulram, and Alfred Grausgruber, "The Decline of '*Lager* Mentality' and the New Model of Electoral Competition in Austria," in *Politics in Austria: Still a Case of Consociationalism?*, ed. Kurt Richard Luther and Wolfgang C. Müller (London: Frank Cass, 1992), 16-44; Wolfgang C. Müller, Fritz Plasser, and Peter A. Ulram, "Party Responses to the Erosion of Voter Loyalties in Austria," in *Political Parties and Electoral Change: Party Responses to Electoral Markets*, ed. Peter Mair et al. (London: Sage, 2004), 145-78.

7. Heinz Kienzl, "Die Struktur der Wählerschaft," in *Der durchleuchtete Wähler*, ed. Karl Blecha et al. (Vienna: Europa Verlag, 1964).

8. Plasser, Ulram, and Grausgruber, "The Decline of '*Lager* Mentality'."

9. Fritz Plasser and Peter A.Ulram, "Politisch-kultureller Wandel in Österreich," in *Staatsbürger oder Untertanen*, 2nd ed., ed. Fritz Plasser and Peter A. Ulram (Frankfurt/ Main: Peter Lang, 1993), 103-55. Peter A. Ulram and Svila Tributsch, *Kleine Nation mit Eigenschaften: Über das Verhältnis der Österreicher zu sich selbst und zu ihren Nachbarn* (Vienna: Molden, 2004).

10. Wolfgang Jagodzinski, "Das religiöse Cleavage in Deutschland und Österreich," in *Wahlen und politische Einstellungen in Deutschland und Österreich*, ed. Fritz Plasser et al. (Frankfurt am Main: Peter Lang, 1999), 65-93.

11. This process was intensified by the extensive absence of a modern and economically strong large-scale private industry, as well as by the considerable support for state-oriented attitudes within the population as a whole and among large parts of the ÖVP's voters. Even decades later, an analysis carried out by Kitschelt [*The Radical Right in Western Europe: A Comparative Analysis* (Ann Arbor, MI: U of Michigan P, 1995)] on the World Value Survey 1990 data revealed only minor differences in the position of SPÖ and ÖVP voters as regards socio-economic factors.

12. Müller, Plasser and Ulram, "Party Responses."

13. Kenneth Janda and Tyler Coleman, "Effects of Party Organization on Performance during the 'Golden Age of Parties'," in *Parties and Democracy*, ed. Richard Hofferbert (Oxford: Oxford UP, 1998), 189-210.

14. Peter Mair, Wolfgang C. Müller, and Fritz Plasser, eds., *Political Parties and Electoral Change: Party Responses to Electoral Markets* (London: Sage, 2004).

15. Russell J. Dalton, *Citizen Politics: Public Opinion and Political Parties in Advanced Industrial Democracies*, 4th ed. (Washington D.C.: CQ Press, 2006).

16. Herbert Kitschelt, *The Radical Right in Western Europe*.

17. Fritz Plasser and Peter A. Ulram, eds., *Wechselwahlen: Analysen zur Nationalratswahl 2006* (Vienna: WUV 2007).

18. Mair, Müller, and Plasser, *Political Parties*.

19. Fritz Plasser, "Assessing the Americanization of Austrian Politics and Politicians," in *The Americanization/Westernization of Austria*, ed. Günter Bischof and Anton Pelinka, Contemporary Austrian Studies, vol. 10 (New Brunswick, NJ: Transaction, 2004), 235-54.

20. Jürgen Falter and Harald Schoen, eds., *Handbuch Wahlforschung* (Wiesbaden: VS Verlag für Sozialwissenschaften, 2005).

21. Fritz Plasser, Gilg Seeber, and Peter A. Ulram, "Erdrutschwahlen, Momentum, Motive und neue Muster im Wahlverhalten," in *Wahlverhalten in Bewegung*, ed. Fritz Plasser and Peter A. Ulram (Vienna: WUV-Universitätsverlag, 2003), 97-158.

22. Müller, Plasser and Ulram, "Party Responses."

23. Jagodzinski, "Das religiöse Cleavage," 90.

24. Geoffrey Evans, ed., *The End of Class Politics? Class Voting in Comparative Perspective* (New York: Oxford UP, 1999).

25. In *The End of Class Politics: Class Voting in Comparative Context,* ed. Geoffrey Evans (New York: Oxford UP, 1999).

26. Pippa Norris, *Radical Right: Voters and Parties in the Electoral Market* (New York: Cambridge UP, 2005).

27. Scott C. Flanagan, "Value Change in Industrial Societies," *American Political Science Review* 81.4 (1987): 1303-19.

28. Herbert Kitschelt, *The Transformation of European Social Democracy* (Cambridge: Cambridge UP, 1994) and *The Radical Right*.

29. Dalton, *Citizen Politics*.

30. Patrick Dunleavy, and Christopher Husbands, *British Democracy on the Crossroads* (London: Allen & Unwin, 1985).

31. Ibid.; Kitschelt, *The Transformation of European Social Democracy* and *The Radical Right*.

32. Plasser and Ulram, *Wahlverhalten in Bewegung*.

33. Fritz Plasser and Peter A. Ulram, "Rechtspopulistische Resonanzen: Die Wählerschaft der FPÖ," in *Das österreichische Wahlverhalten*, ed. Fritz Plasser et al. (Vienna: Signum, 2000), 225-41.

34. Plasser and Ulram, *Wahlverhalten in Bewegung*.

35. Fritz Plasser and Peter A. Ulram, *Das österreichische Politikverständnis* (Vienna: WUV-Universitätsverlag, 2002).

36. Christoph Hofinger, Günther Ogris, and Eva Thalhammer, "Der Jahrhundertstrom: Wahlkampfverlauf, Wahlmotive und Wählerströme im Kontext der Nationalratswahl 2002," in *Wahlverhalten in Bewegung*, ed. Fritz Plasser and Peter A. Ulram (Vienna: WUV-Universitätsverlag, 2003), 159-90.

37. Plasser and Ulram, *Wahlverhalten in Bewegung*; Peter A. Ulram, "Strukturelle Mehrheit oder mehrheitsfähige Angebote für offene Wählermärkte?", in Diesmal, *Analysen zur Nationalratswahl 2002*, ed. Clemens Martin Auer and Michael Fleischhacker (Vienna: Molden, 2003), 117-28.

It Ain't Over 'til It's Over:
Electoral Volatility in Austria from
the 1970s through 2006

Christoph Hofinger, Günther Ogris and Eva Zeglovits

Introduction

After times of great stability in the Austrian political system during the 1970s, electoral volatility increased substantially in the 1980s and the 1990s. The rise and fall of the FPÖ led by Jörg Haider greatly shaped electoral dynamics; the Freedom Party's success started with reaching out to former ÖVP voters and continued with attracting former SPÖ voters. The ÖVP managed to compensate for most of its losses in only one election (2002) when 633,000 voters migrated from the FPÖ to the ÖVP. In the recent election of 2006, the ÖVP was the party most affected by demobilization of its members to other parties as well as to nonvoters. Losses to nonvoters, however, were substantial for all parties in 2006. The media and the general public were surprised by both the ÖVP victory in 2002 and the SPÖ victory in 2006, based on a premature consensus about the expected outcome that remained resistant to empirical evidence.

Electoral Volatility in Austria since the 1970s

It seems hard to find electoral "dynamics" in the Austrian party system of the 1970s at all. The Social Democrats' absolute majority prevailed throughout the decade. In the 1975 election, the changes were so small that the parties' shares of the valid votes were more or less the same as in 1971, with a total net electoral change (Pedersen Index) of less than 0.4 percent.[1] However, only the aggregated results showed record stability; survey data suggested gender-specific shifts in voting preferences below the surface. While the Social Democratic Party (SPÖ) had increased its share among women, the People's Party (ÖVP) could have strengthened its position among male voters.[2] However, these two trends apparently neutralized each other in the overall results.

Electoral volatility became more obvious at the beginning of the 1980s. The two major parties, the Peoples' Party and the Social Democrats, saw their traditional hegemony—a common share in valid votes of more than 90 percent[3]—begin to erode, caused by a rise of two originally small parties, one on the left (Greens) and one on the right (FPÖ).

The Green Party passed the 4 percent threshold and entered parliament in 1986, managing to increase its results almost permanently since then. The right side of the political landscape, however, experienced more dramatic changes. After Jörg Haider's takeover of the Freedom Party (FPÖ) in 1986, it grew from a small party to the second strongest party in 1999. The rapid decline of the FPÖ in 2002 also had great impact on electoral volatility in Austria. In fact, the rise and fall of the FPÖ is the single most influential factor on electoral mobility in postwar Austria, followed by flows to and from non-voting. In addition, two split-offs of the FPÖ made it into parliament: the Liberal Forum in 1994 and 1995, and the BZÖ in 2006.

By analyzing electoral volatility based on voter transition analyses, a permanent increase of constant nonvoters is evident in the 1980s, but has been more or less stable since the 1990s (see Table 1). Since then, about 15 percent of the electorate has been *constant nonvoters* (that is, exercising abstention in two consecutive elections).

The percentage of constant party voters also decreased dramatically in the 1980s and beginning of the 1990s, and has been rather stable since then (between 55 percent and 62 percent).

The percentages of mobilized nonvoters and demobilized voters vary widely. Elections with powerful mobilization campaigns resulted in an increasing turnout and, by turning abstainers into voters, in a relatively high numbers of mobilized nonvoters. Despite the long running trend of declining voter participation, the years 1995 and 2002 saw voters' participation increase.

In these two elections, a polarized debate about the future direction of Austrian politics boosted participation.[4] In 2002, an expectedly tight race between the major parties as well as between center-left and center-right majorities served additionally to strengthen turnout.[5]

However, in most recent elections (1994, 1999, and 2006) turnout decreased, and the share of demobilized party voters was high, usually at the expense of the traditional parties, the SPÖ and ÖVP.

Table 1
Electoral Volatility in Austria, 1979-2006, as a Percentage of Eligible Voters[6]

	1979 1983	1983 1986	1986 1990	1990 1994	1994 1995	1995 1999	1999 2002	2002 2006
Party swing	7	13	14	16	12	14	21	15
Mobilized nonvoters	3	1	2	6	7	1	7	2
Demobilized party voters	2	3	7	10	3	8	2	8
Changing voters – total	12	17	23	31	22	24	30	25
Constant nonvoters	6	7	9	14	16	17	15	15
Constant party voters	82	76	68	55	62	59	55	60
Constant voters – total	88	83	77	69	78	76	70	75
Electorate	100	100	100	100	100	100	100	100

Source: SORA voter transition analyses.

The percentage of swing voters has been more or less stable (around 15 percent) since the middle of the 1980s. An obvious exception was the 2002 election, when 21 percent of eligible voters changed between two parties, with a record swing of 633,000 former FPÖ supporters voting for the ÖVP.[7]

Trends have not only shifted over time, but with respect to regional difference in Austria as well (see Table 2). Compared to the Austrian-wide party swing of 15 percent between 2002 and 2006, there is a regional outlier. In Carinthia where Jörg Haider is governor, his newly founded party, the BZÖ, was very successful (as opposed to in all other provinces). Because these voters came mostly from Haider's "old" party, the FPÖ, they accounted for most of the swing voters in Carinthia, (28 percent of the electorate). Mainly because of Jörg Haider's personal involvement in the campaign could the BZÖ obtain the second position in Carinthia.[8]

In all other provinces, party swing varied slightly from 12 percent of the electorate (Vorarlberg) to 17 percent (Vienna). Vorarlberg has an outstanding percentage of former party voters deciding for abstention in 2006 (18 percent). After decades of high turnout, the most western prov-

Table 2
Electoral Volatility by Province, 2006, as a Percentage of Eligible Voters

	Au-stria	Carin-thia	Vor-arl-berg	Vien-na	Salz-burg	Tyrol	Bur-gen-land	Lower Au-stria	Styria	Upper Au-stria
Party swing	15	28	12	17	15	14	16	15	13	13
Mobilized nonvoters	2	4	4	3	2	1	3	1	2	1
Demobilized party voters	8	11	18	8	9	11	6	6	7	6
Changing voters – total	*25*	*43*	*34*	*28*	*26*	*26*	*24*	*22*	*22*	*20*
Constant nonvoters	15	14	13	20	16	17	9	11	15	14
Constant party voters	60	43	53	52	59	57	66	67	63	66
Constant voters – total	*75*	*57*	*66*	*72*	*74*	*74*	*76*	*78*	*78*	*80*
Electorate	100	100	100	100	100	100	100	100	100	100

Source: SORA voter transition analyses.

ince in Austria experienced a strong decrease in participation in regional elections as well. In the 2006 election, turnout reached only 70.0 percent in Vorarlberg, for the first time falling far below the national average (-8.5 percent). In the other eight provinces, between 6 percent and 11 percent of the electorate turned from participation to abstention.

In five Austrian provinces, the share of constant party voters was less than 60 percent. Aside from Carinthia (for the reasons discussed above) these "volatile provinces" were Vienna, Vorarlberg, Salzburg, and Tyrol. These four were already the provinces with the fewest constant party voters in 2002. Further research would be necessary to reveal the underlying causes of this pattern. However, it is probably safe to assume that the reasons for the high degree of volatility in Vienna differ from the factors responsible in the western provinces of Vorarlberg, Salzburg, and Tyrol. In Vienna, factors related with the obvious urbanity of the province, such as social mobility, migration, lifestyle, tend to play a crucial role in explaining rapid electoral change. The explanation for the, at first glance, surprisingly high electoral volatility in the western provinces might lie in the historically long dominance of the ÖVP combined with a relatively low degree of organization: party membership and union membership are traditionally lower in the west.[9] In this area, recent societal changes (like the increasing share of the service sector) seem to affect traditional party affiliations more than in other provinces.

The Rise and Fall of the FPÖ as a Driving Factor of Electoral Volatility

The successes and failures of the FPÖ have had a great impact on electoral mobility in Austria. The rise of the FPÖ in the 1980s and 1990s was based on large gains from the SPÖ and ÖVP. Its performance as a powerful opposition party against the grand coalition helped the FPÖ to transform itself from a small-sized party to a medium-sized party and, finally, to the second strongest party in voters' popularity between 1983 and 1999.

In the 1980s and 1990s, the Austrian Freedom Party was rather successful in opposing the grand coalition. The FPÖ gained its voters to the same extent from the Social Democratic Party and the People's Party. Whereas the ÖVP lost most of their voters to the FPÖ in the late 1980s, the SPÖ faced larger voter losses in the 1990s.[10]

Between 1986 and 2006, the SPÖ lost 850,000 voters to the FPÖ (including the BZÖ in 2006) and gained only 371,000 in return. The most dramatic losses occurred between the elections in 1990 and 1994,

Table 3
Party Swing between SPÖ and FPÖ/BZÖ, Gains and Losses

Elections		Losses of SPÖ to FPÖ	Gains of SPÖ from FPÖ	Balance
1983-1986		-122	+30	-92
1986-1990		-107	+44	-63
1990-1994		-244	+6	-238
1994-1995		-39	+66	27
1995-1999		-176	+35	-141
1999-2002		-14	+148	134
2002-2006	to FPÖ	-119	+42	-102
	to BZÖ	-25		
Sum		-846	+371	-475

Source: Based on voter transition analyses, 1983-2006.

84 The Changing Austrian Voter

when almost a quarter of a million voters switched from the SPÖ to the FPÖ. The SPÖ was most successful in regaining voters from the FPÖ in the election of 2002 when the FPÖ was dramatically reduced to a third of its size in 1999. In total, the SPÖ has lost nearly half a million voters to the FPÖ.

Between 1986 and 2006, the ÖVP lost approximately 812,000 voters to the FPÖ, coming close to the social democratic losses to the Freedom Party. However, these losses almost balanced out by the party gaining 754,000 voters in return, most of them in the 2002 election, when 633,000 former FPÖ voters gave their support to the ÖVP. In sum, losses and gains are nearly balanced between the FPÖ and ÖVP.

Electoral Volatility in the 2006 Election

The Campaign

The national parliamentary elections took place on 1 October 2006 after a year of changing fortune for the two major parties. The SPÖ had been enjoying a comfortable lead in the polls until April, when a severe financial crisis of the union-owned BAWAG bank started to dominate the public debate.

From this moment on, all published opinion polls showed the ÖVP ahead of the SPÖ. However, in the weeks before the election, the margin shrank to values between two and five percentage points, in most cases below the limits of statistical sampling error. Although still within the statistical margin of most polling results, the race's results were a surprise for many: at the end of the day, the SPÖ came in first, one percentage point ahead of the ÖVP.

Table 4
Party Swing between the ÖVP and FPÖ/BZÖ, Gains and Losses

Elections		Losses of ÖVP to FPÖ	Gains of ÖVP from FPÖ	Balance
1983-1986		-139	+29	-110
1986-1990		-202	+10	-192
1990-1994		-117	+7	-110
1994-1995		-42	+59	17
1995-1999		-138	+6	-132
1999-2002		-12	+633	621
2002-2006	to FPÖ	-102	+10	-152
	to BZÖ	-60		
Sum		-812	+754	-58

Source: Based on voter transition analyses, 1983-2006.

There is a striking parallel to the election of 2002. In an earlier stage of the campaign, a public consensus about the expected election outcome was formed and, in both cases, lasted until election day, despite (published and non-published) empirical evidence. In 2002, the picture of a close race was established in the public debate, and a narrow lead of the ÖVP in the polls immediately before the election had been more or less neglected.[11] In 2006, a different picture was dominating public perception: the ÖVP was out of reach for the challenger, the SPÖ. Narrow differences in the published polls close to election day could not change that picture; only election day itself did.

In both cases, predicting election outcomes turned out to be premature. Even if surveys during the campaign paint a certain picture of the likely outcome, two facts should be kept in mind when interpreting these polls. First, as shown above, the share of changing voters in the last six parliamentary elections in Austria always amounted to more than a fifth, sometimes almost to a third of the electorate. Second, voters take more time to reach their decision; the group of "late deciders" has been growing more or less steadily to a quarter of the electorate in 2006.[12] Truly, the campaign ain't over 'til it's over.

All Parties Lost to the "Party of Nonvoters"; the ÖVP Lost to All Parties

Turnout was 78.5 percent, significantly lower than in 2002 (84.3 percent), and all parties suffered from heavy losses to nonvoters.[13] Nonmobilization was a problem, especially for the two major parties, the ÖVP and the SPÖ. The ÖVP lost 172,000 voters to nonvoting, the SPÖ 143,000 (see Table 5).

Negative campaigning seemed to have a more demobilizing effect than in past elections.[14] In 2002, there was heavy negative campaigning against the existing center-right coalition (ÖVP-FPÖ) as well as against a hypothetical center-left coalition (SPÖ-Greens). Preventing a "red-green coalition" was one of the strongest reasons why former FPÖ voters supported the ÖVP.[15] Without this motivation, many of them would probably have abstained, for their party, the FPÖ, was going through a deep crisis.

In 2006, negative campaigning against possible coalitions did not play such a central role in the campaign. Parties attacked each other directly which might have had overall and specific demobilizing effects. In addition, the ÖVP's strong emphasis on the BAWAG scandal might have undermined its own campaign engaged in painting a picture of a

Table 5
Voter Transitions, 2002-2006, in Thousands

2002	SPÖ 2006	ÖVP 2006	Greens 2006	FPÖ 2006	BZÖ 2006	Others * 2006	Non- voters 2006	Total 2002
SPÖ	1,472	24	26	119	25	41	143	1,851
ÖVP	96	1,545	112	102	60	59	172	2,147
Greens	19	15	338	15	10	18	72	487
FPÖ	42	10	18	248	75	22	93	508
Others	15	1	12	10	5	37	12	93
Non voters	20	19	14	26	18	17	908	1,022
Total 2006	1,664	1,616	520	520	194	194	1,399	

* Other parties, including the Communist Party and the party of Hans-Peter Martin.
Example: In 2002, 1,472,000 SPÖ voters again voted for the SPÖ in 2006; 24,000 voted for the ÖVP, 26,000 to the Greens, and so forth.
Source: SORA voter transition analyses.

nation headed in the right direction. Many ÖVP voters resolved these conflicting messages through abstention.[16]

Although the SPÖ managed to keep 80 percent of its voters of the 2002 election, losses to nonvoters and to the FPÖ were significant. The exchange with the Greens was low and nearly balanced. The SPÖ won 96,000 former ÖVP voters and lost 24,000 voters to the ÖVP in return. In total, Social Democrats won the election by losing fewer voters than the ÖVP.

Voters chose the SPÖ if they supported its issues, according to an election day poll.[17] The top eight reasons for voting for the SPÖ included a variety of reasons: social justice/social security (28 percent), other social issues (for example pensions, 25 percent), best program in general (19 percent), supporting employees/workers (17 percent), jobs/labor market (17 percent), supporting the poor (15 percent), education (12 percent), and health care (11 percent).

The ÖVP lost to all parties. The most dramatic change was the loss to nonvoters: 172,000 former ÖVP voters chose not to vote in 2006. But the ÖVP also lost more than 100,000 voters to both the Greens and the FPÖ, and a little less than 100,000 to the SPÖ. From these parties, only small numbers of voters changed to the ÖVP in return. In addition, 60,000 voters changed to ÖVP's coalition partner, the BZÖ. In total, the ÖVP kept 72 percent of its former voters. The election day poll showed that the ÖVP's losses were highest among workers, employees, people who had been unemployed, and people aged 30 to 44 years.

Table 6
Voter Transitions, 2002-2006, in Percent of 2002 Votes

2002	SPÖ 2006	ÖVP 2006	Greens 2006	FPÖ 2006	BZÖ 2006	Others * 2006	Non-voters 2006	Total 2002
SPÖ	80	1	1	6	1	3	8	100
ÖVP	4	72	5	5	3	3	8	100
Greens	4	3	69	3	2	4	15	100
FPÖ	8	2	3	49	15	5	18	100
Others	16	2	13	11	6	40	13	100
Nonvoters	2	2	1	3	2	2	89	100

* Other parties, including the Communist Party and the party of Hans-Peter Martin. Example: In 2002, 80 percent of SPÖ voters again voted for the SPÖ in 2006; 1 percent voted for the ÖVP, 1 percent for the Greens, and so forth.
Source: SORA voter transition analyses.

Reasons for voting for the ÖVP reflect the campaign's themes. General satisfaction with the ÖVP and Chancellor Wolfgang Schüssel characterize ÖVP voters' motives. Only a few issues rank among the top eight motives for voting for the ÖVP: best program in general (29 percent), did a good job (21 percent), Chancellor Wolfgang Schüssel (17 percent), economy issues (16 percent), integrity (11 percent), have always voted for the ÖVP (11 percent), public finances/public debts (9 percent), and Christian values (8 percent).

Those voters leaving the ÖVP had three main reasons for doing so. These were dissatisfaction with Chancellor Schüssel, the high importance of issues introduced by the SPÖ, and skepticism regarding a possible coalition of the ÖVP and the Greens.

The Greens achieved their best result in federal elections ever, overtaking the FPÖ by an extremely thin margin of 533 votes. Although the Greens also had significant losses to nonvoters (every seventh Green voter of 2002 abstained in 2006), considerable gains from former ÖVP voters (112,000) helped to increase the absolute number of votes. However, the strongest result in the history of the Austrian Greens was still not able to grant the party a parliamentary majority together with one of the two major parties.

The Greens successfully concentrated on their core competences and their core target group, highly educated people. The election day poll gives evidence that this strategy worked. The Greens were most successful among highly educated people, and voting reasons reflect Green issues: ecological concerns (42 percent), best program in general (22 percent), education (21 percent), integrity (19 percent), social issues (18 percent), energy politics (17 percent), and party spokesperson Alexander Van der Bellen (15 percent).

Although the FPÖ managed to gain votes, they lost third place to the Greens. In 2006, 93,000 former FPÖ voters did not vote. The FPÖ lost 75,000 voters to its split-off and governing party, the BZÖ, not many more than the ÖVP. The FPÖ also lost a significant amount of voters (42,000) to the SPÖ, but its gains were nearly three times as high. Events such as the split-off of the BZÖ, the fact of being way back in the opposition, and the reliance on former successful strategies such as the focus on immigration issues impacted the high amounts of gains and losses: only about half of former FPÖ voters stayed with the FPÖ. The most important gains were from former SPÖ and ÖVP voters, which is, perhaps, a hint that well-established strategies in issues led to the known patterns in voter transition of the 1980s and 1990s. Austrians voted for the FPÖ more or less for one reason: 60 percent of its voters said that they voted for the FPÖ because of immigration issues (such as more restrictions on immigration), while 24 percent voted for the party because of the FPÖ's opposition to Turkey becoming an EU member state. One can say that the FPÖ is a single-issue party.

The first attempt of the BZÖ to get into parliament in elections was a narrow success. They exceeded the 4 percent threshold by just 5,207 votes. The new BZÖ electorate consists of voters from all parties, with strong support from former ÖVP and FPÖ voters. The BZÖ's success is centered in the region of Carinthia, where Jörg Haider is governor. Like the FPÖ, the BZÖ was also elected because of immigration issues (33 percent), but also of Jörg Haider, although the party spokesperson was Peter Westenthaler, not Haider.

All other parties get less than 4 percent of valid votes; thud they are not represented in the Austrian parliament.

Nonvoters were the most successful "party" in this election: 89 percent of nonvoters of 2002—809,000 persons—chose not to vote again. In this election, small numbers of mobilized voters were contrasted by high numbers of demobilized party voters from every single party.

Notes

1. Kathrin Gruetzmann and Christoph Hofinger, "A Master Equation Model to Analyze the Electoral Flow at Austrian National Elections, 1970-1990," in *Analyzing Societal Problems: A Methodological Approach*, ed. Dorien J. DeTombe and Cor van Dijkum (Munich: Hampp, 1996), 279-94.

2. Christoph Hofinger and Günther Ogris, "Achtung, gender gap! Geschlecht und Wahlverhalten, 1979-1995," in *Wahlkampf und Wählerentscheidung: Analysen zur Nationalratswahl 1995*, ed. Fritz Plasser et al. (Vienna: Schriftenreihe des Zentrums für angewandte Politikforschung, 1996), 211-32, here 216.

3. Anton Pelinka, "Decline of the Party State and the Rise of Parliamentarism: Change within the Austrian Party System," in *The Austrian Party System*, ed. Anton Pelinka and Fritz Plasser (Boulder, CO: Westview, 1989), 21-40.

4. Fritz Plasser and Peter A. Ulram, "Kampagnedynamik: Strategischer und thematischer Kontext der Wählerentscheidung," in *Wahlkampf und Wählerentscheidung: Analysen zur Nationalratswahl 1995*, ed. Fritz Plasser et al. (Vienna: Signum, 1996), 47-79.

5. Christoph Hofinger, Günther Ogris, and Eva Thalhammer, "Der Jahrhundertstrom: Wahlkampfverlauf, Wahlmotive und Wählerströme im Kontext der Nationalratswahl 2002," in *Wahlverhalten in Bewegung: Analysen zur Nationalratswahl 2002*, ed. Fritz Plasser and Peter A. Ulram (Vienna: Signum, 2003), 159-90.

6. SORA voter transition analyses are calculated from aggregate data, that is, election results of communities, precincts, and so forth. In 2002 and 2006, election results from more than 2,350 Austrian communities and from almost 2,000 polling stations (*Sprengel*) in Vienna were grouped in clusters and analyzed with multiple regression models. More information about SORA voter transition analyses is available online at <http://www. sora.at/en/start.asp?b=266>; Christoph Hofinger, Marcelo Jenny, and Günther Ogris, "Steter Tropfen höhlt den Stein. Die Wählerströme 1999 im Kontext der 80er und 90er Jahre," in *Das österreichische Wahlverhalten*, ed. Fritz Plasser et al. (Vienna: Signum, 2000), 117-40.

7. Ibid.

8. Christoph Hofinger, Sigrid Nitsch, and Brigitte Salfinger, "Alles BAWAG oder was? Kampagnen, Wählerströme und Motive bei der Nationalratswahl 2006," in *Wahl 2006: Kanzler, Kampagnen, Kapriolen,* ed. Thomas Hofer and Barbara Toth (Münster: Lit, 2007), 135-49.

9. Christoph Hofinger, Brigitte Salfinger, and Sabine Westphal, "Tiroler Wählerdynamik 1945-2003 im österreichischen Kontext," in *Politik in Tirol*, ed. Ferdinand Karlhofer and Anton Pelinka (Innsbruck: Studienverlag, 2003), 309-38.

10. Ruth Picker, Brigitte Salfinger, and Eva Zeglovits, "Aufstieg und Fall der FPÖ aus Perspektive der Empirischen Wahlforschung, Eine Langzeitanalyse 1986-2004," *Österreichische Zeitschrift für Politikwissenschaft 33* (2004): 263-79.

11. Sieglinde Katharina Rosenberger and Gilg Seeber, *Kopf an Kopf. Meinungsforschung im Medienwahlkampf* (Vienna: Czernin), 2003.

12. Fritz Plasser and Peter Ulram, "Die Wahlanalyse 2006: Wer hat wen warum gewählt?" Press conference handout, Vienna, 2 October 2006.

13. With the BZÖ as a logical exception because the party was running for the first time.

14. Hofinger, Nitsch and Salfinger, "Alles BAWAG oder was?".

15. Fritz Plasser, Peter A. Ulram, and Gilg Seeber, "Erdrutschwahlen: Momentum, Motive, und neue Muster im Wahlverhalten," in *Wahlverhalten in Bewegung: Analysen zur Nationalratswahl 2002*, ed. Fritz Plasser and Peter A. Ulram (Vienna: Signum, 2003), 97-157, here 139.

16. Hofinger, Nitsch and Salfinger, "Alles BAWAG oder was?".

17. SORA conducted a telephone poll on the election weekend in cooperation with the IFES (Institut für empirische Sozialforschung, Vienna). A representative sample of eligible voters (n=1.500; 250 on Friday, 750 on Saturday and 500 on Sunday = election day) were asked about voting preference, reasons for voting for a party, and important issues that had characterized the campaigns. All further results refer to this poll. Reasons for voting for a party were asked in an open ended question ("Why did you vote/will you vote for party X?"); answers were coded. Results are published at the SORA web site: <http://www.sora.at>.

Regional Elections in Austria from 1986 to 2006

Herbert Dachs

Presentation of the Problem

One of the crucial characteristics of a federal state is the more or less developed sovereignty of its sub-entities (*Bundesländer, Kantone*, and so forth). In a properly defined polity framework, these sub-entities can act autonomously, and—contrary to decentralized states—their political elites must regularly face general elections.[1] Austria can be identified as such a federal state, though with a very centralistic notion and a strong domination of the central unit concerning competencies and especially budgetary issues. Regional elections (*Landtagswahlen*) to the respective parliaments (*Landtage*) are held every five years. The competing actors and political parties in these arenas usually correspond to those at the federal level. In general, the socioeconomic homogeneity of Austrian society has grown during the Second Republic (*Zweite Republik*). Nevertheless, there still remain certain differences between the "*Bundesländer*" in their political cultures and their policy priorities.[2] The political parties thus face special "environments" in each *Bundesland* with respective demands. "These constellations [are] particular in time and space since there are specific combinations of historical, sociostructural, economic and political conditions in the different *Bundesländer*."[3]

These conditions shape the political landscape of, the challenges for, and the demands on the political parties and bring about different political majorities. The politics of the *Länder* are, however, certainly influenced and determined by the decisions, power relationships, and general mood of political players at the federal level. Consequently, the aim of the following analysis is twofold, namely to reconstruct the developments in and dynamics of regional elections since the mid-1980s and secondly, to relate them to electoral behavior on the federal level.

Specific Framework for Party Competition in the *Bundesländer*

Analyzing the regional elections in the Austrian *Bundesländer* necessitates acknowledging some important institutional conditions, their consequences for the political process, and their impact on eventual political transitions.

First, despite their different sizes (the biggest *Bundesland*, Vienna, has about 1.7 million inhabitants while the smallest, Burgenland, has only about 280,000),[4] the Austrian *Bundesländer* are, in general, easily manageable territories. Emerging problems can be identified very quickly, and communication between the political elites is dense which eases negotiation and facilitates consensus.

Second, until 1998, seven of the nine *Bundesländer* prescribed in their constitutions so-called "proportional governments." The only exceptions were Vienna and Vorarlberg. These "proportional governments" had to include every political party having a certain number of seats in the regional parliament without taking into account their willingness to cooperate or the compatibility of the different political programs. Even in Vienna (until 1973) and Vorarlberg (until 1974), where the constitutions did not oblige the parties to build proportional governments, this consensual style was a compulsory custom over a long period. The consequences of the "proportional constitutions" (which are, however, adequate in situations of national crisis) were so-called "governments of concentration." This system encountered a lot of criticism, especially with regard to lack of control, inefficiency, and so forth,[5] so that in 1998, Tyrol and Salzburg abolished the rule of proportion. Since then, governments are built by the usual principle of majorities,[6] but the grand coalitions of the *Österreichische Volkspartei* (ÖVP) and the *Sozialdemokratische Partei Österreichs* (SPÖ) still command very large majorities.

Third, strong patterns of concordance characterize decision making in the *Bundesländer*. Due to the involvement of all relevant parties in the very early stages of the negotiation process, open conflicts rarely arise. In addition, questions of ideology or *Weltanschauung* hardly arise either. One negative consequence, however, is that—due to the already mentioned informal and early inclusion of all relevant interest groups and political parties (with a minimum number of seats) in the governments (still in at least five of the nine *Bundesländer*)—effective control, the development of alternative policy approaches, and the public presentation of such approaches become difficult. Election campaigns are very often considered as inconvenient necessities which hinder the consensual order of business. Political elites are well aware of the fact "that beyond the short periods of open competition, criticism, struggle over ideas, arguments and voters, they have to return to consensual decision making, compromise in acting and communication."[7]

Since parties, therefore, cannot shape clear profiles with regard to policy approaches and ideological contents, they focus on strategies of personalization. The crucial and most significant institution in this respect is the *Landeshauptmann* (governor) and the person who holds that position. This role is of high importance not only due to the regional constitutions, but also because of the *indirect federal administration* (which means that federal ministries delegate the execution of federal agendas to the executives of the *Länder*). The *Landeshauptmann* is a position of high public attention and media interest, and the office holders usually try to present themselves as communicators, moderators, and agents of different interests. They attempt to act statesmanlike in a way that raises them above the daily political struggles. The so-called *Landeshauptmann* bonus makes it difficult for other competitors to appear as viable, let alone better, alternatives.[8]

The big trade associations—*Arbeiterkammer* (representation of employees), *Wirtschaftskammer* (Chamber of Commerce), *Landwirtschaftskammer* (Chamber of Agriculture) and the Austrian *Gewerkschaftsbund* (Federation of Trade Unions)—are informally, but broadly, involved in the decision making process. The know-how of the respective experts is often used as a kind of think tank for ideologically close parties or ministries in the development of policy. Furthermore, these and other associations are involved in a way that can be called a *non-autonomous corporatism* which applies not only to shaping legislation, but also to the enforcement of laws.[9]

Finally, the media landscape in the *Bundesländer* is still dominated by the public broadcasting institution, the *Österreichischer Rundfunk* (ORF). Its regional reporting was enlarged since the 1970s, both in quantity and quality. Being a public broadcasting station, the ORF is obliged to be objective and balanced. Nevertheless, the *Landeshauptmann* has important influence on the appointment of top positions. Until the mid-1970s, the market of the print media in the *Bundeslän-*

der was dominated by just one big newspaper. Since the tabloid *Neue Kronenzeitung* (currently with a circulation of 42 percent on the whole Austrian territory) began its successful regionalization, the competition in the print media landscape changed insofar as—with the exception of the small Vorarlberg—at least two bigger daily newspapers operate in every *Bundesland*. That opened the market and changed the general operating conditions. The stronger competition also led to more diversity in reporting and coverage, strengthened the critical approach, hampered the press' ability to ignore unpopular and delicate issues, and fostered, in general, critical thinking by and politicization of Austrian citizens.[10]

The Development of Majorities in
Regional Elections *(Landtagswahlen)*[11]
Clear Majorities and Stability until the 1980s

Beginning at the end of the 1940s, important changes took place temporarily on the "election market." The national liberal *Verband der Unabhängigen* (VdU), which stood for elections for the first time in 1949, captured a remarkable share of votes in a range of *Bundesländer* (for example, Carinthia: 20.5 percent, Upper Austria: 20.8 percent, Salzburg: 18.5 percent).[12] In the mid-1950s, however, these votes were lost again when the VdU dissolved. The far-right *Freiheitliche Partei Österreichs* (FPÖ) was founded. Apart from ephemeral irritations in a number of *Bundesländer*, there were clear majorities—either of votes or at least of parliamentary seats—which dominated the political situation until the 1980s. In eight of the nine *Bundesländer*, absolute majorities over long periods existed, namely in Tyrol (ÖVP since 1945), Vorarlberg (ÖVP since 1945), Lower Austria (ÖVP from 1945 to 1993), Upper Austria (ÖVP 1945-1949, 1955-1967, 1979-1991), Styria (ÖVP 1945-1953, 1965-1970, 1975-1991), Burgenland (SPÖ 1968-1972, 1977-1987), Carinthia (SPÖ 1970-1989), and Vienna (SPÖ since 1945). Only in Burgenland (1964) was there a change of majorities, and even this case must be ascribed more to socioeconomic transitions than to political competition. The struggle of political parties was dominated by the ÖVP and the SPÖ, both with a high level of organization and a high membership. The third party, the FPÖ, played a marginal role in the political landscape. The reasons for that ultra-stable voting behavior are two-fold. On the one hand, the political actors—especially the often impressive and charismatic governors—succeeded in arranging and modernizing their policies, thereby facing the political and socioeconomic challenges in a pragmatic and moderate way. On the other hand and not less important, the above mentioned specific structures and conditions of the regional politics assisted with the stabilization and the maintenance of power relations.

An important precondition for this phenomenon was the ability of the regional elites to create a kind of fictional political arena of the regions which was—at least in the perception of the voters—disconnected from the federal political moods and trends. Although the political opposition parties (SPÖ between 1966-1970, ÖVP from 1970, and FPÖ non-stop) tried to capitalize on their position party in federal politics, their success was limited. Between 1968 and 1969, however, the circumstances were favorable for political protest against the then-ÖVP government. Between 1983 and 1986, during the unpopular SPÖ-FPÖ coalition, the opposition parties again benefited. Apart from these short periods, however, the movements of voters remained moderate, and the above-mentioned power relations did not change significantly.

Growth of Voter Mobility in the Mid-1980s

The year 1986 brought a range of drastic changes on the federal level: the SPÖ and ÖVP built a new grand coalition (with restrictions in their budgetary policy), the Greens entered the parliament, and, most importantly, the FPÖ under its new leader Jörg Haider adopted a course of fundamental opposition and far-right populism, a strategy which proved to be very successful until 1999.

What was new for Austria was that these developments on the federal level strongly and directly affected voting behavior in regional elections (*Landtagswahlen*). Until then, the above mentioned local specific structures and political modus of the regions had mitigated the effects of federal politics on the voting market. Now, the situation changed. Table 1 shows the developments in the specific *Bundesländer*.

Two significant characteristics of these changes emerge. First, the ÖVP and the SPÖ lost dramatically from 1986/87 on. As the line "Landtagswahlen T-elections until 1999: Gains/Losses" shows, many regional parties had to be concerned by the losses. The SPÖ suffered losses in Carinthia (-18.7 percent), Lower Austria (-11.0 percent), Upper Austria (-11.0 percent), Vorarlberg (-11.0 percent), and Vienna (-16.3 percent). The ÖVP's heavy losses occurred in Salzburg (-11.4 percent), Styria (-15.5 percent), and Tyrol (-17.4 percent). The absolute majorities were lost bit by bit, and the SPÖ even had to renounce the important position of the *Landeshauptmann* in Carinthia. Moreover, the FPÖ gained votes and seats in all *Bundesländer*. The most significant gains for the FPÖ were in Carinthia (+26.1 percent), Lower Austria (+14.4 percent), Upper Austria (+15.6 percent), Styria (+16.6 percent), Tyrol (+13.6 percent), Vorarlberg (+16.9 percent), and Vienna (+22.5 percent). On the federal level, the FPÖ celebrated similar successes: from 1983 to 1999, they gained not less than 21.9 percent of the vote (thus considerably more than in the most *Bundesländer* with the exception of Vienna and Carinthia). Second, in the years until 1999, the green parties accomplished their goals in most *Bundesländer* and entered the regional parliaments (*Landtage*) in Salzburg, Styria, Tyrol, Vorarlberg, Vienna, and Upper and Lower Austria.

How can one explain these movements which seemed to be impossible to overcome for such a long time in Austrian regional elections? Obviously, the regional particularities and characteristics had lost their importance, although the parties' relative power relations generally remained consistent. Apart from that, a number of reasons for the surprising developments can be identified.[14] First, the party loyalties of voters had already diminished markedly. This can be considered a basic condition for the growth of voter mobility. Second, important policy issues had been influenced and determined for a long time by federal or European politics and were no longer resolvable by the regional political elites (such as environmental, traffic, or economic issues). Furthermore, the supra-regional media began considering regional elections in light of certain aspects of federal tactics and strategies. All these developments made it more and more difficult to delineate an explicit regional political arena. The mood and tactics of politicians and parties at the federal level became ever more influential on regional voting behavior. An illustration of this trend is the answers of a survey in Salzburg 1989 about the upcoming regional elections (*Landtagswahlen*). Of those surveyed, 84 percent said that the elections were about the *Landeshauptmann* while 75 percent said they were about the achievements of the political parties of Salzburg; still 48 percent stated that they would also evaluate "the politics of the grand coalition on the federal level."[15]

Since the mid-1980s, the political climate in Austria has been characterized by a kind of protest culture. The Greens, especially the FPÖ, dictated the themes and the style by their aggressive and critical demeanor. They revolted against the cemented power relations, denounced the

Table 1
Regional *(Landtagswahlen)* Election Results and Federal (Nationalratswahlen) Results in the Austrian *Bundesländer*, early 1980s to 2006

	Burgenland				Carinthia				Lower Austria			
	ÖVP	SPÖ	FPÖ	Greens	ÖVP	SPÖ	FPÖ	Greens	ÖVP	SPÖ	FPÖ	Greens
LTW 1982	430	53.2	3.0									
LTW 1983									54.6	41.4	1.7	0.6
LTW 1984					28.3	51.6	16.0	0.7				
NRW 1986	42.8	49.0	5.4	2.5	27.2	47.2	20.9	3.8	47.3	42.4	6.1	3.6
LTW 1987	41.5	47.3	7.3	2.2								
	-15	-5.9	+4.3									
LTW 1988									47.6	37.3	9.4	2.4
									-7.0	-4.1	+7.7	+1.8
LTW 1989					21.0	46.0	29.0	1.7				
					-7.3	-5.6	+13.0	+1.0				
NRW 1990	35.4	49.9	11.1	2.5	18.5	46.1	30.3	3.0	39.1	42.5	12.2	3.3
	-7.4	+0.9	+5.7	+/-0	-8.7	-1.1	+9.4	-0.8	-8.2	+0.1	+6.1	-3
LTW 1991	382	48.1	9.7	33								
	-33	+0.8	+2.4	+1.1								
LTW 1993									44.2	33.9	12.0	3.2
									-3.4	-3.4	+2.6	+1.8
LTW 1994					23.8	37.4	33.3	1.6				
					+2.8	-8.6	+4.3	-0.1				
NRW 1994	31.5	44.3	16.7	3.8	16.4	39.5	33.5	5.9	33.9	34.8	18.2	5.7
	-3.9	-5.6	+5.6	+1.3	-2.1	-6.6	+3.2	+2.9	-5.2	-7.7	+6.0	+2.4
NRW 1995	31.9	44.6	16.9	2.5	18.5	40.8	32.7	3.5	34.5	37.9	17.3	3.7
	+0.4	+0.3	+0.2	-1.3	+2.1	+1.3	-0.8	-2.4	+0.6	+3.1	-0.9	-2.0
LTW 1996	36.1	44.5	14.6	2.5								
	-2.1	-3.6	+4.9	-0.8								
LTW 1997												
LTW 1998									44.9	30.4	16.1	4.5
									+0.7	-3.5	+4.1	+1.3
LTW 1999					20.7	32.9	42.1	3.9				
					-3.1	-4.5	+8.8	+2.3				
LT-elections until 1999: Gains/Losses	-6.9	-8.7	+11.6	+0.3	-7.6	-18.7	+26.1	+3.2	-9.7	-11.0	+14.4	+3.9
NRW 1999	306	41.9	21.0	3.7	16.3	35.7	38.6	5.5	32.9	33.8	22.5	6.0
	-1.3	-2.7	+4.1	+1.2	-2.2	-5.1	+5.9	+2.0	-1.6	-4.1	+5.2	+2.3
LTW 2000	35.3	46.5	12.6	5.5								
	-8	+2.0	-2.0	+3.0								
NRW 2002	424	45.8	6.4	4.7	30.5	38.3	23.6	6.2	47.8	36.8	6.9	7.2
	+11.8	+3.9	-146	+1.0	+14.2	+2.6	-15.0	+0.7	+14.9	+3.0	-15.6	+1.2
LTW 2003									53.3	33.6	4.5	7.2
									+8.4	+3.2	-11.6	+2.7
LTW 2004					11.6	38.4	42.4	6.7				
					-9.1	+5.5	+0.3	+2.8				
LTW 2005	36.4	52.2	5.8	5.2								
	+1.1	+5.7	- 6.8	-0.3								
NRW 2006	361	450	87	58	212	354	7.2	7.5	39.2	36.2	9.6	9.0
	-63	-8	+ 2.3	+1.1	-9.3	-2.9	-16.4	+1.3	-8.6	-0.6	+2.7	+1.8

98 The Changing Austrian Voter

Table 1 (cont.)

	Upper Austria				Salzburg				Styria			
	ÖVP	SPÖ	FPÖ	Greens	ÖVP	SPÖ	FPÖ	Greens	ÖVP	SPÖ	FPÖ	Greens
LTW 1984					50.2	35.1	8.7	4.3				
LTW 1985	52.1	38.0	5.0	1.7								
LTW 1986									51.7	37.6	4.6	3.7
NRW 1986	41.5	42.0	11.0	4.9	40.9	36.7	15.9	5.9	41.0	44.1	9.9	4.1
LTW 1989					44.0	31.2	16.4	6.2				
					-6.2	-3.9	+7.7	+1.9				
NRW 1990	33.3	42.0	16.0	4.1	32.1	37.8	20.5	7.3	33.2	43.3	16.8	3.9
	-8.2	+/-0	+5.0	-0.8	-8.8	+1.1	+4.6	+1.4	-7.8	-0.8	+6.9	-0.2
LTW 1991	45.2	31.4	17.7	3.1					44.2	34.9	15.4	1.7
	-6.9	-6.6	+12.7	+1.4					-7.5	-2.7	+10.8	-2.0
LTW 1994					38.6	27.0	19.5	7.3				
					-5.4	-4.2	+3.1	+1.1				
NRW 1994	28.9	34.5	22.5	7.6	29.0	31.0	23.9	8.1	27.5	36.6	23.4	6.2
	-4.4	-7.5	+6.5	+3.5	-3.1	-6.8	+3.4	+0.8	-5.7	-6.7	+6.6	+2.3
LTW 1995									36.2	35.9	17.1	4.3
									-8.0	+1.0	+1.7	+2.6
NRW 1995	29.5	38.1	21.6	5.1	29.1	32.6	25.4	5.6	29.5	39.6	21.2	4.0
	+0.6	+3.6	-0.9	-2.5	+0.1	+1.6	+1.5	-2.5	+2.0	+3.0	-2.2	-2.2
LTW 1997	42.7	27.0	20.6	5.8								
	-2.5	-4.4	+2.9	+2.7								
LTW 1999					38.8	32.3	19.6	5.4				
					+0.2	+5.3	+0.1	-1.9				
LT-elections until 1999:												
Gains/Losses	-9.4	-11.0	+15.6	+4.1	-11.4	-2.8	+10.9	+1.1	-15.5	+2.0	+16.6	+0.3
NRW 1999	28.6	33.1	26.8	7.4	27.8	29.0	29.4	8.4	26.8	33.8	29.2	5.8
	-0.9	-5.0	+5.2	+2.3	-1.3	-3.6	+4.0	+2.8	-2.7	-5.8	+8.0	+1.8
LTW 2000									47.3	32.3	12.4	5.6
									+11.1	-3.6	-4.7	+1.3
NRW 2002	42.6	37.0	10.4	8.7	46.6	30.8	10.7	10.4	44.6	37.0	9.6	7.0
	+14.0	+3.9	-16.4	+1.3	+18.8	+1.8	-18.7	+2.0	+17.8	+3.2	-19.6	+1.2
LTW 2003	43.4	38.3	8.4	9.1								
	+0.7	+11.3	-12.2	+3.3								
LTW 2004					37.9	45.4	8.7	8.0				
					-0.9	+13.1	-10.9	+2.6				
LTW 2005									38.7	41.7	4.6	4.7
									-8.6	+9.4	-7.8	-0.9
NRW 2006	35.2	36.1	12.2	10.2	39.2	28.5	12.3	12.5	37.5	37.2	10.4	7.9
	-7.4	-0.9	+1.8	+1.5	-7.4	-2.3	+1.6	+2.1	-7.1	+0.2	+0.8	+0.9

Notes: +/- refers to the respective chronologically last regional or national elections. The general basis of calculation is the election results of the Bundesland Upper Austria and the Ministry of Internal Affairs. Only the results of the parties represented in the Austrian Parliament since 1986 were taken into account in the table. Other parties like the BZÖ (Bündnis Zukunft Österreich), the LIF (Liberal Forum) or the KPÖ (Communist Party) are not listed. The basis of calculation for the data of the Greens are the results of the following regional equivalents: Greens, GAL

99

Table 1 (cont.)

	Tyrol				Vorarlberg				Vienna			
	ÖVP	SPÖ	FPÖ	Greens	ÖVP	SPÖ	FPÖ	Greens	ÖVP	SPÖ	FPÖ	Greens
LTW 1983									34.8	55.5	5.4	2.5
LTW 1984	64.6	25.2	6.0		51.6	24.0	10.5	13.0				
NRW 1986	53.2	29.2	11.3	5.8	53.1	25.5	11.9	8.8	33.2	52.4	5.8	6.1
LTW 1987									28.4	54.9	9.7	4.4
									-6.4	-0.6	+4.3	+1.9
LTW 1989	48.7	22.8	15.6	8.3	51.0	21.3	16.1	5.2				
	-15.9	-2.4	+9.6		-0.6	-2.7	+5.6	-7.8				
NRW 1990	40.7	30.5	17.1	6.3	40.4	28.8	17.2	5.2	21.1	50.7	15.7	7.6
	-12.5	+1.3	+5.8	+0.5	-12.7	+3.3	+5.3	-3.6	-12.1	-1.7	+9.9	+1.5
LTW 1991									18.1	47.8	22.5	9.1
									-10.3	-7.1	+12.8	+4.7
LTW 1994	47.3	19.8	11	107	49.9	16.2	18.4	7.8				
	-1.4	-3.0	+0.5	+2.4	-1.1	-5.1	+2.3	+2.6				
NRW 1994	36.2	24.4	22.1	9.5	37.8	20.9	23.6	9.0	17.1	38.5	22.7	9.8
	-45	-6.1	+5.0	+3.2	-2.6	-7.9	+6.4	+3.8	-4.0	-12.2	+7.0	+2.2
NRW 1995	31.3	27.4	27.0	6.4	34.1	22.9	27.4	7.3	19.5	44.0	20.1	6.0
	-4.9	+3.0	+4.9	-3.1	-3.7	+2.0	+3.8	-1.7	+2.4	+5.5	-2.6	-3.8
LTW 1996									15.3	39.2	27.9	7.9
									-2.8	-8.6	+ 5.4	-1.2
LTW 1999	47.2	21.8	19.6	8.0	45.8	13.0	27.4	6.0				
	-0.1	+2.0	+3.5	-2.7	-4.1	-3.2	+9.0	-1.8				
LT-elections until 1999:												
Gains/Losses	-17.4	-3.4	+13.6	-0.3	-5.8	-11.0	+16.9	-7.0	-19.5	-16.3	+22.5	+5.4
NRW 1999	32.9	23.1	28.0	9.7	35.2	18.2	30.2	10.0	17.0	37.9	24.8	10.3
	+1.6	-4.3	+1.0	+3.3	+1.1	-4.7	+2.8	+2.7	-2.5	-6.1	+4.7	+4.3
LTW 2000												
LTW 2001									16.4	46.9	20.2	12.4
									+1.1	+7.7	-7.7	+4.5
NRW 2002	51.9	24.5	10.0	11.6	49.2	20.1	13.0	14.5	30.6	43.8	8.0	15.1
	+19.0	+1.4	-18.0	+1.9	+14.0	+1.9	-17.2	+4.5	+13.6	+5.9	-16.8	+4.8
LTW 2003	49.9	25.9	8.0	15.6								
	+2.7	+4.1	-11.6	+7.6								
LTW 2004					54.9	16.9	12.9	10.2				
					+9.1	+3.9	-14.5	+4.2				
LTW 2005									18.8	49.1	14.8	14.6
									+2.4	+2.2	-5.4	+2.2
NRW 2006	43.8	23.2	10.8	13.0	42.0	18.5	10.9	16.4	21.8	41.0	13.9	17.4
	-81	-1.3	+0.8	+1.4	-7.2	-1.6	-2.1	+1.9	-8.8	-2.8	+5.9	+2.3

(Burgenland); Greens, GAL, Demokratie 99 (Carinthia); Greens, ALNÖ, GAL, GABL (Lower Austria); Greens, GAL (Upper Austria); Greens, GABL, BL (Salzburg); Greens, VGÖ-AL (Styria); Greens, GAT (Tyrol); Greens, AL-VGÖ, GAV (Vorarlberg); Greens, ALW (Vienna). Furthermore, joint candidature is for the AL-VGÖ in the regional elections in Vorarlberg in 1984, the VGÖ-AL in the regional elections in Styria in 1986, or the candidature in the framework of the Election-Alliance Demokratie 99 in the regional elections in Carinthia in 1999.

Source: Election results of the Bundesland Upper Austria and the Ministry of Internal Affairs.[13]

"overly controlling party-state," and contested the consensual political culture. This strategy of criticism proved to be successful in regional as well as federal, elections, where many of the criticized aspects were especially distinctive. But this was not the only reason for the FPÖ's successful results. Party leader Jörg Haider appeared in many election campaigns as an aggressive and energetic campaigner and populist speaker. Thus the party's brilliant results in regional elections were not the consequence of exceptional achievements, abilities, or leadership in the respective *Bundesland*. The electoral gains were, to a large extent, so-called borrowed votes, which made the abrupt crashes and backslides of the FPÖ after its entry into government in the year 2000 understandable.

The Tide Turns

In February 2000, the FPÖ built a coalition with the ÖVP and, thus, had to cease from its oppositional stance. Due to intra-party conflicts about credibility and the political agenda, the FPÖ faced serious tensions, culminating in the so-called "Knittelfeld event." The FPÖ ministers resigned, and the autumn 2002 elections were a fiasco (c.f. Luther in this volume). Thus, the tide turned for the until-then successful FPÖ, and its electoral results in the regions also deteriorated.

Several key conclusions arise when examining the results of the regional elections since 2000 (see Table 1). First, there are absolute majorities again, namely in Vorarlberg, Tyrol, Lower Austria (ÖVP), and Vienna and Burgenland (SPÖ). Next, the Greens gained seats in all regional parliaments. Third, the FPÖ has lost dramatically in all regions with the exception of Carinthia, where Jörg Haider remains *Landeshauptmann*, and Vienna where the losses are of minor importance. In general, the FPÖ fell back to the level of support it enjoyed in the 1980s. Finally, in two *Bundesländer*, Salzburg (2004) and Styria (2005), the SPÖ gained votes to a degree that was never seen before (+13.1 percent in Salzburg, +9.4 percent in Styria). At the same time, the FPÖ and ÖVP lost many voters; consequently, the position of the *Landeshauptmann* went to the SPÖ. Federal trends and circumstances (such as the bonus the SPÖ received by being the opposition party), might have been relevant for these surprising results, but the main explanatory aspects were, however, linked to regional developments (too few convincing candidates, awkward campaigning and communication, charges of bad economic management, and so forth).[16] Thus the current political situation is that four of the nine *Bundesländer* are governed by the ÖVP (Vorarlberg, Tyrol, Upper Austria, Lower Austria), four by the SPÖ (Vienna, Styria, Salzburg, Burgenland) and one (Carinthia) by the BZÖ (former FPÖ). Neither in the First nor in the Second Republic had the situation been that balanced!

We can hardly answer the question of the degree to which regional and federal issues impacted regional elections. Each election has to be considered and analyzed in its singularity. Fritz Plasser and Franz Sommer are correct when stating that despite the growing importance of external and structural impacts, regional elections must not hastily be "degraded to federal test elections"; "[s]pecific regional factors, regional and local problems, the attractiveness of candidates, and the image of the regional parties still play an important role in the competition of the 1990s (and even after the millennium, H.D.)."[17] The table might have turned after the turbulence of the 1980s and 1990s in most of the *Bundesländer*. Nevertheless, we cannot talk of a stable, long-term voter realignment. The high rate of changing voting behavior will animate regional politics so that contests will remain more contentious and dynamic than before 1986 (see Table 2).

Table 2
Changing Voting Behavior in the Regional Elections, in Percent of Voters[18]

Bundesländer	Year	Voting Mobility (Wechselwähler)
Burgenland	2000-2005	23
Carinthia	1999-2004	30
Lower Austria	1998-2003	23
Upper Austria	1997-2003	27
Salzburg	1999-2004	28
Styria	2000-2005	32
Tyrol	1999-2003	32
Vorarlberg	1999-2004	40
Vienna	2000-2005	29
Middle of all Bundesländer		29

Source: Quoted in Brigitte Salfinger and Alexander Reichmann, "Stürmischer Wahlherbst: Analyse der Wählerströme bei den Landtagswahlen in der Steiermark, im Burgenland, und in Wien," in *Österreichisches Jahrbuch für Politik 2005* (Vienna: Oldenbourg, 2006), 29-45, here 45.

Notes

1. See Heidrun Abromeit, *Interessenvermittlung zwischen Konkurrenz und Konkordanz. Studienbuch zur Vergleichenden Lehre politischer Systeme* (Opladen: Leske + Budrich, 1993), 116 ff.

2. For the state of the art in Austria, see Herbert Dachs, "Parteiensysteme in den Bundesländern," in *Politik in Österreich: Das Handbuch,* ed. Herbert Dachs et al. (Vienna: Manz, 2006), 1008-23; Herbert Dachs, "Politische Parteien in Österreichs Bundesländern- zwischen regionalen Kalkülen und bundespolitischen Loyalitäten," in *Der Bund und die Länder: Über Dominanz, Kooperation und Konflikte im österreichischen Bundesstaat,* ed. Herbert Dachs (Vienna: Böhlau, 2003), 69-138; Herbert Dachs, ed., *Parteien und Wahlen in Österreichs Bundesländern, 1945-1991* (Vienna: Verlag für Geschichte und Politik, 1992). Josef Schmid, *Die CDU: Organisationsstrukturen, Politik, Funktionsweisen einer Partei im Föderalismus* (Opladen: Leske + Budrich, 1990), 285.

3. Schmid, *Die CDU,* 285.

4. Statistik Austria, *Bevölkerung,* downloaded on 26 February 2007 from *Statistik Austria* <http://www.statistik.at/statistische_uebersichten/deutsch/pdf/k14t_1.pdf>, 1.

5. Herbert Dachs, "Der Regierungsproporz in Österreichs Bundesländern—ein Anachronismus?", *Österreichisches Jahrbuch für Politik 1994* (Vienna: Oldenbourg 1995), 623-37.

6. Franz Schausberger, *Vom Regierungsproporz zur Konkurrenz: Die Reform der Salzburger Landesverfassung* (Vienna: Manz, 1999).

7. Herbert Dachs: "Wahlwerbung in den Bundesländern—ein vielfältig gezähmter Wettbewerb," in *Zwischen Wettbewerb und Konsens: Landtagswahlkämpfe in Österreichs Bundesländern 1945 bis 1970.* ed. Herbert Dachs (Vienna: Böhlau, 2006), 455-61, here 460f.

8. See Franz Fallend, "Landesregierung und Landesverwaltung," in *Politik in Österreich: Das Handbuch,* ed. Herbert Dachs et al. (Vienna: Manz, 2006), 974-89, here 979-81.

9. See Herbert Dachs, "Medien, Parteien, Verbände und Wahlen in den österreichischen Bundesländern: Ein Überblick," in *Länderpolitik: Politische Strukturen und Entscheidungsprozesse in den österreichischen Bundesländern,* ed. Herbert Dachs et al. (Vienna: Verein für Sozial- und Wirtschaftsforschung, 1997), 13-72, here 37-53.

10. See Manfred Knoche and Gabriele Siegert, "Die österreichische Medienlandschaft zwischen Zentralisierung, Regionalisierung und Lokalisierung," in *Der Bund und die Länder,* ed. Herbert Dachs (Vienna: Böhlau, 2003), 169-228.

11. See Dachs, "Parteiensysteme in den Bundesländern," 1012 f.

12. See the results of the regional elections, in ibid. 1013 f.

13. Election results are posted online at the Bundesland Upper Austria site <http://www.land-oberoesterreich.gv.at) and at the Ministry for Internal Affairs site <http://www.bmi.gv.at>.

14. See Fritz Plasser and Franz Sommer, "Die Landtagswahlen 1989 und die Neustrukturierung regionaler Parteiensysteme," in *Österreichisches Jahrbuch für Politik* (Vienna: Oldenbourg, 1990), 37-66, here, 37-44.

15. Fessel und GFK, *Landtagswahl Salzburg 1989, Telefonumfrage Nov.1988* (Typoskript), 25f.

16. For Salzburg, see Herbert Dachs, "Machtwechsel! Landtags- und Gemeinderatswahlen in Salzburg 2003," in *Salzburger Jahrbuch für Politik,* ed. Herbert Dachs and Roland Floimair (Salzburg: Residenz, 2004), 9-27; Michael Mair, "Ein verwandelter Elfmeter. Machtwechsel und Kommunikation um die Salzburger Landtagswahl 2004," in *Salzburger Jahrbuch für Politik 2005*, ed. Herbert Dachs and Roland Floimair (Salzburg: Böhlau, 2006), 9-33. For Styria, see Peter A. Ulram and Franz Sommer, "Gebremste und ungebremste Stürze: Gemeinderatswahlen und Landtagswahlen 2005," in *Österreichisches Jahrbuch für Politik 2005* (Vienna: Oldenbourg, 2006), 47-58, here 51 ff.

17. See Fritz Plasser and Franz Sommer, "Die Landtagswahlen 1989 und die Neustrukturierung regionaler Parteiensysteme," in *Österreichisches Jahrbuch für Politik* (Vienna: Oldenbourg, 1990), 37-66, here 37-44, 65.

18. Quoted in Brigitte Salfinger and Alexander Reichmann, "Stürmischer Wahlherbst: Analyse der Wählerströme bei den Landtagswahlen in der Steiermark, im Burgenland, und in Wien," in *Österreichisches Jahrbuch für Politik 2005* (Vienna: Oldenbourg, 2006), 29-45, here 45.

Electoral Strategies and Performance of Austrian Right-Wing Populism, 1986-2006

Kurt Richard Luther

Introduction

Until the early 1980s, Austrian politics was dominated the Christian Democratic *Österreichische Volkspartei* (Austrian People's Party, or ÖVP) and the *Sozialdemokratsiche Partei Österreichs* (Social Democratic Party of Austria, or SPÖ). Together, they usually won well over 90 percent of votes and seats and until 1966 shared power in a series of "grand coalitions." The SPÖ governed alone between 1970 and 1983, when in response to losing its majority, it formed a coalition with the small *Freiheitliche Partei Österreichs* (Freedom Party Austria, or FPÖ). Once in government, the FPÖ lost most of its electoral support, whereupon Jörg Haider took over the leadership and made the FPÖ Western Europe's most successful right-wing populist party. In 1999, it won 26.9 percent of the vote and despite enormous internal and external protest entered government with the ÖVP in February 2000. In the subsequent two years, however, the FPÖ suffered a series of internal crises that triggered a premature termination of the coalition. Although the party re-entered government in February 2003, unresolved internal conflicts resulted in Haider forming the breakaway *Bündnis Zukunft Österreich* (Alliance for the Future of Austria, or BZÖ) in April 2005. The decapitated FPÖ plummeted in the opinion polls, but under its new leader, Heinz-Christian Strache, staged a significant recovery, obtaining 11 percent of the vote at the general election of 1 October 2006. By contrast, the BZÖ only narrowly cleared the 4 percent general election hurdle.

This article identifies the electoral strategies of the FPÖ (and latterly the BZÖ) from 1986 and 2006. Thereafter, it examines these parties' electoral performance, focusing in particular upon the extent to which changes to their goals and to the electoral strategies they employed to achieve them were reflected in the profile and motivations of their vote. The concluding section will reflect on the future prospects of Austrian right-wing populism. It would exceed the scope of this article to engage in a detailed discussion of the literature on the concept of populism.[1] For the purpose of this article, populism denotes a "major structural opposition"[2] that challenges not democracy itself, but the specific organizational form of representative democracy it encounters, doing so by reference to the alleged superiority of popular/populist sentiment.[3] This situational contingency means populist parties will vary—and may be opportunistic—in terms of the electoral strategies and issues they utilize.

Primary Goals and Electoral Strategies, 1986-2006[4]

As Robert Dahl argues, political actors' strategies in the key "arenas" of political competition need to be considered in light of their "controlling goals."[5] Wolfgang C. Müller and Kaare Strøm's rational-choice model conceives of parties being constantly pushed and pulled between the partly conflicting ideal-typical goals of votes, policy, and office.[6] Whether they result mainly from endogenous change, or from exogenous factors, fundamental shifts in a party's "primary goal"[7] are likely to require both organizational adaptation and revised electoral strategies.[8] On the basis of such considerations it is possible to divide the electoral strategies pursued by the FPÖ between 1986 and 2006 into three more-or-less distinct periods: populist vote maximization (19861999); incumbency (2000-2005) and return to populist vote maximization (since 2005). The following pages will deal with these periods in turn, focusing in particular upon (changes in) the party's primary goals and electoral strategies; the main targets of those strategies; and the party's most important campaign themes and the style of its electoral mobilization. Given that the FPÖ's changed orientation in 1986 was in large measure a response to the party's preceding primary goal and associated electoral strategy, we will first briefly review the developments in that earlier phase.

Pre-Haider: Policy-Seeking to Office-Seeking

The FPÖ spent the first decade of its existence prioritizing policy. Its focus was predicated upon structural opposition to Austria's consociational system, as well as an uneasy mix of German-national and conservative liberal values. From the late 1960s, the FPÖ started to shift its primary goal towards office. Norbert Steger, the party's leader from 1980 to 1986, aspired to remold it into an Austrian version of the German Free Democrats: a pivot around which the center-left or center-right governments could alternate. The FPÖ thus adopted a less confrontational discourse and accelerated its programmatic liberalization, emphasizing above all anti-statism, free markets, and individual achievement (*Leistung*). Steger believed programmatic liberalization and responsible behavior in the governmental arena would appeal to Austria's emerging pool of disproportionately white-collar and educated floating voters, whom he hoped would in due course replace the FPÖ's traditionally protest-oriented electorate (and activists). In the event, the FPÖ's office-seeking came to fruition when the party became the SPÖ's junior coalition partner in 1983, but Steger failed both to realign his party electorally and to master the challenges of intra-party adaptation. By 1986, the FPÖ's opinion poll ratings were so low and its activists so unconvinced of the desirability of incumbency that Haider succeeded in ousting him from the leadership.

1986-1999: Populist Vote Maximization under Haider

Haider shared Steger's opposition to Austrian consociationalism and realized office was a prerequisite for structural reform, but was convinced a governing party with merely 5 percent of the vote was inherently incapable of effecting system-level change and was susceptible to being politically neutered. His strategy for the FPÖ was thus "strict competition"[9] in the electoral arena, that is, prioritizing vote-seeking, with a view to achieving a share at least as large as that of its competitors. This would, he calculated, ultimately enable the party to resume office with an intra-governmental weight sufficient to force through structural reform and to ensure that the vote loss that would inevitably result from incumbency would not catapult the party into an existential crisis akin to that it had experienced at the end of its first period in office. The FPÖ thus abandoned Steger's bourgeois-oriented electoral strategy in favor of vote maximization targeted particularly (albeit by no means exclusively) on blue-collar voters traditionally represented by the SPÖ. This reorientation was informed in part by the greater size of this electoral segment. Haider was also aware that the socio-economic changes Austria had been experiencing in recent years (including those linked to globalization) were likely to erode Austrians' hitherto exceptionally stable voting behavior[10] and to be particularly unsettling to blue-collar voters. He judged that no-holds-barred populist agitation would permit the FPÖ to detach from the SPÖ a sizeable share of fearful and insecure "modernization losers."

Central to the FPÖ's populist mobilization from 1986 to 1999 was by definition structural opposition to Austria's allegedly undemocratic political system. This was expressed particularly in constant attacks on grand coalition government and *Proporz* (the system of party-political division of spoils of office). Given the development since the 1960s of an Austrian national identity,[11] the FPÖ's traditional emphasis on German nationalist sentiment soon gave way to Austrian chauvinism (*Österreich zuerst*). This was intertwined with the new and in part opportunistic issues of immigration, crime, and (in a reversal of the FPÖ's traditional position) EU skepticism. The FPÖ's mobilizational style was characterized by rhetorical aggression and anti-intellectualism. The party placed much greater emphasis than its competitors upon professionalized permanent campaigning. Its slick presentation centered not on the party as such, but upon the personality of Haider, who was depicted as the spokesperson of popular sentiment. Between elections, the FPÖ utilized constant provocation and direct democratic instruments (such as popular petitions against immigration and EU integration) to maintain public visibility. It constantly reviewed the efficacy of its vote-maximization strategy and sought to penetrate additional electoral segments.[12]

Having in 1994 achieved 22.5 percent of the vote, the FPÖ decided that were it to obtain sufficient votes at the subsequent general election (scheduled for 1998), it would consider entering government. Prospective incumbency prompted the party to slightly modify its behavior. In 1995, Haider publicly distanced himself from *Deutschtümelei*, that is, the FPÖ's traditional revisionist German nationalist sentiment. This was intended to rehabilitate him in the eyes of those for whom his record of controversial statements on such matters disqualified him for high public office. For the first time since the early 1980s, the FPÖ initiated a detailed policy debate, generating numerous action programs intended to demonstrate its substantive preparedness for government. These predictably included critiques of immigration and European integration policy, but also proposals regarding pensions and social and family policy designed to appeal to blue-collar voters. Since its most likely coalition partner was the ÖVP, the FPÖ was not averse to simultaneously championing policies directed at bourgeois voters, including market liberalization and income tax reform designed to reduce progressivity.

Policy inconsistency was a logical corollary of vote-maximization. Ideological promiscuity caused the FPÖ's more traditional supporters to accuse the leadership of de-ideologization. There are at least two reasons why Haider could nonetheless maintain party unity. He successfully circumvented potential counter-elites by de-emphasizing intermediate party structures in favor of direct dialogue with grassroots functionaries. Furthermore, vote maximization had by 1999 quadrupled the party's public offices and, thus, the selective incentives with which the leadership could mitigate internal dissent.[13]

2000-2005: Office Seeking and Mounting Internal Disunity

In February 2000, the FPÖ abruptly switched its primary goal to (maintaining) office. Operating in both the electoral and governmental arenas required a more differentiated strategy. The leadership decided to reposition the FPÖ in the electoral arena as a responsible party of government that nonetheless retained its common touch and commitment to improving the lot of the "ordinary man" (*kleiner Mann*). Securing a second term, preferably as the senior coalition partner, was to be facilitated in the governmental arena by the FPÖ's control of the finance and social affairs ministries. The latter would champion popular social policy reform (the *Kinderscheck*, for example), while the former would secure the necessary funding and deliver tax reductions shortly before the next election. This dual strategy would, it was hoped, help the party recover from predicted initial electoral losses and then ensure that its vote at the general election scheduled for 2003 would be revived to around its 1999 level.

The party's strategy in the governmental arena was undermined by weaknesses in its ministerial team, programmatic contradictions, the need to support some neo-liberal ÖVP reforms unpopular with blue-collar voters, and its traditional weakness in Austria's important neocorporatist institutions. As for the electoral arena, persuading the voters that a party that had since 1986 pursued aggressive structural opposition was now a reliable steward of the nation's affairs was going to be a struggle. Moreover, the party organization had difficulty affecting the transition from a well-oiled electoral machine to a communicator of the government's policy and alleged achievements. Electoral setbacks and the concomitant reductions in selective incentives greatly exacerbated intra-party conflict. There was dispute over whether the electoral strategy should continue to prioritize blue-collar voters, or be retargeted at white-collar voters, which in turn implied more market-oriented policies. Supporters of the former strategy objected to what they saw as the government's overemphasis on business interests. A more fundamental conflict related to whether the party should be pursuing office at all. After thirteen years of populist agitation, many functionaries had great difficulty accepting the inherent compromises of office and often expressed their frustration with their party's governmental team in terms akin to those used in the period up to 1999 against the "establishment parties." Prominent amongst them was Haider himself, whose repeated criticisms of the FPÖ's government team and provocative actions—such as his visit to Saddam Hussein while FPÖ Vice-Chancellor Susanne Riess-Passer was in Washington DC—emboldened intra-party opponents of the leadership's strategy.[14]

In sum, the FPÖ lacked the party unity required for its new dual strategy.[15] Matters came to a head in the summer of 2002, when the government postponed tax reforms while retaining a commitment to purchasing the most expensive replacement for its aging interceptor jets and taking what some internal critics judged too soft a line on the EU's eastern expansion. Haider was a key actor in the ensuing "Knittelfeld rebellion." This led to the resignation in early September of FPÖ Vice-Chancellor and party leader, Susanne Riess-Passer and of most of her government team.

The party's campaign for the November 2002 election had no over-arching strategy. This was a consequence both of the above mentioned internal divisions and the fact that in the eleven weeks prior to polling day the party had four (interim) leaders. Under Matthias Reichhold's forty-two day leadership, emphasis was placed on government responsibility and alleged policy achievements of its ministerial team. Once Herbert Haupt took over, the FPÖ reverted to an aggressive campaign in which Austrian chauvinism figured prominently, as did trusted issues such as immigration, EU skepticism, and the "ordinary man." The campaign was also the first since 1983 without a central role for Haider. He had lost credibility amongst office-seekers because of his repeated attacks on the FPÖ's ministers, while the "rebels" were infuriated by his refusal to resume the party leadership. He was also widely held to have become an electoral liability.

The "external shock"[16] of massive electoral defeat did not prevent the leadership seeking to resume its twin-track strategy. The FPÖ executive voted unanimously to enter coalition negotiations, in which the party gave way on virtually all the substantive demands of the Knittelfeld rebels. As significant sections of the party objected to what they deemed the pursuit of office at almost any cost, the leadership resisted calls for an extraordinary party conference to debate the coalition agreement. It was passed (with two dissenting votes) in the national executive and ratified in the 240-strong party directorate, albeit with only 121 members attending and eleven of them voting against the agreement.

The FPÖ's reduced intra-coalitional weight undermined its strategy in the governmental arena (where it had *inter alia* lost the finance ministry). Its vicious public infighting had fatally damaged its strategy to present itself in the electoral arena as a responsible party of government. In virtually all elections held in the next two and a half years, its massive general election losses were thus replicated (and in some cases exceeded). The concomitant loss of public offices (and office-oriented activists) strengthened intra-party opposition to the primary goal of a leadership increasingly attacked as a self-serving clique clinging to national office at the cost of not only votes and office at other levels of the system, but also of policy. For these critics, salvaging the FPÖ's electoral prospects required either greater assertiveness in the governmental arena, or exit from office. For its part, the leadership considered the grassroots members' substantive demands unrealistic and was—largely in the absence of an alternative—clinging to the hope that the strategy of demonstrating governing competence would ultimately pay off.

2005 to the Present: Return to Populist Vote Maximization

In April 2005, the FPÖ split along its internal fault line over the party's primary goal and governmental and electoral strategies. Its government team, the majority of its caucus, and its Carinthian provincial party organization left to form the BZÖ. Haider justified the split by reference to the "negative forces" that had "irreparably damaged" the FPÖ brand.[17] He calculated that an internally united BZÖ would be better able to present itself to the electorate as a credible governing party. This would, he thought, allow the BZÖ to marginalize the rump FPÖ and secure a further term in office. He also wrongly assumed that the bulk of FPÖ's organizational units would soon defect to the BZÖ.

Having at a stroke been liberated from the demands of supporting a government (however reluctantly), the FPÖ was returned to the primary goal of vote-maximization. At Vienna's provincial election of October 2005 it thus ran an aggressive populist campaign targeted at blue-collar voters and concentrating primarily on crime and immigration. In light of the party's plummeting poll ratings in the preceding months, its 14.8 percent of the vote (only -5.3 percentage points compared to its 2001 result) was considered a great achievement. Buoyed by this success, in March 2006 the party reverted to mobilization via popular petition: its "Stay free Austria" (*"Österreich bleib frei"*) campaign centered on opposition to Turkish EU-membership and the defense of neutrality. That the FPÖ was campaigning with a virulence that had not been seen for some years was the result of at least two factors. The 2002 crisis and BZÖ split had left protest-oriented activists in the ascendancy and revived the intra-party influence of right-wing student fraternities (*Burschenschaften*). Moreover, the FPÖ's leadership considered unbridled vote maximization justified by the existential threat posed by the BZÖ, which should be "strangled at birth" (Interview).

The FPÖ 2006 election campaign was targeted squarely at blue-collar voters. The predominant themes of the FPÖ's campaign were Austrian and welfare chauvinism, as well as opposition to immigration. Its slogans included "Austria first," "We for you," "Welfare instead of Immigration," "Secure pensions instead of asylum millions" and "Home not Islam" (*Daham statt Islam*). Specific policy demands included preventing Turkey's EU accession, repatriation of long-term unemployed immigrants, and limiting welfare benefits to Austrian citizens. The March 2006 revelation that the trade-union bank (BAWAG) had lost billions of Euros through unauthorized speculation was a gift for the FPÖ's populist structural opposition and utilized to try to discredit the SPÖ, its main rival for the blue-collar vote.

For its part, the BZÖ had, in its first year, made little headway in a governmental arena increasingly dominated by the ÖVP. When it had competed in the electoral arena, its results had been derisory (receiving, for example, 1.15 percent of the vote in Vienna), and polls indicated it was at severe risk of not re-entering the National Council. The BZÖ's primary goal remained office, but its more immediate priority of electoral survival required a radically revised electoral strategy. With an eye on white-collar voters, it warned against a lurch to the left (*Links-ruck*) in the form of an SPÖ-Green coalition and put forward a few neo-liberal policies. The BZÖ tried to distinguish itself from the FPÖ by stating that while the latter was fundamentally opposition-oriented, the BZÖ team that had since 2000 (!) delivered social policy benefits and budget consolidation and was also committed to resuming governmental responsibility. However, its prime electoral target was identical to the FPÖ's: the blue-collar voters who had supported the latter during the 1990s. Accordingly, the BZÖ campaign also focused on immigration, the BAWAG affair and—more prominently than the FPÖ—on crime.[18] Both parties employed rhetorically aggressive campaign styles reminiscent of the (early) 1990s.

There was fierce rivalry between them over the mantle of legitimate heir to the FPÖ of the period of populist vote maximization. The BZÖ brazenly claimed (*inter alia* in a mailing to FPÖ supporters) to be the true embodiment of the "successful path" of FPÖ reform during the 1990s. This was symbolized in the BZÖ's original campaign material, which reverted from its adopted color (orange) to the FPÖ's traditional blue and included the designation "*Die Freiheitlichen*," together with the epithet "the original."[19] In his hour long live television debate of 15 September with BZÖ chair Peter Westenthaler, Strache for his part argued that for the sake of office the BZÖ had abandoned FPÖ commitments on issues such as immigration, crime, and European integration.

Electoral Performance

This section does not aspire to prove a causal link between electoral strategies and outcomes. Its more modest aim is to highlight the pattern of electoral outcomes within and between the periods of electoral strategy identified above, with a view to offering tentative conclusions as to the efficacy of those strategies.

Overall Strength of the Vote

As Table 1 shows, the FPÖ's vote was predictably highest during its period of sustained populist vote maximization and lowest when the party was office-seeking, or constrained by incumbency and internal conflict over primary goals and electoral strategy. At first sight, reverting to populist vote maximization in 2006 brought the FPÖ only a modest recovery, namely one percentage point more than it had won in 2002. Yet a more appropriate benchmark would be the party's 6 percent opinion poll rating following the BZÖ breakaway, since it is only then that it reverted to this electoral strategy. Moreover, the 2006 result is double what the FPÖ achieved when it was office-seeking, and the combined vote of the parties that conducted right-wing populist electoral strategies in 2006 amounted to 15 percent.

Vote Strength in Different Electoral Segments

A more differentiated picture of the impact of the FPÖ's electoral strategies is obtained by an examination of the party's electoral segment support by electoral strategy period (see Table 2).

Table 1
FPÖ and BZÖ Votes and Seats 1983-2006 by Electoral Strategy Period

	Office-seeking	Populist Vote Maximization (pvm)					Incumbency	Return to pvm
	1983	1986	1990	1994	1995	1999	2002	2006
FPÖ:								
% Vote	5.0	9.7	16.6	22.5	21.9	26.9	10.0	11.0
Seats	12	18	33	42	41	52	18	21
BZÖ:								
% Vote	-	-	-	-	-	-	-	4.1
Seats	-	-	-	-	-	-	-	7

Source: Bundesministerium des Inneren.

Populist Vote Maximization under Haider

During this phase, the FPÖ increased its aggregate vote by 17 points. Its electoral progress varied significantly according to gender, age, and occupation, however. Though the FPÖ had latterly targeted women, the increase in its female vote was lower (+14) than that amongst men (+20) and in particular amongst non-gainfully employed males (+23). In terms of age, growth was greatest amongst the oldest and youngest cohorts. By 1999, FPÖ support by age thus exhibited a U-shaped distribution, with a distinct bias to those under thirty (+ 35), where the socializing effects of Austria's erstwhile dominant political subcultures were weakest. Indeed, by 1999 only 25 percent of these voters supported the SPÖ, and a mere 17 percent voted ÖVP.

The FPÖ's electoral strength varied most markedly in relation to occupation. FPÖ growth was the lowest amongst farmers (+5), who remain the ÖVP's most loyal voters. The party's aggressive rhetoric and anti-intellectualism probably contributed to its underperformance in the white-collar segment (+9), amongst civil and public sector workers servants (+11), and amongst students (+14). By contrast, thirteen years of consistent targeting of blue-collar voters had reaped substantial rewards (+37). In 1986, the party's vote in this segment was 10 percent and the SPÖ's 57 percent. By 1999, the SPÖ could only muster 35 percent of the vote, while FPÖ support had surged to 48 percent. In sum, the period of populist vote maximization witnessed an electoral realignment of Austria's working-class.

Incumbency

In the 2002 election, the FPÖ vote collapsed by 17 points. Losses were somewhat higher amongst men (-20) than women (-13), which slightly reduced the party's mobilizational gender gap. They were greatest amongst the youngest and oldest age cohort (-21 and -19 respectively), which meant that the distribution of FPÖ electoral support by age was much "flatter" and the U-shape pattern replaced by a negative correlation of support by age. FPÖ incumbency, two years of public infighting, and an inconsistent election campaign had a markedly uneven impact upon the voting behavior of different occupational groups. It seems to have been least alienating where the party was weakest: amongst farmers, white-collar voters, and public sector workers (-9, -11 and -13 points respectively). However, it was hugely damaging to the party's blue-collar support. The FPÖ vote dropped by 27 points among unskilled and semi-skilled workers and by 33 points among the skilled. The SPÖ resumed its lead among the unskilled and semi-skilled (47 percent), with the ÖVP in second place (26 percent). For the first time ever, skilled worker support was marginally higher for the ÖVP (39 percent) than the SPÖ (37 percent). In sum, the class realignment of the period of populist vote maximization had been nullified.

Return to Populist Vote Maximization

The FPÖ's revised electoral strategy appears to have alienated the younger age cohort (-4 percent), but attracted voters over 60 (+5 percent). For the first time since 1986, FPÖ support is no longer greatest amongst young voters, but virtually identical across all age groups. White-collar voters were the only occupational segment in which the FPÖ's return to populist vote maximization was not marked by a significant change in voting behavior. Support fell in particular among the self-employed and professionals (-10), but also among unskilled and semi-skilled workers (-7), public sector workers, (-4) and housewives (-4). It increased amongst the numerically small farming segment (+8), pensioners (+5), and skilled workers (+5). The FPÖ's targeting of blue-collar voters met with mixed success. Its vote among unskilled and semi-skilled workers is identical to its overall share, but within the skilled worker segment is virtually double that level (20 percent). Conversely, the FPÖ is weak amongst the self-employed and professionals (6 percent) and those working in the public sector (3 percent).

Table 2 also compares the sociodemographics of the FPÖ's support in 1986 and 2006, that is, at the first elections after each periods of

Table 2
FPÖ Electoral Segment Support by Electoral Strategy Period, 1986-2006

	Populist vote maximization			Incumbency		Return to pvm		Change
	1986	1999	1986-1999	2002	1999-2002	2006	2002-2006	1986-2006
Overall	10	27	+17	10	-17	11	+1	+1
Men	12	32	+20	12	-20	12	+/-0	+/-0
Employed	13	33	+20	14	-19	11	-3	-2
Pensioners	11	28		9	-19	14	+5	+3
Women	7	21	+14	8	-13	9	+1	+2
Employed	7	22	+15	9	-13	9	+/-0	+2
Unemployed	8	22	+14	8	-14	7	-1	-1
Pensioners	5	19	+14	5	-14	10	+5	+5
Age								
18-29	12	35	+23	14	-21	10	-4	-2
30-44	11	29	+18	11	-18	10	-1	-1
45-59	6	21	+15	10	-11	10	+/-0	+4
60-69	8	21	+13	7	-14	12	+5	+4
70 plus	9	25	+19	6	-19	11	+5	+2
Occupation								
Self-employed, professionals	15	33	+18	16	-17	6	-10	-9
Farmers	5	10	5	1	-9	9	+8	+4
Civil servants, public service	9	20	+11	7	-13	3	-4	-6
white-collar	13	22	9	11	-11	11	+/-0	-2
Blue-collar skilled	11	48	+37	15	-33	20	+5	+9
Blue-collar un/semi-skilled	8	45	+37	18	-27	11	-7	+3
Housewives	8	25	+17	11	-14	7	-4	-1
Pensioners	7	24	+17	7	-14	12	+5	+5
Students	9	23	+14	7	-16	9	+2	+/-0

Source: Fessel+Gfk Exit Polls (n: 1986 = 2,149; 1999 & 2002 = 2,200; 2006 = 1,982).

incumbency. The party has retained the blue-collar bias it developed in the 1990s: support among the self-employed and professionals is 9 points lower, but that among skilled workers 9 points greater than it was in 1986. The FPÖ's vote among public sector workers is considerably lower (-6) and that of pensioners higher (+5) than it was. The gender gap is slightly narrower, while the significant aging of the FPÖ's electorate hints *inter alia* at a possible cohort effect.

Though merely indicative because of the small sample size, GfK Austria's 2006 exit poll data on the 4 percent of BZÖ voters suggest the lowest levels of support came from those under thirty (2 percent) and the strongest from voters in their 60s (6 percent) and from farmers (6 percent). The BZÖ was perhaps more attractive to men (5 percent) and to pensioners (5 percent), but it performed below average in the worker segment (3 percent). One could speculate that the somewhat greater level of support among those aged 30-44 might point to a transfer of loyalties from the FPÖ to the BZÖ of an age cohort socialized during the Haider-led period of populist vote maximization.

Voter Availability and Motivations

The significant voter shifts that accompanied the FPÖ's 1986-1999 electoral strategy exacerbated an existing trend for Austrian voters to become electorally more available. When the FPÖ was seeking office for the first time, half the electorate was willing to vote for the same party (that is, overwhelmingly for the SPÖ or ÖVP) even when not fully satisfied with it. Nine out of ten decided well before the closing phase of election campaigns which party they would support, and only one in ten changed their vote from one election to another. Populist vote maximization helped to halve unconditional party loyalty and to double the proportions of late deciders and party changers. These trends continued after the FPÖ had changed its primary goal to office (see Table 3). However, the FPÖ was now a less attractive option for Austria's more fickle electorate. At elections held between 1986 and 1999, up to half of all party changers moved to the FPÖ, but in 2002 that fell to 6 percent before reviving to 17 percent in 2006. It seems reasonable to conclude

Table 3
"(Un-)Availability" of Austrian Voters by FPÖ Electoral Strategy Period

	Office-seeking	Populist vote maximization		Incumbency	Return to pvm
	1983	1986	1999	2002	2006
Voter loyalty even if not fully satisfied	47	39	26	25	29
Early deciders	92	84	80	77	76
Late deciders	8	16	20	23	24
Party changers	10	16	18	24	26

Source: Fessel+Gfk Exit Polls (n: 1983 = 2,000; n 1986 = 2,149; 1999 & 2002 = 2,200; 2006 = 1,982)

that the switch from opposition to office and back again changed voters' willingness to support the FPÖ. Greater insight into FPÖ voter motivations during the last two decades is provided by the regular exit polls conducted by GfK Austria (formerly FESSEL-GfK).

Populist Vote Maximization under Haider

Above, we argued that a consistent defining feature of the FPÖ's populist mobilization strategy was structural opposition directed in particular at grand coalition government and *Proporz*. We also pointed to three other elements: the focus on Haider's personality; the interlinking of Austrian chauvinism with issues such as immigration, crime, and EU skepticism; and the development from 1995 onward of policy proposals related to, for example, the family, social affairs, and taxation. Although the FPÖ's chosen campaign themes were undeniably divisive and remain controversial, the data on FPÖ voter motivation suggest they made a significant contribution to the success of the party's 1986-1999 strategy. The proportions of FPÖ voters motivated by the issues the party utilized to tap into structural opposition (rows 1 and 2 in Table 4) varied, but ranged from a quarter to nearly half. In 1986, over half cited Haider as their major motivation, and although this proportion gradually declined, one plausible interpretation is that he was soon so intimately identified with the FPÖ that voting for the party was an implicit indicator of support for Haider. Table 4 also shows how anti-immigrant sentiment became an increasingly important motivating factor. The FPÖ's post-1994 development of policy proposals designed *inter alia* to communicate a commitment to the *kleiner Mann* appears also to have had a positive mobilizational effect. Some 16 percent of its 1999 voters attributed their vote to these policies, while 15 percent cited the party's commitment to ordinary people.[20]

Table 4

FPÖ Voter Motivation during the Populist Vote Maximization Period, 1986-1999

Motivation	1986	1990	1994	1995	1999
Protest, scandal, party weariness	16	38	32	20	13
Time for a change, rejection of grand coalition	10	7	7	12	27
Image and leadership of Haider	54	23	17	19	13
Foreigner resentment	3	7	12	12	15

Source: Fessel+Gfk Exit Polls (n: 1986 = 2,149; 1990 = 2,229; 1994 = 2,200; 1995 =2,333: 1999 = 2,200).

Incumbency

Though permitted to cite multiple motivations, only 15 percent of the FPÖ's much reduced 2002 electorate mentioned the personality of its leader, Haupt. Haider's virtual absence for most of the rudderless party's campaign and Haupt's as yet interim status and make this unsurprising. A mere 5 percent of all "candidate-oriented personality voters"[21] cast their vote for the FPÖ. Considerations of coalition options figured prominently: 37 percent of respondents mentioned a desire to avert a return to grand coalition government, and 56 percent wanted to avoid a possible red-green coalition. Similarly negative orientations underpinned the other major type of voting incentive, namely issues. Some 52 percent of FPÖ voters claimed to have been motivated by the party's opposition to immigration and EU eastern enlargement.

Return to Populist Vote Maximization[22]

According to SORA calculations (1 October 2006 press release), only half (49 percent) of those who voted for the FPÖ in 2002 did so again in 2006. A fifth (18 percent) abstained, and one in seven (15 percent) voted for the BZÖ. Gfk Austria's exit poll (which again permitted multiple responses) shows that, at 12 percent, personality was an even less important motivation for FPÖ voters than in 2002. Westenthaler's personality was named by 26 percent of BZÖ voters as a decisive influence upon their vote, but 22 claimed to have been motivated by the BZÖ being "Haider's party." Just under a third of both FPÖ and of BZÖ voters claimed to have been decisively influenced by their party's commitment to the problems of the "ordinary man." Both parties' voters were motivated, above all, by negative emotions. Immigration was of greater significance to the FPÖ than BZÖ voters (51 percent against 29 percent), while the BZÖ's greater mobilization on crime may help explain why 57 percent of BZÖ voters but "only" 45 percent of those who supported the FPÖ claimed their vote had been decisively influenced by their chosen party's support of harsher action against criminals. Finally, half of each group reported that a decisive factor shaping their voting decision had been considerable discontent with others parties.

The Future of Austrian Right-Wing Populism

The FPÖ's electoral performance has been shown to be closely related to the party's altered primary goals and (the delivery of its) electoral strategies. It was also shaped, however, by a range of factors which this article has not been able to examine. One constitutes the strategies of its competitors. The ÖVP and SPÖ's determination to treat Haider's revitalized FPÖ as a pariah and form a series of defensive grand coalitions arguably had the perverse effect of strengthening the credibility of the FPÖ's claims that the "system" conspired against it. By contrast, the ÖVP's controversial decision to coalesce with the FPÖ in 2000 effectively amounted to the latter's political "co-optation and castration."[23] A second factor is the fundamental transformation since the early 1980s of Austria's electorate. In the early 1980s, Austrian voters were still remarkably stable, with very high levels of attachment to the ÖVP and SPÖ.[24] Since then, the sub-cultural pillars (*Lager*) hitherto underpinning Austrian consociationalism have crumbled, class and partisan de-alignment have grown, a generalized party weariness has become apparent, and there has been a significant increase in anti-party and protest sentiment.[25] In short, Austria's electorate has become much more volatile, a trend accelerated by the FPÖ's own conduct in the electoral market.

A more unpredictable electoral market should increase the potential impact upon electoral outcomes of party strategies, privileging in particular smaller, more mobile parties.[26] Yet to succeed in such markets, parties need to choose an electoral strategy appropriate to their goals and to ensure its consistent and effective application. Between 1986 and 1999, the FPÖ achieved this via the relentless pursuit of populist vote maximization. When in office, however, (between 1983 and 1986, as well as between 2000 and 2005), it was unable to maintain internal unity over goals and strategies. Moreover, there were significant discrepancies with respect to party behavior in the different arenas of political competition and amongst FPÖ functionaries. Many (including Haider) resorted to behaviors that had been successful during the period of populist vote maximization, but were now counter-productive. Such inconsistencies damaged the party's electoral performance and triggered the BZÖ's breakaway. In other words, the FPÖ's ability to achieve its primary goals and desired electoral outcomes has been closely related not only to whether it was in office or the opposition, but also to its leadership and internal discipline.

It would be premature to conclude that the FPÖ's dismal 2002 result and its 2005 split signal the end of Austrian right-wing populism. After all, notwithstanding over four years of, in part, vicious public wrangling within the FPÖ and latterly between it and the BZÖ, these parties succeeded in obtaining a combined 15 percent of the 2002 vote. This suggests the potential for populist electoral appeals is probably greater. The "demand" for right-wing populism is not unrelated to the persistence of anti-party sentiment; the fears of, in particular, "modernization losers"; and the enduring mobilizational capacity of, for example, welfare chauvinism, EU skepticism, immigration, and crime.

Austrian right-wing populism is likely to persist for supply-side reasons also. For now, the FPÖ has reverted to unbridled populist vote maximization targeted at blue-collar voters. It hopes that by emphasizing a commitment to the "ordinary man" it will be well placed to win from the SPÖ voters it feels are likely to be disappointed by the latter's inescapable policy compromises. The recent rise in political scandals should enhance the mobilizational capacity of its traditional structural opposition also. Although it committed the FPÖ to returning to opposition in 2006, the leadership also hinted it might seek to re-enter government after the next election. Even assuming it was to find a willing partner, it is not clear why the party would cope any better with a third period of incumbency.

The BZÖ's future is less secure. It lacks the FPÖ's organizational institutionalization and has been unable to establish significant party structures outside Carinthia. It has also failed to develop a secure electoral following. Early indications suggest that now it has achieved the goal of re-entering parliament, its electoral strategy will be to target a more bourgeois electorate than that of the FPÖ. It is too early to tell whether, if it fails to achieve a significant growth in public support, it might at subsequent elections again revert to populist agitation to ensure its electoral survival.

Future relations between the FPÖ and BZÖ remain uncertain. Reunification would be most attractive for the BZÖ, for unless it can improve its stubbornly low poll ratings (still only about 4 percent), it still risks eviction from the National Council and the concomitant loss of funding and political visibility. If the parties ever wished to re-enter government, their prospects of doing so would be enhanced by reunification, as would their intra-governmental weight. On the other hand, levels of personal animosity between the two leadership groups are still so high that reunification appears unlikely unless at least one set of leaders is replaced. Moreover, the parties appear to be developing somewhat different goals and electoral strategies. As the experience of recent years has shown, seeking to combine such differences within a single party does not augur well for organizational unity or electoral success.

Notes

1. See, for example, Hans-Georg Betz, ed., *Radical Right-Wing Populism in Western Europe* (Basingstoke: Macmillan, 1994); Hans-Georg Betz and Stefan Immerfall, eds., *New Politics of the Right: Neo-Populist Parties and Movements in Established Democracies* (Basingstoke: Macmillan, 1998); Margaret Canovan, "Trust the People! Populism and the Two Faces of Democracy," *Political Studies 47* (1999): 2-16; Paul Taggart, *Populism* (Buckingham: Open UP, 2000).

2. Robert Dahl, ed. *Political Oppositions in Western Democracies* (New Haven, CT: Yale UP, 1966), 341-44.

3. Yves Mény and Yves Surel, eds., *Democracies and the Populist Challenge* (New York: Palgrave, 2002).

4. The following assessment draws upon interviews conducted by the author between 1985 and 2006 with over 200 FPÖ activists, including most key members of the party leadership during this period.

5. Dahl, *Political Oppositions*, 341-47.

6. Wolfgand C. Müller and Kaare Strøm, *Policy, Office, or Votes? How Political Parties in Western Europe Make Hard Decisions* (Cambridge: Cambridge UP, 1999).

7. Robert Harmel and Kenneth Janda, "An Integrated Theory of Party Goals and Party Change," *Journal of Theoretical Politics* 6 (1994): 259-87.

8. Robert Harmel, "Party Organizational Change: Competing Explanations?' in *Political Parties in the New Europe: Political and Analytical Challenges*, ed. Kurt Luther et al. (Oxford: Oxford UP, 2002), 119-42; Kurt Richard Luther, "The FPÖ: From Populist Protest to Incumbency," in *Right-Wing Extremism in the 21st-Century*, ed. Peter H. Merkl and Leonard Weinberg (London: Frank Cass, 2003), 191-219.

9. Dahl, *Political Oppositions*, 344.

10. See Fritz Plasser, Peter A. Ulram, and Alfred Grausgruber, "The Decline of '*Lager* Mentality' and the New Model of Electoral Competition in Austria," in *Politics in Austria: Still a Case of Consociationalism?*, ed. Kurt Richard Luther and Wolfgang C. Müller (London: Frank Cass, 1992), 16-44.

11. Ernst Bruckmüller, "The Development of Austrian National Identity," in *Austria 1945-1995: Fifty Years of the Second Republic*, ed. Kurt Richard Luther and Peter Pulzer (Aldershot: Ashgate, 1998), 83-108.

12. For example, women were numerically the most promising target. The party thus symbolically recruited women to prominent positions on its electoral lists. Since its electoral strategists judged the FPÖ's image as a *Buberlpartei* (boys party) and its "hard" themes (for example, anti-immigration, corruption and crime) to be potential obstacles to recruiting more female voters, from the mid 1990s the FPÖ also deliberately highlighted "softer" issues. These included family policy and increasing child allowances via the so-called "check for children" (*Kinderscheck*).

13. See Luther, "The FPÖ: From Populist Protest to Incumbency," and "Strategien und (Fehl-) Verhalten: Die Freiheitlichen und die Regierungen Schüssel I und II," in *Umbau in Schwarz-Blau (-Orange). Eine Bilanz*, ed. Emmerich Tálos (Vienna: Lit Verlag, 2006), 19-37.

14. Kurt Richard Luther, "The Self-Destruction of a Right-Wing Populist Party? The Austrian Parliamentary Election of 2002," *West European Politics* 26.2 (2003): 136-52.

15. Dahl, *Political Oppositions*, 344.

16. Harmel and Janda, "An Integrated Theory."

17. As he had been the architect of the party's strategy of populist vote maximization and a key instigator of the Knittelfeld rebellion, some commentators considered this rather ironic.

18. This caused the BZÖ's liberal Justice Minister Karin Gastinger to resign from the party just days before the election.

19. On 1 September, a court ruled in favour of the FPÖ's claim that this was a deliberate attempt to deceive voters and required the term '*freiheitlich*' to be deleted from the BZÖ's literature and web site. The BZÖ also failed in its attempt to take over the FPÖ's traditional third ballot paper spot.

20. Fritz Plasser and Peter A. Ulram, "Rechtspopulistische Resonanzen: Die Wählerschaft der FPÖ," in *Das österreichische Wahlverhalten*, ed. Fritz Plasser et al. (Vienna: Zentrum für Angewandte Politikforschung, 2000), 225-41.

21. Fritz Plasser and Peter A. Ulram, eds., *Wahlverhalten in Bewegung: Analysen zur Nationalratswahl 2002* (Vienna: Zentrum für Angewandte Politikforschung, 2003), 150.

22. As mentioned above, the small sample size means data on the BZÖ need to be treated with considerable caution

23. Luther, "The Self-Destruction,' 150.

24. Christian Haerpfer and Ernst Gehmacher, "Social Structure and Voting in the Austrian Party System" *Electoral Studies* 3 (1984): 25-46.

25. That transformation is extensively documented in the contributions to this volume by Plasser and Ulram, Plasser and Seeber, and by Hofinger and Ogris and, thus, will not be considered in detail here.

26. Wolfgang C. Müller, Fritz Plasser, and Peter A. Ulram, "Schwäche als Vorteil, Stärke als Nachteil. Die Reaktion der Parteien auf den Rückgang der Wählerbindungen," in *Parteien auf komplexen Wählermarkten. Reaktiosnstrategien politischer Parteien in Westeuropa*, ed. Peter Mair et al. (Vienna: Signum, 1999), 241-46.

Framing Campaigns:
The Media and Austrian Elections

Günther Lengauer

In Austrian parliamentary election campaigns, labels such as "war room" or "spin doctors" come increasingly and prominently to light in the public discourse. Austrian election campaigns are wrapped up in metaphors of horse races among parties or even candidates (*"Kanzler-Duell"*) supported by at least weekly updated survey results. The recent 2006 election campaign was frequently coined as unprecedentedly "negative" and even "dirty" by political opponents as well as pundits. Over the last years, these labels have also become journalistic synonyms for unmasking and deconstructing the rhetoric of intensifying and professionalizing political marketing and electioneering in Austria. Because the media are the primary source for electoral and campaign information for the Austrian public, they play a central role in putting spotlights on this transformation of political campaigning.

Nevertheless, it is unclear to what extent the Austrian media and their coverage are themselves driven and characterized by transformations of their professional imperatives into the direction of trends we can increasingly diagnose for the election coverage in media-centered democracies, especially in the United States: personalization, confrontational negativity, journalist-centeredness, or game-centrism. Therefore, this study focuses on the media's role in framing the Austrian election campaign discourse.

By focusing particularly on the 2006 Austrian parliamentary election campaign, findings of a content analysis are contrasted with results of earlier Austrian elections (1999) and international studies focusing on the media coverage of recent U.S., German, and British election campaigns. This comparison will give some answers to the question whether the structure of the Austrian media coverage of election campaigns is primarily shaped by specific Austrian systemic and cultural settings, or whether it is more driven by transnational patterns of an emerging postmodern journalistic logic in media-centered democracies.

The Austrian Model of Media and Politics

What Jay Blumler and Dennis Kavanagh introduced as the evolutionary phasing model of political communication systems after World War II[1] can also be applied to Austria.[2] Political communication appears to have passed through three successive phases: *premodern* (until the 1960s), *modern* (through 1960s and 1980s), and the ongoing *postmodern* (since the 1990s). Technological innovation, political deregulation, commercialization, and professionalization increasingly shape the fragmented Austrian information society in the early twenty-first century.

Fritz Plasser and Peter Ulram call the Austrian political communication system in the first phase after World War II between 1945 and the 1960s a "party and press-dominated communication system."[3] Party-owned newspapers reached almost 50 percent of the total newspaper circulation. However, in the mid-1960s, television superseded radio and newspapers as primary source of news. At the same time, the Austrian party-press was diminishing and has almost vanished by the year 2000 with only a two percent of the share of the overall circulation of Austrian newspapers.[4]

Beginning in the 1960s, Austrian society and its public discourse had been substantially transformed by the rise of the television into a TV-centered communication system. In the 1980s and early 1990s, the rapid expansion of cable and satellite technology increased the dominant status of television and created a "multi-channel public."[5]

In 2006, Austrians listen for about three and a half hours radio on an average, watch television for about two hours and forty minutes per day, read their newspapers for half an hour, and surf through the World Wide Web for about twenty-five minutes on a daily basis.[6] Besides that the exponential expansion of the online community rings in the *third age* and thus the *postmodern* phase of political communication in Austria. Whereas in 1996 only 4 percent of the Austrian population used the Internet intensively, this ratio has risen to 52 percent in 2006.[7]

The Austrian Media System

Whereas in the beginning of the 1960s Austrian households were only able to receive one terrestrial TV program limited to a few hours in the evening, in 2005 Austrian cable- and satellite-connected households can even receive, on average, forty-nine channels.[8] Steady growth of cable- and satellite-connected households started in the early 1980s, reaching some 90 percent of Austrian TV households by 2005 (24 percent in 1990).

Table 1
Television and Internet Supply in Austria, 1986-2006

Percentage	1986	1990	1995	2000	2006*
TV Sets	94	97	96	97	97
Satellite	-	2	31	43	50
Cable	13	22	36	38	39
Internet	-	-	-	33	58

*Data refer to the first six months of the year 2006.
Source: IP Deutschland GmbH; ORF-Medienforschung.[9]

The technical supply and equipment of Austrian households in the beginning of the twenty-first century meet the standards of a "multi channel information society."[10] More than eight out of ten Austrians listen to the radio on a daily basis, followed by newspapers, which are read by almost three quarters of the population. Additionally, two thirds of the Austrian public watch television on a day-to-day basis, and about one third use the Internet every day.

Austrian public broadcasting dominates the radio as well as the TV market. However, private and foreign radio and TV stations constantly gain audience shares and increasingly emerge as competitors on the Austrian media market.

Table 2
Daily Media Usage in Austria, 2005

Media	Percentage of the Population
Radio (total)	841
Public Service Radio (ORF)	746
Private Radio Stations (Austrian and	260
Newspapers	742
Television (total)	685
Public Service Television (ORF)	593
Foreign TV Stations (total)	496
Austrian Private Television (ATV)	105
Internet (several times a week)	313

Source: Seethaler and Melischek; Verein Arbeitsgemeinschaft Media-Analysen.[11]

The level of competition on the Austrian broadcasting market has intensified by the opening of the television and radio markets to private suppliers. The Regional Radio Act of 1993 and the Private Television Act of 2001 enabled the granting of licenses to private operators.[12] Consequently, the ORF (the Austrian public service provider of television and radio) lost its monopoly as the last public broadcaster in Europe. With a market share of 48 percent in 2005, Austria is still the country with the second largest public TV sector compared to other Western European countries.[13] However, since 1990 the market share of public television was almost cut in half (from 93 percent to 48 percent). In 2005, public and private stations possess almost equal shares of the audience in all TV households (48 vs. 51 percent). In cable- and satellite-households, private TV stations (market share of 56 percent) already clearly supersede the ORF with 43 percent.[14]

In 2006, Austrian newspapers reach a cumulative readership of 72.7 percent.[15] The tabloid paper *Neue Kronen Zeitung* (with a readership of almost 44 percent) is not only the market leader, but also one of the most widespread newspapers worldwide (in relation to the population). More than three million Austrians read it on a daily basis. The market segment of quality papers is composed of *Der Standard*, *Die Presse*, and *Salzburger Nachrichten* which cumulatively reach a readership of 13 percent. The market of the weekly news magazines is dominated by *News* with a readership of almost 14 percent, followed by *profil* with nearly 6 percent. Beginning in 2005, a couple of local gratis newspapers were launched (for example, *Heute*, *ok*, *Neue Express*, *Oberösterreichs Neue*). Additionally, on 1 September 2006 the new national newspaper *Österreich* was introduced to the press market. At the end of 2006, there were seventeen autonomous daily newspapers on the Austrian press market (including the gratis papers *ok* and *Heute*). In comparison, thirty-six Austrian newspapers existed in 1953.[16]

The Austrian media market is highly and multi-dimensionally concentrated. Thus public stations are market leaders on the radio market (ORF) and reach no less than four quarters of the population. On the television market, the public service channels of the ORF are the most popular platforms as well and reach about 60 percent of the Austrian public (see Table 2). The highly concentrated Austrian newspaper market is characterized by the tabloid *Neue Kronen Zeitung*, which reaches almost half of the population. The marketing and sales consortium *Mediaprint* and foreign (German) investors are also dominating players on the print market.

Table 3
Readership of the Austrian Press, 2006

Newspapers and News Magazines	Percentage of Readership
Neue Kronen Zeitung	438
Kleine Zeitung	122
Kurier	97
Oberösterreichische Nachrichten	56
Der Standard	49
Tiroler Tageszeitung	47
Die Presse	43
Salzburger Nachrichten	38
Vorarlberger Nachrichten	30
Wirtschaftsblatt	15
Neue Kärntner Tageszeitung	11
Die Neue – Zeitung für Tirol	10
Neue Vorarlberger Tageszeitung	7
Österreich* (since 1 September 2006)	15.0*
Heute* (gratis newspaper)	17.0*
News (weekly news magazine)	137
Profil (weekly news magazine)	58

*Data for *Österreich* and *Heute* are focusing on the third quarter of 2006 and are based on a different calculation method by MediaCom.
Source: Verein Arbeitsgemeinschaft Media-Analysen; MediaCom.[17]

Additionally, there exist quasi-monopolies for a couple of regional newspapers (for example, regional market share of 96 percent for *Vorarlberger Nachrichten*, 63 percent for *Tiroler Tageszeitung*).[18] Also, regional weekly and gratis papers reach up to 78 percent of the readership (*Tiroler Bezirksblätter*, for example). These figures indicate the remarkable level of concentration on the Austrian press market, which consequently reflects the "highest level of concentration of all Western democracies."[19]

Austrian News Consumption

The interest in news in the Austrian public is outstanding in the European comparison. Only in Scandinavian countries is the level of news consumption higher. Additionally, about 60 percent of Austrians think that they are well informed about the most serious problems and politics of their country.[20] About one-third of the Austrian public can be categorized as very interested in politics. Another third is moderately interested, and one-third is rather unconcerned about politics.[21]

Television is the most prominent source of political news for the Austrian public (see Table 4). About every second Austrian additionally retrieves political news from newspapers. The significance of newspapers as news source is slightly diminishing, but still of relatively high importance. In contrast, the radio lost substantially in significance as a political news source over time, such as personal conversations did. Recently, the Internet superseded magazines as a primary news source, and its popularity is still on the rise.

Table 4
Primary Sources of Political News in Austria, 1961-2006

Source	1961	1981	1995	2001	2003	2006
Television	11	55	69	79	75	71
Newspapers	61	38	44	52	49	55
Radio	59	20	25	45	38	22
Magazines	-	-	-	-	-	5
Personal	17	15	12	11	8	2
Internet	-	-	-	-	4	10

Note: Multiple answers were accepted.
Source: Filzmaier and Hajek; Plasser and Ulram.[22]

Austrian mass media in general and television in particular are not only the most prominent sources of political news; they are also the most trustworthy ones. In comparison to other EU member states, the Austrian public trusts its media coverage more than citizens of other countries do; this trust is rated above average[23] (see Table 5).

Referring particularly to election campaigns, we can also state that the electorate gathers most of its information from television, followed by newspapers and radio. Personal talks and conversations as well as campaign events have lost importance for voters. Contrastingly, televised debates are highly recognized by the Austrian electorate.

Not only is the Austrian media system sustainable as transformed by technological innovations and political deregulation; journalistic logic is also constantly adapting to larger social, cultural, and economic changes. Intensifying professionalism a well as competitive and commercial pressure within the Austrian media system puts transformative pressure on journalistic logic also. During the last few decades, Austrian political journalism is moving into the direction of a more politically detached and critical journalism that follows the U.S.

Table 5
The Trustworthiness of the Austrian News Sources, 1976-2006

Source	1976	1989	1995	1999	2003	Sept. 2006
Television	66	56	47	54	51	32
Newspapers	27	16	20	14	14	14
Radio	17	9	8	7	8	4
Magazines	5	5	7	3	2	1
Personal	-	5	16	12	-	1
Internet	-	-	-	-	2	3

Note: Data for 2006 was gathered by a different survey conception. Thus the data are not directly comparable with preceding years.

Sources: Filzmaier; Filzmaier and Hajek; Plasser and Ulram.[24]

Table 6
Sources of News about Austrian Election Campaigns, 1962-2002

Sources Consulted	1962	1999	2002
Television reports	23	89	90
Television debates	-	86	-
Newspaper reports	48	79	74
Radio reports	65	55	47
News magazines reports	0	15	10
TV spots	0	30	-
Internet reports	-	5	9
Campaign events	11	7	-
Personal conversations with party	18	10	-

Note: There are no directly comparable data for the 2006 election campaign available.

Source: Plasser, Ulram, and Sommer.[25]

model.[26] The latest study comparing journalistic roles and self-definitions in Austria and the United States concludes that a "kind of 'homogenization' of journalistic cultures—beyond divergent institutional and market constraints within given media systems" is taking place.[27]

The Austrian Election System and Campaigning

In direct comparison to highly dynamic changes and transformations within the media system and logic, the Austrian political and institutional framework is relatively stable. The Austrian election system represents a proportional representation model and is thus clearly party-centered. The Austrian party system is a moderate multi-party system. After the 2006 elections, five parties are represented in the Austrian Parliament.[28]

Parties and campaigns are publicly financed. However, the transparency of the campaign costs is low, yet they are increasing significantly from election to election. The advertising budgets of the parties in the 2006 election campaign were mostly spent for newspaper advertisements and poster campaigns. TV and radio spots still play a marginal and underdeveloped role. Contrastingly, the Internet is a rising platform of political campaigning over the last few years. Especially in regard to internal communication (Intranet), the World Wide Web plays an increasing role in Austrian election campaigning. Also targeted emails, candidates' web logs, video downloads and tools of negative campaigning are increasingly launched via the Internet.

As far as election campaigning on Austrian television and radio is concerned, there is no free airtime provision for political parties. Furthermore, political advertisements on public broadcasting are prohibited. Consequently, only a handful of TV and radio spots were aired by political parties on private stations and in movie theaters during their 2006 campaigns. In 1994, TV debates (*TV-Konfrontationen*) among major candidates were introduced. Consequently, party representatives were allowed to confront each other in a series of TV debates on the ORF in the final stage of election campaigns. Since then, these TV confrontations are the most dominant feature of televised Austrian election campaigns. Altogether 3.6 million Austrians (60 percent of the electorate) followed at least partially one of the TV debates in 2006. The largest audience was reached by the "elephant round" among all frontrunners of the parties represented in the Austrian parliament with 1.4 million viewers.[29]

The Austrian Electorate

On a longitudinal perspective, pundits report a steady increase of mobility and fragmentation within the Austrian electorate.[30] Despite the party-based political system, partisanship among the electorate is on the decline. Whereas in 1975 only 3 percent of the voters had been categorized as floating voters, this group of flexible voters rose to 26 percent in 2006. In the same period, the ratio of late deciders (those making their voting decision within the final days) has risen from 5 to 24 percent.[31] Accordingly, we can discern a significant reduction of party identification. Whereas in 1969 three quarters of the Austrian population stated a party identification, this amount fell to 53 percent in 2006. The ratio of party membership was nearly cut in half from 23 to 12 percent in the same period.[32]

Table 7
A Framework of the Austrian Political Communication System

Political Communication Logic	Party-centered – However increasingly Media- and Candidate-centered
Media System and Markets	High competition; dual television and radio markets; high level of foreign investment on the press market; high newspaper circulation; high level of concentration on the press market; vanishing of an historically strong party press
Characteristics of the Media System	Strong public service sector; quasi-monopoly of public broadcasting on the political news sector; tabloid *Kronen Zeitung* highly dominates the newspaper market; quasi-monopolies of regional newspapers; consortium *Mediaprint* highly dominates the marketing and distribution sector on the press market; highest level of concentration on the print market among Western democracies
Relationship between Media and Politics	Highly intertwined; high level of interaction; low distance between political actors and journalists; increasing conflict potential and decreasing political parallelism; shift toward neutral commercial press; professionalization towards critical and active journalism
Political and Election System	Parliamentary system; proportional representation model; party-centered; corporatist- and consensus-oriented with, however, increasing conflict potential; moderate multi-party system
Political Campaigns – Organization	Highly centralized; nationwide; labor intensive, but also increasingly capital intensive; parties and campaigns are publicly financed, however with no spending limits; party campaign managers supported by special party campaign units and external political consultants
Political Campaigns – Transmission	Party- and functionary-centered, however also increasingly media-centered; on television free-media centered (TV debates); rising significance of the Internet
Political Campaigns – Advertising	Marketing logic; nationwide poster campaigns and newspaper advertisements; since 2002 increasing TV advertisements on private channels; no political airtime on public broadcasting; purchase of airtime only on private channels allowed
Political Campaigns / Style	Personalization: moderate, generally party-centered, however increasingly candidate-centered; Negativism: modest on an international scale, however intensifying
Electorate	Increasing social and partisan dealignment; below average on the EU level, however increasing public distrust; intensifying political volatility and social fragmentation
Channels of Political and Campaign News	Television is the leading source of news; newspapers still play a substantial role; Internet is a rising factor

Source: Own compilation, according to various sources.[33]

To summarize, all these outlined transformations and trends referring to the media, to the political and election system, and to political and journalistic logic as well as to the electorate contribute reciprocally to the formation of the contemporary Austrian political communication system and its logic. We can synoptically outline a framework that comprises its specific characteristics.

Transnationalization of the Media Logic?

Daniel Hallin and Paolo Mancini classify the Austrian model of media and politics as "Northern European or Democratic Corporatist Model" along with Germany, the Scandinavian countries or Switzerland. According to Hallin and Mancini, the major differences to the "North Atlantic or Liberal Model" (Britain, United States, Canada, and Ireland) are lower market pluralism as well as less political liberalism in terms of higher levels state intervention, corporatism and a stronger welfare state.[34] However, the authors conclude that "by the beginning of the twenty-first century, the differences have eroded to the point that it is reasonable to ask whether a single, global media model is displacing the national variation of the past, at least among the advanced capitalist democracies."[35] Although Hallin and Mancini also state a series of countertendencies (stable variations of political systems and restrictions on political broadcasting advertising), they come to the conclusion that the liberal model has become dominant across Europe as well as North America. In this context, Austria is not so much an exceptional case, as it is a late developer: party newspapers have been eroded and commercialization and deregulation as well as technological innovations have displaced the formal public service monopoly in favor of a mixed and so-called dual system in which commercial media increasingly dominates. Traditional patterns of political communication have also been transformed away from party-centered imperatives toward more media-centered patterns that bring marketing strategies and professional news management into the forefront of political campaigning. Additionally, political parties increasingly tend to blur their ideological identity and so does the Austrian electorate. However, in the light of ubiquitous trends in media-centered democracies, the modes of communication and interaction within national communication systems still reflect system-and culture-specific characteristics.[36] The few transnational and comparative studies that have investigated this topic so far suggest that although campaigning techniques in Western and media-centered democracies become more alike, election coverage in those countries still displays divergence due to different contextual, institutional, and systemic settings.[37] Only a few studies identify at least partially cross-national trends referring to political coverage in general and campaign coverage in particular.[38]

In the light of substantial transformation and partially converging trends of political communication in general and campaign discourse in particular in the United States and other media-centered democracies over the last decades, this study investigates to what extent Austrian election coverage is marked by the emergence of common patterns and traces of a transnational media logic. The almost completely deregulated U.S. commercial media system, its imperatives and operational logic, serves as a "role model" for journalism in media-centered and postindustrial democracies. In order to operationalize these major theses and trends, this study applies a set of indicators that can be drawn from earlier U.S. studies and for which long-term trends are reported: "personalization," "journalist-centeredness," "confrontational negativism" and "game-centrism."

Indicators of a Transnational Media Logic

The phenomenon of *personalization* refers to an increasing focus on candidates at the expense of parties or policy issues in the election coverage.[39] It also refers to the appearance of front-runners in comparison to other politicians and their parties. Jürgen Wilke and Carsten Reinemann coin the term "hierarchization" to describe the phenomenon of frontrunners increasingly becoming the dominant carrier of political messages and superseding other politicians.[40] In addition to this, "individualization" stands for an evolving superseding of collective political institutions (such as parties) by individual political actors (front-runners, for example), even in campaigns based on party-based election systems where parties rather than individual candidates are elected.

Over the last decades, empirical evidence also supports the hypothesis that political and election coverage in the United States is increasingly becoming "more mediated" and "more journalist-centered."[41] Whereas the "air time" of politicians shrinks, the number of journalistic evaluations concerning political actors increases.[42] These trends can be summarized as *journalist-centeredness* or *de-authentication* of political media messages.[43] Previous studies offer a series of indicators of de-authentication that can be applied here. These include "air time" and "sound bite lengths" of political actors.

Pundits also frequently conclude that political news is dominated by an intensifying negative tone and disdain based on "an automatic skepticism—some call it cynicism."[44] Thomas Patterson speaks of an increasing "antipolitics bias" of the U.S. media.[45] Lance W. Bennett states that the news focus has increasingly shifted away from trusted authorities to portrayals of mistrusted and failing politicians; additionally, "news drama emphasize crisis over continuity."[46] Thus dramatization via conflict-centered reporting is another prominent feature of the political coverage. These indicators frame a phenomenon that can be labeled as *confrontational negativity*.[47]

One of the most prominent indicators of the electoral media logic that can be extracted from previous research is the so-called *game schema*[48] or *strategy focus*.[49] It describes a portrayal of politics in a de-politicized way, lacking policy relevance. Politics is portrayed as a game or horse race and a journalistic search for the story behind the story to deconstruct political public relations strategies (strategy focus). The *game/strategy schema* is contrasted by the policy focus. This perspective describes a policy and issue-centered reflection of campaigns "within the context of policy and leadership problems and issues" and their potential solutions.[50] Another feature of the *game-centeredness* of reporting is highly intertwined with increasing personalization, that is, a de-emphasis of the policy dimension in reporting about politics by the concentration on personal and non-professional traits such as outward appearance or style of candidates. It is hypothesized that portrayals of professional traits (competence, leadership ability) are superseded by the coverage of non-professional characteristics of the candidates.[51]

The above introduced indicators that have been identified as dominant or increasingly emerging features of campaign coverage in previous—predominantly U.S.—studies can, therefore, be seen as a set of potential and reliable indicators representing the contemporary media logic in media-centered and post-industrial political communication systems.

Austrian Election Coverage

This study contrasts the results of content analyses of the 1999 and 2006 Austrian election coverage with data retrieved from similar content analyses referring to the recent national election coverage in Germany, Great Britain, and the United States. For the content analysis of the 2006 Austrian election coverage, a sample of 3,138 reports (published between 15 July and 20 September 2006) that refer to domestic and foreign politics in general and the election in particular was drawn. The analysis represents the coverage of the five leading national daily Austrian newspapers (*Neue Kronen Zeitung, Kleine Zeitung, Kurier, Der Standard, Die Presse*) with the highest circulation, the two dominant political newsmagazines (*profil, News*) and the most popular television evening newscast (*Zeit im Bild 1*). Because television is the most dominant source for political and electoral information, a special focal point of the analysis is the political coverage of the public-service evening newscast *Zeit im Bild 1*.

For the 1999 content analysis, the same sample of media outlets was observed, and the final six weeks of the campaign were analyzed.[52] The conception of the content analyses and their operationalization were equal in 1999 and 2006. For both content analyses, tests of reliability and validity were conducted. For the 1999 data, the average intracoder-reliability reaches 0.991.[53] The coding of the 2006 reports was conducted by a team of coders.[54] The accordance of this coding is reported by an intercoder-reliability coefficient of 0.853. Additionally, a validity test was computed that shows the correspondence of the conception of the researchers and its operationalization by the coders. The validity-coefficient reaches 0.921 and thus reflects a high level of accordance.

In order to offer a contextual framework of the 2006 Austrian election campaign, its main issues, and public discussion elements (including the non-political public discourse) are briefly outlined. In late summer 2006, an Austrian UN peacekeeper was killed by an Israeli rocket attack during the Israel-Lebanon conflict. Beginning with 23 August, the surprising end of the kidnapping of Natascha Kampusch cast its shadow over all other public affairs.[55] Besides the election campaign itself, above all the domestic BAWAG-ÖGB scandal[56] and the public dispute about geriatric nursing[57] were dominant. Additionally, the discussion in the run-up to the election of the ORF general manager turned into a prominent public issue in August 2006.[58]

The media-transmitted election campaign itself was imprinted by analytical assessments of the twelve aired TV debates among the front-runners of the parties (Who is the winner; who is loser? Who gained ground; who lost ground?). The media also focused on speculations about the possible outcome of the election (Which coalitions are possible? Who is going to be the next chancellor?); however, pre-election surveys and assessments by pundits did not indicate that the ÖVP would fall behind the SPÖ and come in second. Media reflections on the election campaign also prominently focused on the negative tone of the parties' campaigns. "Negative," "dirty" or even "mud-slinging campaigning"[59] were labels that have been frequently used by members of the Austrian media. Not only did political opponents accuse each other of a mud-slinging style of campaigning; journalists were also focusing on this feature of political campaigning. The intensive discussion was heated up by the statement of the SPÖ publicity expert Alois Schober who labeled the campaign of the Social Democrats that was drafted by him as "napalm, pure napalm."[60] As a counter-move, the SPÖ prime minister of Styria, Franz Voves, compared the ÖVP to a "cancer cell" (17 September 2006). Additionally, the SPÖ and ÖVP attacked each other mutually in confrontational and negative TV advertisements.

The following sections comparatively outline the results of the content analyses of recent Austrian election campaigns and thereby focus on the above outlined indicators of a transnational media logic.

Personalization

In order to analyze the level of personalization in the Austrian election coverage, two central indicators are applied: "individualization" and "hierarchization." First, the level of "individualization" of the portrayal of politics is analyzed by comparing the share of "personal profiles" and "party profiles" in the election coverage. Personal profiles refer to the coverage of characteristics of individual politicians (competence, leadership ability, integrity, character, style, or fitness), whereas party profiles reflect characteristics of parties as institutional political actors. This distinction is a central indicator for identifying traces of personalization in party-centered democracies as Austria. Taking the specific Austrian contextual framework into consideration, it can be hypothesized that party profiles should play a bigger role in the election coverage than personal profiles, for in Austrian parliamentary elections (a proportional representation system), parties are elected. However, the empirical evidence draws a different picture. Party profiles account for only 2 percent of all political reports in the final stages of the 2006 Austrian election campaign. However, in almost 7 percent of all stories, personal profiles dominate the media portrayal of politics. The ratio of personal profiles in contrast to party profiles was two to one in 1999 and increased to three to one in 2006.

In comparison, the 2000 U.S. presidential election coverage reflected personal profiles in about 15 percent of all national newspaper reports and in 5 percent of the network news.[61] These figures illustrate that the level of candidate-centered reporting in Austria is quite comparable to the one in the 2000 U.S. election coverage. Over a long-term perspective, we can also trace a steady increase of personal profiles in the U.S. coverage. A study by the Committee of Concerned Journalists shows a moderate increase of personal profiles in the newspaper as well as in the network news coverage between 1977 and 1997.[62] Similarly, in the 1998 German election coverage, a majority of personal profiles over party profiles is reported in a ratio of four to one.[63]

Personalization may also refer to a journalistic concentration on front-runners at the expense of their parties. This phenomenon is labeled as "hierarchization."[64] This dimension of investigation reveals that in the Austrian TV election coverage (*Zeit im Bild 1*) 36 percent of all political sound bites (speech elements) of parties are covered by their frontrunners. Thus, Austrian election coverage is characterized by a similar level of elite-centrism that characterized the 2005 British election coverage on television. David Deacon et al. indicate a level of elite-centrism (frequency of appearance of main party leaders in comparison to all other candidates) that equals about one third. In both countries, TV election coverage is highly dominated by party leaders and frontrunners.[65] The parties' representation is highly hierarchized on TV, although the electoral systems differ significantly (majority and candidate-centered vs. party-centered, proportional representation).

Additionally, one third of all sound bites contributed by Austrian politicians on *Zeit im Bild 1* are concentrated on the front-runners of the seven competing parties on a national level. In comparison, in the 1998 German TV election coverage, one third of all political sound bites were limited to the two chancellor candidates, Helmut Kohl and Gerhard Schroeder.[66] Additionally, Andreas Genz et al. state an increasing level of front-runner centrism in German TV election coverage over the 1990s.[67] It is hardly surprising that an even higher level of candidate-centeredness can be reported for the 2000 U.S. election coverage: three quarters of all political sound bites were from either Al Gore or George W. Bush.[68]

Despite their party-centered representational systems, Austrian as well as German news coverage displays a significant level of personalization in terms of hierarchization and individualization. This institutional and systemic party-centrism is not correspondingly reflected by its election coverage. Parallelism between more candidate-centered political reporting in the United States or Great Britain and Austria or Germany is evident; however, at this stage of analysis we can recapitulate that the systemic context may moderately limit the level of concordance referring to elite-centrism on a transnational scale.

Journalist-Centeredness and De-Authentication

The "air time" of Austrian politicians in the 2006 TV election coverage totals 6 percent of the overall coverage. Journalists themselves cover about 90 percent of sound bites within the newscasts. The remaining 4 percent are covered with statements of other public actors (experts and so forth). In contrast, the 2004 U.S. election coverage on network news was a little less journalist-centered. Stephen J. Farnsworth and Robert S. Lichter show that 67 percent of all statements are made by journalists themselves; 12 percent of all sound bites are due to political candidates and 21 percent to other actors.[69] Thus journalist-centeredness is even higher on Austrian TV. Comparatively, in the 1998 German TV election coverage, political candidates are responsible for 16 percent of all sound bites.[70] Clearly, journalist-centrism cannot be interpreted as a unique American phenomenon. Journalists themselves clearly dominate the election coverage in all of the investigated countries.

As an additional indicator of de-authentication, the shrinkage of soundbites[71] of political actors can be investigated. On this element for comparison, the analysis reveals an extraordinarily high level of similarity. *Zeit im Bild 1* reports containing speech elements of one of the Austrian front-runners allowed the candidate to talk for about nineteen seconds on an average in 2006. This corresponds exactly to the average sound bites of presidential candidates in the 2000 U.S. election coverage on *ABC World News Tonight* and in the 1998 German election coverage on television referring to the chancellor candidates. [72] In comparison, in the 2005 British TV election coverage, party leaders spoke for about 28 seconds per report on *BBC 1* or *ITV* evening news.[73] Deacon et al. also state a longitudinal decrease of about 20 percent since 1992 as far as the length of these average sound bites is concerned. An overall as well as substantial decrease of candidates' sound bites over time is also repeatedly reflected in analyses investigating U.S. election coverage[74] as well as German election coverage. Genz, Schoenbach and Semetko show that the average airtime of chancellor candidates on German TV has shrunk per 20 percent from 1990 to 1998.[75] Similarly, Wilke and Reinemann illustrate a dramatic decrease of candidates' statements in the German quality press.[76] Compared to the late 1980s, in the 2006 election coverage, candidates statements per report were cut in half.

On this comparative level, the front-runners get little time to pitch for themselves on a transnational level. Altogether the total portion of political sound bites reaches similar levels in U.S., German, and Austrian TV election coverage. These findings underscore the fact that the state of "de-authentication" as far as sound bites are concerned is similar and that the phenomenon of de-authentication and journalist-centeredness is not limited to coverage in the United States. It seems to be a transnational phenomenon.

Confrontational Negativity

"Only bad news is good news": this statement seems to hold true for the 2006 Austrian election news. Conflict-centered reporting clearly dominated over consensus with a ratio of ten to one. Whereas 21 percent of all reports mainly reflect conflict and controversy, only 2 percent predominantly focus on elements of consensus and agreement. Even in the 1999 Austrian election coverage, conflict-centered stories clearly outnumbered consensus-centered ones. This underscores the reality that conflict-centeredness is not so much dependent on specific campaign settings and dynamics; it is, rather, a substantial news value that frames political and electoral coverage in general. A similar pattern of confrontation—however on a less dramatic scale (with a ratio of four to one)—is also reported for the 1998 German election coverage.[77] Additionally, Michaela Maier illustrates in her longitudinal content analysis of German TV evening news between 1992 and 2001 that there is a substantial increase in conflict-centered reporting.[78] Referring to the U.S. coverage, Marion Just et al. state that, for the election coverage in 1992,t 28 percent of all newspaper reports and 27 percent of all reports on network evening news focused on conflict.[79] Corresponding results are also reported for the 2000 U.S. presidential election coverage on *ABC World News Tonight*. Conflict-centered stories are aired eleven times more often than stories regarding consensus.[80]

Evaluations of political actors in political reports can be seen as a further indicator illustrating the state of confrontational negativity. The 2006 Austrian election coverage is characterized by a predominantly negative tone. Evaluations of candidates and parties are simply negative. At least seven out of ten reports containing evaluations of candidates and politicians (72 percent negative, 12 percent positive),[81] parties (77 percent negative, 8 percent positive) or politics in general (90 percent negative, 6 percent positive) are clearly unenthusiastic in tone. On a longitudinal perspective, there can also be identified an increase of a negative tonality concerning Austrian party leaders. The 1999 election coverage explicitly referring to the party leaders was in 63 percent of the cases negative in comparison to 72 percent in 2006.

On a transnational level, evaluations of the chancellor candidates as well as the presidential candidates and their parties reflect a negative balance (more negative than positive evaluations). Although there may be some individual cases of positive coverage reporting on candidates,[82] the overall evaluation of individual and institutional political actors is clearly negative in tone. Wilke and Reinemann confirm an increasingly negative evaluative tendency toward chancellor candidates in the German quality press over the last decades.[83] Genz et al. additionally state an increase of negative evaluations of politicians in German TV election coverage during the 1990s.[84] That the dominance of negative evaluations is not limited to candidates, but is also effective for their parties is confirmed by Wolfgang Donsbach in his analysis of the 1998 German election coverage on TV and in the press.[85] Correspondingly, Deacon et al. diagnose a dominance of negative evaluations referring to parties for the 2005 British election coverage.[86] Donsbach found for the 1992 U.S. election coverage that political parties in the United States are even more negatively portrayed than the presidential candidates.[87] This trend to report negatively on the candidates but even more so on the parties was also evident in the 2000 U.S. TV election coverage.[88] On a longitudinal perspective, Patterson additionally outlines a trend toward an increasingly negative picture of presidential candidates drawn by the U.S. media; whereas in 1960 only one quarter of all references to the candidates was negative, this has been steadily on the rise and reached over 60 percent in the year 2000.[89]

To summarize, universally dominating patterns of confrontation and negativity are visible in all investigated election coverage settings. On a transnational level, longitudinal studies additionally confirm a basic trend towards negativity and confrontation over the last decades. There seems to be a transnational and transatlantic schema and prevailing perspective of confrontational negativity in covering campaigns and political actors in diverging cultural and communicational settings. Conflict dominates clearly over consensus, and negative evaluations of political actors prevail over positive ones.

Game-Centrism

Almost half of the political stories in the Austrian media during the 2006 campaign (48 percent) predominantly focused on non-policy and thus game-centered views on politics and elections. Contrastingly, only about one third (35 percent) of all political stories predominantly feature policy information. This preference for game-centered reporting is also empirically confirmed for the 1999 Austrian election coverage. Game-centered stories mainly contained portrayals of (potential) winners and losers, horse race scenarios, speculations and predictions about the possible election outcome, campaign strategies, and style. That election coverage is dominated by a game focus is also confirmed for the 2005 British coverage. Deacon et al. outline that, on average, less than one third of the election coverage reflects policy descriptions and issue-based debates.[90] For the U.S. coverage, Patterson shows that the dominance of game reporting is not limited to election coverage; he illustrates that between 1980 and 1999 game-centrism has increased from 35 to 50 percent of the political coverage.[91] Referring to the election coverage on network news, Farnsworth and Lichter additionally show that since 1988 game reporting has continuously outnumbered policy-centered reporting; in the 2004 election, horse race or game and policy coverage was balanced with portions of 48 and 49 percent respectively.[92] Findings of a longitudinal content analysis conducted by Andreas Genz et al. substantiate high levels of transnational similarity and confirm an underlying long-term trend towards game-centered reporting on German TV. They found for the election coverage during the 1990s that the portion of game-centered reporting has not only become the dominant feature of campaign coverage, but that it also has intensified significantly and steadily over time.[93] In the 2005 TV election coverage, the German chancellor candidates were portrayed in the context of *politics* instead of *policy* by about two thirds of the reports.[94] Additionally, Wilke and Reinemann state that the game focus is also a dominant feature in covering politics in German quality papers; in the 2006 German election coverage, 58 percent of all stories focused on the campaign itself instead of on policy issues.[95]

As a further indicator that outlines the level of de-emphasis of policy-centered political information in election coverage, we can investigate the level of "privatization" in the journalistic portrayal of candidates. In the 2006 Austrian election coverage, the level of "privatization" is substantial. No less than 70 percent of all candidate-centered reports mainly focused on their non-political and non-professional traits (integrity, style, outward appearance). Since 1999, we can also notice a significant increase of such non-political portrayals of candidates. In the 1999 Austrian election coverage, 41 percent of all candidate-centered reports focused on professional and political characteristics such as competence or leadership ability, whereas in 2006 this level fell to 30 percent. A similar and steady decrease of political and professional characteristics in journalistic portrayals of candidates is also reported for the German TV election coverage since 1990 by Winfried Schulz and Reimar Zeh; they find that about one third of all candidates' evaluations in the 2005 election coverage referred to their professional and political traits.[96] Wilke and Reinemann computed that 31 percent of all reports focused on candidates' competence or leadership ability in the 2005 election coverage in German quality papers.[97] Regarding U.S. election coverage, Doris A. Graber notes that in the late 1960s and the early 1970s a focus on the personal lives of presidential candidates dominated coverage by about three quarters.[98]

To summarize, political reports in the final stages of election campaigns predominantly focus on politics as a competitive game and thrust public policy information into the background. Additionally, the media portrayal of candidates is merely framed by their non-professional traits. This conclusion holds true on a transnational level, and the phenomena of game-centered reporting and "privatization" are not limited to the United States. Thomas E. Patterson's argument that the dominance of the game schema in covering U.S. elections is mainly due to the exceptionally long lasting, media-centered, and candidate-driven campaign in the United States thus cannot be maintained.[99] Similar phenomena of election coverage in light of the game schema are also applicable to Austrian or German election coverage where the official campaign is much shorter and traditionally more driven by parties instead of individual candidates.

Conclusion

Although this study only provides a snapshot of a few selected indicators, it offers valuable insights about the current state of political and electoral discourse culture in post-modern information societies by using recent Austrian election coverage as an empirical and analytical example. It can be concluded that the Austrian election coverage is characterized by significant levels of personalization and journalist-centeredness and that it is clearly dominated by game foci as well as a negative perspective on politics. Therefore, the recent Austrian media portrayal of politics and elections is similar to patterns and trends that have recently been identified in U.S., U.K., and German election coverage. What seems to be emerging is a form of a transnational medial logic in media-centered democracies.

Hallin and Mancini conclude that the "media system increasingly operates according to a distinctive logic of its own," and they name it a "professional or commercial logic."[100] However, besides the lack of transnational comparative empirical evidence, most of the previous investigations in this field of study concluded that the systemic and contextual framework of the American political communication system is characterized by an exceptional status among post-modern democracies. Its politically deregulated contextual features; its professionalized and commercialized, money- and media-centered style of campaigning; and its candidate-centered political and electoral system have been interpreted as unique contextual features that foster a dynamic transformation which can not necessarily be applied and transferred to other Western democracies. Thus it has been widely argued that higher degrees of political regulation and protection, other specific structures of national media systems, and differing historical, cultural, and legal frameworks would limit the degree of transnational convergence and homogenization among political communication cultures.[101]

However—based on the empirical evidence presented here—transnational forces of convergence concerning technological innovation, professionalization, and commercialization may not only change the formal structure of media systems, but could also affect their operational logic. The data outline that the coverage of campaigns seems to be not so much driven by systemic conditions, but more by transnational professional news values of postmodern political journalism. Persistent institutional and systemic differences such as party-centeredness or strong public service sectors and cultural differences do not halt the emergence of basic structures of a transnational media logic that mainly operates according to its business logic: "What I have in mind here is simply the redefinition of politics in market categories."[102] Hence, it is reasonable to speak of a solid foundation of a postmodern media logic that is inherent in Western media-centered democracies and is dominantly characterized by elements of confrontational negativity, journalist-centrism and entertainment features of personalization or game-centrism on a high level of accordance. In this context, Austria is not an exceptional case.

The outlined manifestations of transnational media logic are, however, not characterized by a perfect state of universal harmonization. Therefore, the ongoing trends should not be interpreted as tendencies toward a universal standardization. It is reasonable to state that unique national as well as cultural settings may limit the level of transnational coherence to some extent. What best characterizes the ongoing transformation of covering election campaigns is a form of hybridization[103] that reflects transnational trends of homogenization as well as national or cultural norms and specifics.

Notes

1. Jay G. Blumler and Dennis Kavanagh, "The Third Age of Political Communication: Influences and Features," *Political Communication* 16.3 (1999): 209–30.

2. Pippa Norris, *A Virtuous Circle: Political Communications in Post-Industrial Societies* (Cambridge: Cambridge UP, 2000); Fritz Plasser, *Global Political Campaigning: A Worldwide Analysis of Campaign Professionals and their Practices* (London: Praeger, 2002).

3. Fritz Plasser and Peter A. Ulram, "Öffentliche Aufmerksamkeit in der Mediendemokratie," in *Politische Kommunikation in Österreich: Ein praxisnahes Handbuch,* ed. Fritz Plasser (Vienna: WUV Universitätsverlag, 2004), 37-99, here 40.

4. Thomas Steinmaurer, *Konzentriert und verflochten: Österreichs Mediensystem im Überblick* (Innsbruck: StudienVerlag, 2002), 18.

5. Winfried Schulz, "Wahlkampf unter Vielkanalbedingungen," *Media Perspektiven* 8 (1998): 378-91.

6. ORF-Medienforschung, *Teletest* (Vienna: 2006).

7. INTEGRAL Markt- und Meinungsforschung, *Austrian Internet Monitor 2006* (Vienna: 2006).

8. "Fasching und Opernball," *Horizont,* 14 January 2005, p. 7.

9. IP Deutschland GmbH, *Television 2005—International Key Facts* (Cologne: 2006); ORF-Medienforschung, *Teletest.*

10. Schulz, "Wahlkampf."

11. Josef Seethaler and Gabriele Melischek, "Die Pressekonzentration in Österreich im europäischen Vergleich" *Österreichische Zeitschrift für Politikwissenschaft* 4 (2006): 337-60, here 346; Verein Arbeitsgemeinschaft Media-Analysen, *Media-Analyse 2005* (Vienna: 2006).

12. Since 1 June, 2003, ATV broadcasts as the first private and terrestrial Austrian television program.

13. ORF-Medienforschung, *Teletest.*

14. Ibid.

15. Verein Arbeitsgemeinschaft Media-Analysen, *Media-Analyse 2006.*

16. Peter Filzmaier, "Das österreichische Politik- und Mediensystem im internationalen Vergleich," in *Mediendemokratie Österreich,* ed. Peter Filzmaier et al. (Vienna: Böhlau, 2007), 119-42.

17. Verein Arbeitsgemeinschaft Media-Analysen, *Media-Analyse 2006;* MediaCom, *MediaScan 2006* (Vienna: 2007).

18. See Seethaler and Melischek, "Die Pressekonzentration in Österreich im europäischen Vergleich," 355.

19. Filzmaier, "Das österreichische Politik," 138.

20. Plasser and Ulram, "Öffentliche Aufmerksamkeit," 38.

21. Ibid., 64.

22. Peter Filzmaier and Peter Hajek, "Die Nationalratswahl 2006: Ergebnisse und Wahlverhalten," in *Mediendemokratie Österreich*, ed. Peter Filzmaier et al. (Vienna: Böhlau, 2007), 63-90, here 82; Plasser and Ulram, "Öffentliche Aufmerksamkeit in der Mediendemokratie," 73.

23. Ibid., 90.

24. Peter Filzmaier, "Wag the Dog? Amerikanisierung der Fernsehlogik und mediale Inszenierungen in Österreich," in *Politik und Medien, Medien und Politik*, ed. Peter Filzmaier et al. (Vienna: Facultas Universitätsverlag, 2006), 9-50, here 13; Filzmaier and Hajek, "Die Nationalratswahl 2006," 83; Plasser and Ulram, "Öffentliche Aufmerksamkeit in der Mediendemokratie," 92.

25. Fritz Plasser, Peter A. Ulram, and Franz Sommer, "Do Campaigns Matter? Massenmedien und Wahlentscheidung im Nationalratswahlkampf 1999," in *Das österreichische Wahlverhalten*, ed. Fritz Plasser et al. (Vienna: Signum, 2000), 141-73, here 144; and ibid., "Kampagnendynamik, Mediahypes und Einfluss der TV-Konfrontationen 2002," in *Wahlverhalten in Bewegung: Analysen zur Nationalratswahl 2002*, ed. Fritz Plasser and Peter A. Ulram (Vienna: WUV Universitätsverlag, 2003), 19-53, here 20.

26. Fritz Plasser, Günther Lengauer, and Wolfgang Meixner, "Politischer Journalismus in der Mediendemokratie," in *Politische Kommunikation in Österreich*, ed. Fritz Plasser (Vienna: Facultas WUV Universitätsverlag, 2004), 237-308.

27. Fritz Plasser, "From Hard to Soft News Standards? How Political Journalists in Different Media Systems Evaluate the Shifting Quality of News," *The Harvard International Journal of Press/Politics* 10.2 (2005): 47-68, here 47.

28. Key: Social Democrats: SPÖ, People's Party: ÖVP, Greens: Die Grünen, Freedom Party: FPÖ, Alliance for the Future of Austria: BZÖ.

29. Peter Filzmaier and Peter Hajek, "Die Nationalratswahl 2006," 81.

30. Fritz Plasser and Peter A. Ulram, *Das österreichische Politikverständnis: Von der Konsens- zur Konfliktkultur?* (Vienna: WUV Universitätsverlag, 2002).

31. Filzmaier and Hajek, "Die Nationalratswahl 2006," 65; Fritz Plasser and Peter A. Ulram, *Die Wahlanalyse 2006: Wer hat wen warum gewählt*, (Vienna: GfK Austria, 2006), 6.

32. Plasser and Ulram, *Die Wahlanalyse 2006*.

33. Filzmaier, 2007: 19; Daniel C. Hallin and Paolo Mancini, *Comparing Media Systems: Three Models of Media and Politics* (Cambridge: Cambridge UP, 2004); Barbara Pfetsch, *Politische Kommunikationskultur: Politische Sprecher und Journalisten in der Bundesrepublik und den USA im Vergleich* (Wiesbaden: VS Verlag für Sozialwissenschaften, 2003); Plasser, *Global Political Campaigning*, 83; Fritz Plasser, ed., *Politische Kommunikation in Österreich: Ein praxisnahes Handbuch* (Vienna: Facultas WUV Universita(tsverlag 2004).

34. Hallin and Mancini, *Comparing Media Systems*, 67-68.

35. Ibid., 251.

36. Plasser, *Global Political Campaigning*.

37. Holli Semetko, "Political Balance on Television: Campaigns in the United States, Britain, and Germany," *The Harvard International Journal of Press/Politics* 1.1 (1996): 51-71; Holli Semetko, et al., *The Formation of Campaign Agendas: A Comparative*

Analysis of Party and Media Roles in Recent American and British Elections (Hillsdale, NJ: L. Erlbaum Associates, 1991); Jürgen Wilke and Carsten Reinemann, "Do the Candidates Matter? Long-term Trends of Campaign Coverage, A Study of the German Press since 1949," *European Journal of Communication* 16.3 (2001), 291-314.

38. Andreas Genz, et al., "'Amerikanisierung'? Politik in den Fernsehnachrichten während der Bundestagswahlkämpfe 1990-1998," in *Wahlen und Wähler: Analysen aus Anlass der Bundestagswahl 1998*, ed. Hans-Dieter Klingemann and Max Kaase (Wiesbaden: VS Verlag für Sozialwissenschaften, 2001), 401-13; Günther Lengauer, *Postmoderne Nachrichtenlogik: Redaktionelle Politikvermittlung in medienzentrierten Demokratien* (Wiesbaden: Vs Verlag, 2007).

39. Lance W. Bennett, *News: The Politics of Illusion*, 4th ed. (New York: Addison Wesley Longman, 2001).

40. Wilke and Reinemann, "Do the Candidates Matter?".

41. Kevin G. Barnhurst and Diana Mutz, "American Journalism and the Decline in Event-centered Reporting," *Journal of Communication* 47.4 (1997): 27-53; Daniel C. Hallin, "Sound Bite News: Television Coverage of Elections, 1968-1988," *Journal of Communication* 42.2 (1992): 5-24.

42. Catherine A. Steele and Kevin G. Barnhurst, "The Journalism of Opinion: Network Coverage in U.S. Presidential Campaigns, 1968-1988," *Critical Studies in Mass Communication* 13.3 (1996): 187-209.

43. Wilke and Reinemann, "Do the Candidates Matter?"

44. Bennett, *News: The Politics of Illusion*, 6.

45. Thomas E. Patterson, *Out of Order* (New York: A. Knopf, 1993), 19.

46. Bennett, *News: The Politics of Illusion*, 36.

47. Lengauer, *Postmoderne Nachrichtenlogik*.

48. Patterson, *Out of Order*.

49. Joseph N. Cappella and Kathleen Hall Jamieson, *Spiral of Cynicism: The Press and the Public Good* (New York: Oxford UP, 1997); Kathleen Hall Jamieson, *Dirty Politics: Deception, Distraction, and Democracy* (New York: Oxford UP, 1992).

50. Patterson, *Out of Order*, 74.

51. Doris A. Graber, "Personal Qualities in Presidential Images: The Contribution of the Press," *Midwest Journal of Political Science* 16 (1972): 46-76; ibid., "Press and TV as Opinion Resources in Presidential Campaigns," *Public Opinion Quarterly* 40 (1976): 285-303.

52. The content analysis of the 1999 Austrian election coverage comprises the full coverage of the final six weeks of the election campaign. The population consists of 2,919 political reports between 23 August and 3 October 1999 (election day).

53. All coefficients reported here are average coefficients computed for ordinal (Spearman's Rho), ratio- (percent agreement) and nominal-scale variables (Scott's Pi). The coding for 1999 was conducted by the author himself. Therefore, the intracoder reliability was computed by comparing the coding of a 5 percent sample of reports in the beginning and in the end of the coding process.

54. Special thanks to the coding team consisting of Mag. Iris Höller, Josef Kofler, Christoph Tauber, and Mag. Martin Straganz.

55. After eight years of captivity, the eighteen-year-old kidnapping victim was able to escape.

56. The BAWAG bank, owned by the Austrian labor union ÖGB, speculatively lost money, and the ÖGB gave its guarantee. Consequently, the Austrian finance market inspector and the public prosecutor launched investigations. The BAWAG general manager Helmut Elsner was arrested. In the final stages of the election campaign, the arrest of Elsner as well as the allegation that former SPÖ Chairman Franz Vranitzky had received consulting payments from BAWAG investment banker Wolfgang Flöttl dominated the BAWAG discussion. Additionally, a few days before election day it was publicized that Josef Taus, former ÖVP chairman, visited Helmut Elsner in France and that BAWAG flew Chancellor Wolfgang Schüssel to Sofia.

57. The public debate about a "state of emergency" concerning geriatric nursing in Austria was stoked by a letter to the editor in *Der Standard* which uncovered that even the chancellor's mother-in-law was cared for by an illegal foreign nurse.

58. The election campaigns for the position of the general manager of the Austrian Public Broadcasting (ORF) as well as the discussion about the role and the responsibility of public broadcasting in general were dominating themes. On 17 August, Alexander Wrabetz was elected as the new ORF general manager.

59. Examples include "mud-slinging campaign" (*Salzburger Nachrichten* 29 August 2006, p. 3; "raging mud-slinging" (*Neue Kronen Zeitung*, 3 September 2006, p. 4; "brutal election campaign" (cover story in *News*, 17 August 2006).

60. *profil,* 7 August 2006, p. 22.

61. Project for Excellence in Journalism, *The Last Lap: How the Press Covered the Final Stages of the Presidential Campaign.* 31 Oct. 2000 <http://www.journalism.org/node/ 309>.

62. Committee of Concerned Journalists, *Changing Definitions of News: A Look at the Mainstream Press over 20 Years* (Washington, D.C.: 1998).

63. Lengauer, *Postmoderne Nachrichtenlogik,* 164.

64. Frank Marcinkowski and Volker Greger, "Die Personalisierung politischer Kommunikation im Fernsehen," in *Trans-Atlantik, Trans-Portabel? Die Amerikanisierungsthese in der politischen Kommunikation,* ed. Klaus Kamps (Wiesbaden: Westdeutscher Verlag, 2000), 179-97.

65. David Deacon, et al., *Reporting the 2005 U.K. General Election* (Loughborough: 2005), 18.

66. Lengauer, *Postmoderne Nachrichtenlogik,* 161.

67. Genz et al., "'Amerikanisierung'?", 407-08.

68. Lengauer, *Postmoderne Nachrichtenlogik,* 171.

69. Stephen J. Farnsworth and Robert S. Lichter, *The Nightly News Nightmare: Television's Coverage of U.S. Presidential Elections, 1998-2004* (Lanham, MD: Rowman & Littlefield, 2006), 92.

70. Lengauer, *Postmoderne Nachrichtenlogik,* 266.

71. In this comparison sound bites are defined as direct speech elements per report (cumulative) and not as uninterrupted single speech elements within the reports.

72. Calculated by the author (referring to the final six weeks of the election campaign).

73. Deacon et al., *Reporting,* 15.

74. Farnsworth and Lichter, *Nightly News Nightmare,* 83; Hallin, "Sound Bite News."

75. Genz et al., "'Amerikanisierung'?".

76. Jürgen Wilke and Carsten Reinemann, "Die Normalisierung des Sonderfalls? Die Wahlkampfberichterstattung der Presse 2005 im Langzeitvergleich," in *Die Massenmedien im Wahlkampf: Die Bundestagswahl 2005*, ed. Christina Holtz-Bacha (Wiesbaden: VS Verlag fu(r Sozialwissenschaften, 2006), 306-37, here 327.

77. Lengauer, *Postmoderne Nachrichtenlogik*, 236.

78. Michaela Maier, "Analysen deutscher Fernsehnachrichten 1992-2001," in *Der Wert von Nachrichten im deutschen Fernsehen*, ed. Georg Ruhrmann et al. (Opladen: Vs Verlag, 2003), 61-98.

79. Marion Just, et al., "Voice, Substance, and Cynicism in Presidential Campaign Media," *Political Communication* 16 (1999): 25-44, here 36.

80. Lengauer, *Postmoderne Nachrichtenlogik*, 248.

81. Missing values are due to reports that equally contain negative as well as positive evaluations.

82. Farnsworth and Lichter, *Nightly News Nightmare*.

83. Wilke and Reinemann, "Do the Candidates Matter?", 330-31.

84. Genz et al., "'Amerikanisierung'?"

85. Wolfgang Donsbach, "Drehbücher und Inszenierungen: Die Union in der Defensive," in *Kampa: Meinungsklima und Medienwirkung im Bundestagswahlkampf 1998*, ed. E. Noelle-Neumann et al. (Freiburg: K. Alber, 1999), 141-80.

86. Deacon et al., *Reporting*, 32.

87. Wolfgang Donsbach, "Täter oder Opfer—Die Rolle der Massenmedien in der amerikanischen Politik," *Beziehungsspiele—Medien und Politik in der öffentlichen Diskussion: Fallstudien und Analysen*, ed. Wolfgang Donsbach et al. (Gütersloh: Bertelsmann, 1993), 221-82.

88. Lengauer, *Postmoderne Nachrichtenlogik*, 250; Project for Excellence in Journalism, *The Last Lap*.

89. Thomas E. Patterson, *Doing Well and Doing Good: How Soft News and Critical Journalism are Shrinking the News Audience and Weakening Democracy—and What News Outlets Can Do about It* (Cambridge: Cambridge UP, 2000), 10.

90. Deacon et al., *Reporting*, 20.

91. Patterson, *Doing Well*, 3.

92. Farnsworth and Lichter, *Nightly News Nightmare*, 52.

93. Genz et al., "'Amerikanisierung'?"

94. Winfried Schulz and Reimar Zeh, "Die Kampagne im Fernsehen – Agens und Indikator des Wandels. Ein Vergleich der Kandidatendarstellung," in *Die Massenmedien im Wahlkampf*, ed. C. Holtz-Bacha (Wiesbaden: Vs Verlag, 2006), 290.

95. Wilke and Reinemann, "Die Normalisierung des Sonderfalls?", 316.

96. Schulz and Zeh, "Die Kampagne im Fernsehen," 298.

97. Wilke and Reinemann, "Die Normalisierung des Sonderfalls?", 323.

98. Graber, "Personal Qualities in Presidential Images" and "Press and TV as Opinion."

99. Patterson, *Out of Order*.

100. Hallin and Mancini, *Comparing Media Systems*, 253.

101. See, for example, Richard Gunther and Anthony Mughan, eds., *Democracy and the Media: A Comparative Perspective* (Cambridge: Cambridge UP, 2000); Gianpietro Mazzoleni and Winfried Schulz, "'Mediatization' of Politics: A Challenge for Democracy?", *Political Communication* 16 (1999): 247-61; and Pfetsch, *Politische Kommunikationskultur*.

102. Jürgen Habermas, "Political Communication in Media Society: Does Democracy Still Enjoy an Epistemic Dimension?", page 26. Paper presented at the annual meeting of the International Communication Association, Dresden, 20 June 2006.

103. See also Plasser, *Global Political Campaigning*.

Austrian Electoral Behavior in International Comparison

Fritz Plasser and Gilg Seeber

International comparisons of election studies are rare because the state of research on the whole continues to be unsatisfactory despite improved possibilities for using national data sets.[1] This applies particularly to Austria where only recently an initiative was started to participate in the *Comparative Study of Electoral Systems* (CSES).[2] Consequently, the literature dealing with trends and patterns of comparative electoral behavior is quite minimal. In Germany, Rüdiger Schmitt-Beck and Harald Schoen carried out comparative analyses; Schmitt-Beck explored the influence of political communication upon the individual voting decision in Germany, Great Britain, Spain, and the United States, while Schoen dealt with the political competence of party changers in Germany, Great Britain, and the United States.[3] A milestone of comparative election research is the study edited by Jaques Thomassen, *The European Voter: A Comparative Study of Modern Democracies*, where long-term changes of election behavior in Denmark, Germany, the Netherlands, Norway, and Sweden have been analyzed systematically on the basis of available national elections studies for the first time.[4]

Comparative insights into trends and changes in election behavior are also offered by Russell J. Dalton who focuses on Germany, France, Great Britain, and the United States.[5] Newer studies approach special questions like the change of cleavage structures, gender and religious determinants of election behavior,[6] the erosion of class-voting,[7] and the influence of top candidates on the voting decision,[8] as well as the influence of election campaigns on voter behavior[9] and the electoral success of right-wing populist parties from a comparative perspective.[10] Additional studies deal with voter behavior at elections to the European Parliament in country comparison,[11] but their sophisticated findings can only be transferred to a limited extent to national parliamentary elections due to the "second order" status of European elections and deplorably low turnout rates.

The status of the research is much more satisfactory regarding the long-term development of voter participation in country comparison[12] as well as the institutional context of election procedures[13] and campaign practices[14] in international comparison. It need not be mentioned that Austrian election behavior is only addressed perfunctorily in the publications mentioned and that the comparative status of knowledge is anecdotal.

This is the basic approach of the present contribution, which tries for the first time to investigate patterns of Austrian election behavior comparatively. Based on data of a representative election-day survey at the Austrian parliamentary elections in 2006, a comparison is made between central determinants of Austrian election behavior and comparative patterns of the election behavior in Germany, France, Great Britain, Italy, and the United States. The following data sets have been available: the exit poll of the research group for elections to the German parliamentary elections of 2005 as well as the data of the German National Election Study 2002 (CSES), the French Election Study 2002 (CES), the British Election Study 2005 (BES), the Italian National Election Studies 2001 and 2006 (ITANES), and the American National Election Study 2004 (ANES), as well as the data of the National Exit Poll at the American Congressional Elections 2006 (National Election Poll).

These six countries vary greatly regarding their political systems and election procedures. Austria represents a parliamentary, party-centered democracy. The Austrian parliament consists of two chambers, the second chamber of which is only elected indirectly and has only marginal legislative competence. In the National Council—the first and legislatively decisive chamber of parliament—five parties are currently represented. They are in the left center the Greens (11 percent) and the Social Democratic Party of Austria (*Sozialdemokratische Partei Österreichs*, or SPÖ), which became the strongest party at the parliamentary elections 2006 with 35.3 percent. In the right center there is the conservative Christian Democratic Austrian People's Party (*Österreichische Volkspartei*, or ÖVP), which had nominated the chancellor during the coalition government with the Austrian Freedom Party (*Freiheitliche Partei Österreichs,* or FPÖ) between 2000 and 2006, but fell back to second place after losing 8 percent to its present 34.3 percent representation, and is part of a great coalition government with the SPÖ under a Social Democratic chancellor since January 2007. To the right stands the populist FPÖ with 11 percent of the votes, and the Alliance for the Future of Austria (*Bündnis Zukunft Österreich*, or BZÖ)—a party split off in 2005 from the FPÖ—which was barely able to exceed the national 4 percent threshold with 4.1 percent. The Austrian election procedure is party-centered. Main attention is paid to the party lists, only a minority makes use of preferential votes for party candidates. Valid votes are allocated to party lists in a three-step procedure based on the principle of proportional representation.

In the Federal Republic of Germany, personalized proportional representation has been established. Every voter has a vote for candidates (primary vote) and a party vote (secondary vote). With the primary vote, 299 district candidates are elected on a plurality basis. However, decisive are the secondary votes, since they determine the distribution of all 598 parliamentary seats on the party lists. The Federal Republic of Germany is, like Austria, a party-centered parliamentary democracy. The second chamber—the Federal Council—is appointed indirectly as it is in Austria, but has considerable legislative powers. In the first chamber of the German parliament—the *Bundestag*—five parties are currently represented. In the left center—but isolated on the left edge—stands the former East German Leftist Party of Democratic Socialism (PDS) with 8.7 percent of the votes. The left further consists of the Greens (*Bündnis 90/Die Grünen*) with 8.1 percent of the votes. The left center is represented by the German Social Democratic Party (SPD) with 34.2 percent of the votes. Right of the center stands the Christian Democratic Union (CDU) in alliance with the Christian Social Union (CSU), which—being the strongest faction, together sharing 35.2 percent—nominates the chancellor since the parliamentary election in 2005. Along with the CDU/CSU, the right center is also represented by the rightist liberal Free Democratic Party (FDP) with 9.8 percent. The Union parties and the FDP intended to form a coalition government in 2005, but failed to reach a majority. The result is a coalition government of CDU/CSU with the SPD since 2005. Based on the logic of the secondary votes, German election law conforms to the principles of proportional representation with a federal 5 percent clause.

With the election reform of 2006, Italy returned to a PR system, which has a built-in mechanism to strengthen majorities for the election to the first and second chamber—a majority bonus for the winning coalition—and, moreover, animates small parties to engage in alliances with larger parties due to reasons of election arithmetic. During the parliamentary election of 2006, the results were two contesting party coalition blocs:

the *Centrosinistra* (center left) or *Unione* under Romano Prodi, which consisted of the strongest party *Ulivo* (Olive Tree) in alliance with the Communist Refoundation, the Italian Communist Party, and the Greens (10.5 percent) as well as other smaller left of the center parties (7.4 percent). The *Centrodestra* (center right) or House of Liberties was led by Silvio Berlusconi. The strongest party of the center right alliance is *Forza Italia* (Go Italy) with 24.0 percent of the votes. Second is the National Alliance (An) with 12.6 percent. The House of Liberties also includes a successor party of the Christian Democrats which had dominated for decades—the Union of Christian Democrats (Udc)—with 6.8 percent as well as the nationalist populist Northern League (Ln) with 4.6 percent. With an advantage of only 0.02 percent (expressed alternately as 49.8 percent to 49.7 percent), the center left alliance reached a narrow majority and nominated the minister president in the person of Romano Prodi, who only found a fragile majority in the second chamber, the senate. Italy also represents a type of party-centered parliamentary democracy. The technically complex election law is oriented on the principle of proportional representation and is a majority strengthening system of voting based on national coalition lists and a threshold. The decisive vote is the one for the party.

France has a semi-parliamentary system based on the strong position of the directly elected president. However, the voting practice at elections to the National Assembly—the first chamber of parliament—is completely oriented on the rules of parliament. Contrary to Austria, Germany, and Italy, France votes according to a majority-plurality system; the French only vote for candidates. Those getting more than 50 percent of the valid votes in the first round join the National Assembly. The second round of French parliamentary elections is—after pre-electoral deals—only made up of the most promising candidates of left and right parties. During the second round, a plurality is sufficient, such that the voting recommendations of parties forgoing an independent candidature can make the difference. At the French parliamentary elections in 2002, among left parties, the Party of the Extreme Left (EL) got 2.8 percent of the vote, the French Communist Party (PCF) 4.8 percent, the Greens (*Verts*) 4.5 percent, and the strongest left party, the French Socialist Party (PS), got 24.1 percent. The strongest party right of the center was the Union for a Popular Movement (UMP), a newly formed alliance of Gaullists and the rightist liberal Union for French Democracy (UDF), with 33.3 percent. The extreme right—the National Front (FN) and its offshoot, the list Megret—together reached 12.2 percent without being represented in the National Assembly with a single seat.

Great Britain stands for the "Westminster Model" of a parliamentary democracy. The election law is a plurality system in single member districts. In the 646 election districts, votes are cast for candidates only, whereby, according to the First-Past-the-Post System, a candidate one single vote ahead of the next candidate is elected to a parliamentary seat. Due to the majority supporting mechanics of the plurality system, Great Britain, in terms of government responsibility, does, in fact, have a two-party system, whereby a third party—the Liberal Democrats—with 22 percent of the votes, certainly plays a relevant role in the election competition. A series of regional parties also received a share of the votes at 10.4 percent. The strongest party in the British General Elections of 2005 with 35.2 percent of the vote was, again, the Social Democratic Labour Party (Lab) in spite of a loss of 5.5 percent. The Conservatives (Con) remained in opposition with 32.4 percent.

Different from the election systems described above, the United States has a presidential system in which the elected president takes over the function of the executive. The parliament—the Congress—consists of two chambers with equal weight: the House of Representatives with 435 seats and the Senate consisting of 100 senators. The representatives of the first chamber—the House of Representatives—are newly elected every two years. The also directly elected senators have a six-year term, whereby about one-third of all senatorial seats are up for election every two years. The American election law follows the British tradition of plurality elections in single-member districts. There are no party lists, votes are for candidates only who qualified themselves previously in primaries. The American election system represents a pure two-party system. Third parties are more or less negligible for congressional elections. To the left of the center—according to the American understanding of "liberal"—stand the Democrats (Dem), who won the majority in both chambers at the Congressional elections of 2006. In the House of Representatives, the Democrats reached a 57.7 percent majority, while the conservative Republicans (Rep) fell back to 41.8 percent and lost their majority which they had held since the Congressional elections of 1994.

The countries chosen for this comparison all show strong national characteristics in their institutional arrangements, the logic of competition, and their election systems which consequently influence election behavior. Currently, four of the six countries selected have coalition governments. Only in Great Britain are the prime minister and the government nominated by only one party. In the United States, on the other hand, congressional elections do not determine the composition of the executive branch of government, but the majority in the legislative branch, which defines the range of action of the president. Additionally, there are always national topics, the personalities of candidates, and general sentiments making a direct comparison of short-term determinants and factors for the voting decision impossible. However, characteristic patterns of voting behavior as well as in-depth structures of the voting decision can be examined comparatively for similarities and differences, just as the influence of selected structural variables for the individual voter decision can be modeled and calculated comparatively.

The present contribution approaches its topic in three steps. In the first step, long-term trends in Austrian voting behavior are related to the developments in other countries. In a second step, a comparison is made between the patterns and determinants of Austrian voting behavior with similar data from election studies of the selected reference countries. In the third and final step, the effects of selected variables are modeled and estimated within the frame of a multivariate analysis of the data sets. The comparison of effectual parameters is supposed to answer the core question of this contribution: Does Austrian voting behavior represent an exceptional case after all, or is the voting behavior of Austrians characterized by structures and patterns that can also be observed in voting behavior in Germany, Italy, France, Great Britain, and the United States despite the political-institutional differences between the national election systems?

Erosion of Party Affiliations and Increasing Voter Mobility

Characteristic of Austrian election behavior is the erosion of traditional party loyalty which is also expressed in declining voting participation, but also in the continually increasing mobility and readiness for change among Austrian voters. During the 1980s, Austria in international comparison represented a country with above average turnout rates at parliamentary elections. A comparison of voter participation at parliamentary elections in twenty-two countries between 1945 and 1999 shows that Austria was positioned in the uppermost segment with an average turnout rate of 92.1 percent. Only in Australia and Belgium (both of which have compulsory voting) and in Italy was the average turnout rate at parliamentary elections higher than in Austria.[15] Since the late 1980s, however, the turnout rate has been declining and reached a new low at the parliamentary elections in 2006 with only 78.5 percent voter turnout.

During the last thirty years, the turnout rate has declined by 14.4 percentage points. Similar declines also took place in Germany—where the turnout rate at the parliamentary election in 2005 also reached a historic low of 77.7 percent—and in Great Britain and Italy since the middle of the 1970s. In the United States, the turnout rate at midterm elections slid from 53.3 percent in 1974 to 40.4 percent in 2006, though the decline was not linear, but cyclical. The turnout rate remained comparably most stable in Italy, which is remarkable given the turbulences in the Italian party system during the early 1990s, which led to the collapse of the first Italian party system. The strongest decline of the turnout rate can be found in France with negative 21.0 percentage points. A look at Table 1 shows, with the exception of France, a parallel course of decline regarding the voting turnout in all six countries, which can only in part be reduced to national context factors and points to a change of cultures as well as the political participation repertoires of new generations of voters.[16]

The political participation repertoire of the countries investigated show interesting patterns that are tangentially also reflected in the turnout rates at parliamentary elections. Countries whose eligible voters show a restrictive participation repertoire where the participation in the political process primarily concentrates on the participation in elections, like Italy, are, despite considerable generative changes and a general softening of the voting and participation discipline, characterized by comparatively high turnout rates. Countries whose eligible voters show an expanded participation repertoire—like France or Great Britain—also have a comparatively low turnout rate at parliamentary elections. The United States is, in fact, an exception regarding participation in national elections. On the one hand, the United States has a traditionally "low turnout

Table 1
International Comparison of Voter Turnout at Parliamentary Elections, in Percent

Country		2002-2006	1974-1976	Change in Percent
Italy	(2006)	836	93.4	-9.8
Germany	(2005)	77.7	90.7	-13.0
Austria	(2006)	78.5	92.9	-14.4
Great Britain	(2005)	61.4	72.9	-11.5
France	(2002)	60.3	81.3	-21.0
USA	(2006)	40.4	53.5	-13.1

Note: Germany until 1976 includes only West Germany. United States voter turnout is for congressional mid-term elections.
Source: International IDEA (2006).

culture"; on the other hand, institutional and regulative factors contribute to turnout rates far beyond Western European standards—with the exception of Switzerland. These factors are the definition of eligible voters as members of the "voting age population" which on the basis of census data also include persons without American citizenship; the barriers of the registration procedure, for in the United States the eligible voter is supposed to take the initiative to register for voting; and the incomparable density and frequency of local, state, and national elections.[17]

Austria not only follows the trend in Western democracies regarding the declining voter turnout, but a significant decline of party affiliations among the Austrian electorate has developed over time as well. What is referred to as *dealignment* in international literature—an erosion of long-term, emotional attachments to a certain party—started in Austria during the early 1980s and left deep marks in the political competition. Party identification in Austria has actually been declining since the 1980s. While in the 1970s 65 percent of voters still identified themselves with a particular party, ten years later they were barely 60 percent. During the 1990s, party attachment continued to weaken further and reached its lowest point in 1994 with a share of only 44 percent of party affiliated voters. During the late 1990s, party identification restabilized at a share of 50 percent. The end of the great coalition government in 2000 and the formation of a coalition between the ÖVP and the FPÖ increased the political competition and led to a polarization between supporters of the ÖVP-FPÖ coalition government and supporters of the parliamentary opposition parties (SPÖ and Greens).

Party identification increased again after 2000. Of all voters at the national elections in 2006, 57 percent were emotionally inclined to support

Table 2
Political Participation Repertoire, in Percent

Country	Focus on Participation in Elections	Mixed Repertoire	Focus on Other Forms of Participation	Politically Passive
Italy	59	29	2	9
Austria	34	54	5	7
United States	28	43	11	17
Germany	27	58	7	9
Great Britain	21	51	15	13
France	21	42	21	16

Source: European Social Survey 2002/2003; Citizenship, Involvement, Democracy (CID) Survey Project 2005.

a particular party. In 2006, 89 percent of voters with party affiliations voted for the same party they supported four years ago; 11 percent voted for another party. This pattern conforms to the findings of comparative election research. In Great Britain, an average 13 percent of "party loyalists" at general elections vote for another party because they prefer it emotionally. In German parliamentary elections, these voters are on the average 12 to 14 percent. In Italy in 2006, 11 percent of the voters with party identification voted for another party.[18]

Upright party affiliations are still contributing to the stabilization of voting behavior. However, their contribution gradually lessened during the last decades, and party identification and the actual voting decision partially drifted apart.[19] In addition, the share of voters with an upright party affiliation declined over time.[20] As expected, the erosion of long-term party attachments occurred, too; this was especially true in Italy, since the collapse of the traditional party system at the beginning of the 1990s caused traditional parties like the DCI to vanish from the political stage. While in Germany the level of party identification only changed minimally over time, the recession of voters with strong party affiliation in Germany points to a declining stabilization effect of existing party attachments. A comparable pattern can also be found in Austria. Just as in other Western democracies, Austrian parties operate on an open and volatile electoral market.[21]

The most conspicuous consequence of the erosion of stable party affiliations is the increasing share of those voters who decide on their definite vote for a party only during the campaign or even shortly before election day. While in Austria during the 1970s on the average only 5

Table 3
Party Identification in Comparison, in Percent

Country		2002-2006	1974-1976	Change
Germany	(2005)	68	70	-2
France	(2002)	68	70	-2
United States	(2006)	61	63	-2
Austria	(2006)	57	65	-8
Italy	(2006)	57	77	-20
Great Britain	(2005)	51	66	-15

Note: The wording of questions is only partially comparable. Germany refers to Western Germany only. The United States is a percentage of strong or weak identifiers. Great Britain is a percentage of very strong or fairly strong identifiers. France is a percentage of persons with a *proximite partisane*.

Source: National election studies or Eurobarometer and European Social Survey Data.

percent belonged to the group of "late deciders," they increased to 24 percent in 2006. Regarding the time when a person makes a definite voting decision, existing party affiliations play an essential role. Of voters with party identification, 92 percent had already decided long before the campaign for which party they would vote. Among voters without a stable party attachment, only 60 percent decided upon a particular party prior to the campaign. Forty percent of non-party-affiliated voters—in total 43 percent of the Austrian electorate—made their definite decision only during the campaign or a few days before the election. The highest share of "late deciders" is found with 64 percent among inconsistent voters who voted for a party in 2006 other than the one they principally prefer. Concerning the time of the individual voting decision, Austrian voting behavior approximated the international trend and conforms to patterns that can also be found in Italy, Germany, France, Great Britain, and the United States.

Weakened party affiliations, a gradual split of one's party affiliation from one's voting decision, as well as the postponement of the time of voting decision to the final phase of the campaign consequently result in increased voter mobility. In fact, the rate of party shifters at parliamentary elections increased continually since the middle of the 1980s. While in 1983 10 percent voted for a party other than the one voted for at previous elections, the share of volatile voters already reached 20 percent ten years later. In 2006, a total of 26 percent of all voters changed the party for which they voted. This was the highest rate of party shifting in the newer Austrian history of elections so far.

The continuing increase of party shifters at parliamentary elections started in Austria later than in Germany or Great Britain, just as the dealignment in Austria was on the whole delayed. While the rate of party

Table 4
Time of Definite Voting Decision, in Percent

		Long before the Campaign (Early Deciders)	During the Campaign or shortly before Election Day (Late Deciders)
Italy	(2006)	77	23
Austria	(2006)	76	24
Germany	(2005)	71	29
France	(2002)	71	29
Great Britain	(2005)	68	32
United States	(2006)	50	49

Source: National election studies.

shifting in Germany had already begun fluctuating in the 1970s and 1980s roughly between 10 and 16 percent,[22] the rate of shifts in Austria ranged between 3 and 7 percent until the middle of the 1980s.[23] In Germany, the rate of party shifting had exceeded 20 percent in the 1990s. At the federal parliamentary elections in 1998, the share of volatile voters amounted to almost one-fourth of the electorate, while at the national parliamentary elections 1999 in Austria the same rate only reached 18 percent. In the meantime, the electoral mobility in Austria has approached the shifting rates seen at German parliamentary elections. During the federal parliamentary elections in 2005, 28 percent of German voters changed the party for which they had previously voted.[24] In Austria, the shifting rate at the national parliamentary elections in 2006 reached 26 percent. In Sweden at the parliamentary elections in 2006, more than 30 percent changed the party for which they had previously voted.

Even the rates of change at the British General Elections increased earlier than in Austria.[25] In the 1980s, the British rates of party shifters fluctuated around 20 percent and increased during the course of the 1990s to an average of 25 percent.[26] At the General Election in 2005, 19 percent changed their voting behavior. In the United States, the shifting rates developed cyclically. During the 1980s, party shifters represented on the average one-fifth of the American electorate.[27] In the following years, these rates stabilized at around 25 to 30 percent,[28] so their share can periodically exceed 30 percent at landslide elections—like the Congressional elections in 1994 and 2006. Rates of change between 20 to 25 percent are also in no way exceptions in French parliamentary elections since the 1990s.[29] Even in the Italian parliamentary elections can a continuous increase of shifting rates be observed.[30] Though lagging behind the trend slightly, Austrian voting behavior has also approached international trends toward higher electoral mobility and readiness to change parties.[31] Whether this approximation also includes the patterns of voting behavior will be subject of the following section.

Patterns of Voting Behavior

During the 1970s, a *gender gap* regarding election behavior could be observed first in the United States and in the Scandinavian countries, then later in numerous other industrialized countries.[32] Only in the middle of the 1980s were gender-specific deviations in voting behavior noticed in Austria, such deviations bloomed in the 1990s. These deviations were the consequence of younger men supporting the right populist FPÖ, which during the 1990s was increasingly successful during elections, but was also due to the attraction that issues raised by the Greens had for women. The national election of 1999, when the FPÖ led by Jörg Haider rose to become the second strongest party, marks the culmination of electoral gender splitting until now. If the gender gap is calculated as the sum of the percentage difference between votes of men and women for parliamentary parties, the gender gap index in 1999 reached 24 points. In the meantime, the decline of the FPÖ and the restabilization of both traditional parties (SPÖ and ÖVP) led to a reduction of the gender-specific splitting in Austrian voting behavior. At the national election in 2006, the gender gap index reached 12 points and again approached internationally comparable values. Gender-specific differences in electoral behavior remained in the two right-wing populist parties (the FPÖ and BZÖ). Together they got 18 percent of the male votes, but only 13 percent of female votes. A similar pattern is also found in Italy, where at the parliamentary election in 2006, 20 percent of the men voted for the rightist National Alliance or the right populist Northern League, while only 13 percent of the female voters chose one of these two parties. Even in France in 2002, 14 percent of the men but only 10 percent of the women voted for the National Front or its offshoot, the list Megret.

The gender gap is particularly visible in American voter behavior. At the Congressional elections in 2006, 55 percent of the women voted for Democratic candidates, and only 43 percent of the female electorate gave their vote to a Republican candidate. Even more pronounced was the gender gap among younger, unmarried women, of whom 66 percent voted for a Democratic candidate and only 32 percent for a Republican candidate; this behavior is referred to as the "marriage gap" in the United States. In France, Italy, Great Britain, and Germany, no comparably strong divisions can be observed in the voting behavior of men and women.

In Italy and France, the gender gap expressed itself in a stronger support of conservative parties among women. In France in 2002, 44 percent of the women, but only 37 percent of men voted for the conservative party alliance Union for a Popular Movement (UMP). In Italy in 2006, 28 percent of females cast ballots for the conservative *Forza Italia* compared to only 21 percent of the males. A similar pattern was also noted at the British general elections in 2005, when 34 percent of the women voted for conservatives while only 29 percent of the men elected the conservative party.

In Germany and Austria, however, the social democratic parties got significantly more votes among women than among male voters. At the German parliamentary election in 2005, 36 percent of the women, but only 33 percent of the men, voted for the social democratic SPD. In Austria at the national parliamentary elections in 2006, 38 percent of female voters compared to only 34 percent of male voters cast votes for the SPÖ.

Gender-specific differences in electoral behavior have clearly gained importance, and such gender effects are more pronounced in the younger generation of voters than in the older generations. The country-specific variations in gender-specific behavior do not, however, show a common pattern which would justify identifying a definite gender splitting in electoral behavior; exceptions might be the obvious distance of female voters to militant right populist parties and a gradually more pronounced affinity of younger women for green parties, which can be observed in the voting behavior in several European countries.

Austrian electoral behavior is more strongly characterized by differences between generations rather than by gender-specific differences. Since the 1980s, the voting behavior of the younger and older generations has been drifting apart and now has resulted in a pronounced *generation gap*. At the height of the right populist momentum at the end of the 1990s, the FPÖ under Haider became the strongest party among voters under thirty years-old at the parliamentary elections in 1999;[33] the party then lost its attraction for younger voters in the following years.[34] In the meantime, the Greens caused a generation-specific realignment of the Austrian electorate. At the parliamentary elections in 2006, 22 percent of those under thirty years old voted for the Greens while only 4 percent of the oldest voter generation voted for the Greens. The SPÖ and ÖVP, as well as the two right populist parties (FPÖ and BZÖ), however, found support in the middle-aged and older voting generations. A tangentially comparable pattern is also found in German election behavior, but there it is primarily the Union parties that are negatively affected by the generation gap. In France, the generation gap concentrates primarily upon the conservative UMP. In Great Britain, the generation gap in electoral behavior is particularly manifested among the Conservatives who in the general election in 2005 were the strongest party among voters above sixty years old, but only reached third place among voters under thirty years old.[35] This generation-specific differentiation in election behavior is similarly severe in the United States: 60 percent of voters under thirty years of age cast their ballots in the Congressional elections of 2006 for Democratic candidates, and only 38 percent voted for Republican candidates.

The generation-specific pattern in Austrian voting behavior fits, with some variations, into the picture of an age-specific reorientation of the electorate, which in the international literature is referred to as "gender-generation realignment." Generally the green, left-libertarian parties exert a particularly strong influence on members of the younger voting generations. In some countries like France or Italy—just as in an impressive way in Austria during the 1990s—right populist parties also strongly attract younger—especially male—voters. Conservative parties are obviously affected more strongly by generation-specific differentiations of election behavior than social democratic parties, with the exception of Austrian and French voting behavior, where during the last parliamentary elections social democratic parties were less successful among younger voters than with those in the older population.

The generation-specific reorientation of the electoral behavior is reinforced by educational effects.[36] At the Austrian national elections in 2006, 20 percent of all younger males and 25 percent of younger males with a university degree voted for the Greens. Among younger women, 24 percent decided for the Greens, but among degreed younger women, it was 31 percent. Although the ÖVP is still the strongest party for voters in the upper educational group, the leading position in this voter segment is increasingly challenged by the growing attraction of the Greens for degree-holding young voters.

A similar pattern can be noted in Germany if education is added to the generation factor. In Italy, too, young qualified groups of voters tend ever more strongly to support parties of the left spectrum.[37] This trend is less pronounced in France although left parties are also increasingly favored over time. In Great Britain, however, it is not so much the Labour Party that profits from this generative reorientation as it is the Liberal Democrats. Finally, in the United States a great majority of younger, degree-holding voters prefer the Democrats. The Austrian version of a "gender-generation-education realignment" as it showed during the parliamentary elections in 2006 clearly fits an international pattern whose outlines point in the direction of "postmodern" election behavior.[38] However, retarding influences should not be underestimated without sufficient qualification, for contrary trends among members of the youngest voter generation, who in Austria, the Federal Republic of Germany, Italy, and France are also mobilized by right populist parties.

Austria, together with Germany and the Netherlands, is among those countries where confessional voting behavior is especially pronounced;

164 The Changing Austrian Voter

however, in Austria it is less the denominational affiliation that influences the voting decision (76 percent of the Austrian electorate are Catholics, 6 percent Protestants, and 3 percent belong to other religions) than the church attachments. The great majority of voters with strong religious affiliations—operationalized as regular participation in religious service—votes for the conservative, Christian Democratic ÖVP, while those distant from the church or not practicing a faith mostly vote for the social democratic SPÖ. For decades, the ÖVP has been able to count on roughly

Table 5
Generation Gap in Electoral Behavior, in Percent Voted

	Over 60 Years Old	Under 30 Years Old	PPD
Austria (2006)			
Greens	4	22	+18
SPÖ	41	32	-9
ÖVP	38	30	-8
FPÖ+BZÖ	16	11	-5
Germany (2005)			
Left parties	7	8	+1
Greens	5	10	+5
SPD	34	35	+1
CDU+CSU	43	29	-14
FDP	9	11	+2
United States (2006)			
France (2002)			
EL+PCF+Verts	8	18	+10
PS	25	19	-6
UMP+UDF+DVD	52	37	-15
FN+Megret	8	12	+4
Great Britain (2005)			
Lab	36	45	+9
Lib. Dem.	18	30	+12
Con	41	20	-21
Italy (2006)			
Altri Sinist	8	4	-4
RC+CI+Verdi	6	16	+10
Ulivo	33	27	-6
Udc	10	4	-6
FI	28	26	-2
An+Ln	16	23	+7

Source: National election studies.

60 percent of the votes of regular church goers, so the SPÖ only receives about 22 percent of the votes of persons with church affiliations.

Even stronger than in Austria, the patterns of religious voting can be observed in Germany where the Christian Democratic Union in 2005 received 67 percent of the votes of confessional voters. In France, again it was the conservative UMP which was able to convince 64 percent of regular church goers to support their party at the parliamentary elections in 2002. In Italy, the pattern of confessional voting is less pronounced. During the parliamentary elections in 2006, two parties—the *Forza Italia* as well as the Christian democratic Udc—received disproportionately higher support from voters with strong confessional ties.

In the United States, however, an ever deepening religious divide of the American electorate can be observed since the 1980s. A majority of steady church goers—55 percent—voted at the Congressional elections in 2006 for Republican candidates, only 43 percent for Democrats, who, on the other hand, found support among occasional church goers gaining 60 percent of their vote and among those distant from the church gaining 67 percent of their vote. Still more pronounced was the confessional splitting among evangelical voters in the United States, 70 percent of whom voted for Republican candidates. Deep-seated social, moral, and cultural value conflicts polarizing the American people are at the source of this "god gap" in U.S. electoral behavior. In the United Kingdom, this confessional factor plays a minor role, and only partially favors the electoral chances of the conservative party.[39]

Confessional determinants of election behavior are apparently more consistent than class voting,[40] which in the Western democracies including Austria continuously weakened during the last decades.41 By comparison, the pattern of union voting proved to be relatively robust. Union members mostly vote for social democratic parties, yet even this relationship gradually weakened over time. Only 51 percent of Austrian union members voted for the SPÖ in 2006 compared to 62 percent in 1990. However, the pattern of union voting continues to be a constant factor in Austrian voting behavior which can also be observed in other countries. The German SPD ranks 15 percentage points higher among union members than among non-members, just like the SPÖ in Austria. On the other hand, the conservative parties, the ÖVP as well as its German counterpart the CDU/CSU, reached a plurality among non-union members. While in Great Britain the Labour Party also received more support from union members than from non-union members, the Conservatives stayed behind the Labour Party among non-members, too.

In the United States, union membership marks a constant division in electoral behavior. Yet the relevance for electoral politics should not be overestimated due to the continuous decline of union membership in the United States where only 9 percent of all employees in the private sector are union members. Nevertheless, union member voting patterns can still prove to be decisive because of the higher rate of voting participation among union members. Sixty-eight percent of union members voted for a Democratic candidate at the Congressional elections in 2006; only 30 percent voted for Republican candidates. However, with a share of 48 percent of the votes among non-union members, even in this voter segment the Republicans still remained behind the Democrats whose overwhelming victory in closely contested, highly competitive races can still be reduced to the union gap in U.S. electoral behavior.

The pattern of union voting is, to a lesser degree, also reflected in the voting behavior of the working class. At the U.S. congressional elections in 2006, 60 percent of the blue collar-vote concentrated on Democratic candidates. The British Labour Party received similar support from the working-class vote in 2005. During the French parliamentary elections in 2002, the parties belonging to the left received more than 60 percent of the working-class vote. The trend of class-voting was, however, much more erratic in Austria. During the 1990s, a spectacular reorientation of the labor vote took place, when these voters left the SPÖ and changed to the right populist FPÖ. Between 1986 and 1999, the share of Austrian workers who voted for the FPÖ quadrupled. At the parliamentary elections in 1999, the FPÖ became the strongest party among workers with 47 percent of the vote. Only 35 percent of the working class voted for the social democratic party.[42] The following decline of the FPÖ led to a reorientation of electoral behavior among workers, who again voted predominantly for the social democrats at the parliamentary elections in 2002. In 2006, 47 percent of the blue-collar workers voted for the SPÖ, 25 percent for the conservative ÖVP, and 18 percent for the FPÖ. However, the FPÖ again succeeded in getting protest votes from the working class in 2006. Among male workers, the FPÖ received a disproportionate share of 24 percent of the votes. Regarding the pattern of class voting, Austria represents an exception in spite of the gradual return of the blue-collar vote to the SPÖ. The patterns are in no way as stable as in other Western European countries.

In Germany, class voting has comparably weakened. At the national election in 2005, 37 percent of the blue-collar vote went to the SPD and 30 percent to the CDU/CSU. Class voting in Germany appears even

Table 6
Church Attendance and Electoral Behavior, in Percent Voted

	Regular Church Goers	Occasional Church Goers	Non-Church Goers	PPD
Austria (2006)				
Greens	6	9	18	-12
SPÖ	22	39	40	-18
ÖVP	59	33	15	+44
FPÖ+BZÖ	8	16	18	-10
Germany (2005)				
Left parties	0	1	5	-5
Greens	6	12	10	-4
SPD	21	34	46	-25
CDU+CSU	69	45	32	+37
FDP	3	8	5	-2
United States (2006)				
Dem	43	59	67	-24
Rep	55	39	30	+25
France (2002)				
EL+PCF+Verts	6	11	14	-8
PS	16	19	28	-12
UMP+UDF+DVD	64	50	33	+31
FN+Megret	9	13	13	-4
Great Britain (2005)				
Lab	41	38	41	0
Lib. Dem.	25	25	29	-4
Con	34	38	30	+4
Italy (2006)				
Altri Sinistra	7	12	14	-7
RC+CI+Verdi	3	6	14	-11
Ulivo	27	35	35	-8
Udc	14	4	2	+12
FI	30	23	17	+13
An+Ln	17	16	16	-1

Source: National election studies.

more complex if a differentiation is made between western and eastern Germany. Diverging trends in the old and new provinces as well as the attraction of the Left Party (PDS) for workers in the eastern regions result in a stratified picture of professionally related voting behavior in Germany.[43]

Table 7
Union Membership and Electoral Behavior, in Percent Voted

		Union Members	Non-Members	PPD
Austria	(2006)			
Greens		10	11	-1
SPÖ		51	26	+25
ÖVP		21	41	-20
FPÖ+BZÖ		10	17	-7
Germany	(2005)			
Left parties		13	8	+5
Greens		8	8	0
SPD		47	32	+15
CDU+CSU		24	37	-13
FDP		6	11	-5
United States	(2006)			
Dem		68	50	+18
Rep		30	48	-18
Great Britain	(2005)			
Lab		50	40	+10
Lib. Dem.		25	24	+1
Con		25	36	-9

Source: National election studies.

Besides factors like gender, generation, education, confession, union affiliation, and profession, an accurate predictor of the voting decision is the ideological position of voters—their self-positioning on the left-right-continuum. "Voters' left-right positions are strongly related to party choice";[44] this relationship can be stronger or weaker in different countries. This can also be reduced to the degree of ideological polarization of contesting parties and their respective positions in the party systems. Although the ideological polarization of the electorate in Austria is only moderate compared to other countries and the majority is positioned close to the ideological center, the patterns result in a clearly differentiating picture. Three-quarters of the voters who positioned themselves left of the center also voted for a party in the left segment (55 percent for the SPÖ, 22 percent for the Greens) at the parliamentary elections in 2006. Conversely, 80 percent of the voters positioned right of the center decided for a party in the right segment (54 percent for the ÖVP, 25 percent for the FPÖ or BZÖ). Comparable relationships can also be found in other European countries and are even more pronounced and divisive than in Austria.

In the United States, 87 percent of self-declared liberals voted for Democratic candidates at the Congressional elections in 2006, while 78 percent of self-declared conservatives preferred Republican candidates. In Germany, 90 percent of all voters who positioned themselves left of the center also voted for a party in the left segment, which in Germany consists of the Left Party (PDS), the Greens, and the SPD. The patterns are similar in France and in Great Britain.

The left-right continuum still defines the interpretation and evaluation of societal problems to a high degree as "super issues" or ideological "short cuts,"[45] whereby the positioning of voters on the left-right continuum can only in part be reduced to sociocultural characteristics.[46] Austrian voting behavior is—although less so than in more polarized countries—characterized by ideological views and attitudes. Due to a greater polarization of parties and of the electorate in the United States, France, and Italy, such ideological positioning leads to a stronger ideological differentiation of the voting decision than in Germany or Great Britain, where the majority of voters—just like in Austria—are positioned close to the ideological center. In 2006, 33 percent positioned themselves left of the center, 32 percent in the middle, and 28 percent right of the center. In the United States in 2004, however, only 24 percent of the voters positioned themselves in the middle; 43 percent took a position right of the center, and only 19 percent took a position left of the center.[47]

The findings described above have drawn a dynamic picture of Austrian voting behavior which clearly differs from the view of a traditional, party-loyal, and calculable electorate. In fact, national deviations from international trends in electoral behavior are smaller than similarities and concordance. This is true for constant as well as variable factors of voting behavior. Traditional determinants like those found in the election behavior of other countries appear beside new patterns, pointing to a lasting transformation of Austrian voting behavior, which—and this is particularly unusual—only became visible in Austria with considerable delay. In addition, there are temporary turbulences in voting behavior, which were caused by the electoral increase of a right populist party—the FPÖ under Haider—during the 1990s and left their traces on Austrian electoral behavior. While Austrian voting behavior had briefly—at the height of the right populist impact at the national parliamentary elections in 1999—distanced itself from European electoral trends, it again approximated Western European standards and patterns thereafter. How far this approximation took place, how deep-seated the shown similarities really are, if and how Austrian electoral behavior will still differ from

170 The Changing Austrian Voter

that in Germany, Italy, France, Great Britain, and the United States, will be examined in the final section on the basis of multivariate models and estimates.

Comparative Modeling of Austrian Electoral Behavior

Multinomial logit regressions models, as described, for example by Alan Agresti,[48] allow the simultaneous assessment of various effects

Table 8
Ideological Position and Electoral Behavior, in Percent Voted

	Very Left	More Left	Center	More Right	Very Right
Austria (2006)					
Greens	32	21	10	3	0
SPÖ	58	54	35	15	14
ÖVP	5	14	39	54	53
FPÖ+BZÖ	0	4	17	24	33
Germany (2005)					
Left parties	20	4	1	0	0
Greens	18	23	7	1	2
SPD	48	64	34	4	16
CDU+CSU	7	8	49	88	74
FDP	4	0	8	5	2
United States (2006)					
Dem	94	78	60	35	33
Rep	6	22	40	65	67
France (2002)					
EL+PCF+Verts	58	26	7	0	3
PS	25	59	16	2	0
UMP+UDF+DVD	3	6	59	76	9
FN+Megret	0	2	7	13	89
Great Britain (2005)					
Lab	69	62	43	25	31
Lib. Dem.	29	33	30	12	6
Con	2	5	27	63	64
Italy (2001)					
Rifundazione Communista	40	15	2	0	0
Democratici Sinistra	35	53	20	0	0
La Margherita	11	17	20	2	1
Forza Italia	1	5	33	58	53
An+Ln	0	0	6	28	40

Source: National election studies.

on a categorical outcome variable—vote choice in this case. The probability of voting for a particular party is compared to the probability of voting for a specific party chosen as a point of reference by using a logit transformation and assuming a linear effect of independent variables on these logits. Model parameters are interpreted much like parameters in linear regression, except that they operate on a logit scale rather than a linear scale.

First, a model is fitted to the Austrian 2006 election data, including some basic variables of interest, that have deliberately been chosen to allow comparison with similar or identical variables in the other national election data sets. In a second step, the same model is fitted to the national data, dropping effects that appear not to be significant.

As a reference category, parties on or right of the political center have been chosen: ÖVP for Austria, CDU/CSU for Germany, Republicans for the United States, UMP/UDF/DVD for France, Conservatives for Great Britain, and Forza Italia for Italy.

As it turns out, Austrian voters are not a species very different to citizens in those advanced Western democracies that have been analyzed. In particular, we find evidence for the existence of a gender gap in all six countries except France. Overall, women are more likely to vote for left leaning or green parties. As an Austrian peculiarity, the gender effect is moderated by education: better educated women tend to favor the Greens. An almost identical pattern shows up for citizens of thirty years of age or younger. Ideological orientations and voters' self-positioning on the left-right continuum prove to be a highly significant predictor for voting behavior in all six countries studied. The intensity of religious beliefs measured by the frequency of church attendance does have a strong effect on voting behavior, although the patterns differ in the various countries. Members of trade unions in all countries voted in a significantly higher proportion for left leaning parties.

In spite of the effects of societal modernization on voting behavior and independent from different electoral party systems in the respective countries, church attendance, union membership, and the left-right orientations of voters affect electoral choices to a significant degree. Austrian electoral behavior fits into this pattern to a remarkable extent. Focusing on central patterns of electoral behavior, Austria conforms to the mainstream trends that are observable in advanced Western democracies.

Table 9
A Multinomial Logit Model for the Austrian Elections, 2006

Effects	Grüne			SPÖ			FPÖ/BZÖ		
	Parameter		SE	Parameter		SE	Parameter		SE
Women	-0.57		0.78	0.56	*	0.34	0.10		0.42
Secondary	-0.60		0.63	-0.09		0.31	0.45		0.37
Secondary Education × Women (interaction)	1.36		0.86	-0.60		0.39	-0.37		0.47
Higher Education	0.63		0.59	-0.88	***	0.32	-0.57		0.39
Higher Education × Women (interaction)	0.60		0.81	-0.58		0.40	-0.21		0.51
Age < 30	0.34		0.27	0.01		0.24	0.19		0.29
Age > 60	-1.23	***	0.31	0.32	**	0.15	0.08		0.19
Left-Right-Position	-3.40	***	0.31	-2.46	***	0.24	0.91	***	0.24
Close to a Party	-0.21		0.19	-0.27	**	0.13	-0.80	***	0.16
Attached to Trade Union	0.41	**	0.20	1.36	***	0.14	0.37	**	0.18
No Religious Denomination	0.20		0.65	-0.75		0.52	0.01		0.60
Protestant	-0.62		0.73	-1.39	**	0.57	-0.29		0.64
Catholic, Regularly Attending Servicess	-1.48	**	0.66	-2.85	***	0.51	-2.39		0.60
Catholic, Sporadically Attending Services	-1.15	*	0.63	-1.73	***	0.49	-1.08	*	0.57
Constant	-0.61		0.84	1.58	***	0.57	0.46		67

Deviance: 3503.2 (5211 d.f.), AIC: 3593.2 Significance Levels: *: p=0,1, **: p=0,05, ***: p=0.01

Source: Austrian Election Study 2006, GfK.

Table 10
A Multinomial Logit Model for the German Elections, 2002

Effects	PDS		Grüne		SPD		FDP	
	Parameter	SE	Parameter	SE	Parameter	SE	Parameter	SE
Women	0.23	0.25	0.31 *	0.17	0.25 **	0.11	-0.13	0.18
Secondary Education	-0.30	0.32	0.25	0.23	-0.56 ***	0.14	-0.16	0.21
Higher Education	0.38	0.31	1.23 ***	0.22	-0.23	0.15	0.06	0.23
Age < 30	0.51 *	0.30	-0.19	0.21	-0.27 *	0.16	-0.38	0.25
Age > 60	0.45	0.31	-0.73 ***	0.23	-0.29 **	0.13	-0.48 **	0.21
Left-Right-Position	-4.81 ***	0.34	-3.42 ***	0.24	-3.00 ***	0.17	-0.88 ***	0.24
Close to a Party	-0.73 ***	0.25	0.17	0.19	0.05	0.12	-0.55 ***	0.18
Attached to Trade Union	0.81 **	0.32	0.36	0.25	0.75 ***	0.17	-0.19	0.31
Protestant, Regularly Attending Services	-1.74 ***	0.32	-0.13	0.21	-0.21	0.15	0.48 *	0.26
Protestant, Sporadically Attending Services	-1.76 **	0.76	0.32	0.40	-0.44	0.30	0.07	0.50
Catholic, Regularly Attending Services	-2.27 ***	0.40	-0.68 ***	0.24	-0.68 ***	0.17	-0.16	0.29
Catholic, Sporadically Attending Services	-2.77 ***	0.56	-1.94 ***	0.38	-1.82 ***	0.21	-0.51	0.33
Constant	-1.96 ***	0.40	-1.94 ***	0.30	0.38 **	0.19	-1.02 ***	0.30

Deviance: 4729.9 (9092 d.f.), AIC:4833.9 Significance Levels: *: p=0,1, **: p=0,05, ***:p=0.01
Source: German Election Study 2002, Zentralarchiv für empirische Sozialforschung, Universität Köln (ZA3861).

174 The Changing Austrian Voter

Table 11
A Multinomial Logit Model for the U.S. Midterm (House) Elections, 2004

	Democrats	
Effects	Parameter	SE
Women	0.33 *	0.18
Secondary Education	-0.48 **	0.24
Higher Education	-0.61 ***	0.21
Age < 30	0.47 *	0.27
Age > 60	0.19	0.21
Left-Right-Position	-1.83 ***	0.22
Close to a Party	-0.18	0.19
Attached to Trade Union	-0.05	0.26
Regularly Attending Religious Services	-0.11	0.20
Sporadically Attending Religious Services	0.53 *	0.29
Constant	0.61 ***	23

Deviance: 750.6, AIC:772.6
Significance levels: *: p=0,1, **: p=0,05, ***:p=0.01
Source: ANES 2004.

Table 12
A Multinomial Logit Model for the French Parliamentary Elections, 2002

	EL+PCF+Verts		PS		FN+Mégret	
Effects	Parameter	SE	Parameter	SE	Parameter	SE
Women	0.34	0.30	0.15	0.25	-0.38	0.26
Secondary Education	-0.81 *	0.46	-0.64 *	0.39	-0.53	0.37
Higher Education	-1.16 **	0.46	-0.53	0.38	-0.92 **	0.40
Age < 30	0.52	0.40	-0.28	0.36	-0.77 **	0.39
Age > 60	-0.94 **	0.38	-0.48	0.29	-1.05 ***	0.34
Left-Right-Position	-5.36 ***	0.49	-4.55 ***	0.41	1.09 ***	0.40
Close to a Party	0.94 ***	0.32	1.25 ***	0.28	0.24	0.28
Without Religious Denomination	-0.10	0.58	-0.39	0.51	0.78	0.65
Protestant	-0.89	0.92	-1.31 *	0.79	0.95	0.84
Catholic, Regularly Attending Services	-1.64 **	0.68	-1.51 ***	0.54	-0.53	0.69
Catholic, Sporadically Attending Services	-1.10 *	0.62	-1.23	0.53	-0.18	0.66
Constant	0.30	0.72	0.72 **	0.62	-0.74	0.75

Deviance: 1270.9 (2424 d.f.), AIC:1342.9 Significance Levels: *: p=0,1, **: p=0,05, ***:p=0.01
Note: Trade union membership not available.
Source: Panel électoral français 2002, Centre de données socio-politiques, Sciences Po.

Table 13
A Multinomial Logit Model for the UK General Elections, 2005

Effects	Labour		LibDem	
	Parameter	SE	Parameter	SE
Women	0.37 ***	0.11	0.32 ***	0.12
Secondary Education	-0.42 ***	0.14	-0.04	0.16
Higher Education	-0.47 ***	0.12	0.16	0.13
Age < 30	0.18	0.15	0.46 ***	0.16
Age > 60	-0.31 **	0.13	-0.07	0.15
Left-Right-Position	-1.15 ***	0.11	-1.29 ***	0.12
Close to a Party	0.06	0.11	-0.80 ***	0.12
Attached to Trade Union	0.45 ***	0.11	0.42 ***	0.12
Regularly Attending Religious Services	-0.10	0.17	-0.31 *	0.19
Sporadically Attending Religious Services	-0.34 **	0.14	-0.31 **	0.15
Constant	0.56 ***	0.13	0.28 *	0.14

Deviance: 4600.6 (4500 d.f.), AIC: 4644.6

Significance levels: *: p=0,1, **: p=0,05, ***:p=0.01

Source: Comparative Study of Electoral Systems UK 2005.

Table 14
A Multinomial Logit Model for the Italian Parliamentary Elections, 2001
(Proportional Vote for the Chamber)

Effects	RC+CI+Verdi		Margherita+DS		AN+LN	
	Parameter	SE	Parameter	SE	Parameter	SE
Women	-0.35	0.22	0.07	0.15	-0.55 ***	0.14
Secondary Education	0.23	0.33	0.08	0.21	0.79 ***	0.21
Higher Education	0.35	0,46	0.08	0.33	1.35 ***	0.30
Age < 30	-0.97 ***	0.31	-0.63 ***	0.20	-0.09	0.18
Age > 60	0.22	0.27	-0.16	0.20	0.06	0.17
Left-Right-Position	-7.34 ***	0.39	-5.39 ***	0.30	1.23 ***	0.20
Close to a Party	0.59 **	23	43 ***	16	0.19	0.14
Attached to Trade Union	0.40	0.28	0.58 ***	0.20	-0.02	0.21
Catholic, Regularly Attending Services	-0.25	0.29	-0.19	0.21	-0.30	0.20
Catholic, Sporadically Attending Services	-0.55 **	0.28	-0.36 *	0.21	0.00	0.19
Constant	-1.72 ***	0.44	0.27	0.29	-1.71 ***	0.29

Deviance: 3280.8 (5784 d.f.), AIC:3346.8; Significance levels: *: p=0,1, **: p=0,05, ***:p=0.01

Source: ITANES 2001, Istituto Carlo Cattaneo Research Foundation.

Notes

1. Oscar W. Gabriel and Silke J. Keil, "Empirische Wahlforschung in Deutschland: Kritik und Entwicklungsperspektiven," in *Handbuch Wahlforschung*, ed. Jürgen W. Falter and Harald Schoen (Wiesbaden: VS Verlag für Sozialwissenschaften, 2005), 611-641, here 640.

2. The initiative was started by the SORA Institute in Vienna. The data set is not yet available.

3. Rüdiger Schmitt-Beck, *Politische Kommunikation und Wählerverhalten: Ein internationaler Vergleich* (Wiesbaden: Westdeutscher Verlag, 2000); Harald Schoen, *Wählerwandel und Wechselwahl: Eine vergleichende Untersuchung* (Wiesbaden: VS Verlag für Sozialwissenschaften, 2003).

4. Jaques Thomassen, ed., *The European Voter: A Comparative Study of Modern Democracies* (Oxford: Oxford UP, 2005).

5. Russell J. Dalton, *Citizen Politics: Public Opinion and Political Parties in Advanced Industrial Democracies*, 4th ed. (Washington, D.C.: CQ Press, 2006).

6. Paul Nieuwbeerta and Jeff Manza, "Klassen-, Religions- und Geschlechterspaltung: Parteien und Gesellschaften im Vergleich," in *Das Ende der politisierten Sozialstruktur?*, ed. Frank Brettschneider et al. (Opladen: Leske + Budrich, 2002), 247-78; Oddbjorn Knutsen, "Education and Party Choice in Eight West European Countries: A Comparative Longitudinal Study," *Das Ende der politisierten Sozialstruktur?*, ed. Frank Brettschneider et al. (Opladen: Leske + Budrich, 2002), 315-46; Martin Elff, "Social Structure and Electoral Behavior in Comparative Perspective," *Perspectives on Politics* 5(1): forthcoming.

7. Geoffrey Evans, ed., *The End of Class Politics? Class Voting in Comparative Perspective* (Oxford: Oxford UP, 1999).

8. Frank Brettschneider, *Spitzenkandidaten und Wahlerfolg. Personalisierung—Kompetenz—Parteien: Ein internationaler Vergleich* (Wiesbaden: Westdeutscher Verlag, 2002); Anthony King, ed., *Leaders' Personalities and the Outcome of Democratic Elections* (Oxford: Oxford UP, 2002) Kees Aarts et al., eds., *Political Leaders and Democratic Elections* (Oxford: Oxford UP, forthcoming 2008).

9. David M. Farrell and Rüdiger Schmitt-Beck, eds., *Do Political Campaigns Matter? Campaign Effects in Elections and Referendums* (London: Routledge, 2002).

10. Herbert Kitschelt, *The Radical Right in Western Europe: A Comparative Analysis* (Ann Arbor, MI: U of Michigan P, 1995); Terri E. Givens, *Voting Radical Right in Western Europe* (New York: Cambridge UP, 2006); Pippa Norris, *Radical Right: Voters and Parties in the Electoral Market* (New York: Cambridge UP, 2005).

11. Cees Van der Eijk and Mark N. Franklin, eds., *Choosing Europe? The European Electorate and National Politics in the Face of Union* (Ann Arbor, MI: U of Michigan P, 1996); Cees Van der Eijk, Mark Franklin, and B. Guy Peters, *Voters and Elections* (London: forthcoming 2008).

12. Pippa Norris, *Democratic Phoenix: Reinventing Political Activism* (New York: Cambridge UP, 2002); Mark N. Franklin, *Voter Turnout and the Dynamics of Electoral Competition in Established Democracies since 1945* (New York: Cambridge UP, 2004).

13. Pippa Norris, *Electoral Engineering: Voting Rules and Political Behavior* (New York: Cambridge UP, 2004).

14. Fritz Plasser with Gunda Plasser, *Global Political Campaigning: A Worldwide Analysis of Campaign Professionals and Their Practices* (Westport CT: Praeger, 2002).

15. Franklin, *Voter Turnout*, 11.

16. See Norris, *Democratic Phoenix*; Franklin, *Voter Turnout*.

17. Dalton, *Citizen Politics*, 38-42.

18. See ITANES, ed., *Dov'è la vittoria? Il voto del 2006 raccontato dagli italiani* (Bologna: Il mulino, 2006).

19. Frode Berglund et al., "Party Identification and Party Choice," in *The European Voter: A Comparative Study of Modern Democracies*, ed. Jacques Thomassen (Oxford: Oxford UP, 2005), 106-24, here 122-23.

20. Dalton, *Citizen Politics*, 189.

21. Peter Mair, Wolfgang C. Müller, and Fritz Plasser, eds., *Political Parties and Electoral Change: Party Responses to Electoral Markets* (London: Sage, 2004).

22. Schoen, *Wählerwandel und Wechselwahl*, 131.

23. Fritz Plasser and Peter A. Ulram, eds., *Wahlverhalten in Bewegung: Analysen zur Nationalratswahl 2002* (Vienna: WUV-Universitätsverlag, 2003), 106.

24. Eckhard Jesse and Roland Sturm, eds., *Bilanz der Bundestagswahl2005* (Wiesbaden: VS Verlag für Sozialwissenschaften, 2006).

25. Harold Clarke et al., *Political Choice in Britain* (Oxford: Oxford UP, 2004).

26. Schoen, *Wählerwandel und Wechselwahl*, 128.

27. Ibid., 125.

28. Alan Abramowitz, *Voice of the People: Elections and Voting in the United States* (New York: McGraw-Hill, 2004); William H. Flanigan, *Political Behavior of the American Electorate*, 11th ed. (Washington, D.C.: CQ Press, 2006).

29. John Gaffney, ed., *The French Presidential and Legislative Elections of 2002* (London: Ashgate, 2004); Michael S. Lewis-Beck, ed., *The French Voter: Before and After the 2002 Elections* (London: Palgrave Macmillan, 2003).

30. See James Newell, ed., *The Italian General Election of 2001* (Manchester: Manchester UP, 2002); ITANES, ed., *Dov'è la vittoria?*

31. The higher mobility also shows in the volatility (one-half of the sum of voting changes for all parties). It amounted to 8.1 points in Germany 2005, to 9.3 in France 2002, to 5.4 in Great Britain 2005 and to 8.6 points in Austria 2006.

32. Nieuwbeerta and Manza, "Klassen-, Religions- und Geschlechterspaltung"; Ronald Inglehart and Pippa Norris, *Rising Tide: Gender Equality and Cultural Change around the World* (New York: Cambridge UP, 2003).

33. Fritz Plasser, Peter A. Ulram, and Franz Sommer, eds., *Das österreichische Wahlverhalten* (Vienna: Signum, 2000).

34. Plasser and Ulram, eds., *Wahlverhalten in Bewegung*.

35. Pippa Norris and Christopher Wlezien, eds., *Britain Votes* (Oxford: Oxford UP, 2005).

36. Knutsen, "Education and Party Choice in Eight West European Countries," 315-46.

37. See ITANES, ed., *Dov'è la vittoria?*.

38. See Dalton, *Citizen Politics*.

39. Andrew Geddes and Jonathan Tonge, *Britain Decides: The UK General Election 2005* (London: Palgrave Macmillan, 2006).

40. Maria Oskarson, "Social Structure and Party Choice," in *The European Voter: A Comparative Study of Modern Democracies*, ed. Jacques Thomassen (Oxford: Oxford UP, 2005), 84-105, here 96.

41. See Evans, *The End of Class Politics?*

42. Plasser and Ulram, *Wahlverhalten in Bewegung*, 123-31.

43. Jürgen W. Falter, Oscar W. Gabriel, and Bernhard Wessels, eds., *Wahlen und Wähler: Analysen aus Anlass der Bundestagswahl 2002* (Wiesbaden: VS Verlag für Sozialwissenschaften, 2005); Frank Brettschneider, Jan van Deth, and Edeltraud Roller, eds., *Die Bundestagswahl 2002* (Wiesbaden: VS Verlag für Sozialwissenschaften, 2004).

44. Cees Van der Eijk, Hermann Schmitt, and Tanja Binder, "Left-Right Orientations and Party Choice," in *The European Voter: A Comparative Study of Modern Democracies*, ed. Jacques Thomassen (Oxford: Oxford UP, 2005), 167-91, here 180.

45. Dalton, *Citizen Politics*, 209-12.

46. Van der Eijk et al., "Left-Right Orientations," 180-82.

47. American National Election Studies, *2004 National Election Study Dataset* (Ann Arbor, MI: U of Michigan, Center for Political Studies, 2004) <www.electionstudies.org>.

48. Alan Agresti, *Categorical Data Analysis*, 2nd ed. (New York: Wiley-Interscience, 2002), Chapter 7.

FORUM

Austrian Experts Interpret the National Elections of October 1, 2006

Political Discontent, Negative Campaigning, and an Overrated Monster: A Short Comment on the Austrian Parliamentary Elections of 2006

Rudolf Bretschneider

The Austrian parliamentary elections of 2006 were characterized by a decrease of electoral turnout, heavy losses of the incumbent ÖVP, and smaller losses of the oppositional SPÖ. The FPÖ and BZÖ (the "successor parties" of the "old FPÖ") increased their share of votes (a combined 15 percent compared to 10 percent). Minor gains were made by the Greens and the Communist Party. The latter did not enter parliament, nor did the new party of the European Parliament MP Martin which polled less than 3 percent.

Campaigning and events during the campaign period proved to be decisive for the final outcome of the two great parties, the ÖVP and SPÖ. The ÖVP entered the race from a leading position, but lost many voters during the campaign and came in second albeit by a small margin. The ÖVP had concentrated the campaign on its past merits, but was not able to formulate new political directions or to appease the latent discontent of a sizable share of the electorate by adapting its substantive and/or personnel propositions. Furthermore, the party did not succeed in influencing the dominant public agenda or countering the campaign strategy of the SPÖ. The ÖVP thus lost voters in all directions, mainly to the growing number of non-voters but also to all other competing parties. The SPÖ, on the other hand, ran two parallel campaigns: a positive one combining social populist requests with demands for a cut in taxes, and a negative one accusing the ÖVP and the chancellor of not having kept past electoral promises. The SPÖ's primary aim was to reinforce the negative mood of a part of the electorate and direct it against the ÖVP and to mobilize social democratic core voters. The strategy was relatively successful. Although the SPÖ convinced only a small number of people to switch their vote in its favor, the party was able to damage the incumbent and to limit its own losses.

However, the SPÖ had to pay a price for the populist and negative campaigning after election day. Lacking sufficient strength to govern alone and flinching from the prospect of a minority government, the SPÖ had to form a coalition government with its former adversary. At this point, it became clear that many electoral promises had been unrealistic and the "read my lips" strategy of the SPÖ's top candidate and new chancellor backfired: the party lost much of its former credibility and suffered a severe decline in the polls in the first months of 2007. Perhaps more important will be the overall effects on campaigning in Austria. Until now, hard and very personalized negative campaigning had been restricted to the fringes of the political spectrum. With the elections of 2006, it has become firmly established and will be the rule rather than the exception in the future.

As mentioned above, the parties of the radical populist right increased their share of votes. However, this should not be overestimated. Radical right-wing populism had been most successful in the late 1990s when the FPÖ (then under the leadership of Jörg Haider) mobilized discontent about the traditional parties and the grand SPÖ-ÖVP coalition which had become a symbol for featherbedding, cronyism, spoil system politics, political deadlock, and resistance to change. The FPÖ also exploited and highlighted fears especially among members of the lower educational and social strata concentrating on the issue of foreign immigration. After the FPÖ entered government in 2000, it soon became clear that the party could not deliver, lacked qualified programs and personnel, and was torn between populist appeals and the necessities and constraints of governmental politics. As a consequence, the FPÖ lost about 60 percent of its former voters in 2002 and split three years later. The stronger successor party (the FPÖ) was voted for mostly because of its stand on the issue of immigration. Nevertheless, even the combined vote of the

FPÖ and BZÖ in 2006 was far less than the FPÖ's result in 1999 (26.9 percent). One thing holds true for both the old and the new FPÖ: their electoral support depended and depends mainly on the performance of the governing parties and its ability to focus on emotionalized issues, while ideological considerations were and are largely absent. In this as well as in many other respects, Austria is not a special case, but Austrian politics and voters are deeply embedded in the West European mainstream.

Note

1. For a detailed analysis, see Fritz Plasser and Peter A. Ulram, eds., *Wechselwahlen: Analysen zur Nationalratswahl 2006* (Vienna: forthcoming 2007), and Thomas Hofer, "Der Triumph des Negative Campaign," in *Wahl 2006: Kanzler, Kampagnen, Kapriolen*, ed. Thomas Hofer and Barbara Toth (Vienna: Lit Verlag, 2007).

Europeanization in Disguise

Peter Gerlich

> *Die internationalen Entwicklungen haben die öster-*
> *reichische Politik stärker beeinflusst, als man in der*
> *Hektik des Tagesgeschehens wahrnimmt.*
> *Gerfried Sperl*

If it is true that political systems demonstrate their dominant character-istics during election time, one has to conclude that the political system of Austria has not yet arrived in Europe. Looking at the process of the 2006 election in a broader sense, at the campaign, at the actual voting, and at the negotiations leading to the formation of a new government, one can observe trends toward an Americanization and possibly a Reaustrifica-tion of Austrian politics, but hardly any orientation towards the European Union or towards patterns of politics in other member states.

All observers agree that the 2006 campaign was characterized by an import of experts, strategies, and techniques from the United States. That was particularly true for the campaign of the SPÖ. It closely followed U.S. models, even imitating television spots from recent American elec-toral contests, applying negative campaign strategies (accusing the repre-sentatives of the incumbent government of lying), and careful coaching and training of the top candidate, Alfred Gusenbauer, for his appearance in the many television confrontations. In contrast, the campaign of the incumbent People's Party (ÖVP) tried to rely only on past successes and appeared rather passive and uninspired. Nevertheless, even this party as well as the smaller parties tried to organize their campaigns according to the U.S.-inspired rules of media politics: they practiced personaliza-tion, dramatization, and scandalization. The campaigns were organized not so much around issues, but around the top candidates. Maybe it was a weakness of the ÖVP campaign that Chancellor Wolfgang Schüssel participated only in a few of the many television confrontations and allowed himself to be represented by various politicians in others. A sense of drama was heightened by carefully trying to manipulate the continuing political show in order to represent one's own candidates in the best way. Great emphasis was placed on the emotionalization of issues and conflicts. Continuing references to failures and problems of one's contenders served the need of the media for the daily scandal.

It was remarkable to observe how the issues raised were not only not the most pressing let alone the most relevant problems which the country faced (like, for example, politics discussed or promoted by the European Union), but that campaign issues seemed, rather, to appear almost by chance. Some of the controversies involved the size of school classes or the cost of university tuitions, a situation obviously related to the fact that the campaign did take place while schools and universities happened to start their respective academic years. Likewise, the issue of illegal foreign workers in the private care of old people was raised almost by chance because of a letter to the editor of a newspaper which alleged that such help had been used by the family of Chancellor Schüssel. Europeanization of the electoral campaign would not only have meant that elections in other European countries rather than in United States should have served as models but also that issues decided by the European Union should have been made central to the campaign. That did not, however, happen except in very negative and populist anti-European ways by the smaller right-wing parties.

The outcome of the election surprised almost everyone. It certainly constituted a defeat for pollsters, journalists, and many other partly self-declared experts who had predicted that Schüssel's ÖVP would be ahead. While both big parties lost votes, the ÖVP admittedly more than the SPÖ, the real winners in terms of seats gained were the Greens (who managed to achieve third place) as well as the FPÖ. The SPÖ, however, undoubtedly managed to dominate on the election's eve by successfully defining itself as the winner.

All kinds of expert theories were brought forward by commentators to explain the rather unexpected result. The most plausible reason seemed simply to be that voters as so often before and in other systems had decided not so much to embrace a new government but rather to register dissatisfaction with the old one. But the definition of the election result as a victory for the SPÖ once again had more than a touch of U.S.-inspired media management to it. A European orientation would have prepared the public for the unavoidable next phase, namely the negotiation to form a new government coalition.

The results did not allow for many possibilities. If one wanted to form a coalition of only two parties, only the traditional Austrian model of a grand coalition seemed possible. After some back and forth, other possibilities, such as three-party coalitions, were rejected. The country visibly seemed to relax, as the two main parties, carefully prompted by Federal President Heinz Fischer agreed to try the old pattern again. It then became painfully apparent that the SPÖ victory was not so clear after all. Gusenbauer was not able to make his new partner accept most of his campaign promises to the great dissatisfaction of his followers. While in public opinion the ÖVP had lost the election, it most certainly had won the game of forming a government by occupying the most important seats in the cabinet and getting a government program mutually accepted that contained most of its own political priorities.

With the formation of a grand coalition government holding a 70 percent majority in the National Council, a certain Reaustrification of Austrian politics can be observed. This Reaustrification also found its expression in the reemergence of the traditional weaknesses of this traditional form of government: a careful division of mutual spheres of influence, continuous public attacks against the other party in the sense of *Bereichsopposition*, and the inability to tackle big problems, even if one has so far to give the new government the benefit of doubt on that. If one remembers the performance of previous grand coalition governments, an eventual breakup of the coalition and an early new election seems rather likely as soon as really difficult decisions will have to be made. One influential journalist maintained that the Austrian electorate, by making a grand coalition the only viable possibility, had voted for political standstill.

In one sense, however, one could say that the new government implies a Europeanization of Austrian politics after all. Since the priorities in most policy areas are set in Brussels (many observers estimate that as much as 70 percent of political decisions relevant for Austria are made there) the government has now returned to face this reality. It does not do so front stage—there is a tendency to criticize the EU in the Austrian public—but backstage day to day negotiations with Brussels have been resumed, and the government is acting accordingly, trying, in fact, to forget some of its campaign promises or to promote different policies as if they did fulfill these promises.

To sum up, one could say that while the 2006 election and to some extent its results were dominated by a trend towards Americanization, the formation of a government and its mechanisms show a trend towards

Reaustrification, a tendency to return to traditional patters of Austrian politics with all their strengths and weaknesses. But behind that looms the fact that for a small member state of the European Union there is no alternative to following the European line. A Europeanization of the Austrian political system does take place, but it does not show on the outside, is rarely discussed publicly, and is not apparent during the electoral process. Maybe that is one of the reasons why the approval rates for the European Union in Austria are the lowest of those of all EU member states.

References

Hofer, Thomas, and Barbara Toth, eds. *Wahl 2006: Kanzler, Kampagnen, Kapriolen.* Vienna: Lit Verlag, 2007.

Plasser, Fritz, and Peter A. Ulram. eds. *Wahlverhalten in Bewegung.* Vienna: WUV-Universitätsverlag, 2003.

Rosenberger, Sieglinde K., and Gilg Seeber. *Kopf an Kopf: Meinungsforschung im Medienwahlkampf.* Vienna: Czernin, 2003.

Sperl, Gerfried. *Die umgefärbte Republik.* Vienna: Zsolnay, 2003.

Did the ÖVP Lose, or Did the SPÖ Win the 2006 National Parliamentary Election?

Imma Palme

Austria's political course during the last two years of the ÖVP-led coalition didn't find a majority of the voters. Over a long period, all the polls showed a significant advantage for the Social Democrats (SPÖ). This changed drastically the day the BAWAG affair started to affect both the trade unions, dominated by SPÖ, and the party itself. For months, the SPÖ did not recover. The Austrian race changed gears and saw a triumphant ÖVP leading all the polls.

The SPÖ seemed paralyzed and unable to shake off the BAWAG yoke. One of the main misgivings people had about the Social Democrats—their presumed inability to manage Austria's economy and administer a budget without deficit spending—was more or less confirmed. Both the incumbent government, especially Chancellor Wolfgang Schüssel himself, and the opposition parties pointed out this weakness. Maybe this was one of Schüssel's decisive tactical errors, for BAWAG was not the only bank scandal at that time, and the majority of voters was convinced that something like this might happen in any political camp. By merely pointing a finger at the SPÖ and exaggerating the risks that the bank's clients might face with their savings, the ÖVP's fear tactics simply went to far, alienating voters.

The issues that voters associated strongly with the SPÖ, though, remained the same and steadily gained importance for the people. Public debates on the Austrian health system and the education system (test results in the PISA assessment showed Austria's pupils lagging far behind those in the leading countries) were favorable for social democratic platforms. All of a sudden, an intense debate about the elderly's care put a focus even on Chancellor Schüssel's family. He appeared to be a man out of touch with the average Austrian's needs and problems. His status as chancellor solidified his credibility as a politician who is respected and who, in fact, had much higher ratings in his overall performance than Alfred Gusenbauer, but who at the same time couldn't win the people's hearts. His coolness worked against him; people had always had doubts about him in that respect, and the public debate about the eldercare showed his emotional coldness.

Despite these circumstances, the ÖVP campaign had only one agenda item: to promote the idea that everything is good, beautiful, and fine in the country if, it suggested, the electorate would allow the Schüssel-led government to continue its mission to reduce further public debts. This feel-good campaign failed to connect to the voters' concerns. Schüssel's basic weaknesses—his arrogance, self-consciousness, and obsession with power—shone brightly.

At the same time, and step by step, the SPÖ tried to overcome the negative effects of the BAWAG affair. Gusenbauer participated in all TV debates, in a sharp contrast to the chancellor who appeared only in the closing debate. Gusenbauer was able to reach a broader public by introducing the concept of a "new fairness."

Nevertheless, Schüssel was the main asset of the ÖVP. He had excellent ratings for his performance as chancellor, and he was seen as the key player of a balanced team with the financial star Karl-Heinz Grasser. Gusenbauer had at this point no team to offer, but during the campaign, he was able to overcome a lot of his former weaknesses. His lack of governmental experience—something for which the ÖVP criticized him—was very well compensated for by his social behavior: Gusenbauer was seen as very close to the people, the candidate who really knew what people were talking about.

Another element in the SPÖ's favor was that the top issues in its campaign corresponded to the main concerns of the Austrian voters, as Table 1 shows.

Table 1
Main Concerns of Austrian Voters, Fall 2006

Issue of Concern	Percentage
Education	90
Unemployment amongst young people	86
Jobs	84
Guaranteed fair pensions	80

Note: n=1.500

Source: IFES poll, 29 September–1 October 2006.

Contemporary Austrian Studies

In sharp contrast, Schüssel and the ÖVP repeated that Austria has it better because Austria does it better. But this statement did not express the public's assessment of things. Despite economic growth, the majority of the Austrian electorate felt that their living standard was declining. All IFES polls over the last two years preceding election day showed that the majority of adults saw Austria heading in the wrong direction. While the ÖVP held onto its feel-good campaign, the SPÖ differed sharply and attacked in a very open-minded way the failures and shortcomings of the ÖVP.

ÖVP voters from the 2002 election who had been won from the Freedom Party, as well as traditional social democratic voters, saw a lack of social responsibility in the ÖVP. Fears of a two-tier health system, of an ever-widening gap in educational standards between Austria and comparable countries, and of a stagnation of real income growth were issues that benefited the SPÖ.

The Austrian electorate remained undecided, not only regarding which party to support, but also whether it was at all worthwhile to participate actively in the election. The choice that many saw was not between two political parties with their distinct concepts and personnel, but between the lesser of two evils.

As a result, this election produced the lowest turnout in Austrian history. Only 78.5 percent of voters cast a ballot. This low turnout did not favor any party in particular. The gains and losses were rather evenly distributed. The SPÖ could only win one state, but its losses were significantly less than the ÖVP's. This pattern could be seen all over Austria.

On election day, a combination of emotions let the SPÖ win 47,493 votes more than the ÖVP. Gusenbauer was eventually seen as the candidate who really was willing to fight for the needs of Austrians, who cared about them. The issues of health and eldercare, education, and the Eurofighter contract, together with rising ratings of Gusenbauer's performance, softened the support for the ÖVP. Obviously, the election results came as a big surprise for Schüssel and his team. Once more, their reaction showed how out of touch they were with the Austrian populace.

The very long, tenacious, and tough negotiations for the formation of a coalition government led by the SPÖ—and the months thereafter—show that a more explicit swing to one of the two sides had made life easier for any government.

Who Is the Winner?: The Strategic Dilemma of "the People's Choice"

Anton Pelinka

The Austrian general elections of 1 October have resulted in one loser and many winners. The loser is obvious: the moderate right, represented by the conservative Austrian People's Party (ÖVP) and its leader, Federal Chancellor Wolfgang Schüssel. The ÖVP fell from 42.3 percent (2002) to 34.3 percent.

The winners represent a broad spectrum. The left-of-center Green Party had the best result in its history: 11.1 instead of 9.5 percent (2002). The Social Democratic Party (SPÖ) received 35.3 percent of the votes, a slight decline from 36.5 (2002), but because the SPÖ regained the number one position ahead of the ÖVP, the SPÖ's jubilation is understandable.

The real winner is the extreme right. The Freedom Party (FPÖ) got 11.0 percent, and the BZÖ (Alliance for Austria's Future), a splinter from the FPÖ, 4.1 percent. The "old" FPÖ, still united in 2002, had only 10.0 percent of the votes.

Because Austria uses proportional representation with a 4 percent threshold and because the government now to be built needs a majority in parliament, in the National Council, the result must be called ambiguous. The outcome of elections of 1999 and 2002 was a rightist coalition: the ÖVP and the FPÖ were able to form a cabinet; the SPÖ and the Greens stayed in the opposition.

The situation is different now. The split within the FPÖ is a split between those who wanted to stay in government together with the ÖVP and those who prefer the successful recipe of a fundamentalist opposition which was so successful for the FPÖ in the 1990s. The pro-ÖVP wing founded the BZÖ in 2005. The remaining FPÖ behaved more and more like an opposition party, criticizing the Schüssel government from the far right. After 1 October, the BZÖ is not strong enough to give the weakened

ÖVP a majority. But the combined left—the SPÖ and Greens—doesn't have a majority either.

The result gives the SPÖ sixty-eight seats, the ÖVP sixty-six, the Greens and the FPÖ twenty-one each, and the BZÖ seven seats. That means that there is a potential majority right of the center. But this would include the FPÖ, and such an inclusion has been ruled out by the ÖVP—at least for the moment. It has also been ruled out by the FPÖ itself—again, for the moment.

The implication of such a result is that the only possibilities to form a cabinet, backed by a majority in the National Council, are either the inclusion of the FPÖ or a grand coalition.

Pros and Cons of a Grand Coalition

According to an unwritten rule, the Austrian Federal President, Heinz Fischer, has entrusted the SPÖ's leader, Alfred Gusenbauer, with the formation of a cabinet. During the campaign, Gusenbauer expressed his intention to form a coalition either with the Greens or with the ÖVP. Because the first possibility—as a consequence of the 1 October elections—is not feasible due to the lack of a majority, Gusenbauer has been required to start negotiations with the ÖVP, the party he has opposed for more than six years. After weeks of wavering, the ÖVP has decided to negotiate with Gusenbauer. After weeks of negotiations, the formation of a grand coalition was possible—in January 2007, more than three months after the elections.

Behind the scenes, intense networking—especially between the ("red" as well "black") governors of the Austrian provinces and between the "social partners" (labor and business)—had its impact: whatever the legendary "Austrian voter" had in mind, he or she will get a coalition between the two major parties. The Federal President, Heinz Fischer, has made his preference for a Gusenbauer-led grand coalition very clear, given the (lack of) alternatives. Fischer's constitutional options are not far reaching; he cannot force the forming of a coalition against the will of the National Council's majority. But atmospherically, he can use his still significant popularity to push the major parties in the direction of a compromise.

Austria has a long tradition of grand coalitions. From 1945 to 1966 and, again, from 1987 to 2000, the country was governed by a coalition between the SPÖ and ÖVP. In the beginning, this coalition was seen as a necessity. To stabilize democracy, the economy, and Austria's international standing, the grand coalition was perceived as a kind of national government.

But this changed after the task of such a government was fulfilled. Later on, the grand coalition existed first and foremost out of a lack of alternatives or to be more precise, to keep Haider's far-right FPÖ out of power. Jörg Haider and his populist message of anti-elitism, anti-immigration, and anti-European Union, mixed with down-playing Nazi crimes, became the defining "other" of the grand coalition in the 1990s.

The grand coalition's strategic dilemma of the 1990s was reflected by the FPÖ's rise and the major parties' decline. In the end, the ÖVP left the grand coalition to side with Haider.

There was a lot of talk that Schüssel successfully domesticated Haider. But in 2006, the FPÖ and the BZÖ are still and even more decisive factor in Austrian politics. Haider himself may be out as a national figure due to the BZÖ's disastrous showing outside Haider's home province, Carinthia. But Haiderism is very much in.

In many respects, the situation in 2006 has been reminiscent of the situation before 2000. The grand coalition would not be the result of a common agenda, but the least of all evils. To keep the FPÖ out, the two major parties would build a negative coalition. A high probability exists that the FPÖ would profit now as it did before.

In the meantime, the negotiations between the SPÖ and ÖVP to form a grand coalition have underscored that there is not much love within both parties for such a coalition. Some comments about changing the electoral law to enable one major party to govern alone and to prevent a grand coalition based on nothing else but the lack of any alternative have surfaced. But it is obvious that both major parties are lacking the strength to make such a decisive step towards a two-party system.

Why is the Extreme Right so Successful?

Austria's democracy is taken hostage by the extreme right. The dilemma is that the extreme right has to be included into a coalition government, or a grand coalition has to be formed just to keep the extreme right out. How is it that the country's rather good economic performance counter-intuitively allows such an angry sentiment consisting of xenophobia and general protest to have such broad appeal?

Electoral research gives some answers. It is the lesser educated male voter who disproportionately votes for the FPÖ. It is modernization's loser who is tempted to follow the FPÖ's battle cry against "them": the political class, the European Union, foreigners in general, and Muslims in particular.

But the existence of a social segment afraid of the future in a more and more globalized economy is not a special Austrian phenomenon. There are some Austrian preconditions permitting the success of right-wing populism. It is the existence of a traditional structure and of a traditional social milieu providing that resentment with an articulated leadership.

The FPÖ is an old party. Its roots go back to the Pan-German movement of the beginning of the 1900s. Georg Ritter von Schönerer is one of Haider's forbearers. This tradition also includes the Austrian Nazi Party. After 1945, when the NSDAP was outlawed, the hard core of former Nazis created their new platform: the FPÖ. Differently from in Germany, the Austrian mainstream parties did not shy away from making deals with such a party in a common candidate for the Federal Presidency in 1957 and in coalition agreements in 1983, 2000, and 2003. What was not respectable in Germany was respectable in Austria. There was no *cordon sanitaire* forbidding the center to bring the far right into the political game.

The center is challenged once more. If the two major parties are unable to write a common platform convincingly enough, a grand coalition would be once more the nourishing ground for the far right. A successful grand coalition needs more of a justification than the lack of any kind of alternatives.

Two possible outcomes of the strategic dilemma resulting from the 1 October elections had surfaced once more: a grand coalition with all the resulting negative implications if a "grand agenda" cannot be developed, or early elections in 2007, possibly after a brief stint with a minority cabinet of the SPÖ. But early elections would probably have been just a postponement of the consequences of the dilemma mentioned above.

After three months of negotiations about negotiations and of playing the "blame game," a grand coalition had been formed at the beginning of 2007. That means that early elections in 2007 will not take place. But this does not change anything with respect to the strategic dilemma the Austrian political system has to face.

The most decisive consequence of that dilemma is that it is not a particular party that is losing. It is the credibility of Austrian democracy which would be in further decline.

References

Pelinka, Anton, "Die Italianisierung Österreichs? Der 1.Oktober und die Folgen." *Europäische Rundschau* 4 (2006): 3-10.

Plasser, Fritz, and Peter A. Ulram, *Die Wahlanalyse 2006. Wer hat wen warum gewählt?* Presseunterlage, Vienna, 2 October 2006.

The Conservative Turn to Socialism

Manfred Prisching

It was a surprising election. Social researchers and political scientists, journalists and other observers had been wrong. Nobody thought that the Social Democratic Party would win the election since it had been shaken by scandals which were damaging central parts of its self-conception. Nobody thought that the People's Party would be overtaken given the excellent economic statistics, an adequate record of reforms, and a qualified top candidate.

The Loyalty of Socialist Party Supporters

Political scientists have announced that political camps are becoming "liquid," that voters are floating and party identification is declining. However, socialist voters seem to have stronger ties to their political "homeland" than adherents of other parties. During the last years, a temporary "emigration" from "red" to "blue" areas occurred, with a further journey to the "black" camp, but the 2006 election was a return "home," an act of "normalization." The homecoming was not impeded by the topical scandal; apparently, whatever the socialist party leadership does, its followers show a high level of patience.

The scandal which shaped the election campaign did not concern corrupt practices at the periphery of the socialist party. It was all about a bastion of social democracy.[1] The trade union was at stake. Its wealth was gambled away. The general perception was that core institutions of the socialist movement have betrayed their people by implementing dirty financial speculations, a kind of activity which officially has never been fiercely fought by the party. Important party functionaries did what rotten capitalists used to do. Finally, partisans realized that there had been a broad acceptance of corrupt practices and lifestyles in the party, as long as outward success was visible. Penthouse stories had not been a secret. But in the current case, the feeling seemed to prevail that a penthouse is all right as long as one of "our guys" owns it. Champagne is a "proletarian drink" as long as we drink it ourselves. Some groups expressed their uneasiness when the scandal exploded, but in the end, loyalty was strong enough. Ranks closed.[2]

The People's Party Distant from the People

In the election, the People's Party did not have to answer for bad politics. Altogether, journalists and experts certified that the federal government had performed well during the last years. International organizations praised reform initiatives. In European or global comparisons, economic indicators placed Austria, as a country of luxury, in the topmost ranks. Essential and inevitable projects had been tackled, even at the risk of unpopularity, such as the reform of the pension system. However, the government occasionally dipped into the box of tricks, for instance in the design of federal budgets and in the postponement of realizing important goals, such as the reduction of the ratio of government expenditures to the social product. Other projects were left to languish, for instance, health system reform. In addition, school and university policy is a disaster, and some other issues remain to be tackled.

Statistics are not enough, for the objective reality does not correspond to the subjective one. The data may show a satisfying picture, but this does not suffice to win the elections. The everyday experience of the people is that they live in a "liquid society."[3] Everything which seemed stable and firm is being dissolved. Jobs are no longer secure. Careers are unforeseeable. Families are disintegrating. Parties and trade unions are losing supporters; convincing ideologies no longer exist. Even religion cannot unify Austria which is no longer a Catholic, but actually a quite secularized country.[4] When all institutions are eroding, timidity grows in the midst of luxury.

Of course, the government is not to blame for these developments, and actually no government could do much in response to them. But voters want their anxieties to be taken seriously. They do not want to hear that everything is excellent and gets even better. But this was exactly the predominant message on which the People's Party built its election campaign. Clearly, "strategic euphoria" is not always effective.[5]

In fact, economic growth rates do not guarantee that individuals have a successful life, in a comprehensive sense. When everything is crumbling and politicians rejoice because of the excellent conditions in all areas of life, people get the impression that the incumbents are out of touch, that they do not know how the "real life" of "real people" has to be managed. The election outcome was the result of a social-political cleavage: party leadership no longer knew how people really felt.

From the Conservative Turn to the Conservative Turn

The opposition was unprepared. During the campaign, Social Democrats were busy sealing the breaking dams. They were not able to develop political objectives or programs; scandals overshadowed everything. Actually, there was no need for developing a blueprint for government policy because nobody thought that the Social Democrats could win the elections. However, after the elections, a delay in the development of fruitful trend-setting ideas occurs. Some people even say that it's not a delay, but simply an impossibility.

It is not clear if the programmatic or visionary deficit will damage the ruling socialist party. Austria is a conservative country, and paradoxically, the Social Democrats represent the conservative stance much better than the People's Party. The People's Party may be oriented towards traditional values (this is the benevolent interpretation; some would say that it has already lost its conservative values, partly in favor of neo-liberal elements). But it began some structural reforms that had become urgent after long years of social democratic governments, because the SPÖ holds onto a "structural conservatism." The structural inertia of the leftist camp in Austria refers primarily to welfare state guarantees, but there are also other historical reflexes, like a bias against the armed forces, against the family, and against performance-related outcomes in the educational system.[6]

At the starting line of the new legislative period, the basic promise of the social democratic government is that nothing will change, that pensions are guaranteed, that all health expenditures are paid, that free education at all levels should be provided, that poverty will be removed soon, that care services for older people will be paid for, that research will get more money, just like the arts. There are the usual ideas for financing these plans: "rich people" and enterprises shall pay. In fact, taxes will grow, in spite of a public spending ratio close to 50 percent of the social product. It will still last for a while until the incumbents understand that a further expansion of the welfare state is not so easy to implement in a globalized world in which other countries, the admired Scandinavian countries included, head in the other direction.

When Austria is labeled a conservative country, this does not mean that conservative values are really appreciated.[7] Austrians want to maintain and expand their welfare privileges. They do not take into account demographic shifts and global pressures. They believe that a comfortable social network can be established at political discretion. While this state of consciousness of the electorate is not in accordance with reality, the political attempt to evolve the economic and political system beyond the present state has failed. The coalition government even tries to retreat from some reform steps, for instance by eliminating "cruelties" of the pension system reform. Early retirement is made more attractive again, in spite of the fact that there is only a very small group of Austrians who work beyond the age of 60. International organizations consider measures making early retirement easier steps into the wrong direction. Anyhow, the attention of the public is not directed to the "large problems" (like the project to design a sustainable "European Social Model," in contrast to Anglo-American versions of capitalism), but to trifles like the question of academic tuition fees.

If the "sovereign" is short-sighted, his political representatives will not be pushed to be farsighted, and they will not be able to take in a broad horizon. Therefore, the electoral success of the SPÖ was a conservative turn. For the moment, we are heading towards the "old world" characterized by generous social expenditures financed by debts, and the SPÖ is satisfied by telling the Austrian electorate that a faster move back is impeded by nothing but the unwillingness of the ÖVP.

Ideological Confusions on All Sides

The two large parties are living in a state of increasing ideological confusion,[8] and voters are confused, too. Almost nothing has been left from classical socialist ideas: no Marxist analysis of society, no confidence in the work of the laws of history, no class theory. Socialism today means a bundle of inconsistent sentiments: a feeling of egalitarianism which is difficult to sustain when faced with pressures of the world market; a statism which is rather old-fashioned; and a diffuse humanism which is as friendly as it is naive.[9] The urban factions utter progressive statements, but are actually content to cultivate a mood of bohemia, consumption, and design which they mistake for modernity.

The People's Party does not come to terms with the problem that a conservative inventory cannot easily be reconciled with neo-liberal market ideas. The unconstrained market destroys what is dear for a conservative. The ÖVP counts on continuities and reliabilities which are nothing but obstacles for market euphoria's eagerness to customize everything, and it counts on virtues which appear quite dusty in a narcissistic society. Nevertheless, it is astonishing that the party has surrendered traditional fields like the universities and more generally the concept of *Bildung* which has constituted the high reputation of the German-speaking countries.

The populist groups in the Austrian political scene confine themselves to two issues: resentment against "those people above" who finance their good life by exploiting the decent common man and xenophobia. The Greens do not know where they should locate themselves between leftist social policy and clumsy ecological proposals. It is no wonder that electoral behavior is becoming unpredictable.[10]

The Conquest of Socialism by Populism

The advisors for the election campaign of the SPÖ delivered their post-electoral interviews, conceding that they have patterned their strategy after American election campaign methods: dirt, lies, hypocrisy.[11] This is not an assessment by reluctant observers, but a confession of the proud producers themselves. Their confession has been received in Austria's media with calmness, even by those journalists who previously used to worry rather sensitively about the decay of political culture and Austrian democracy. In this case, they have not sneered at "dirty Alfred"; rather, they have considered the use of dirty campaigning to be a type of "political professionalization."

The success of the method will not remain without consequences. Adherents of the ÖVP have already aired their grievances that the party's election campaign had been conducted too nobly, too modestly, too decently, and too objectively. They admonish their party that it should have taken the socialists as an example because the ÖVP will lose the fight if it regards itself as too high-minded when confronted with dirt. There will be learning effects. Actually, Jörg Haider has conquered Social Democracy: his successful policy of resentment, his strategy of deriding and expressing contempt for other people, his permanent generation of political balloons and simple gags intended to gain the attentiveness of the media—this repertoire has been gratefully accepted and applied by the SPÖ. The People's Party will follow these patterns when the next election campaign approaches.

Notes

1. Christian Dickinger, *Die Skandale der Republik. Haider, Proksch & Co.* (Vienna: Ueberreuter, 2001).

2. Loyalty is a valuable resource before and after elections. Commentators refer to the capability of suffering on the side of party supporters in order to explain the acceptance of the "lost negotiations" that established a coalition government between the ÖVP and SPÖ. They assume that it is predominantly important for the party leaders to win the chancellory; in case of success, the rank and file are content with any deviance from election pledges. Success is more important than keeping promises.

3. Zygmunt Bauman, *Liquid Modernity* (Cambridge: Polity, 2000).

4. Günter Bischof, Anton Pelinka, Hermann Denz, eds., *Religion in Austria*, vol. 15, Contemporary Austrian Studies (New Brunswick, NJ: Transaction, 2004).

5. "Strategic euphoria" is a mode of communication which has become characteristic for several fields of public life, not only for marketing campaigns of firms. The European Union predicts that it will be the strongest economic area in 2010, and it bolsters this aspiration with quantitative goals that will be impossible to achieve. Universities herald that they are on the way to global importance and excellence. Public institutions promulgate that they are just a few steps away from becoming the best or greatest or most efficient entity on the continent. But in most cases, the "semantic generation" of reality does not work if it is not accompanied by a realistic strategy of transformation.

6. The sentiments may be summarized in some statements: "Neutrality is fine; therefore, we do not really need an army because in a case of emergency others will fight for us. Unwed mothers are everyday heroes, while a housewife with five children is simply reactionary, a holdover reminding of non-emancipated times. A modern school system should certify everyone; to refuse a doctorate to a student simply because he is stupid is an act of obvious discrimination."

7. Manfred Prisching, *Die zweidimensionale Gesellschaft. Ein Essay zur neokonsumistischen Geisteshaltung* (Wiesbaden: VS Verlag für Sozialwissenschaften, 2006).

8. Manfred Prisching, "Zur Zukunft von Volksparteien in Österreich. Die Epoche einer Volkspartei," in *Zukunftsfest. 60 Jahre Österreichische Volkspartei*, ed. Andreas Khol et al. (Vienna: Molden Verlag, 2005), 227-50.

9. Norbert Leser, *Salz der Gesellschaft. Wesen und Wandel des österreichischen Sozialismus* (Vienna: Orac, 1988).

10. Manfred Prisching, "Produktive Verwirrungen der Weltanschauungen," in *Die Macht des Geistes. Festgabe für Norbert Leser zum 70. Geburtstag*, ed. Erwin Bader (Frankfurt am Main: Peter Lang Verlag, 2003), 171-199.

11. Kathleen J. Jamieson, *Dirty Politics. Deception, Distraction, and Democracy* (New York: Oxford UP, 1992).

NON-TOPICAL ESSAYS

A New Perspective from Moscow Archives: Austria and the Stalin Notes of 1952*

Peter Ruggenthaler[1]

In spring 1952, when it was plain to see what progress West Germany was making towards integration into the Western alliance, Joseph Stalin captured the world's attention with the proposal of an initiative regarding the German question. On 10 March, he dispatched identical notes to the Western allies containing the draft of a peace treaty with Germany: the Soviet "offer" provided for Germany to be restored as a "unified nation." For decades, historians have been unable to agree on the nature of this so-called Stalin Note (which was to be followed by several others). Was it a genuine opening gambit, or merely a tactical and diplomatic one, a kind of smoke screen? Would it have been in Stalin's interest to restore Germany's unity, or was his real aim quite the reverse, namely making the partition of Germany irreversible? On 13 March 1952, the Western powers submitted to Moscow a proposal regarding Austria. In a manner that bore a striking resemblance to Stalin's German initiative, the West tabled a shortened draft treaty "*Kurzvertrag*" (the so-called "Abbreviated Treaty" or "Evacuation Instrument"), which called for a resumption of the state treaty negotiations. The alleged aim was the withdrawal of all troops from Austrian soil. What needs to be stressed here is the fact that the Abbreviated Treaty was not the first reaction of the Western powers to the Stalin Note, even though the diplomatic tit-for-tat might tempt one to reach that conclusion. Yet the Abbreviated Treaty, even if it was no immediate reaction to Stalin's move, was nevertheless closely connected to the German question. The result of long-term planning, it had been conceived purely as a propaganda manoeuvre on the part of the Western powers. The Evacuation Instrument contained no serious intention to turn Austria into a neutral country. The Western powers goal in making this move was to test how flexible Stalin was likely to be in the resolution of the German question. In the end, Stalin beat the West to the post by three days—without being aware of the West's plans to re-open the Austrian question.

There were operatives in the Soviet Ministry of State Security (MGB) who knew of preparations in the West related to this issue, but Semen Ignatiev, the minister in charge, did not report this development to Stalin and Molotov. This becomes evident from an analysis of the reports. The West's propaganda move was, therefore, made without being influenced by the timing of the dispatch of Stalin's Note. Documents on Soviet policy regarding Austria and Germany that have recently come under historical scrutiny, most notably those from the Molotov files, make it appear increasingly plausible that the Stalin Note from 10 March 1952 and the Soviet "offer" of a peace treaty for Germany, which was linked to that country taking up a neutral, equidistant position between West and East, were without genuine substance. Austria would have provided an opportunity for the Kremlin to demonstrate its goodwill in the German question and to flesh it out with a concession. However, Stalin was not (yet) in a position in early 1952 to neutralize Austria. It was felt that Austria must not become a blueprint; according to Andrey Vyshinsky, the Soviet foreign minister, in a note to Stalin, "attention should remain focused on the discussion of the German question." Austria's neutralization only became a genuine option after the consolidation of the German Democratic Republic (GDR). It was the allegedly irrevocable partition of Germany that opened up the road for Austria to neutrality and not, as has so often been asserted, Stalin's death in 1953. Carving up Austria was never seriously contemplated as far as the Soviets were concerned. It would ultimately only have resulted in strengthening (West) Germany, something Moscow was determined to avoid at all costs.

The Soviet secret services had succeeded, as will be shown in greater detail below, in getting copies on a regular basis telegraphic exchanges between French embassies, high commissioners, and the Quai d'Orsay as well as occasional directives from the State Department to American diplomatic representatives abroad; a Soviet spy had been installed in the immediate vicinity of the head of the press department of the French Ministry for Foreign Affairs.[2] This put the Kremlin consistently a step

Austria as a Prop to the Stability of the Eastern Bloc

Behind the closed doors of the Kremlin, the notion that the Austrian State Treaty was going to deprive the Soviet Union of its right to station troops in Hungary and Romania began to dominate the discussion. The West's willingness to sign this treaty, which had been displayed openly enough even though the U.S. president had not yet made plain his approval, was interpreted by Stalin as evidence that this step was linked for the West with collateral support for Yugoslavia.[18] The Soviet bracketing together of the question of Austria with that of Trieste and, in the last resort, of Germany, as well as the Soviets' repeated demands for the de-Nazification and demilitarization of Austria ultimately spelled the end for the Austrian State Treaty for the time being. All these issues were "repeatedly used to block progress in the state treaty negotiations."[19] For the sessions of the deputies scheduled for 1950, the Soviet team was given zero negotiating range by Stalin.[20] There were at least two reasons why Stalin considered it imperative to continue with the occupation of eastern Austria. The West, as was only too obvious, supported Josip Tito with regard to the question of Austria, which appalled Stalin. Secondly, the occupation of Austria contributed significantly, as Stalin saw it, to the consolidation of the Eastern bloc on two fronts: on one hand, the conclusion of a state treaty with Austria following on the heels of the foundation of the GDR might have encouraged certain circles to seek a similar solution for Germany; on the other, perhaps Stalin specifically wanted no closure regarding Austria in order to reach his overriding aim of consolidating the GDR while continuing to appear ready to return to the negotiating table to settle the subordinate issue of Austria. Nor was Stalin seriously interested in the implementation of the peace treaty with Italy regarding the question of Trieste, that is, the appointment of a UN High Commissioner. In this way, Trieste remained an ace up the sleeve of the USSR that could be played at any time to trump the obligation of concluding the Austrian treaty and to enable the Soviet Union to firmly anchor Hungary and Romania in its orbit.[21]

The continued delays in the treaty negotiations made the Communist Party of Austria (KPÖ) embrace neutrality slogans for the first time in 1950.[22] It is rather improbable that they had Moscow's backing for this initially. The first exploratory move in this direction might have been initiated by Mikhail Koptelov, the Soviet political representative, and by Georgi Tsinev, who later rose to the rank of assistant high commissioner in Austria. At around this time, these two submitted a "proposed solution to the question of Austria" to the Soviet Ministry of Foreign Affairs that would have required Austria "to abstain from joining any politico-military bloc."[23] However, Mikhail Gribanov, the head of the Foreign Ministry's Third European Department (and as such also in charge of Austria), an outspoken advocate of German neutrality in 1951/52 according to Wilfried Loth,[24] gave the proposal short shrift because such obligations signaled "to a certain extent a discriminatory attitude (!) toward Austria" and might lead the Western powers to conclude that the Soviet Union was viewing NATO with "great concern." Gribanov's choice of words is remarkable. In the draft of a peace treaty in the so-called Stalin Note dated 10 March 1952, Germany would have been saddled with the obligation "not to join any kind of coalition or military pact."[25]

With regard to the German question, we may note that in 1950/51 Moscow remained outwardly ready to return to the negotiating table to discuss the question of Austria, but did not, in fact, want any progress on a substantive level. In January 1952, even this ostensible readiness disappeared; it had in any case always been compromised by preconditions throughout its lifetime. The Soviet representative repeated in London the well-known Soviet demands to the Western powers as a matter of routine and wound up by declaring himself unable to take part in the session of the deputies scheduled for 21 January. In a note to the Kremlin, the Western powers accused the USSR of having blocked the conclusion of the Austrian State Treaty for two years. The Kremlin did not even bother to reply and issued no official communiqués on Austria for several months. This casts a revealing light on the Kremlin's alleged willingness to take part in substantive negotiations during those same weeks and on its near-enthusiasm in elaborating plans for a neutral Germany. Yet one needs to remember that Stalin's death was not a necessary precondition for Austria's neutral status to materialize;[26] this would have been possible under certain circumstances even during the dictator's lifetime.[27] Once a consolidated GDR was a *fait accompli*, there was nothing to block the road forward as far as the Soviets were concerned.

Nothing had changed on the Eastern bloc's south-eastern flank; rather, it was more of the same. Tito was courted even more by the Western powers. Reports about NATO's plans concerning Yugoslavia that included the installation of military bases on Yugoslavian soil must have set off alarm bells in Moscow.[28] Eastern Austria would still have been needed as a troop deployment area in a war with Yugoslavia, yet as we now know as a fact rather than as a matter of speculation,[29] Austria's (military) neutralization would not only have been made possible by the shoring-up of the GDR through the Battle of the Notes in 1952, it ahead of the Western powers throughout 1951/52. The planning that centered on the Stalin Note took more than a year.[3]

This paper,[4] which undertakes the clarification of an episode in the overall context of Soviet policy towards Germany and Austria in 1951/52, is based on hitherto inaccessible documents in the Vyacheslav Molotov files; Molotov's role in the Kremlin up to and including the last years of Stalin's life was far more important than has been realized to date.[5] These files were part of the Archives of the President of the Russian Federation (AP RF); in 2004, they were re-opened and handed over to the Russian State Archive for Social and Political History (RGASPI).[6] The files relevant to Austria were systematically mined for information for the first time in *Die Rote Armee in Österreich* (*The Red Army in Austria*), which was published in 2005.[7] Prior to this, the files in the archive were accessible only to Russian researchers in the 1990s. The most significant publications produced under these auspices are Nataliya Egorova on NATO from the Soviet point of view[8] and Mikhail Narinsky on the Soviet attitude towards the Marshall Plan.[9] No analytical studies of Soviet policy regarding Germany were published at the time that made use of the 1951/52 files referring to Germany.[10] The pertinent works on the subject were all based on documents from the Archives of the Ministry for Foreign Affairs of the Russian Federation (AVP RF);[11] they were mining data, in other words, in a sphere that was further removed from where the action was. They were of relevance only in those cases where Stalin's or Molotov's intentions could be deduced from their handwritten comments preserved in the files. In their efforts to identify the goals and underlying intentions of Soviet policy regarding Germany, historians had to resort to the analysis of circumstantial evidence, which was, and indeed continues to be, made all the more difficult by the fact that the indexes of the Archives of the Ministry for Foreign Affairs are not accessible to researchers, who in consequence must make do with the pre-selected files supplied to them. For this article, the author has been able to make use of the indexes of the Russian State Archive of Social and Political History, which makes focused research possible. It was possible, for instance, to establish the important role Molotov played particularly in the last year of Stalin's life. There was hardly a document of importance that did not cross Molotov's desk. The Soviet secret services reported directly to Molotov: Semen Ignatiev for the Ministry of State Security, MGB, and Ivan Tugarinov for the "Small" Committee of Information. Owing to his poor state of health, Stalin was arguably unable to read all documents personally.[12] At the Party Congress of the CPSU in the autumn of 1952, Stalin finally accused Molotov of being a British spy. At this point, the Molotov files end and do not resume until after Stalin's death, when Molotov was re-appointed as Foreign Minister.

After Hermann Graml, Hans-Peter Schwarz and Gerhard Wettig had based their conclusion that the so-called Stalin Note was without genuine substance not only on a linguistic analysis of the note[13] but also on the first use of U.S. sources, the most stringent line of argumentation prior to the partial opening of the Soviet archives was put forward by Günter Bischof in 1991. Basing his research on material drawn from U.S. files, Bischof compared Soviet policies in 1952 towards Germany and Austria respectively and convincingly concluded that the offer of agreeing to a neutralized Germany was a propaganda ploy on the part of the Kremlin leaders, who continued at the same time to maintain a stubborn silence on the question of Austria.[14] All subsequent analyses of Soviet policies towards Germany paid scarce attention, if any, to the question of Austria, even though in late 1951 and early 1952 this issue primarily concerned the German question rather than the fate of Austria itself. Austria had become a Cold War weapons testing site that the Superpowers used for their experiments to gauge how far the other side was prepared to go regarding the German question. In a 1994 article, Michael Gehler by and large validates Bischof's conclusions.[15]

"Attention Should Remain Focused on the German Question": The Austrian Abbreviated Treaty (13 March 1952)

In 1949, the first genuine possibility arose for the withdrawal of Allied occupation forces from Austria. The Austrian State Treaty, which had been the subject of negotiations since 1947, was about to be concluded. On 20 June 1949, the last day of the session of the Council of Foreign Ministers that had been convened in Paris, the four Great Powers declared their intention to finalize the Austrian State Treaty and to have it ready for signing by 1 September. Deputies were assigned to the task and charged with hammering out the remaining articles.[16] As we now know, Stalin was prepared for a brief period to agree to a withdrawal of Soviet troops from Austria.[17] Yet by the time President Truman finally overruled a skeptical Pentagon and signaled his approval of the State Treaty on 26 October 1949, that particular window of opportunity had already swung shut. On 24 October, a mere two days earlier, the Politburo had instructed the Soviet negotiators to break off the talks at the earliest opportunity.

would even have offered certain advantages in the Kremlin's view. It would have been made possible because the German question had been "settled"; after breaking with Tito, Stalin was also said to have lost interest in Italy.[30] One of the consequences of this was that the occupation of Austria ceased to be of great importance. The advantages of a neutral Austria were clearly in evidence even before Stalin's death. Top priority was given to preventing a renewed "Anschluß" of Austria or its western states to Germany and its subsequent entry into the fold of NATO.[31] These were also the overriding considerations for the ultimate conclusion of the State Treaty in 1955.

As is well known, Molotov's opposition to releasing Austria remained in place until he ceded to pressure exerted by Nikita Khrushchev and Anastas Mikoyan. From 1949 onward, the Kremlin had bracketed together the questions of Austria and Trieste; according to Mikoyan's testimony, this was done because of rising international tension, which made withdrawal from Austria impossible for the Soviets. Molotov, as Khrushchev remembered, remained opposed to a withdrawal from eastern Austria even after a settlement of the Trieste question had been reached by Italy and Yugoslavia,[32] possibly because his attitude towards Tito remained the same. The Soviet political priorities with reference to Germany and Austria were not affected by the death of Stalin. The neutralization of Austria pre-empted a renewed "Anschluß" together with the attendant strengthening of West Germany and the devaluation from the Soviet point of view of the carving up of Germany. When he signed the Austrian State Treaty on 15 May 1955, Molotov had to bear in mind the directive that barred him from engaging the Western foreign ministers in negotiations touching on the German question.[33] Presumably he had no problems following this directive as it coincided with his personal convictions. This was, of course, not the case with the release of Austria, even though Molotov is said to have been brought around to seeing its merits in the light of rational arguments.[34]

Austria as a Pawn in a Cold War Endgame

Three days after they had received the Stalin Note, the Western powers embarked on what could be passed off as an initiative. On 13 March, they submitted a new proposal to the Soviet side, the so-called "Abbreviated Treaty" or "Evacuation Instrument." This provided for the four occupying powers to commit themselves to withdrawing from Austrian soil within 90 days of the proposal becoming effective; this is why the term "Evacuation Instrument" has also been applied to it. None of the moot points that had resisted resolution in the past were mentioned in the Abbreviated Treaty. This "initiative" of the Western powers had the full weight of Washington's support behind it, yet Austria itself was "the last of the priorities"[35] it addressed. What might have appeared in the eyes of the public as an immediate response to the Soviet proposal regarding the German question had, in fact, been brewing for a long time. The conference of the foreign ministers from the United States, Great Britain, and France that took place in Washington between 12 and 14 September 1951 issued a final communiqué saying there was no reason for any further delays in concluding the Austrian State Treaty.[36] A few days later, the draft of an abbreviated state treaty prepared by the State Department was presented to the Austrian ambassador in Washington, Ludwig Kleinwächter. A first analysis led Kleinwächter to conclude that the proposal was, for all intents and purposes, unacceptable to the Soviets. He was also quick to realize that the Western powers' new initiative was in reality angled at addressing the German question.[37]

Prior to the presentation of the Abbreviated Treaty, the deputies for the negotiations of the Austrian State Treaty were summoned in January 1952 to a session in London that was to be the last one in the series before a long intermission.[38] Even though the MGB possessed the relevant information, neither the Soviet Ministry for Foreign Affairs nor Molotov had been informed that the Western powers were preparing a new move with the Abbreviated Treaty. The only topic touching on the Austrian question which Semen Ignatiev, the head of the MGB, reported to Molotov and Gromyko at this stage was the talks between Sam Reber, the U.S. deputy for the negotiations of the Austrian State Treaty, and the three high commissioners in Vienna. The MGB had gleaned the substance of these talks from the French high commissioner's dispatches to Paris: Reber was personally prepared to go "very far" to accommodate the Soviets, but the U.S. administration had not yet reached a definitive stance. In addition, the administration was determined to reject any Soviet proposals that involved "further concessions" on the part of the United States. According to Ignatiev's report, the high commissioners unanimously agreed that it was "better to sign the present treaty" than to maintain the status quo.[39] Andrey Gromyko was briefed accordingly on 9 January. He based his preparations for the U.S.-convened London session of the deputies for the negotiation of the Austrian State Treaty on the premise that the Western powers were poised to conclude the Austrian State Treaty. One week into those preparations, he submitted to Molotov a draft addressed to Stalin. "In view of the fact that we are at this moment not interested in bringing forward the conclusion of the Austrian treaty,"[40] Gromyko recommended making Soviet willingness to take part in a further session contingent upon the West overruling the Italian peace treaty with regard to Trieste and upon the de-Nazification and demilitarization of Austria. He proceeded from the assumption that if negotiations were to continue, the Western powers would go out of their way to remove all obstacles to the Austrian State Treaty in order to be able to blame the breakdown of negotiations on the USSR.[41] The Kremlin was in a quandary.

This is why the Politburo issued a directive for the Soviet deputy in London that limited him to repeating the well-known Soviet formulae (Trieste, de-Nazification, demilitarization) and to announcing that he would be unable to attend the session scheduled for 21 January 1951. No further move from the Kremlin was forthcoming.[42]

The Abbreviated Treaty was not needed, as can be seen, to create a situation that would provoke the Soviets into finally walking away from the negotiating table. At the beginning of 1952, Moscow was simply not ready to talk about Austria.

The Abbreviated Treaty, which was conceived in the summer of 1951 by the Austrian Desk of the State Department,[43] caused concern among diplomats in Vienna as well as in London and Paris; negative Soviet reactions were expected.[44] At the NATO meeting in Lisbon in February 1952, which saw the admission of Greece and Turkey as members, the French side managed to have a clause inserted that explicitly provided against Austria ever again becoming part of Germany.[45] The French were keen from the start to let the Soviets know that their agreement to the treaty had been conditional upon the insertion of this clause and also that they had opposed locking out the Soviet Union for good. Presentation of the Abbreviated Treaty in Moscow was scheduled in the period of 29 February to 15 March. The Austrians had no possibility of not approving the proposal, and the three Western powers rose to the occasion in a fine show of unity.[46] The Abbreviated Treaty was a tool designed, above all, for Washington to put Soviet intentions regarding the German question to the test. In case the Soviets rejected the treaty, the Americans were hoping that this would be considered sufficient proof of the "insubstantial nature of Stalin's proposals concerning Germany." The logic may appear bizarre at first sight,[47] but was not entirely irrelevant. Conceived exclusively for use in the propaganda skirmishes, the Abbreviated Treaty was formulated in such a way that the West could count on Moscow re-

208 The Changing Austrian Voter

jecting it out of hand. For this reason, it met with initial resistance from Britain and France, which was ultimately overcome by the Americans. Neutral status for Austria brought about by the Western powers' offer of military withdrawal was clearly an idea to which the Kremlin could not (yet) commit.

On 10 March, the Kremlin pre-empted and surprised the West with the Stalin Note and the alleged offer of neutrality for Germany; the relevant actors in the Kremlin were not aware,[48] as has already been mentioned, of the West's intentions centering on the Abbreviated Treaty, which was presented at the Soviet Ministry for Foreign Affairs by the ambassadors of the three Western powers.[49]

The presentation of the Abbreviated Treaty on 13 March appears to have caused a certain amount of irritation in the Kremlin, as is evidenced by the fact that Valerian Zorin, the deputy minister of foreign affairs of the USSR, did not report to the Soviet leadership on the matter of the treaty until 19 March; the possibility of some earlier report on the subject reaching the leadership may safely be discounted, as will be demonstrated below.[50] Only then did Molotov learn that, according to a note dispatched by the French embassy in Washington to the Quai d'Orsay on 14 September 1951, the American Secretary of State, Dean Acheson, speaking at the conference of foreign ministers of the United States, Great Britain, and France on 13 September, had proposed injecting the Abbreviated Treaty into the Austrian State Treaty negotiations in order "to put the Soviet government in a difficult position."[51] Zorin's analysis as presented to Molotov suggests that he himself had only then become aware of the trail left by the Abbreviated Treaty, presumably after he had ordered a search for intercepted relevant information at the MGB. He told Molotov:

> It is obvious that the governments of the Western Powers are in a hurry as regards the presentation of the note on the Austrian treaty: their Moscow ambassadors were most anxious to secure appointments at the Foreign Ministry of the USSR at a date no later than 13 March, i.e., immediately after the publication of the Soviet note on the basis of a peace treaty with Germany. With their note on the Austrian treaty the Western Powers are trying to deflect the world's attention away from the important new initiative of the USSR regarding the German question.

In light of his newly acquired knowledge, it was obvious to Zorin that the Western powers had planned to table the Abbreviated Treaty at the session scheduled for 21 January 1952. That the Soviet leadership had been unaware of the existence of the Abbreviated Treaty is demonstrated by the fact that the Soviet Foreign Ministry based their internal preparation for this session on the assumption that it would be possible "to finalize all outstanding articles" and that the Austrian State Treaty would then be ready for signing.

While the Soviet Foreign Ministry was closely monitoring Western reactions to the Stalin Note after 10 March,[52] the MGB reported to the Soviet leadership with a frequency that reflected the urgency of the situation on the Western powers' internal deliberations and discussions on the subject. France in particular became very explicit. Circles in the Quai d'Orsay sympathetic to the Soviet cause pointed out to the Soviets in no uncertain terms that it was the Americans who were opposed to all kinds of negotiations with the Soviets and had also pressured the French into agreeing to the Abbreviated Treaty. These same circles, about which Ignatiev incidentally failed to be more specific, let the Soviets know that Washington intended to confront "the Soviet government with the choice" of either "accepting the draft of the Abbreviated Treaty in the form prepared by the Western Powers or rejecting it. [. . .] The French thought it was imperative to 'keep the door open' for the USSR in case it became necessary to resurrect the former draft [of the Austrian State Treaty]."[53] This was presumably how elements within the French government shared with their old ally their dissatisfaction with the official French foreign policy. Subsequent to the presentation of the note in Moscow, Paris became convinced that the Stalin Note was much "more than a red herring": it amounted to "a sincere if highly dangerous attempt to settle the German question."[54] According to Georges-Henri Soutou, "only a few top officials" in the Quai d'Orsay considered "neutral status for Germany within a new European security framework of the kind advocated by Moscow between 1952 and 1955" acceptable. As a rule, "the possibility of a re-united, bloc-free Germany was what France dreaded most." The doctrine of double security on the basis of a lasting partition of Germany (in tacit agreement with Moscow) provided for the solution of two problems "with one stroke," as the integration of the Federal Republic into the Western bloc also enhanced security with regard to the Soviet Union.[55] For the same reason, France had always militated for the Austrian treaty to contain a clause that provided against a future "Anschluß" of Austria or parts thereof to West Germany.[56] In their communications with Moscow, the French "top officials" vaguely referred to in the MGB documents claimed that this clause had been inserted into the Abbreviated Treaty at their insistence against opposition from Washington and London.[57]

The Kremlin Keeping Mum on Austria

Because the Kremlin's priorities in early 1952 precluded completing work on the Austrian State Treaty, the Soviet deputy was instructed not to appear at the session scheduled in London for January. The rationale behind this move was not, as has already been said, Soviet awareness of the impending presentation of the Abbreviated Treaty by the Western Powers; it was purely and simply the Soviets' lack of interest at this stage in the conclusion of a treaty for Austria.[58] Britain concluded at the time that the Soviets must have been warned of the impending diplomatic maneuver that was the Abbreviated Treaty. Rumor had it that Indian diplomats were the source of this piece of intelligence; it seemed to follow quite naturally that the Soviets had boycotted the session to deprive the Americans of presenting the Abbreviated Treaty; this was going to put the Soviets in the position of branding the Abbreviated Treaty as a "unilateral act by the Western Powers."[59] None of this had, in fact, been the case. The Indian information nuggets were nothing but the figments of a mistaken interpretation of Soviet policy.

The MGB's failure to brief the Soviet leadership in late 1951 and early 1952 on the West's plans for a diplomatic maneuver in the guise of the Abbreviated Treaty did not work to the detriment of Soviet policies towards Germany and Austria. Moscow was in any case unwilling to agree to neutral status for Austria until spring 1952 at the earliest. Until then, at least one obstacle was blocking the road to further progress: the German question. If the Soviets had reached an agreement with the Western powers regarding neutral status for Austria against their inclination, this would, in fact, have produced a blueprint for Germany. This is why the Kremlin at that stage ultimately dropped even its *pro forma* readiness to take part in talks on the subject for the first time in the course of the State Treaty negotiations. As Zorin pointed out to Molotov, a rejection of the Abbreviated Treaty by the USSR might result in a referral of the Austrian question to the UN. Moreover, he feared that the Western powers might go it alone with a unilateral declaration on Austria and begin to withdraw their troops from Austria's occupation zones: this would have necessitated the withdrawal of Soviet troops from eastern Austria.[60]

In the case of Germany, the Kremlin could rule out anything of the kind being considered by the Western powers. Given the circumstances, Moscow was in a tight corner. On the question of Austria, the Kremlin subsequently played for time, which was the only option available. In the meantime, what had become clear in Moscow was that the Abbreviated

Treaty, while it was no direct answer to the Stalin Note dated 10 March, was going to be exploited by the West in order to direct attention away from the German question. The most expedient course to take was for Moscow to ignore the Abbreviated Treaty. The question of Austria had become too hot. If Stalin had really and truly wanted neutral status for Germany, he could have, with relative ease, removed the relatively minor Austrian issue from the equation. As long ago as 1991, Günter Bischof pointed out the interdependence existing between the Stalin Notes and the Western note which was used as the vehicle for the Abbreviated Treaty;[61] until then, this interdependence had gone unnoticed by historians, and its significance has remained grossly underrated to this day. From the Soviet point of view, the German question could not be solved until after the partition of Germany had reached a point of no return.[62] In the meantime, Moscow was reduced to playing up the obstacles with reference to the Austrian question, particularly its demands for de-Nazification and demilitarization and the question of Trieste.[63]

After almost two months of Soviet non-reaction, the Western Powers contacted the Foreign Ministry of the USSR via diplomatic channels asking the Soviets "to elucidate their point of view with regard to the settlement of the issue of Austria at their earliest convenience."[64] The Soviets were still unable to reply. Any reply other than a positive one would have come as a great surprise to the other parties involved. Yet Moscow was unable to extend an offer of neutral status to Austria as well, even though it would have vindicated Moscow's putative readiness to enter into talks on the German question. Three days after the receipt of the missive urging a reply regarding the Abbreviated Treaty, Vyshinsky told Stalin that attention should remain focused on the discussion of the German question, "I would deem it advisable in principle not to react to the note [. . .] concerning the Abbreviated Treaty for Austria at this stage in order not to deflect attention away from the discussion of the German question, which, as we know, also has a high priority for the governments of the US, England and France."[65]

It became obvious in 1952 that Austria had become a pawn in the Cold War scenario of world politics. The West exploited the Austrian question to check out whether Stalin really meant business regarding the German question. For the Kremlin, on the other hand, it was advisable to keep mum on Austria in order not to create a precedent for Germany. Put more simply, Austria was used as a test case to explore the hidden agenda of the other side. The Western powers had "fathomed" what could be expected of Stalin and how far he was prepared to go.

Austria held its first post-war parliamentary elections at the end of 1945, which resulted in a coalition of the ÖVP, Austria's conservatives, and the socialist SPÖ. In the interim government that preceded the first democratically elected one, the communists, the KPÖ, had gained a complimentary share of one-third of the available seats; in the November election of 1945, the party was almost wiped out completely, getting a pitiful 5 percent of the vote. Although the KPÖ at least held on to one ministerial post until 1947, the Soviet political representatives in Austria concluded that the government was a bunch of Western puppets that gravitated more and more towards a pro-American stance and consisted of American and British agents anyway.[66] In the eyes of the Kremlin, the so-called "secret ally"[67] had already come out of the closet and was taking up a position openly opposed to the Soviet Union. The enlargement of NATO that took place in the early 1950s presumably caused a great deal of concern in the Kremlin.[68] At least in the eyes of Soviet diplomats, membership in NATO was a perfectly viable option for Austria—or at least for parts of it.[69] For this reason, the Soviet High Commissioner in Austria, Vladimir Sviridov, did not support the idea of neutral status for Austria in 1952. At that time, the countdown to the final launch of a consolidated GDR, this idea simply did not make sense in Soviet eyes; nor were the future prospects in the form of Austria's ongoing and accelerating orientation towards the West, with a worst-case scenario of the country being integrated into NATO, any more encouraging. According to Sviridov, the latter project met with stiff resistance from the Austrian coalition government, as American military planning would have involved the partitioning of Austria. He claimed that the Americans had been considering creating a new political entity by tacking western Austria onto Bavaria, which would have strengthened West Germany as well as the United States; these plans, however, had to be scrapped due to British and French opposition. Sviridov also stressed the strategic importance of the west of Austria for the Americans, who needed to be able to ship supplies to their troops stationed in Germany via the route from Trieste to Bavaria. He came to the conclusion that "American interest in the Austrian treaty was focused solely on the prospect of Austria becoming a member of the Atlantic alliance and not on the country's neutrality or independence."[70]

Austria in Finland's Footsteps?

Austrian diplomats and politicians had realized early on that the country was being cast in the role of a pawn in the great game of the

West's German policy and that the Abbreviated Treaty had been conceived with priorities in mind that were at odds with Austria's best interests. Yet it was impossible for Austria not to support the West's "proposals." After the Stalin Note had resulted in a complete eclipse of Austria on the international political stage, the only countermove left to Vienna was to reanimate and finally implement the long cultivated plans of a referral of the Austrian question to the United Nations; this move had been coordinated closely with Washington. At this stage, in view of the fact that negotiations on the Austrian question had ground to a halt, a group of politicians in Vienna headed by the leader of the ÖVP, the future Federal Chancellor Julius Raab, began to question the wisdom of predicating Austria's foreign policy exclusively on the two key elements of an unqualified orientation towards the United States on the one hand and unconcealed antagonism towards the USSR on the other. Raab started signalling ÖVP flexibility to Moscow long before his well-known speech of 1953, in which he declared it was a mug's game "rhetorically to tweak the stumpy tail of the Russian bear, who has ensconced himself plumb in the middle of the Austrian garden."[71] On 23 February, only a few weeks after the first extraordinary party congress of the ÖVP, the "Party Congress of New Ideas,"[72] Josef Dobretsberger, the leader of the *Demokratische Union* and something of a dark horse in Austrian postwar politics, whose name had been floated in 1947 in the wake of the so-called "Figl-Fischerei" as the candidate for the post of federal chancellor supposedly endorsed by the Soviets—his leanings had earned him the nickname "*Sowjetsberger*"[73]—told Raab there was no other option for him but to become a "second Kekkonen" and none other for Austria "but to follow exactly in Finland's footsteps." By way of reply, Raab asked Dobretsberger, whose next trip to Moscow was imminent, to pass on the message to representatives of the Soviet Foreign Ministry "that there was a group of politicians in the ÖVP [. . .] who were casting around for a route that would lead to neutral status for Austria without it turning into a People's Democracy."[74] It has been impossible to date to establish who led off in this direction. Dobretsberger certainly maintained close contacts with the Soviets and the KPÖ. What is important to note is that this is the first documented suggestion that Austria model itself on Finland. Finland, as is well known, claimed a far larger share of the Soviet Union's interest than Austria, yet for many reasons the country was spared the fate of ending up in the Soviet orbit. In 1948, Stalin had contented himself with concluding the Treaty of Friendship with the Finns.[75]

In the ensuing months, while the Battle of the Notes was at its height, there was a steadily increasing trickle of reports on how Austria was distancing itself more and more from its former position of unconditionally supporting a confrontational course towards the USSR. It was still too early for the Kremlin to react to Vienna's overtures, but they were the beginning of a process that led, still in Stalin's lifetime, to the first Soviet-Austrian talks in the autumn of 1952.[76]

On 19 March 1952, Molotov learned from Zorin that Julius Raab had received assurances from the Americans during his visit to Washington that Austria "would soon be rid of the Russians"; for the United States to couch assurances in such blunt terms was an entirely new development. According to Zorin, Raab had been given the advice to ensure there was a strong Austrian government on which the United States could rely at the decisive moment. Zorin felt "that in case the Soviet Union rejected the draft of the Abbreviated Treaty, the Western powers might refer the Austrian question to the UN together with a declaration unilaterally granting Austria freedom and sovereignty; the withdrawal of their troops from Austrian territory would equally necessitate the withdrawal of Soviet troops."[77] This was, of course, a purely theoretical solution to the problem of Austria. The Austrian Foreign Minister, Karl Gruber, calling this possibility "unthinkable" and potentially "the end of Austria," had already precluded it in a meeting of ÖVP parliamentarians on 12 February 1952. In Vienna, everyone was aware that a withdrawal of all Allied troops was unconditionally tied to global détente, which would have been more than welcome on all counts.[78] In Zorin's eyes, the fact that Figl promptly reshuffled his government in January 1952 signaled his opting for a "tough" course towards the USSR and the KPÖ in order to prepare the ground for the United States co-opting Austria into NATO.[79] In order to support measures for the "defense of Europe against the USSR and its allies," the Socialist International had issued marching orders in Brussels in 1951 to Austria's Socialist Party, the SPÖ, as well as to all other European socialist parties "to vote in parliament unreservedly in favour of all budgetary items to do with defence and armament."[80] The ÖVP, still according to Zorin, was losing its hold on Austrian politics; since 1951, its appeal to the masses had definitely diminished. This was the reason why the ÖVP had held an extraordinary party conference early in 1952, which was characterized by its consistent anti-Soviet tenor.[81] Finally, in May 1952 the USSR criticized the Austrian government "openly to an extent that was without precedent [...] since the beginning of the Cold War."[82]

For Raab this was, of course, grist to his political mill.

The Referral of the Austrian Question to the United Nations

Austria's Federal Chancellor, Leopold Figl, subsequently advocated referring the Austrian question to the United Nations. Moscow was aware that the Austrian government would be unable to take this step unless it had the West's backing to do so.[83] Brazil's forthcoming initiative to have the Austrian question put on the agenda of the Seventh Plenary Session of the United Nations[84] was regarded as having originated with the Americans.[85] The French had suggested that care be taken lest the UN initiative "look like a maneuver directed against the USSR."[86] The USSR's official role remained confined to that of an observer of the Austrian development. On 7 June 1952, Molotov learned from Semen Ignatiev, the head of the MGB, of Raab's speech in which he had asserted that there was no need "to be afraid of standing up to the Americans [. . .] or of taking the sympathies seriously that existed in Austria for Russia."[87] A few days later, on 18 June, Molotov had Zorin analyze to what extent recent changes within the Austrian government were due to the impact of the Abbreviated Treaty.[88] On 29 July, Ignatiev reported that Raab considered the Abbreviated Treaty a "cheap ploy" of the Americans angled at the USSR; according to Ignatiev, he thought that the Americans were completely at a loss concerning "what course to take." Raab thought, moreover, that the approaching elections in the United States were having a paralyzing effect on U.S. politics. In the run-up to the elections, the Austrian government should "create the impression" as if "it was following all American instructions to the letter" while, in fact, all major decisions should be put on hold until after the presidential elections.[89] Around the middle of August, Ignatiev reported that Dean Acheson, whose term of office as Harry S. Truman's Secretary of State was drawing to a close, had asked the Austrian government to speed up the creation of an army to "fill the [strategic] vacuum between Yugoslavia and West Germany."[90] Vienna, as we know, promptly complied. The creation of the so-called B-gendarmerie,[91] the beta version as it were of the Austrian *Bundesheer*, and the installation of arms depots in Austria by the U.S. and the British secret services are by-products of the East-West confrontation in this particular phase of the initial stages of the Cold War.[92]

It was not until five months later, on 14 August 1952, that Moscow articulated its rejection of the Abbreviated Treaty for the first time in a note;[93] in the same breath, it proposed a resumption of the state treaty negotiations on the basis of the old draft. Four days earlier, Molotov had been extensively briefed by Ignatiev on the exchange of telegrams between the Foreign Ministry in Vienna and Austria's political representative in Moscow, Norbert Bischoff. According to the relevant document, Bischoff had told Karl Gruber, Austria's foreign minister, that the Soviet Union was not planning to launch a war of aggression against Europe or to start World War III.[94] On 24 September, Moscow rejected the Abbreviated Treaty for a second time.[95] Moscow signaled—or appeared to signal—its readiness to take part in talks on Austria in a phase when it claimed—or appeared to claim—to be similarly disposed with regard to the German question. Today we know that in early 1952 Moscow was not interested in signing a state treaty with Austria or in permitting it to assume the status of a neutral country. In the autumn of 1952, however, the Soviet Union was again ready to return to talks on the Austrian question with the proviso that the subject of the Abbreviated Treaty not be broached.

On 20 December 1952, the UN plenum adopted a resolution calling for an early conclusion of the Austrian State Treaty.[96] The Soviet delegation had received the directive to abstain from voting.[97] The delegation had already been unable to prevent the Austrian question from being put on the agenda of the UN plenum.[98]

Conclusion

The Abbreviated Treaty, which had been conceived as an instrument directed against the interests of the USSR (a fact also commented on by Molotov in the paper presented to him by Vyshinsky),[99] provided an almost ideal diplomatic pretext for the Soviets not to have to enter into negotiations on the Austrian State Treaty. The West wanted to exploit the Austrian question to probe Soviet intentions regarding the question of Germany. The Abbreviated Treaty was presented at the Foreign Ministry in Moscow on 13 March 1952, three days after the publication of the Soviet "offer" of German reunification, the Stalin Note, which took the world by surprise and caused considerable irritation among the Soviet leadership. The MGB possessed information on the West's propaganda coup, which had been long enough in the making, but had failed to pass this information on to Stalin, Molotov, or the Foreign Ministry. The Soviets proceeded in January 1952 from the erroneous assumption that the Western powers were interested in the conclusion of the Austrian State Treaty. As Moscow had no intention at this stage of withdrawing militarily from Austria, the London talks were aborted by the Soviets in accordance with directives issued by Stalin.

Immediately after the presentation of the Abbreviated Treaty, Molotov gave orders to Ignatiev to investigate the rationale behind the treaty. On the basis of intelligence information obtained from the French Foreign Ministry and of intercepted telegrams, Ignatiev reached the conclusion that the West's objective was to maneuver the USSR into the dilemma of having to choose whether to accept or reject the treaty in the form as presented. The presentation had been timed, according to Ignatiev, with a view to deflecting the world's attention away from the Soviet initiative regarding the German question. After a note from the Western powers urging a reply, Vyshinsky advised Stalin not to respond to the Abbreviated Treaty. Non-reaction was, it must be said, the only option open to the Kremlin. A solution of the problem of Austria would not only have affirmed a readiness on Stalin's part to enter into negotiations, which seemed to transpire also from the plethora of notes in 1952, but was, in fact, non-existent; it would also have demonstrated that solid results were to be gained in the end. Stalin was in no position in 1952 to authorize negotiations on Austria, for this might very well have led to the creation of a blueprint for Germany. From the point of view of the Kremlin, Austria was needed as a prop to shore up Eastern Europe in two ways: first of all, it legitimized the presence of Soviet troops in Hungary and Rumania and, second, if Austria had been released, voices in Germany would inevitably have demanded the same, which would, in addition to everything else, have amounted to an existential threat to the GDR.

Germany was partitioned, yet Austria was not. East Germany was sovietized, yet in occupied eastern Austria, Sovietization measures were never even attempted. Nevertheless, Soviet policy towards Germany and Austria was predicated on the same priorities. In the one case, Soviet security and political considerations led to an enforced partition and to Sovietization; in the other, the same considerations precluded either of these measures. The establishment of a communist regime in East Germany was a means to an end for the Soviet Union, yet in this case, security and political goals went hand in hand with ideological ones; the two complemented each other. In Austria, it was not only possible to play down the importance of the ideological goal of spreading communism, but to discard the goal altogether.[100]

The partition of Germany finally opened up the road forward to neutral status for Austria. In the Kremlin's eyes, neutrality was a more advantageous solution in the case of Austria than partition, which would only have resulted in strengthening West Germany. Western Austria on its own would not have constituted a viable entity. The Kremlin had achieved all of its goals in Central Europe: Germany was weakened for the foreseeable future: the partitioning of the country, which appeared irreversible at the time, and the neutral status of Austria guaranteed this. Whether this had been the minimum Soviet foreign policy had set itself to achieve or the maximum is another question altogether.

Appendix

Document 1: Report of the Minister of State Security of the USSR, S. Ignatiev, to V. Molotov (Oral Communication).

Ignatiev: According to information received from officials in the top echelons of the French Foreign Ministry, a resolution regarding the question of the Austrian State Treaty has been passed at the conference of the foreign ministers of the USA, England, and France. The resolution provides for the previous draft of the treaty to be regarded merely as a preliminary version drawn up by experts that does not have binding force for the governments of the Western powers. The same source had also passed on the information that France's position in the talks on the draft of the Abbreviated Treaty had differed from the positions of the US and England. The Americans asserted that it was necessary to confront the Soviet government with the choice of either accepting the draft of the Abbreviated Treaty in the form as presented by the Western powers or of rejecting it. The French on the other hand felt that the "door had to be kept open" for the USSR so that a return to the previous draft was possible should the need arise. Despite objections from American and British officials the French insisted on introducing an anti-Anschluß clause into the text of the Abbreviated Treaty.

Forwarded to Comrade Stalin and the other comrades in the Committee of Eight as well as to Comrades Vyshinsky and Zorin. RGASPI, F. 82, op. 2, d. 1042, S. 78, 18.3.1952.

Document 2: Report of the Deputy Foreign Minister of the USSR, V. Zorin, to V. Molotov. (Oral Communication).

Zorin: According to a communication from the French ambassador in Washington, Bonnet [Henri Bonnet, ambassador from 1944 to 1954], to the French Foreign Ministry dated 14 September 1951, [Dean] Acheson made a proposal during the discussion of the Austrian question by the foreign ministers of the United States, England and France; he proposed tabling at the forthcoming session of the Deputies for the Negotiation of the Austrian [State] Treaty an abbreviated version [of the previous treaty], in which all concessions made by the Western powers to the Soviet Union in the course of the negotiations in the past were to be declared null and void. The object of the American proposal was, in Bonnet's words, to put the Soviet government in a "difficult" position. Morrison [Herbert Morrison, later Lord Morrison of Lambeth, British Foreign Secretary from March to October 1951] insisted that there was no hurry implementing the American plan. The party leader of the *Österreichische Volkspartei* told the members of his party's inner circle in September 1951 that the Americans had promised him to "rid Austria of the Russians" within the next few months and to integrate Austria into the system of the North Atlantic Treaty Organisation. According to Raab, the Americans felt, on the evidence of the "feeble response of the USSR in the context of the Japanese treaty," that the Soviet Union was unlikely to risk a war because of Austria. Raab also pointed out that the Americans wanted a "strong government" to be in charge of Austria when the time came, one that was capable of bringing "passive resistance" to bear against the orders of the Soviet occupation force. By the end of 1951, the American proposal regarding the question of the Austrian Treaty was finalized among the three Western powers; as a next step they proposed convening the next session of the four deputies for 21 January 1952 with the intention of presenting the abbreviated version of the treaty at that session. The governments of the Western powers displayed symptoms of being pressed for time regarding the presentation of the note: their ambassadors were most insistent that they be given an appointment at the Foreign Ministry of the USSR on 13 March, i.e. immediately after the publication of the Soviet note on the conditions for a peace treaty with Germany. With their note on the Austrian treaty the Western powers tried to deflect the attention of the world away from the important new initiative of the USSR regarding the German question. Comrade Zorin has pointed out that a rejection of the Abbreviated Treaty by the USSR might result in a referral of the Austrian question to the UN by the Western powers. Moreover, according to him, the Western powers might go it alone with a unilateral declaration on "granting Austria freedom and sovereignty" and, by withdrawing their troops from Austria's territory, also necessitate the withdrawal of Soviet troops from eastern Austria.

Forwarded to all the members of the Committee of Eight as well as to Comrades Vyshinsky and Gromyko. RGASPI, F. 82, op. 2, d. 1042, S. 82, 19.3.1952.

Notes

* I am grateful to state government of Carinthia for financially supporting my archival research for this article.

1. Otmar Binder translated this essay from German into English. This article is based on Peter Ruggenthaler, ed., *Stalins großer Bluff: Die Geschichte der Stalin-Note in Dokumenten der sowjetischen Führung*, Schriftenreihe der Vierteljahrshefte für Zeitgeschichte, vol. 95 (Munich: 2007).

2. Ignatiev to Molotov, 10 October 1952, Russian State Archives of Social and Political History (henceforth: RGASPI), F. 82, op. 2, d. 1348, 175.

3. For more details see, Gerhard Wettig, *Bereitschaft zu Einheit in Freiheit? Die sowjetische Deutschland-Politik 1945-1955* (Munich: Olzog, 1999), 205-06.

4. I would like to thank Professor Stefan Karner for the unstinting support he has given over the years to young historians like me. I also want to convey my gratitude to my colleagues at the Ludwig Boltzmann-Institute for Research on War Consequences in Graz, to Wolfram Dornik, Walter M. Iber, Harald Knoll, Barbara Stelzl-Marx, and Silke Stern, who have read this article and offered many helpful suggestions. I am deeply indebted to Kirill Anderson, Olga Pavlenko, Mikhail Prozumenshchikov and Aleksey Filitov in Moscow and to Vladislav Zubok in Philadelphia for many interesting discussions and exchanges of ideas. Finally, I would like to thank Günter Bischof in New Orleans for accepting this article for publication in *Contemporary Austrian Studies*.

5. This is already hinted at in Alexey M. Filitov, "SSSR i germanskij vopros: Povorotnye punkty (1941-1961gg.)," in *Kholodnaya vojna 1945-1963gg. Istoricheskaya retrospektiva. Sbornik statej*, ed. Natalija I. Egorova and Aleksandr O. Èubar'jan (Moscow: Olma, 2003), 342-43; Stefan Creuzberger, Manfred Görtemaker, "Das Problem der Gleich-schaltung osteuropäischer Parteien im Vergleich. Eine Synthese," in *Gleichschaltung unter Stalin? Die Entwicklung der Parteien im östlichen Europa 1944-1949*, ed. Stefan Creuzberger and Manfred Görtemaker (Paderborn: F. Schöningh, 2002), 434; Wilfried Loth, "Die Entstehung der 'Stalin-Note.'" Dokumente aus Moskauer Archiven," in *Die Stalin-Note vom 10. März 1952. Neue Quellen und Analysen. Mit Beiträgen von Wilfried Loth, Hermann Graml und Gerhard Wettig*, ed. Jürgen Zarusky (Munich: R. Oldenbourg, 2002), 19-115; and, finally, Bernd Bonwetsch and Sergej Kudrjašov, "Stalin und die II. Parteikonferenz der SED," in *Stalin und die Deutschen. Neue Beiträge der Forschung*, ed. Jürgen Zarusky (Munich: Oldenbourg, 2006), 182.

6. In the AP RF [Archives of the President of the Russian Federation], the holdings in question had the shelf mark F. 56, op. 1, in RGASPI this has been changed to F. 82, op. 2.

7. Stefan Karner and Barbara Stelzl-Marx, eds., *Die Rote Armee in Österreich. Beiträge Sowjetische Besatzung 1945–1955* (Graz: Oldenbourg, 2005); Stefan Karner, et al., eds., *Die Rote Armee in Österreich. Sowjetische Besatzung 1945–1955. Dokumente. Krasnaja Armija v Avstrii. Sovetskaja okkupacija 1945-1955. Dokumenty* (Graz: Oldenbourg, 2005).

8. Natalija Egorova, "Evropeyskaya bezopasnost' i 'ugroza' NATO v ocenkach stalinskogo rukovodstva in Stalinskoe desjatiletie cholodnoj vojny," in *Stalinskoe desyatiletie. kholodnoi voiny: Fakty i gipotezy*, ed. Alexander O. Chubaryan (Moscow: Nauka, 1999), 56-78. Identification of the sources used by her and by those who came after her was limited to F. [holdings] 82 without further details.

9. Mikhail M. Narinsky, "The Soviet Union and the Marshall-Plan." *Cold War International History Project*. Working Paper No. 9. (Washington, D.C., 1994), 41-51.

10. The evidence that can be gleaned from the files is presented by Wladimir K. Wolkow, "Die deutsche Frage aus Stalins Sicht (1947-1952)," *Zeitschrift für Geschichtswissenschaft* 48 (2000): 20-49.

11. See above all the contributions of Stein Björnstad, Alexey Filitov, Voytech Mastny, and Gerhard Wettig. Individual documents from the AP RF are quoted from Loth, "Die Entstehung der 'Stalin-Note,'" 59. Most publications written within the last fifteen years have also tapped the holdings of the *Zentrales Parteiarchiv der SED*, the SED Party Archive.

12. Zubok points out that it is doubtful whether Stalin read all the information given to him by the Secret Services. Vladislav Zubok, "Soviet Intelligence and the Cold War: The 'Small' Committee of Information, 1952-53," in *CWIHP, Working paper 4* (Washington D.C., 1992), 455. Even condensed reports sometimes only reached him if Alexander Pos krebyshev, his personal secretary, read them out to him. For this information, I am indebted to Olga Pavlenko in Moscow.

13. For an overview, see Gerhard Wettig, "Die Stalin-Note vom 10. März 1952 als geschichtswissenschaftliches Problem. Ein gewandeltes Problemverständnis," *Deutschland Archiv* 25 (1992): 159.

14. Günter Bischof, "Karl Gruber und die Anfänge des 'Neuen Kurses' in der österreichischen Außenpolitik 1952/53," in *Für Österreichs Freiheit. Karl Gruber—Landeshauptmann und Außenminister 1945-1953*, ed. Lothar Höbelt and Othmar Huber, Innsbrucker Forschungen zur Zeitgeschichte, vol. 7 (Innsbruck: Haymon, 1991), 147-49.

15. Michael Gehler, "Kurzvertrag für Österreich? Die westliche Staatsvertrags-Diplomatie und die Stalin-Noten von 1952," *Vierteljahreshefte für Zeitgeschichte* 42 (1994): 243-78.

16. Vgl. Gerald Stourzh, *Um Einheit und Freiheit: Staatsvertrag, Neutralität und das Ende der Ost-West-Besetzung Österreichs 1945-1955*, 5th ed., Studien zu Politik und Verwaltung, vol. 62 (Graz: Böhlau, 2005), 154-55; Audrey Kurth Cronin, "Eine verpasste Chance? Die Großmächte und die Verhandlungen über den Staatsvertrag im Jahre 1949," in *Die bevormundete Nation: Österreich und die Alliierten, 1945-1949*, ed. Günter Bischof and Josef Leidenfrost, Innsbrucker Forschungen zur Zeitgeschichte, vol. 4 (Innsbruck: Haymon, 1988), 347-51.

17. For details, see Peter Ruggenthaler, "Warum Österreich nicht sowjetisiert wurde: Sowjetische Österreich-Politik 1945 bis 1953/55," in *Die Rote Armee in Österreich. Beiträge Sowjetische Besatzung 1945–1955* (Graz: Oldenbourg, 2005), 649-726; Stefan Karner and Peter Ruggenthaler, "Stalin und Österreich. Sowjetische Österreich-Politik 1938 bis 1953," in *Jahrbuch für Historische Kommunismusforschung 2005* (Berlin: Akademie Verlag, 2005), 102-40.

18. Ruggenthaler, "Warum Österreich nicht sowjetisiert wurde," 680.

19. Bischof, "Karl Gruber und die Anfänge des 'Neuen Kurses' in der österreichischen Außenpolitik 1952/53," 144; Stourzh, *Um Einheit und Freiheit*, 178.

20. Ruggenthaler, "Warum Österreich nicht sowjetisiert wurde," 683-85.

21. Ibid., 686. For the question of Trieste see Stourzh, *Um Einheit und Freiheit*, 178-89.

22. Ibid., 267; Karner and Ruggenthaler, "Stalin und Österreich. Sowjetische Österreich-Politik 1938 bis 1953," 124-25.

23. Gribanov to Vyshinsky on the proposals of Tsinev and Koptelov from 28 February 1950, Archives on Foreign Policy of the Russian Federation (henceforth: AVP RF), F. 66, op. 29, p. 49, d. 11, 25–27.

24. Loth, "Die Entstehung der 'Stalin-Note.'"

25. See note. 23. In February 1951, Chuykov and Semenov advocated adopting this central demand of the "neutralist" movement.

26. The same view is taken by Gerald Stourzh, most recently in "Der österreichische Staatsvertrag in den weltpolitischen Entscheidungsprozessen," in *Der österreichische Staatsvertrag 1955. Internationale Strategie, rechtliche Relevanz,* ed. Arnold Suppan et al., *Nationale Identität, Archiv für österreichische Geschichte, vol. 140* (Vienna: Verlag der Österreichischen Akademie der Wissenschaften, 2005), 973-74. Wolfgang Mueller takes a different view; see "Gab es eine verpasste Chance?", in ibid., 116.

27. Khrushchev pointed this out in his closing speech at the plenary session of the Central Committee of the CPSU in July 1955. He reminded the CC that in the year preceding his death Stalin had asked several times why the treaty with Austria was not yet concluded. Stourzh, *Um Einheit und Freiheit*, 458-59; *CWIHP 10, Plenum Transcripts, 1955-1957*, 42-43.

28. Zorin reporting to Stalin, to all the other members of the Committee of Eight, and to Suslov, Vyshinsky, Grigoryan, Bogomilov, and Pushkin, 5 June 1952, RGASPI, F. 82, op. 2, d. 1043, 198.

29. Stourzh, *Der österreichische Staatsvertrag in den weltpolitischen Entscheidungsprozessen*, 973-74. A question awaiting further research is to what extent a militarily neutral status for Austria was also relevant to the reconciliation process that was taking place between the Kremlin and Tito. According to Bruno Kreisky's testimony, Belgrade had named the solution of the Austrian question as the top priority precondition for a reconciliation; see ibid., 979-80.

30. Victor Zaslavskij, *Lo stalinismo e la sinistra italiana dal mito dell' URSS alla fine del comunismo. 1945-1991* (Milan: Mondadori, 2004).

31. Voytech Mastny, "Die NATO im sowjetischen Denken und Handeln 1949 bis 1956," in *Konfrontationsmuster des Kalten Krieges 1946 bis 1956*, ed. Voytech Mastny and Gustav Schmidt, Entstehen und Probleme des Atlantischen Bündnisses bis 1956, vol. 3 (Munich: R. Oldenbourg, 2003), 440-41.

32. Stourzh, *Um Einheit und Freiheit*, 454-456.

33. Ibid 478; most recently, Stourzh, Der österreichische Staatsvertrag in den weltpolitischen Entscheidungsprozessen, 990-991.

34. This is how Mikoyan put it to the July Plenum of the CPSU. See the stenographic minutes of the July Plenum of the Central Committee of the CPSU published in Karner et al. eds., *Die Rote Armee in Österreich*, 841-43.

35. On the subject of the Abbreviated Treaty in general, see the publications of Günter Bischof. His most recent ones take the most up-to-date research into account, for example, "'Recapturing the Initiative' and 'Negotiating from Strength': The Hidden Agenda of the 'Short Treaty' Episode—The Militarization of American Foreign Policy and the Un/Making of the Austrian Treaty," in *Der österreichische Staatsvertrag 1955*, ed. Arnold Suppan et al., (Vienna: Verlag der Österreichischen Akademie der Wissenschaften, 2005) 217-47, with appended bibliographies. Also cf. Gehler, "Kurzvertrag für Österreich?", 253; Stourzh, *Um Einheit und Freiheit*, 184-92. Soviet files (Politburo decisions from the Special Portfolio and the Molotov files concerning Austria) touching on the Abbreviated Treaty have been mined for the first time in Ruggenthaler, "Warum Österreich nicht sowjetisiert wurde. Sowjetische Österreichpolitik," 698-701.

36. Gehler, "Kurzvertrag für Österreich?," 244.

37. Ibid.

38. See Stourzh, *Um Einheit und Freiheit*, 183.

39. Ignatiev reporting to Molotov and Gromyko, 9 January 1952, RGASPI, F. 82, op. 2, d. 1042, 7.

40. Ruggenthaler, "Warum Österreich nicht sowjetisiert wurde," 698; Gromyko to Stalin, 16 January 1952, RGASPI, F. 82, op. 2, d. 1115, 62-64. Drafts with Molotov's emendations, ibid. 38-39, 67-69.

41. Ibid. By late summer 1951, the Soviet Foreign Ministry had learned that Washington intended resuming negotiations on the Austrian State Treaty and giving financial aid to Austria to repay its debts to the USSR. Zorin to Gromyko, 1 August 1951, RGASPI, F. 82, op. 2, d. 1041, 153.

42. Ruggenthaler, "Warum Österreich nicht sowjetisiert wurde" 699; Stourzh, *Um Einheit und Freiheit*, 183.

43. Günter Bischof, *Austria in the First Cold War, 1945-55: The Leverage of the Weak*, Cold War History Series (Houndmills: Macmillan, 1999), 123-29 and, "Karl Gruber und die Anfänge des 'Neuen Kurses' in der österreichischen Außenpolitik 1952/53," 146.

44. Gehler, "Kurzvertrag für Österreich?," 248-49.

45. Bischof, "Karl Gruber und die Anfänge des 'Neuen Kurses' in der österreichischen Außenpolitik 1952/53," 147; most recently, Günter Bischof, "'Recapturing the Initiative'," 243.

46. Gehler, "Kurzvertrag für Österreich?," 248-50.

47. Ibid., 253.

48. The real purpose behind the Abbreviated Treaty was not the only piece of intelligence to be withheld from the Soviet leadership. In none of the reports on the 9th Meeting of the NATO Council—or at least in none that are accessible to researchers—is there any mention of the Western powers having publicly announced "new proposals" on the Austrian question. For the deliberations on the Austrian question in Lisbon, see Bischof, "Karl Gruber und die Anfänge des 'Neuen Kurses' in der österreichischen Außenpolitik 1952/53," 146-47.

49. RGASPI, F. 82, op. 2, d. 1115, 95-109.

50. Mention of the Abbreviated Treaty is also absent from all reports on the Lisbon meeting of the NATO Council, where the decision was taken to present it to the USSR. Zorin reporting to all the members of the Committee of Eight as well as to Vyshinsky, Vasilevsky, Gromyko, and Grigoryan, 2 March 1952, RGASPI, F. 82, op. 2, d. 1042, 58; Gromyko to Stalin (Draft to Molotov), 3 March 1952, RGASPI, F. 82, op. 2, d. 1170, 4852; Ignatiev to all the members of the Committee of Eight and to Vyshinsky, 17 March 1952, RGASPI, F. 82, op. 2, d. 1042, 77; Ignatiev to all the members of the Committee of Eight and to Vyshinsky, 17 March 1952, RGASPI, F. 82, op. 2, d. 1042, 76.

51. Ignatiev to all the members of the Committee of Eight as well as to Vyshinsky and Zorin, 19 March 1952, RGASPI, F. 82, op. 2, d. 1042, 82.

52. Loth, "Die Entstehung der 'Stalin-Note'," 57.

53. Ignatiev to Stalin and all the members of the Committee of Eight as well as to Vyshinsky and Zorin, 18 March 1952, RGASPI, F. 82, op. 2, d. 1042, 78.

224   **The Changing Austrian Voter**

54. Rolf Steininger, *Deutsche Geschichte 2: 1948-1955, Darstellung und Dokumente in vier Bänden,* (Frankfurt am Main: Fischer Taschenbuch Verlag, 2002), 180.

55. Georges-Henri Soutou, "Frankreich und der Albtraum eines wiedervereinigten und neutralisierten Deutschlands 1952-1990," in *Neutralität – Chance oder Chimäre? Konzepte des Dritten Weges für Deutschland und die Welt 1945-1990*, ed. Dominik Geppert and Udo Wengst (Munich: R. Oldenbourg, 2005), 265-66.

56. The most recent publication on the subject is Thomas Angerer, "Französische Freundschaftspolitik in Österreich nach 1945: Gründe, Grenzen und Gemeinsamkeiten mit Frankreichs Deutschlandpolitik," in *Die Gunst des Augenblicks. Neuere Forschungen zu Staatsvertrag und Neutralität*, ed. Manfried Rauchensteiner and Robert Kriechbaumer, Schriftenreihe des Forschungsinstitutes für politisch-historische Studien der Dr.-Wilfried-Haslauer-Bibliothek (Vienna: Böhlau, 2005), 134-38.

57. Ignatiev to Stalin, all the members of the Committee of Eight as well as to Vyshinsky and Zorin, 18 March 1952, RGASPI, F. 82, op. 2, d. 1042, 78. For the French insistence on a clause banning another "Anschluß," see Bischof, "'Recapturing the Initiative,'" 243.

58. For more details, see Ruggenthaler, "Warum Österreich nicht sowjetisiert wurde," 698-701.

59. Bischof, "'Recapturing the Initiative,'" 242-43.

60. Zorin to all the members of the Committee of Eight as well as to Vyshinsky and Gromyko, 19 March 1952, RGASPI, F. 82, op. 2, d. 1042, 82.

61. Bischof, "Karl Gruber und die Anfänge des 'Neuen Kurses' in der österreichischen Außenpolitik 1952/53," 147-49.

62. Bischof, "'Recapturing the Initiative,'" 219.

63. Neither the question of Trieste nor de-Nazification nor demilitarization had any genuine priority for the Kremlin, as was already pointed out in 1991 by Bischof, "Karl Gruber und die Anfänge des 'Neuen Kurses' in der österreichischen Außenpolitik 1952/53," 144. What is of interest in this context is the course regarding Austria that Gribanov proposed the Soviet Union should follow as of the beginning of 1950. Gribanov laid out arguments with which the conclusion of the State Treaty could be postponed *ad infinitum*. Soviet diplomacy took his advice to heart, as was demonstrated by the direction further negotiations took. Gribanov to Vyshinsky, 28 February 1950, AVP RF, F. 66, op. 29, p. 49, d. 11, 25-27. On internal Soviet positioning and on Soviet preparation for the State Treaty negotiations, see Ruggenthaler, "Warum Österreich nicht sowjetisiert wurde," 698-705. Michael Gehler suggested as early as 1994 that a solution of the Austrian question would have come in handy for Stalin to demonstrate that his avowed readiness for talks on the German question was, in fact, genuine. The situation was made difficult for him by the Western powers' inflexible insistence on the Abbreviated Treaty; see Gehler, "Kurzvertrag für Österreich?," 277. Zubok comes to the same conclusion in *Soviet Intelligence and the Cold War*, 402.

64. Vyshinsky to Stalin, 12 May 1952, RGASPI, F. 82, op. 2, d. 1115, 110.

65. Ibid., 110. It is interesting in this context how the Abbreviated Treaty is portrayed in a confidential progress report filed by the Soviet High Commissioner, Vladimir Sviridov, to the Central Committee of the CPSU. In it, he called the Abbreviated Treaty an American "maneuver" undertaken with a view to engineering a final breakdown of State Treaty negotiations and confronting Austria with "the prospect of a long period of occupation and possibly ultimate partition." There was no doubt that the Abbreviated Treaty was against the Soviet Union's interests, yet this was, as has been shown,

not what mattered most for Vyshinsky in his reports to Stalin. Vyshinsky even advised Stalin to acknowledge the receipt of the proposals contained in the Abbreviated Treaty. Ibid., 112.

66. Ruggenthaler, "Warum Österreich nicht sowjetisiert wurde," 662.

67. The phrase that Austria evolved into "a sort of secret ally of the West" was coined by Gerald Stourzh. See Günter Bischof, "Österreich—'ein geheimer Verbündeter' des Westens? Wirtschafts- und sicherheitspolitische Fragen der Integration aus der Sicht der USA," in *Österreich und die europäische Integration, 1945-1993: Aspekte einer wechselvollen Entwicklung,* ed. Michael Gehler and Rolf Steininger (Vienna: Böhlau, 1993), 425-50.

68. RGASPI, F. 82, op. 2, d. 1042, d. 1043.

69. Zorin analyzed for Molotov the U.S. Balkans policy in terms "of the consolidation of an anti-Soviet Mediterranean deployment area" that might not stop short of including Italy and Austria. Zorin to Molotov, Stalin, all the members of the Committee of Eight and to Suslov, Vyshinsky, Grigoryan, Bogomilov, and Pushkin, 5 June 1952. RGASPI, F. 82, op. 2, d. 1043, 198. Cf. on the same subject the report of the "lesser" Cominform to Stalin dated 23 August 1952; according to this report, the United States was envisioning the conclusion of a separate treaty with Austria and the country's integration into NATO. Zubok, "Soviet Intelligence and the Cold War," 458.

70. V. Sviridov and S. Kudryavtsev to the Central Committee of the VKP(b) [All-Union Communist Party (Bolsheviks)], c/o. A. Smirnov. Annual report 1952 on the activities of the Soviet members of the Allied Commission and of the political representatives of the USSR in Austria, Vienna, 28 February 1953, RGASPI, F. 17, op. 137, d. 918, 74-201, here 104.

71. Stourzh, *Um Einheit und Freiheit,* 225.

72. Ludwig Reichhold, "Julius Raab als Bundesparteiobmann," in *Julius Raab: Eine Biographie in Einzeldarstellungen,* ed. Alois Brusatti and Gottfried Heindl (Linz: R. Trauner, 1986), 201-11, here 203. The party leadership was criticized first within the ÖVP following the presidential elections of May 1951. Rising internal criticism led to "a gradual takeover of power in the party leadership by the business wing of the ÖVP around Julius Raab." Stefan Karner, "Die Österreichische Volkspartei. Ein Abriss ihrer Entwicklung 1945-1995," in *ZUKUNFTsFEST. 60 Jahre Österreichische Volkspartei,* ed. Andreas Khol et al. (Vienna: 1995), 38.

73. The so-called "Figl-Fischerei" was one of Austria's major postwar political scandals and consisted of secret talks between Ernst Fischer, a communist parliamentarian and member of the Central Committee of the KPÖ, and the Austrian Federal Chancellor, Leopold Figl. "Figl-Fischerei" is a pun on Fischer's name and can be understood on one level as "trying to hook Figl." The talks were regarded as a communist attempt to bring about a Soviet-friendly government reshuffle. In retrospect, Fischer was discovered to have acted alone; he had not even accorded his move with his party comrades. Dobretsberger was still classified as a Western spy in Soviet reports of the time. For details, see Ruggenthaler, "Warum Österreich nicht sowjetisiert wurde," 667-69.

74. Ignatiev to Molotov, Malenkov, and Vyshinsky, 31 March 1952, RGASPI, F. 82, op. 2, d. 1042, 104.

75. Ruth Büttner, *Sowjetisierung oder Selbständigkeit? Die sowjetische Finnlandpolitik 1943-1948* (Hamburg: Verlag Dr. Kovac, 2001). For a comparison of Soviet policy towards Finland and Austria, see Peter Ruggenthaler, "Warum Österreich nicht sowjetisiert werden sollte," in *Die Rote Armee in Österreich,* ed. Karner et al., 81-84.

76. For more details, see Stourzh, *Der österreichische Staatsvertrag in den weltpolitischen Entscheidungsprozessen*, 973-74.

77. Zorin to Molotov, all Politburo members, Vyshinsky, and Gromyko, 19 March 1952, RGASPI, F. 82, op. 2, d. 1042, 82.

78. Gehler, *Kurzvertrag für Österreich?*, 250.

79. Zorin to Molotov, Stalin, all Politburo members, Vyshinsky, and Gromyko, 23 February 1952, RGASPI, F. 82, op. 2, d. 1042, 51.

80. Ignatiev to Molotov, Malenkov, and Zorin, 18 March 1952, RGASPI, F. 82, op. 2, d. 1042, 78.

81. Ignatiev to Molotov, Stalin, and all Politburo members, 1 March 1952, RGASPI, F. 82, op. 2, d. 1042, 61.

82. Ignatiev to Molotov, 1 July 1952, RGASPI, F. 82, op. 2, d. 1043, 236.

83. Ignatiev to Molotov, Malenkov, Vyshinsky, and Zorin, 29 February 1952, RGASPI, F. 82, op. 2, d. 1042, 187.

84. For more details, see Klaus Eisterer, "Die brasilianische UNO-Initiative 1952," in *Die Gunst des Augenblicks*, ed. Rauchensteiner and Kriechbaumer, 321-58; Josef Leidenfrost, "Die UNO als Forum für den österreichischen Staatsvertrag? Vom Wiener Appell 1946 bis zur Brasilien-Initiative 1952," in *Geschichte zwischen Freiheit und Ordnung. Gerald Stourzh zum 60. Geburtstag*, ed. Emil Brix et al. (Graz: Styria, 1991), 261-75.

85. Tugarinov to Molotov, Stalin, all Politburo members, Suslov, Vyshinsky, Grigoryan, Pushkin, and Podtserob, 23 August 1952, RGASPI, F. 82, op. 2, d. 1043, 299. The State Department conveyed to the Austrians that Brazil was well placed for putting forward a resolution at the United Nations. Mexico, which had protested against Austria's Anschluß in the League of Nations in 1938, also joined the initiative, but did not in the end become active in putting the Austrian question on the agenda of the UN plenum. For more details, see Stefan A. Müller, "Die versäumte Freundschaft. Österreich-Mexiko 1901-1956: Von der Aufnahme der Beziehungen bis zu Mexikos Beitritt zum Staatsvertrag." *Lateinamerikanistik* 3 (2006): 228-43.

86. Ignatiev to Molotov, Malenkov, and Vyshinsky, 15 August 1952; RGASPI, F. 82, op. 2, d. 1043, 288.

87. Ignatiev to Molotov, Malenkov, and Vyshinsky, 7 June 1952, RGASPI, F. 82, op. 2, d. 1043, 200.

88. Zorin to Molotov, Vyshinsky, and Pushkin, 1 July 1952, RGASPI, F. 82, op. 2, d. 1043, 215.

89. Ignatiev to Molotov, Malenkov, Beria, Bulganin, and Vyshinsky, 29 July 1952, RGASPI, F. 82, op. 2, d. 1043, 268.

90. Ignatiev to Molotov, Stalin, all Politburo members, and Vyshinsky, 14 August 1952, RGASPI, F. 82, op. 2, d. 1043, 286.

91. For more details, see Walter Blasi et al., eds., *B-Gendarmerie, Waffenlager und Nachrichtendienste: Der militärische Weg zum Staatsvertrag* (Vienna: Böhlau, 2005).

92. Ibid., particularly the papers Blasi/Etschmann, "Überlegungen zu den britischen Waffenlagern in Österreich," 139-53, and Ortner, "Die amerikanischen Waffendepots in Österreich," 155-70.

93. Appropriate replies were prepared in July and submitted twice to Molotov for vetting before being passed on to Stalin. Vyshinsky to Molotov asking for instructions, 31

July 1952, RGASPI, F. 82, op. 2, d. 1115, 113-19; Vyshinsky to Molotov asking for instructions, 5 August 1952; ibid., 120-27.

94. Report by Ignatiev, 10 August 1952, RGASPI, F. 82, op. 2, d. 1043, 282. Bischoff, who served first as Austria's political representative in Moscow and then as its ambassador, was criticized by the Austrian Ministry for Foreign Affairs for having been out of touch with reality. His political reports are punctuated by his expressions of sympathy for the country and its people as well as of his admiration for the "achievements" of the Soviet Union. The Austrian government nevertheless continued to place its trust in Bischoff. According to the memoir of his then secretary, Herbert Grubmayr, and according to Raab's personal secretary, Ludwig Steiner, Bischoff was convinced that the Secret Service had ways and means to overhear every word uttered in the Austrian embassy and to intercept and read every line that was written. In conversation with his closest collaborators, Bischoff is said to have been highly critical of the Soviets. I would like to thank Dr. Ludwig Steiner and Dr. Herbert Grubmayr for information on this subject and for many stimulating conversations. A report of the counterintelligence unit Smersh filed before Bischoff was dispatched to Moscow confirms this basic disposition. AVP RF, F. 06, op. 8, p. 22, d. 305, 39-40; Herbert Grubmayr, "Norbert Bischoff, Beschaffer des Staatsvertrages und/oder 'unguided missile' am österreichischen Polithimmel? Persönliche Erinnerungen," in *"Österreich ist frei!" Der österreichische Staatsvertrag 1955: Beitragsband zur Ausstellung auf Schloss Schallaburg 2005,* ed. Stefan Karner and Gottfried Stangler (Vienna: Berger, 2005), 376-79.

95. Politburo decision no. 89 (316) of the Central Committee of VKP(b) [All-Union Communist Party (Bolsheviks)], 27 September 1952, RGASPI, F. 17, op. 3, d. 1096, 151-53; draft of the first note to Stalin in: RGASPI, F. 82, op. 2, d. 1115, 128-35, draft of the second note ibid., 152-58. On the rejection of the Abbreviated Treaty by the USSR, see Stourzh, *Um Einheit und Freiheit,* 187.

96. Eisterer, "Die brasilianische UNO-Initiative 1952," 354.

97. Directives to Molotov drafted by Vyshinsky, September/October 1952, RGASPI, F. 82, op. 2, d. 1083, 114, 133, 154.

98. Eisterer, "Die brasilianische UNO-Initiative 1952," 351-54.

99. "Abbreviated Treaty—Infringement of the rights of the USSR (according to the Potsdam Agreement)." Draft of a reply to the Western powers on the subject of the Abbreviated Treaty by Vyshinsky with Molotov's handwritten emendations, 31 July 1952, RGASPI, F. 82, op. 2, d. 1115, 114.

100. For a perspective based exclusively on the Molotov files touching Austria see Ruggenthaler, "Warum Österreich nicht sowjetisiert wurde," 700-05.

The Birth of the N+NA:
Austrian and Swiss Foreign Policy in the CSCE

Thomas Fischer

Introduction[1]

The first half of the 1970s saw a remarkable period of relaxation of Cold War tensions. The flowering of this so-called "détente" was exemplified above all by the convening of the Conference on Security and Cooperation in Europe (CSCE) that culminated in the signing of the Helsinki Final Act on 1 August 1975. The Helsinki Document was at the same time sort of a substitute for a "final peace treaty" of World War II and a new basis for the future relations between East and West in Europe. Although by the end of the decade little was left of the spirit of détente, the Helsinki process that emerged from the original CSCE provided an important long-term framework for the peaceful winding down of the Cold War. So far, détente in Europe has mainly been understood as a consequence of West German "*Ostpolitik*" in the late 1960s under Chancellor Willy Brandt, which opened up new paths to discuss the central issue of international and mutual recognition of the two German states, a development that was abetted by emerging superpower negotiations on arms control and disarmament (SALT and MBFR). However, détente was more than German *Ostpolitik* and arms control negotiations on a superpower level.

Notably in the framework of the CSCE, smaller states and nonmilitary alliance members found a forum in which to express their views on East-West issues and influence the course of the Cold War in Europe. For the first time, East-West-relations were not exclusively discussed by the military alliances, but in a conference reuniting all thirty-three

European states (except Albania) as well as the United States and Canada, with every country having the same right to voice its opinion. This provided the neutral and non-aligned states with new possibilities for activating their foreign policy in the East-West context. Thus the "N+NA," as this group of states later came to be known, became of the most active participants and contributors to the CSCE. In fact, the negotiations leading up to the Helsinki Final Act were the first time the N+NA countries were formulating common positions and proposals in a multilateral negotiation forum.

The close collaboration between the neutral and non-aligned states in the CSCE can indeed be understood as a driving force of European détente. However, little attention has been paid so far to the development and influence of the N+NA group in the Helsinki process. In a sense, they were natural partners in confronting the military alliances with their demands concerning European security. Yet the fact that the neutral and non-aligned states formally joined together in the course of the CSCE needs further explanation. The question of how the N+NA group came about is more than academic and can be illustrated by examining the security conference involving the two neutral states Austria and Switzerland.

When Switzerland wanted to introduce the "right of neutrality" following the notion of sovereign equality into the Declaration of Principles of the CSCE, this, rather surprisingly, raised an objection by the Austrian Foreign Ministry.[2] On 20 February 1974, Ambassador Müller of the Swiss Foreign Ministry reported a phone call from the Austrian Ambassador in Berne saying that the Austrian delegation to the CSCE negotiations in Geneva had been advised by Vienna to ask urgently their Swiss colleagues to abstain from the idea of mentioning of neutrality in the Declaration of Principles. Withstanding the Austrian objections, the Swiss would have to face open resistance in the subcommittee dealing with the question.[3]

This stern Austrian reaction to the Swiss proposal of including of neutrality amongst the principles of the CSCE caused an immediate political intervention on the highest bilateral level. The very same day the Austrian resistance was reported to him, the Swiss Foreign Minister, Federal Councillor Pierre Graber, in a rather unusual move cabled his Austrian counterpart, Foreign Minister Rudolf Kirchschläger in Vienna, asking for the Austrian consent to the Swiss initiative. Since the final document of the CSCE would not be legally binding but simply of political character, the mentioning of neutrality would not jeopardize the international standing of the two countries—on the contrary, such an inclusion would most likely contribute to strengthening the notion and international acceptability of neutrality, a status freely chosen by Switzerland and Austria.[4]

After further discussion on the matter between the two delegations in Geneva Kirchschläger signaled in his answer to Graber's telegram, on 28 February, that—for reasons of friendship between the neighboring countries—the Austrian side would no longer object to the initiative:

> Even if I personally think that from an Austrian point of view there is no need for such a reference [to neutrality in the Declaration of Principles] and that we do not expect any advantages of a discussion of questions of neutrality within the CSCE, I notice with interest that you attribute great importance to such a mention. We would therefore not stand in the way of an initiative that is—as discussions between our two delegations in Geneva have shown—of concern to your country.[5]

Contrary to what the Swiss diplomat and member of the delegation in Geneva, Hans-Jörg Renk, later wrote in his detailed report on the negotiations, it was obviously not the Austrians (and the Finns) who had the greatest interest in a reference to neutrality in the Declaration of Principles of the CSCE, but the Swiss themselves.[6] As the head of the Swiss delegation Rudolf Bindschedler noted in an internal paper listing the arguments to counter the objections to the Swiss proposal, Austria, attributed less importance to including the right to neutrality in the Helsinki Final Act than Switzerland.[7] Austria had incurred a much greater risk in this respect when joining the United Nations, so far, however, without any negative consequences for their status of neutrality. Now the country could not be interested in opening a new discussion on the subject in the CSCE. Furthermore, as the later head of the Austrian delegation to the conference, Ambassador Franz Ceska in an interview with the author confirmed, Austria always considered its status of neutrality a matter of autonomous decision. Therefore, it had no interest whatsoever in making it an obligation of international agreements.[8] Switzerland on the other hand, not being a member of the UN, attributed considerable importance to a reference to neutrality in the first multilateral conference uniting all the great powers it participated actively in a long time.[9]

I mention this episode not because I think that the inclusion of the right to neutrality was a particularly important element of the Helsinki Final Act; in fact, as the subsequent head of the Swiss delegation, Edouard Brunner, admitted later on, the Swiss proposal was to be seen mainly in a domestic context.[10] However, it exposes the riddle of the group of the neutral and non-aligned participating states in the CSCE.

As the Swiss-Austrian quarrel over the inclusion of a reference to the right of neutrality in the Declaration of Principles shows, their common status of neutrality as such did not make the neutral states partners in every question in the CSCE as it might appear in hindsight—and as the "legend" of the N+NA group might suggest.

With a special focus on the "classic" neutrals, Switzerland and Austria, this contribution asks why these two states decided to participate in the CSCE in the first place, what role they perceived for a neutral state in the Conference, what their ambitions were, and at what point they effectively began to form a group with the rest of the neutral and non-aligned states. In order to answer these questions, the paper examines the different perspectives on détente of the two countries and their understanding of neutrality in the context of world politics in the 1970s. The N+NA-group was established rather late during the Conference based on a common position with regard to the military aspects of the agenda and notably in response to the Mutual and Balanced Force Reductions (MBFR) talks that the big powers held distant from the European Security Conference. Special attention will, therefore, be paid to Switzerland and Austria's position on this issue.

The article is structured as follows. In the first section it deals with the differing motivations of the two countries for choosing to participate in the CSCE, explaining their geographical, political, and historical background defining their attitude towards the general idea of an East-West détente and the more specific project of the Security Conference. The second section shows how their understanding of neutrality at first led to a conservative interpretation of their role in the Conference, a role that began to change gradually only after the opening of the Multilateral Preparatory Talks (MPT) in Helsinki. Section three then outlines the major projects Austria and Switzerland tried to introduce to the Conference agenda. Austria was more innovative with its demands to integrate the MBFR talks and the discussion on the Middle East problem into the CSCE, while Switzerland originally opposed a link of MBFR to the military and security aspects of the Conference and pursued more traditional goals by promoting a system for the peaceful settlement of disputes. Finally, section four highlights the major steps that established the N+NA-states first as important individual actors at the Conference through their active participation in procedural matters and later as a group by combining their individual proposals on security matters to a common proposal during Stage II. A final assessment of this development is made in the conclusion.

A word on the sources of this article has to be added. While the documents concerning the Swiss CSCE policy until 1975 of the Department of Foreign Affairs in Switzerland are fully archived and freely accessible at the Federal Archive in Berne, the situation regarding the Austrian archives is somewhat more obscure. The files of the Austrian Foreign Ministry are currently only deposited up to the year 1971 with the *Archiv der Republik* in Vienna and do not include any material of the *Völkerrechtsbüro* (Bureau for International Law) where the main bulk of information concerning the CSCE preparations and negotiations from 1969 onward is possibly to be found.[11] For these documents as for all records concerning the period after 1971, the thirty-year regulation for archival access does not yet apply since they are still physically with the Ministry of Foreign Affairs.[12]

Overall, the availability of material is much better on the Swiss side. Besides the open access to the documents in the Federal Archives, there exists a lengthy conference report from a Swiss perspective published by former diplomat Hans-Jörg Renk and an extensive oral history interview by Victor-Yves Ghébali with the former head of the Swiss CSCE delegation Edouard Brunner, whose transcript is accessible on the Internet.[13] Compared to these sources, the articles published by Austrian members of the CSCE delegation remain rather general concerning the specifics of the Austrian policy in the Conference.[14]

The Decision to Participate in the CSCE

Switzerland and Austria were at the outset both hesitant about participating in an eventual conference on European security. The Swiss government reacted negatively to the early invitations from Moscow to attend such a conference during the 1950s, but signaled its willingness to make Geneva available as a venue for the event, if required.[15] Switzerland's geographical and historical position clearly stood against the participation in any substitute for a "peace treaty conference" after the Second World War. Having avoided the turmoil of two world wars through its long-standing policy of neutrality, Switzerland in the 1950s had become a clearly Western-oriented, anti-communist state. Surrounded by "friendly" democracies and strategically and geographically located under the shield of NATO defense, any Eastern inspired European security conference trying to re-draw the balance in Europe at that time could only undermine Switzerland's well established Western position in the Cold War. Détente was mainly seen as an attempt by Moscow to achieve its geo-strategic goals of expanding its propaganda and influence with little to no advantages for neutral Switzerland.[16]

The situation was somewhat different for Austria. Lying on the very Eastern border of the NATO defense perimeter, protection from Eastern attempts of influencing the country's policy was much less sure. Neutrality as established with the Austrian State Treaty of 1955 had not yet proven it was able to guarantee the country's independence in Cold War struggles. The German scenario of being split between East and West had been avoided, but the experience of ten years of occupation after the Second World War had marked the country. Neutrality was merely guaranteed by the goodwill of the former occupying powers (Soviet Union, United States, Great Britain, France), which meant that their political requests had to be handled with great circumspectness. This was particularly true with regard to the Soviet Union, which watched Austria's Western-oriented policy with great alertness. Historical ties dating back to the Habsburg monarchy with bordering Czechoslovakia, Hungary, and Yugoslavia, which had come under communist rule after 1945, also called for a good neighbor policy across the blocs. In this context, relaxation of East-West-relations in the early 1970s was seen as a chance to enhance Austria's room for political maneuvering as a neutral state in a delicate geo-strategic position on the outskirts of the Western world.

Not surprisingly, however, skepticism towards the Soviet overtures with regard to the European security conference project was still to be found in Austria until the 1960s.[17] When Soviet Prime Minister Alexei Kossygin in March 1967 called upon the visiting Austrian Chancellor Josef Klaus to support the idea of a European security conference, the latter remained cautious, indicating that any attempt to launch talks on European security issues would clearly surpass the possibilities of neutral Austria.[18]

This rather hesitant attitude in Austria towards the idea of a European security conference began to change with the nomination of Kurt Waldheim as the new foreign minister in 1968. He pushed the idea of an active neutrality policy, including the promotion of international détente and the active participation of Austria in international collaboration.[19] When the Swiss Foreign Minister Willy Spühler and Waldheim discussed the issue of a European security conference on a bilateral level for the first time on 26 April 1968, the Austrian Minister stated that his country was positive about the idea of convening such a conference, pointing out that Austria had been stressing the importance of the inclusion of the United

States in the talks in Moscow earlier that year. While Spühler agreed with the last point, he emphasized that Switzerland would not be able to participate in the conference for reasons of neutrality if it were to establish a new system of collective security.[20]

The decisive change in attitude towards the security conference in both countries came in the wake of the Budapest Appeal of March 1969 and the subsequent NATO communiqué in April of the same year. In extensive bilateral contacts, the Swiss Foreign Minister began to explore the attitude of a number of Eastern and neutral European states and to explain the position of his government towards the idea of convening a pan-European conference.[21] With the Finnish Memorandum of 5 May 1969, all European states as well as the United States and Canada were definitely called upon to state their position on the matter. When Waldheim and Spühler met again on 20 May 1969, however, the common vision of the conference still remained vague, and both representatives assured each other that neither of their respective governments would undertake an initiative on the issue at the moment. The only thing they explicitly agreed on was the importance of the inclusion of the United States and Canada as participants in a European security conference.[22]

While the Swiss Foreign Ministry remained skeptical about the idea and anticipated little chance for success of the conference, the official response to the Finnish initiative in summer 1969 was generally positive.[23] Switzerland manifested its interest in the security conference mainly for the reason "that it could not be indifferent to any issue concerning peace in Europe."[24] However, it pointed out that it could only participate in the conference along the lines of its status of permanent neutrality and provided that it would be taken into consideration that Switzerland had not participated in World War II.

Austria was more forthcoming with its response to the Finnish initiative. In fact, when the government informed the public on 28 May it was the first country to react positively. It indicated its general interest in convening a conference, but stated that only a detailed preparation could prevent it from failure.[25] Austria subsequently began intensive bilateral consultations with other governments, and when Waldheim and his Swiss colleague Spühler met again in October 1969 in Vienna, the Austrian government had clearly taken the decision to participate in the security conference and was ready to play an active role in its preparation.[26] Waldheim further explained the Austrian position to the public in a speech to the Austrian Association of Foreign Policy in November 1969, where he confirmed the interest of his government in a European security conference. Austria would be positive about the convening of a conference; however, only a detailed preparation could prevent it from failure.[27]

The decision to participate was reinforced with the ascent to power of the new Austrian Chancellor Bruno Kreisky in 1970. Like the newly elected Swedish Prime Minister Olof Palme, Social Democrat Kreisky was a strong supporter of the idea of European détente.[28] When he and his new Minister of Foreign Affairs, the crossbench Rudolf Kirchschläger, for the first time discussed the matter of the European security conference with the Swiss government in Berne on 3 and 4 July 1970, the Austrian side explained that they would plead for convening a European security conference in the near future; therefore, the Austrian government had prepared a memorandum to all interested states explaining their position.[29]

While the Swiss government in the talks with the Austrian Chancellor and Foreign Minister still showed some reticence about actively preparing the conference, the general decision to participate in the conference—if it were to take place after all—by that time seems to have been reached in both countries, provided that the United States and Canada would take part with full rights.[30] The Austrian side perceived a fair chance that the conference would contribute to a real détente in Europe and was actively contributing to its preparation. The Swiss, on the other hand, remained skeptical about the outcome of such an exercise; nevertheless, as Federal Councillor Graber explained to the national Parliament in summer 1970, Switzerland could not be the only European state to "not participate" in a conference concerning pan-European security issues and was, therefore, carefully preparing its position and possible contributions to the conference.[31] Not being a member of the United Nations nor of the European integration process, Switzerland was used to seeing international affairs managed by forums in which it was not represented. In the CSCE, the Swiss recognized an occasion to participate effectively in world politics and to defend their interests.[32]

The different geographic and historical situations of Switzerland and Austria obviously produced slightly different approaches to the idea of a European security conference in the two countries.[33] While both generally endorsed the project, the Swiss showed great reluctance to actively engage in common activities together with the other neutrals in preparation for the conference.[34] Austria under Kreisky and Kirchschläger, on the other hand, displayed a more genuine interest in the concept of détente in Europe and was eager to contribute to it through active participation in the CSCE.[35]

The Role of a Neutral State

As early as May 1969, the Austrian Foreign Minister Waldheim and his Swiss colleague Spühler for the first time discussed the possible role of the neutral states in a future European security conference. It was the Swiss representative who voiced the opinion that it was not unthinkable that the small neutral states perform a specific task in the conference, be it only in the function of creating a balance.[36] The idea of a special role for the neutrals was further discussed between Austria and Switzerland in July 1970 when both sides generally approved the important role they had to play if the conference were to take place.[37]

Asked by a Swiss member of parliament whether Switzerland and the other neutrals should not play a central role in the preparation of the conference and, therefore, call a meeting of all European neutral states in advance to find a common position, Foreign Minister Graber replied that the status of neutrality would prevent Switzerland from looking for an overly dominant role in the conference. However, his government would seek to play an active role in collaboration with the other neutrals. Therefore, intense bilateral contacts had already been initiated on the matter.[38]

While the Swiss and Austrian representatives further agreed in their subsequent bilateral meetings that the neutrals had to play a role in a European security conference, they were not yet anticipating the future establishment of the group of the N+NA as it was to emerge later in the CSCE. The non-aligned countries were not engaged in a collaboration of such wide scope, and as Renk has pointed out, the Swiss at that time showed little interest in a form of coordination with the other neutrals closer than bilateral meetings to inform each other of their respective projects and initiatives.[39]

The perspective for a collaboration of the neutrals during this pre-conference phase is possibly best summarized by a statement of the Swiss Foreign Minister Graber in a meeting with his Austrian colleague Kirchschläger in January 1972, when the convening of the European security conference had finally become a fact:

> The security conference being conceived as a conference of states and not of groups of states, the participation of the neutrals will be very important. However, they should not form a bloc themselves, which on the other hand does not exclude a minimum of coordination among us. Our collaboration should neither be systematic nor institutionalized, but conceived step by step like an exchange of good proceedings.[40]

Despite this cautious approach to collaboration, the future role of the neutral states had become quite clear during the bilateral contacts in preparation for the CSCE. By 1972, the neutral countries had come to the conclusion that they had to play a certain role and that it was in their own interest to participate actively in the conference. Austrian neutrality, according to a speech by Foreign Minister Kirchschläger at the Wilton Park Conference in February 1972, was precisely agreed upon by the four former occupying powers in 1955 to separate the military blocs in Europe by a neutral zone running from the Pannonian Plain to the Swiss Jura. It was Austria's belief that in this role of a strategic balancer it could—even as a small state—make a positive contribution to security and peace in the Central Europe region.[41] Détente and the opening of CSCE talks provided a new forum where Austria could play the role of an "intercultural" interpreter between East and West and door opener for its neighboring countries behind the Iron Curtain.[42] Furthermore, an active role in the conference was likely to give Austria a higher international status and to show that Austria—largely by virtue of her "active neutrality" and the fact that she was not formally a member of either bloc—had an individual role to play in European and world affairs.

The Swiss shared the Austrian idea that the neutrals should make the broadest use of the forum to strengthen their image and role as mediators in the power game of international politics. However, a traditional understanding of neutrality was seen to impose certain limits to the possibilities of acting in the multilateral context of an East-West conference. Much of this attitude was motivated by domestic politics. On the other hand, Swiss neutrality constantly needed to prove its usefulness to the other states in order to gain recognition of this status in the changing context of world politics in the 1970s. For Switzerland, this was even more important since it was not a member of the UN and since it was not participating in the European integration process. A European security conference, in the eyes of Swiss decision makers, provided the country with a perfect occasion to strive for international recognition of its status of neutrality. Finally, both Switzerland and Austria shared the conviction that the CSCE touching upon the very questions of security in all Europe should not be left to NATO and Warsaw Pact states exclusively. Only the participation of the neutral states, as Federal Councillor Graber in August 1972 explained to a national parliamentary Committee on Foreign Affairs, would make sure that, in the end, the conference would not be reduced to a confrontation between the two blocs, which ignored the interests of the other states.[43]

Initiatives in Preparation for the Conference

While the neutrals agreed that the role of a catalyst would most likely fall to them in the CSCE, they were keen to elaborate their own national proposals in the conference according to their different understanding of détente. After the Social Democrat government of Chancellor Kreisky gained power, the Austrians soon announced their ideas in a memorandum of 24 July 1970, sent to all European states (except Liechtenstein and San Marino) and to the United States and Canada.[44] It stated that Austria, given its geographic and military position as well as the general political situation, was expecting a positive long-term influence on détente only if the question of Mutual and Balanced Force Reductions (MBFR) in Europe was treated thoroughly within the conference. The Austrian national military budget had never quite been up to the standard of their neutral companions Sweden and Switzerland, and taking into consideration the limits the State Treaty of 1955 imposed on the country with respect to military hardware,[45] the CSCE and its possible link to MBFR talks now seemed to offer a promising possibility for improving Austrian security. However, Austria, like all non-bloc states, was afraid to be left out of this discussion by the big powers and, therefore, had a clear interest that the MBFR talks be held within the scope of the security conference. The memorandum further demanded the endorsement of the non-use of force or threat of force as a basic principle in European relations, and thirdly stipulated the enhancement of mutual commercial, economic, scientific, technical, and cultural relations with the aim of developing political cooperation between all European states.[46] Austria welcomed the Finnish initiative of May 1969 to prepare a European security conference, but offered at the same time Vienna as a venue for high-level expert talks as an alternative to the idea of an "Ambassadors Tea Party" (convening the ambassadors to the Finnish capital to a "cup of tea" for talks) as a suitable next step to enter the multilateral phase of the preparations. Although the Austrian representatives stressed that they did not want to challenge Helsinki as a venue, they explained that Vienna would be available for pre-conference talks of high-level civil servants and diplomats, which they favored.[47]

Around the same, the Swiss time were about to define their position with regard to a future European security conference. After the initial decision of the Federal Council to respond positively to the Finnish initiative, made public in a press communiqué on 24 July 1969,[48] the government had asked the Foreign Ministry to elaborate possible Swiss contributions to the conference.[49] The Ministry, in turn, created an internal working group to draw up the lines of a future CSCE policy. The attitude within the working group towards the idea of a European security conference was generally skeptical; notably the group's leader, Ambassador Rudolf Bindschedler, later to become the head of the Swiss delegation to Helsinki and Geneva, was rather negative about the concept of détente. Bindschedler was particularly critical of the idea of a force reduction in Europe since Switzerland, in fact, profited from the current bloc-structure and the security the NATO alliance provided. He was of the opinion that the current strategic situation would prevail for a long time and that under such circumstances any reduction of Swiss troops was out of the question. This was also the main reason why Switzerland early on opposed a participation in MBFR and any link of these talks to the CSCE. This "realistic" worldview clearly contrasted with Kreisky's vision of détente in Europe, which was inspired by a more "idealistic" view of current world affairs.[50] The only positive result Bindschedler expected from a European security conference was the possibility of gaining recognition for Switzerland's status of neutrality from the big powers, notably the United States and the USSR.[51]

On 7 July 1970, the working group presented its report to the government.[52] The document, over 100 pages long, was still skeptical about whether the security conference would be convened at all and suggested that Switzerland should take an "interest free of illusions" in the project. While it should abstain from taking any initiatives in the preparation of the conference, Switzerland should actively make use of the conference if it were to take place and should promote—besides the right to neutrality—the following issues: the specification of the non-use of force and, as a specific Swiss initiative, the idea of a system for the peaceful settlement of disputes. This proposal fitted the Swiss perception of the actual state of détente much more. The degree of acceptance of the obligatory dispute settlement system would be a good indicator of how serious the big powers were about détente and its benefit for the European small states. Apart from that, Switzerland should concentrate on its traditional role as a mediator between the blocs and a provider of good offices to the conference; in general, it should act along the lines of its traditional neutrality policy. These recommendations of the report would become the general guidelines of the future Swiss CSCE policy.

From the summer of 1971 onward, Switzerland began to make its project to develop a system for the peaceful settlement of disputes known to the other possible participating states of the security conference in informal talks.[53] Meanwhile, Chancellor Kreisky amended the

Austrian July 1970 memorandum with a public proposal in his speech to the consultative assembly of the European Council on 25 January 1971, namely to include the problem of the Middle East in the future agenda of the conference.[54] The discussion of the Arab-Israeli conflict in the framework of the CSCE was subsequently to become his very personal ambition.[55] When the Foreign Ministers of the two countries met again from 27 to 29 January 1972 to discuss their respective proposals for the CSCE to improve security in Europe, the cards had, thus, already been revealed.[56]

By that time, Austria had also adopted the Western demand for a freer movement of people and exchange of ideas across the blocs. Yet in his exchange with the Swiss Minister Graber, Kirchschläger particularly stressed the Austrian request for the mutual force reduction in Europe that would lead, in his government's opinion, to greater security. Not surprisingly, however, Graber explained that Switzerland had great reservations vis-à-vis this proposal, as already indicated on the occasion of their last meeting in January 1971.[57] The Austrian representative, on the other hand, showed serious doubts about whether the Swiss proposal for a system for the peaceful settlement of disputes should be included in the conference agenda, since his government attributed very little chances of success to the idea, "Don't take our position as a denial of a constructive co-operation from our side. If you really introduce the proposal on the conference agenda, we will have little choice but to lend it our support. However, we hesitate to climb on the barricades with you."[58] Agreement on a common position was mainly reached with respect to the fortification of the principle of the non-use of force.

It is interesting to see that these early disagreements on the feasibility of the respective proposals (the inclusion of the MBFR talks and the Middle Eastern problem in the CSCE on the Austrian side and the proposal of a system for the peaceful settlement of disputes on the Swiss side) had not been obliterated by the time the interested states were beginning to seriously envisage the form of the preparatory talks for the CSCE in Finland in early 1972. Austrian Foreign Minister Kirchschläger discussed the Swiss proposal with regard to the peaceful settlement of disputes briefly in a speech on 27 March 1972, but still showed clear skepticism about its chances of success.[59] Switzerland, on the other hand, while beginning to show some interest at last in the MBFR talks by spring 1972,[60] did not yet advocate their inclusion in the CSCE and abstained from making any reference to the introduction of the Middle East question on the agenda.

The Birth of the N+NA

Despite their increased exchange of information on a bilateral level at an early stage, the four neutral states—Austria, Finland, Sweden and Switzerland—certainly did not form a group of their own when the Multilateral Preparatory Talks (MPT) began on 22 November 1972 in Dipoli near Helsinki. Brunner as well as Renk stressed that it was not planned before the opening of the MPT that the neutrals would act together as a group within the CSCE.[61] It was, in fact, only during the course of the preparatory talks that they would develop common positions and a more coordinated policy within the conference. The establishment of the group of the N+NA would, nevertheless, not occur until early 1974, during Stage II of the negotiations in Geneva.

MPT and Stage I

It did not take long for the neutrals to make a first concerted effort in the MPT to assert their influence in procedural matters. After the Finnish hosts had designated their State Secretary Richard Tötterman as president and Ambassador Jaakko Iloniemi as permanent vice-president of the talks (to be elected), Romania vigorously protested the arrangement in the opening session of the MPT and demanded a daily rotating chairmanship with the president and vice president coming from different countries. The Swiss, who shared the Romanian discomfort about the Finnish tandem, which very much resembled a permanent conference secretariat, proposed a compromise with a permanent Finnish president but a rotating vice-chair. The Swedish Ambassador Göran Ryding gave immediate support to this scenario, and the Austrians, in turn, emphatically backed a subsequent Romanian amendment to apply the principle of rotation of the chair in future working groups. This way, the Swiss, in close coordination with the Romanian delegation and together with the help of the skillfully placed interventions of the Swedish and the Austrian delegates, were able to secure the influence of the smaller delegations in procedural matters at this early stage of the conference.[62]

The neutrals further enhanced their decisive role in the MPT when, in December 1972 and early 1973, the question of how to establish a future conference agenda was discussed. By the various proposals the different participating states had formally or informally uttered so far, it had become clear that the agenda would generally be developed around the following issues: security, including political and military aspects; economic and environmental cooperation; cultural and human relations;

and the question of the follow-up to the conference. The delicate task of grouping all proposals under a definite agenda, however, was yet to be tackled. After the delegations had agreed on a three-stage conference as a "working hypothesis" on 12 December 1972, Sweden and Switzerland were again among the first to voice their opinion on the subject in late 1972.[63]

When the talks in Dipoli resumed after the Christmas break on 15 January 1973, the delegations began definitely laying out the proposals for the agenda and the terms of reference for future committees of the Conference. According to the Austrian head of delegation, Helmut Liedermann, it was his idea at this point to group several diverse subjects under broad headings termed "baskets," in order not to prejudice the importance of any single subject. It was a proposal that gained wide support and a term that was to have great success in the future Conference vocabulary.[64]

The Swiss diplomat Renk, however, claims that the copyright for the basket concept belongs to the Swiss Ambassador to Finland, Samuel Campiche, who had introduced the term to the discussion first on 18 January when he spoke for the Swiss delegation in Dipoli. According to Renk, Campiche had explained the concept of using "baskets like a housewife to separate the laundry of different colors" to organize the agenda; each country could add all the points it wanted to the non-enumerative list. Following this exercise, one could start grouping similar proposals together.[65]

As documents from the German Foreign Ministry Archives illustrate, Liedermann had, indeed, already proposed on 11 December 1972 that the Finnish Chairman Tötterman draw up a "list" to which ambassadors could add their agenda suggestions. One day later, Campiche—still according to West German reports—"seized the Dutch and Austrian proposals of previous sessions" and suggested to group the agenda items into four main chapters ("political problem," "follow-up and Mediterranean," "economic cooperation," "human contacts").[66] After all, it seems, the originality of the term "baskets" neither belongs to the Austrian nor the Swiss head of delegation to Dipoli, but as Luigi Vittorio Ferraris notes, to the Dutch delegation which had already proposed "putting the various proposals of each delegation into a *basket*" in early December 1972.[67] Therefore, the term seems to have been a part of the Conference vocabulary well before January 1973, but as British documents show, it was the Austrian delegate who (in close coordination with the British delegate) formally suggested using baskets marked with numbers at the plenary session of the MPT on 23 January in order to avoid objections regarding titles.[68] The Swiss, according to the same British source, were meanwhile encouraged by the EC Nine to prepare a catalogue of proposals so far submitted to the agenda and the terms of reference.[69]

In the end, it was Spain, which formally suggested on 24 January 1973, that Switzerland should be asked to prepare the synopsis of all the documents collected into a compendium. Switzerland, as had been previously arranged, accepted this task and on 29 January was able to present its compendium as a working paper. The document of nearly thirty pages grouped the proposals into four numbered baskets, dealing with 1) political and security matters; 2) economic and related issues; 3) human contacts, culture, and information; and 4) follow-up to the Conference.[70]

While the neutrals, and this time particularly Austria and Switzerland, through their initiatives to establish a conference agenda by using and expanding the concept of baskets, gained influence and a higher profile in the talks in Dipoli, they still did not form a homogeneous group. As mentioned above, the two neighboring neutral countries even became opponents at times in claiming the merits for the invention of the basket system.[71]

However, in the course of the drawing up of the agenda, the neutrals—in response to the more actively interpreted role of the EC Nine[72]—began to promote their initiatives on security issues more decidedly by supporting each other.[73] After the EC Nine and NATO had introduced their proposals, Austria, on 17 January, presented its elaborate proposals for the agenda (emphasizing the possible "European contribution to détente in the Middle East"). Switzerland did the same thing by specifying its proposal (on the system for the peaceful settlement of disputes) for greater political security, while Sweden introduced a document on the military aspects of security and arms control.[74] All three were now openly backing the proposals of the other neutrals.[75] The fact that Switzerland began to change its position on the question of linking MBFR to the CSCE was chiefly due to the fact that by early 1973 it had become clear that the force reduction talks, which were to take place in Vienna from October 1973 on, would exclusively be held by NATO and Warsaw Pact states. Between the opening of the MPT and Stage I, Switzerland had advocated the possibility for participating under certain circumstances in the MBFR; however, it also advocated for keeping these talks strictly separated from the CSCE. Now that the neutral and non-aligned states would be denied a direct participation in the MBFR talks, Switzerland joined Sweden and Austria in their demand to have at least a link to the matter of force reduction in Europe via the CSCE.[76]

From March 1973 onward, Austria, Sweden, and Switzerland also began to play a decisive role in the Conference as coordinators for the drafting of documents. As the MPT were entering the stage of drafting texts, a working group with representatives of all delegations was established. This working group proved immediately to be too cumbersome to execute the task effectively. The Swiss hence proposed the formation of mini-groups consisting of a very limited number of delegates. This solution was accepted, and the Swiss diplomat Edouard Brunner was to become coordinator of the first informal group on the problems of political security. A second mini-group on confidence-building measures was soon after entrusted to a Swedish coordinator, and Austria performed a similar function in the drafting of a text for basket two, economic and related issues.[77] When in April 1973 the working group finally arrived at drafting a text for basket three—human contacts, culture, and information—the neutral states again (now for the first time together with Yugoslavia) were the driving force behind the exercise.[78]

Thus, when the Austrian Foreign Minister Kirchschläger and his Swiss counterpart Graber met once more on a bilateral level in Vienna on 28 and 29 May 1973, they were happy to observe, as Kirchschläger put it, that the collaboration between the Swiss and the Austrian delegation in Dipoli had so far been "particularly good and positive."[79] Graber noted with great satisfaction that the neutrals in Dipoli had played a role far beyond anyone's expectations. For Switzerland, contrary to Austria and Sweden, who were both members of the United Nations, the multilateral meetings in Dipoli were a particularly new experience. While the two statesmen largely agreed in their talks on their positions concerning the relevant questions in the CSCE, a closer cooperation of the neutrals was not yet planned. This was only to happen during the course of the negotiations of Stage II in Geneva.

Geneva (Stage II)

With the beginning of Stage II in Geneva, Finland was suddenly free of the political restrictions it had had to take into consideration during the Helsinki stages and was willing to play a more active role.[80] While it had previously been careful not to associate itself with the delegations of its fellow neutrals Austria, Sweden, and Switzerland, Finland—and

Yugoslavia—now joined the group, particularly with regard to the discussion on military security.

Any link between the MBFR talks in Vienna and the CSCE as advocated by Sweden and Austria during the preparatory talks, however, had bluntly been rejected by NATO and the Warsaw Pact delegations.[81] In response, the neutrals and non-aligned, led by Yugoslavia, Sweden, Austria, Switzerland, and Finland, sought recognition for the principle that European states not participating in arms control negotiations in Europe had at least the "right" to be informed of the developments in this domain and to have their views taken into consideration. Even more important for the foundation of the N+NA, the fact that MBFR were not linked to the CSCE had caused a vacuum on the subject of military questions in the Conference, a vacuum the neutrals and the non-aligned states were now ever more eager to fill with proposals of their own.

This, in fact, seems to be the very moment of the birth of the N+NA group in the CSCE. First, proposals on the subject of confidence-building measures from their side were introduced on an individual basis by Yugoslavia (24 September 1973) and Sweden (23 October 1973). Activities of Yugoslavia, Sweden, and Austria subsequently remained intensive in the respective Sub-Committee, but as Ferraris notes, "[C]oordination between these delegations began extremely late and they were thus only in a position to produce joint documents at the end of the general discussion."[82] In fact, it was not before February 1974 that the N+NA presented for the first time a common draft.

Encouraged by various delegations, Sweden on behalf of Austria, Cyprus, Finland, Switzerland, and Yugoslavia presented a "Project for a Resolution on the Military Aspects of Security" to the sub-committee.[83] It was the drafting of this proposal that ultimately led to the creation of the N+NA group. Malta had been involved in the formulation of the proposal and would lend it its full support, but for tactical reasons did not want to figure among the co-sponsors. Liechtenstein and San Marino, who were later to join the N+NA group, as unarmed micro-states would not participate in the military discussion. According to Renk, the sequence of events which led to the creation of the N+NA was totally unplanned; however, the situation in the CSCE negotiations in late 1973 and early 1974 seems to have provided the necessary conditions to foster and to galvanize this new group.[84]

This version of the constitution of the N+NA group is, in essence, confirmed by Brunner and the report of the American CSCE diplomat John J. Maresca.[85] Maresca indicates that since the neutrals at the outset of the CSCE clung to the principle that each state should participate as an independent entity in the Conference, they did not enter into negotiation as a bloc for a long time. According to an Austrian source, it was the Austrian side that in late 1973 invited a number of neutral and nonaligned representatives to explore the possibilities of a closer collaboration by forming a group of their own in the Conference.[86]

Even though their proposal on confidence-building measures was considerably tempered down by the East in the end, the N+NA from now on was a force with which to be reckoned in the Conference. Their "moment of glory" ultimately arrived when the negotiations over the drafting of the principle of non-intervention came to a complete standstill in May 1974. The USSR was mainly trying to make up for concessions in basket three (admittance that human rights become the subject of international dialogue) by bringing the conceded powers back under national authority in a preamble to this chapter. It was Finland that tried to break the deadlock first by proposing on 4 June 1974, a compromise formula on the principle of non-intervention, stating that "every participating State respects the political, economic and cultural foundations of the other participating States, including their right to establish their own legislative systems and regulations."[87] The Finnish proposal, however, was not acceptable to the Western countries at that time.

With the Conference on the verge of breakdown, the N+NA, who by now had a clear interest in a substantial closing document of the CSCE, began to build on the Finnish proposal and on 23 June, word was uttered, that a "neutral package deal" was being prepared.[88] The package was trying to meet the Western requirements against the insertion of non-intervention in internal affairs in a preamble to basket three by an undertaking to insert the Finnish sentence (with minor alterations) within the general principle of sovereign equality, and a reference to *all* the principles in the preamble of the Third Committee instead. Thus the provisions of basket three would not only be carried out with respect to the principles of national sovereignty and non-intervention of internal affairs (as advocated by the Soviets), but also in keeping with the principles of respect for human rights and fundamental freedoms, and fulfillment of international obligations (as demanded by the West).[89]

It is interesting to note that in May 1974, in a bilateral Austrian-Swiss meeting in Berne attended by Foreign Ministers Graber and Kirchschläger as well as the heads of the CSCE delegations Liedermann and Bindschedler (and his collaborator Brunner), there was still substantial disagreement between the two sides on how to break the impasse in

Geneva. Austria wanted to put the Conference on hold for a period of four years and try to find a basis for common ground on a bilateral level to reopen the talks. The Swiss were more optimistic about finding a way out of the current stalemate and strongly pleaded to strive for the closing of the Conference with a substantial document as early as possible.[90]

However, these differences seem to have been overcome by June 1974, and the neutrals now worked closely together over a period of several weeks well into July 1974 to find a general acceptance of the arrangements outlined in their package, building on the Finnish initiative. Maresca describes how the neutrals in careful proceedings finally reached agreement on the package deal, "To lay the groundwork, neutral delegates first contacted key delegations privately, then formulated their proposal. They presented a first draft to separate, informal gatherings of Eastern, Western, and independent delegations, then sought to improve on their draft to make it fully acceptable. Both East and West moved reluctantly."[91] In a general atmosphere of increasing negotiating pressure, the Gordian knot of problems relating to the content of basket three was finally broken on 26 July 1974, when the neutral package deal was accepted by all sides and agreement was reached on the "overall solution" in the Coordinating Committee of the Conference.[92]

Although the success of the package deal was, in the end, only temporary, it contributed a great deal, as Renk notes, to the consolidation of the N+NA group and to its acceptance as a decisive force in the Conference.[93] After the summer break when the CSCE convened again in September 1974, however, the quarreling over the final provisions of basket three resurfaced. Throughout September and October, the Soviets stonewalled again on a central issue in the Third Committee. The neutrals, and according to a British source namely the Swiss diplomat Brunner, were soon "toying with the idea of a[nother] package deal with Basket III."[94] However, the Soviets, this time, discouraged such an effort.[95]

While the N+NA and notably the neutrals during the summer 1974 had discovered their "increased power" acting as a group on some issues of special concern to all of them, they soon had to learn the limits of their possibilities of maneuvering the Conference, as this last example shows. Even if the N+NA group began to strengthen its collaboration by regular meetings first by their State Secretaries for Foreign Affairs and later by their Foreign Ministers,[96] it remained a product of the specific East-West interplay in the European security conference and was, thus, always limited to the functions that the great powers were ready to let it perform.[97]

Conclusion

As a closer examination of the early days of the N+NA collaboration in the CSCE shows, it was not a given fact that these states would end up acting as a group in the negotiations. While they were somewhat natural partners in not being members of either one of the military alliances, they would not form a group of their own until very late in the negotiation process leading up to the Helsinki summit. We can, in fact, only speak of a "N+NA group" from early 1974 onward, the very moment the neutral states together with Yugoslavia and Cyprus for the first time introduced a common project on the security aspects of the Conference.

The steps leading up to the fostering of the N+NA group can clearly be illustrated by the examples of Austrian and Swiss foreign policy in the CSCE. Both countries were hesitating to react positively to the original Soviet idea as long as the United States and Canada were not included. Once this obstacle was removed in 1969, the Austrians (particularly after the ascent to power of the Kreisky government in 1970) actively engaged in preparing the conference that was seen as a chance to improve European détente. Switzerland, meanwhile, remained much more reluctant to the general concept of détente and for reasons of neutrality would not take any initiative in engaging in the conference project early on. A decision to participate was mainly made for the reason that Switzerland did not want to deprive itself of the possibility to participate in the only first pan-European forum dealing with security issues.

The European security conference became a regular subject in Austria and Switzerland's bilateral talks from 1968 onward, and an agreement between the Swiss and Austrian representatives that if the conference were to take place the neutrals had to play a role in asserting their own rights was soon reached. The possibility of acting as a group together with the other neutral states was repeatedly discussed; however, the coordination between them at this early stage remained on a strictly bilateral level in the form of mutual information on each other's position in preparation of the conference. The actual role they perceived for the neutral states in the CSCE was that of a balancer and catalyst in the negotiations between East and West.

As a consequence, Austria and Switzerland would, at first, launch their substantial proposals at the conference individually without coordinating their policy with the other neutrals. According to its different understanding of détente, Austria would stress the importance of the inclusion of the MBFR talks in the forum of the CSCE while Switzerland would advocate a project for the peaceful settlements of disputes, which was completely in line with its "realistic" view of current world affairs. As the documents show, both countries originally attributed little chance for success to the other's proposal and were not yet backing each other when the MPT opened in November 1972.

It was only in the course of the preparatory talks to the CSCE that the neutrals discovered their role and a common interest in closer collaboration. As different sources document, the building of the N+NA group was still not in the scope of the respective decision makers and was only to happen during stage II in Geneva when the four neutrals began endorsing their respective proposals and, partly in reaction to the stronger role of the EC Nine and the exclusion of the MBFR talks from the conference agenda, when they embraced closer cooperation, namely on security issues. Finally, it was less a conscious decision taken in a long-term perspective by the governments of the N+NA states than a combination of various push-and-pull factors within the CSCE that ultimately led to the tabling of a first common project for a resolution on the military aspects of security on 25 February 1974. This date can be seen as the moment when the character of the N+NA changed from a non-institutionalized, loose cooperation to a quasi-institutionalized coalition. While the N+NA group was further consolidated with the success of the neutral package deal to break the conference deadlock in July 1974, it remained a heterogeneous group, which at times also had to overcome considerable dissent. Nevertheless, despite their different individual starting points, by joining together in the course of the CSCE the N+NA became a major driving force of détente in Europe during the mid-1970s and persistently worked in this direction in the follow-up process of the Conference. Austria, due to its particular historical and geo-strategic position, can even be seen as one of the countries at the forefront of this development.

While the neutrals and non-aligned states during the Geneva phase of the original conference discovered their increased power by forming a group of their own, the N+NA in the course of the subsequent follow-up meetings in Belgrade (1977/78) and Madrid (1980-83) also had to realize the limits of their involvement in East-West negotiations. During that time, it was mainly through their mediating efforts that the N+NA played a crucial role in keeping the process alive when the talks were more than once on the verge of a total breakdown in an atmosphere of renewed Cold War tensions between Moscow and Washington.

Still, the CSCE was a unique opportunity for the neutral and non-aligned states to participate in European Cold War politics, and it became an important forum in which to express their views on East-West issues. During the most difficult times in the 1980s, the role of the neutrals was possibly essential for keeping the Helsinki process on track, a process, many are convinced today, that contributed considerably to the peaceful end of the Cold War.

Notes

1. This article is based on a draft paper first presented to the conference *At the Roots of the European Security System: Thirty Years since the Helsinki Final Act* in Ruschlikon/Zurich, 8-10 September 2005. Research for this study has been made possible by a fund of the *Jubiläumsfonds der Österreichischen Nationalbank* (Project No. 11435).

2. This episode was first disclosed in Thomas Fischer, *Die Grenzen der Neutralität: Schweizerisches KSZE-Engagement und gescheiterte UNO-Beitrittspolitik im Kalten Krieg, 1969-1986* (Zürich: Chronos-Verlag, 2004), 148-50.

3. Schweizerisches Bundesarchiv, Bern [hereafter: BAR], E 2001(E) 1987/78, 190, EPD, Politische Direktion: Notiz Botschafter Müller an Bundesrat Graber, Botschafter Thalmann und Bindschedler (vertraulich), 20 February 1974. It is worth noting that already in talks between Foreign Ministers Graber and Kirchschläger in July 1970, the Austrian representative pointed out that his country had no interest in a discussion on neutrality in the CSCE and, therefore, did not wish a notion on the "right to neutrality" to be introduced into the talks. Österreichisches Staatsarchiv /Archiv der Republik, Wien [hereafter: ÖStA/AdR], BMfaA, II-Pol/Schweiz, [non-registered box Nr. 45], Zusammenfassendes Protokoll über die Arbeitsgespräche anlässlich des Besuches von Bundeskanzler Dr. Kreisky und Bundesminister Dr. Kirchschläger am 3 and 4 July 1970 in Bern.

4. BAR, E 2001(E) 1987/78, 191, EPD, Politische Direktion: Telegramm Bundesrat Graber an den österreichischen Aussenminister Kirchschläger, 20 February 1974.

5. Original German quotation: *"Wenn ich auch weiter der Ansicht bin, dass vom österreichischen Standpunkt aus keine Notwendigkeit zu einem solchen Hinweis besteht und wir uns keine grossen Vorteile aus einer Diskussion erwarten, die auf der KSZE oder in ihrem Gefolge über Neutralitätsfragen entstehen könnte, nehme ich mit Interesse zur Kenntnis, dass Sie einem Hinweis auf die Neutralität grosse Bedeutung beimessen. Ich möchte daher nicht einer Initiative im Weg stehen, die sich – wie die Gespräche zwischen unseren Delegationen in Genf zeigen – als ein Anliegen Ihres Landes herauskristallisiert hat."* BAR, E 2001(E) 1987/78, 191, EPD, Politische Direktion: Telegramm Aussenminister Kirchschläger an Bundesrat Graber (vertraulich), 28. February 1974.

6. Cf. Hans-Jörg Renk, *Der Weg der Schweiz nach Helsinki: Der Beitrag der schweizerischen Diplomatie zum Zustandekommen der Konferenz über Sicherheit und Zusammenarbeit in Europa (KSZE), 1972-1975* (Bern: Paul Haupt, 1996), 81-83.

7. BAR, E 2001(E) 1987/78, 191, EPD, Politische Direktion: Neutralität und Sicherheitskonferenz, Notiz Botschafter Bindschedler an Generalsekretär Thalmann, 26 February 1974.

8. Interview with Franz Ceska, Vienna, 2 August 2005.

9. The Swiss proposal in February 1974 for the inclusion of a reference to neutrality under the principle of sovereign equality is to be seen in the context of the discussion on the problem of the relationship between the Declaration of Principles and the

documents of the United Nations: The Western and the other neutral countries—all members of the United Nations—considered it necessary to clearly subordinate the principles of the CSCE to the Charter of the United Nations and to connect them to the United Nations Declaration of Friendly Relations. The Swiss, however, not recognizing the priority of the UN Charter over the classic right of neutrality, had a special interest in getting some kind of recognition of their special status of neutrality in the final document of the CSCE. A reservation by Switzerland concerning a future mention of the right to neutrality had formally been included in the draft of the first principle (sovereign equality) on 26 February 1974. See Luigi Vittorio Ferraris, *Report on a Negotiation: Helsinki-Geneva-Helsinki, 1972-1975*, Trans. Marie Claire Barber (Alphen aan den Rijn: Sijthoff & Nordhoff International Publishers BV, 1979), 113.

10. *Le rôle de la Suisse à la Conférence pour la Sécurité et la Cooperation en Europe (CSCE)*, témoignage de l'Ambassadeur Edouard Brunner, recueilli par le Professeur Victor-Yves Ghébali (Institut universitaire de hautes études internationales – HEI). Entretiens réalisés à l'Institut HEI du 5-13 August 2002 <http://www.isn.ethz.ch/osce/networking/secondary_literature/coc/Interview_Amb_Brunner.PDF>, 4, 25.

11. The author is hoping to gain access to this material in the context of an ongoing project of the collaboration of the neutral states in the CSCE between 1969 and 1975.

12. Some materials concerning the Austrian CSCE policy from the British National Archive have been brought to light by Erwin A. Schmidl in "L'Autriche et le processus d'Helsinki," in *Vers la réunification de l'Europe: Apports et limites du processus d'Helsinki de 1975 à nos jours*, ed. Elisabeth du Réau, and Christine Manigand (Paris: L'Harmattan, 2005). Additional material has been collected in October 2006 by the author of this article at the Archives in London.

13. Details fn. 6 and 10.

14. Helmut Liedermann, "Die Schlussakte der Konferenz über Sicherheit und Zusammenarbeit in Europa (KSZE)," *Österreichische Zeitschrift für Aussenpolitik 16/1* (1976): 3-22; Helmut Liedermann, "Die Konferenz über Sicherheit und Zusammenarbeit in Europa (KSZE) aus österreichischer Sicht," in *Kirche und Staat: Fritz Eckert zum 65. Geburtstag*, ed. Herbert Schambeck (Berlin: Duncker & Humblot, 1976), 555-78; Helmut Liedermann, "Von Helsinki über Belgrad nach Madrid: Die Konferenz über Sicherheit und Zusammenarbeit in Europa aus der Sicht eines österreichischen Konferenzteilnehmers," in *Völkerrecht und Philosophie: Internationale Festschrift für Stephan Verosta zum 70. Geburtstag*, ed. Peter Fischer et al. (Berlin: Duncker & Hum-blot, 1980), 427-44; Helmut Liedermann, "Österreichs Rolle beim Zustandekommen der KSZE," in *Mit anderen Augen gesehen: Internationale Perzeptionen Österreichs 19552000*, Österreichische Nationalgeschichte nach 1945 Bd. 2, ed. Oliver Rathkolb et al. (Vienna: Böhlau Verlag, 2002), 487-506; Franz Ceska, "Détente und KSZE-Prozess—Österreich zwischen Helsinki (1975) und Madrid (1983)," in *Mit anderen Augen gesehen: Internationale Perzeptionen Österreichs1955-2000*, Österreichische Nationalgeschichte nach 1945 Bd. 2, ed. Oliver Rathkolb et al. (Vienna: Böhlau Verlag, 2002), 507-22; Franz Ceska, "Vom Kalten Krieg zur Europäischen Union—Die KSZE als Geburtshelfer des Europa der '25 plus'," in *Europa auf Friedenssuche: Vom Europarat zur Osterweiterung der Union*, ed. Otto M. Maschke (Vienna: Molden, 2004), 159-80.

15. Cf. Christoph Breitenmoser, *Sicherheit für Europa: Die KSZE-Politik der Schweiz bis zur Unterzeichnung der Helsinki-Schlussakte zwischen Skepsis und aktivem Engagement*, Zürcher Beiträge zur Sicherheitspolitik und Konfliktforschung Nr. 40 (Zürich: ETH, 1996), 78-81, available online at <http://cms.isn.ch/public/docs/ doc_278_290_de.pdf>.

250 The Changing Austrian Voter

16. See Fischer, *Die Grenzen der Neutralität*, 86-90.

17. Schmidl, "L'Autriche et le processus d'Helsinki," 90; the first signs of a positive reaction to the idea under certain circumstances were given in 1964 and 1966. See Michael Zielinski, *Die neutralen und blockfreien Staaten und ihre Rolle im KSZE-Prozess*, Nomos Universitätsschriften, Politik Bd. 13 (Baden-Baden: Nomos Verlagsgesellschaft, 1990), 132.

18. ÖStA/AdR, BMfaA, II-Pol/USSR 2, 1967, Die Neutralität – der neue politische Weg Österreichs, Vortrag gehalten von Dr. Josef Klaus vor der Akademie der Wissenschaften Moskau, 16 March 1967 [Klaus' speech is reprinted in *Sicherheitskonferenz in Europa: Dokumentation 1954-1972*, ed. Friedrich-Karl Schramm et al. (Frankfurt am Main: Metzner, 1972), 653f.]; cf. Konrad Ginther, *Neutralität und Neutralitätspolitik: Die österreichische Neutralität zwischen Schweizer Muster und sowjetischer Koexistenzdoktrin*, Forschungen aus Staat und Recht 31 (Vienna: Springer Verlag, 1975), 55f.

19. Ibid., 61-63.

20. BAR, E 2001(E) 1980/83, 363, EPD, Politische Direktion: Protokoll schweizerischösterreichischen Arbeitsgespräche mit Aussenminister Waldheim in Bern, 26 April 1968.

21. Breitenmoser, *Sicherheit für Europa*, 81-83. Minister Willy Spühler had met in spring 1969 with his Romanian and Swedish colleagues; bilateral meetings with his Austrian and Yugoslavian counterparts were to follow during the same year. Fischer, *Die Grenzen der Neutralität*, 81.

22. BAR, E 2001(E) 1980/83, 363, EPD, Politische Direktion: Gespräche mit dem österreichischen Aussenminister Waldheim in Bern, 20 May 1969; ÖStA/AdR, BMfaA, II-Pol/Schweiz, 1547, Österreichisch-schweizerische Arbeitsbesprechung auf Aussenministerebene vom 20 May 1969 in Bern.

23. BAR, E 2001(E) 1980/83, 136, EPD, Abteilung für politische Angelegenheiten: Bundesratsentscheid zur europäischen Sicherheitskonferenz (vertraulich), 6 July 1969. Cf. Fischer, *Die Grenzen der Neutralität*, 81f; Breitenmoser, *Sicherheit in Europa*, 84f.

24. BAR, E 2001(E) 1980/83, 136, EPD, Abteilung für politische Angelegenheiten: Presse Kommuniqué zur Antwort des Bundesrates auf den Budapester Appell vom 17 March, 24 July 1969. (Printed in *Sicherheit und Zusammenarbeit in Europa (KSZE)*, ed. Jacobsen et al. 150.)

25. The government declaration of 28 May was made public in the *Wiener Zeitung* on 29 May 1970.

26. BAR, E 2001(E) 1980/83, 364, EPD, Politische Direktion: Besuch von Bundesrat Spühler in Vienna, Protokoll der Arbeitsgespräche (vertraulich), 26 and 27 October 1969; ÖStA/AdR, BMfaA, II-Pol/Schweiz, 1547, Zusammenfassendes Protokoll der österreichisch-schweizerischen Arbeitsgespräche anlässlich des Besuches von Bundesrat Dr. Willy Spühler in Vienna, 27 October 1969.

27. Speech by the Austrian Foreign Minister, Kurt Waldheim, to the Austrian Association of Foreign Policy, *Österreichische Zeitschrift für Aussenpolitik 10* (1970): 47-49.

28. Cf. Renk, *Der Weg der Schweiz nach Helsinki*, 30.

29. BAR, E 2001(E) 1980/83, 364, EPD, Politische Direktion: Protokoll der schweizerisch-österreichischen Arbeitsgespräche mit Bundeskanzler Kreisky und Aussenminister Kirchschläger in Bern, 3./4. Juli 1970; ÖStA/AdR, BMfaA, II-Pol/Schweiz,

[non-registered box Nr. 45], Zusammenfassendes Protokoll über die Arbeitsgespräche anlässlich des Besuches von Bundeskanzler Dr. Kreisky und Bundesminister Dr. Kirchschläger am 3 and 4 July 1970 in Bern. According to Ceska, it was Foreign Minister Kirchschläger, backed by State Secretary Ludwig Steiner, who showed considerable interest in the conference from the beginning while Chancellor Kreisky at first was rather indifferent to the idea. However, he soon developed a particular interest in the conference as a means to promote his very personal goals in Austrian foreign policy such as the improvement of the good neighbor policy, the idea of an internationalized European network of waterways, and his ambition to play a decisive role as a mediator in the Middle East conflict. Interview with Franz Ceska, Vienna, 2 August 2005.

30. The Austrian decision to participate in the European Security Conference seems, in fact, to have been a decision that was not actively taken. According to Ceska, it was certain that Austria would participate the moment it became clear that the conference would be convened under the prerequisite of participation of the United States and Canada. Interview with Franz Ceska, Vienna, 2 August 2005.

31. BAR, E 2001(E) 1980/83, 136, EPD, Abteilung für politische Angelegenheiten: Réponse du Conseil fédéral à l'interpellation Renschler du 2 June 1969, 15 July 1970; and Réponse du Conseil fédéral à l'interpellation Hefti du 27 November1969, 26. July 1970. For a discussion of the Swiss attitude towards the idea of a European security conference at this early stage, see Fischer, *Die Grenzen der Neutralität*, 86-90.

32. *Le rôle de la Suisse à la CSCE*, témoignage de l'Ambassadeur Edouard Brunner, 2.

33. Cf. Renk, *Der Weg der Schweiz nach Helsinki*, 31.

34. One of the reasons Graber gave to his Austrian counterpart Kirchschläger as an explanation was the skepticism of the Swiss people vis-à-vis the East in general and his government's view that a conventional force reduction in Europe as advocated by Sweden and Austria would be seen more as a security risk than as a sign of détente. BAR, E 2001(E) 1982/58, 291, EPD, Politische Direktion: Protokoll der Gespräche im Aussenministerium in Vienna zwischen Bundesrat Graber und dem österreichischen Aussenminister Kirchschläger, 21/22 January 1971.

35. A report by the British Ambassador to Vienna in 1972 explained the Austrian attitude early on toward the idea of a European security conference as follows: "Austria was one of the first countries to welcome the Warsaw Pact proposal for a European Security Conference. They have no illusions about Soviet aims but they genuinely believe that Austria can act as a window on the West for the countries of Eastern Europe and that this role is best served in conditions of *détente* which a Conference might help to promote." National Archives London, FCO 33/1673: Diplomatic Report No. 439/72, Denis S. Laskey to Foreign and Commonwealth Office, Austria's Role in the World of the Seventies, Vienna, 4 October 1972.

36. BAR, E 2001(E) 1980/83, 363, EPD, Politische Direktion: Gespräche mit dem österreichischen Aussenminister Waldheim in Bern, 20 May 1969.

37. BAR, E 2001(E) 1980/83, 364, EPD, Politische Direktion: Protokoll der schweizerischen-österreichischen Arbeitsgespräche mit Bundeskanzler Kreisky und Aussenminister Kirchschläger in Bern, 3/4 July 1970; ÖStA/AdR, BMfaA, II-Pol/Schweiz, [non-registered box Nr. 45], Zusammenfassendes Protokoll über die Arbeitsgespräche anlässlich des Besuches von Bundeskanzler Dr. Kreisky und Bundesminister Dr. Kirchschläger am 3 and 4 July 1970 in Bern.

38. BAR, E 2001(E) 1980/83, 136, EPD, Abteilung für politische Angelegenheiten: Réponse du Conseil fédéral à l'interpellation Renschler du 2 June 1969, 15 July 1970.

254   The Changing Austrian Voter

(Printed in *Sicherheit und Zusammenarbeit in Europa (KSZE)*, ed. Jacobsen, Mallmann, and Meier, 218-224.)

39. Renk, *Der Weg der Schweiz nach Helsinki*, 31f.

40. Original French quotation: "*La conférence de sécurité devant être une conférence d'Etat et non de groupes d'Etats, la participation des neutres sera très importante. Mais ceux-ci ne devraient pas former un bloc eux-mêmes, ce qui toutefois n'exclue pas un minimum d'action coordonnée entre nous. Notre collaboration devrait être ni systématique ni institutionnalisée, mais conçue de cas en cas comme un échange de bon procédés.*" BAR, E 2001(E) 1982/58, 291, EPD, Politische Direktion: Besuch des österreichischen Aussenministers Kirchschläger in Bern, 27-29 January 1972.

41. National Archives London, FCO 41/1344: An Austrian view on the future of All-European Co-operation and Security, Talk given by Foreign Minister Rudolf Kirchschläger at the 139th Wilton Park Conference, 11 February 1972 (printed in *Wilton Park Journal* 47 (December 1972).

42. The "window function" of Austria for the Eastern European states was a recurring theme in Austrian statements on the CSCE. See the National Archives London, FCO 33/1248: Record of conversation between the Foreign and Commonwealth Secretary and the Austrian Foreign Minister at the Waldorf Astoria (Towers), New York at 6.15 p.m. on Tuesday, 28 September 1971.

43. BAR, E 1050.12 1995/512, 3, Aussenpolitische Kommission, Ständerat: Sitzungsprotokoll (vertraulich), 14 August 1972.

44. The intention of the memorandum was explained by an Austrian diplomat to his British counterpart the following way: "They had no ambition to act as a mediator between the great powers or to aspire to a leading role, but they have a vital interest in European security and thought that they could make a helpful contribution." National Archives London, FCO 41/752: Telegram Scott (Vienna) to FCO, 25 June 1970.

45. Notably, this included certain restrictions on the air force with regard to anti-ballistic missile systems.

46. Memorandum of the Austrian Government on the Project of a European Security Conference, 24 July 1970, *Österreichische Zeitschrift für Aussenpolitik 10* (1970): 250f.

47. When it became clear later on that Helsinki would host these preparatory talks, Austria would repeat its offer for Vienna as a meeting place for a later stage of the Conference. According to a report of the British ambassador to Vienna, the Austrians in talks with Soviet Foreign Minister Gromyko by October 1971 "regarded Helsinki as a foregone conclusion for the opening stages; but they were quite ready for Vienna to be considered for future meetings of any organ which might emerge from the CES." National Archives London, FCO 33/1280: Julian Hartland Swinn to Peter W. Unwin in the Foreign and Colonial Office/Western Department, Vienna, 18 October 1971. Cited in Schmidl, "L'Autriche et le processus d'Helsinki," 93.

48. BAR, E 2001(E) 1980/83, 136, EPD, Abteilung für politische Angelegenheiten: Presse Kommuniqué zur Antwort des Bundesrates auf den Budapester-Appeal vom 17 March, 24 July 1969. (Printed in *Sicherheit und Zusammenarbeit in Europa (KSZE)*, ed. Jacobsen et al, 150).

49. For the internal preparation of the security conference in Switzerland see Breitenmoser, *Sicherheit in Europa*, 98-106; Fischer, *Die Grenzen der Neutralität*, 86-90.

50. As Ginther has noted, Kreisky's concept of "active neutrality" came, in fact, much closer to the Soviet notion of peaceful coexistence than the Swiss model. Ginther, *Neutralität und Neutralitätspolitik*, 50-53.

51. BAR, E 2001(E) 1980/83, 136, EPD, Abteilung für politische Angelegenheiten: Sitzungsprotokoll der Arbeitsgruppe Europäische Sicherheitskonferenz (vertraulich), 16 December 1969.

52. BAR, E 2001(E) 1980/83, 138, EPD, Abteilung für politische Angelegenheiten: "Die Schweiz und die Europäische Sicherheitskonferenz", Bericht der Arbeitsgruppe (streng vertraulich), 7 July 1970.

53. Breitenmoser, *Sicherheit für Europa*, 131, note 359. The project was first made public in an answer by the Federal Council to a parliamentary interpellation in the Swiss National Council on 15 June 1970, printed in *Sicherheit und Zusammenarbeit in Europa (KSZE)*, ed. Jacobsen et al., 218-24.

54. Speech by Chancellor Kreisky to the Assembly of the European Council, 25 January 1971, in *Sicherheit und Zusammenarbeit in Europa (KSZE)*, ed. Jacobsen et al., 262.

55. The British ambassador to Vienna, Julian Hartland-Swann, in May 1972 called this idea the "pet hobby-horse" of Kreisky. National Archives London, FCO 33/1674: Report 3/23 by Julian Hartland-Swann to Peter W. Unwin of the Foreign and Colonial Office/ Western Department, Vienna, 31 May 1972. Cited in Schmidl, "L'Autriche et le processus d'Helsinki," 92f.

56. BAR, E 2001(E) 1982/58, 291, EPD, Politische Direktion: Besuch des österreichischen Aussenministers Kirchschläger in Bern, 27-29 January 1972.

57. BAR, E 2001(E) 1982/58, 291, EPD, Politische Direktion: Protokoll der Gespräche im Aussenministerium in Wien zwischen Bundesrat Graber und dem österreichischen Aussenminister Kirchschläger, 21/22 January 1971.

58. Original quotation in German: *"Betrachten Sie unsere Haltung nicht als Absage unsererseits, nicht konstruktiv mitarbeiten zu wollen. Es wird uns gar nichts anderes übrigbleiben, als Ihren Vorschlag zu unterstützen, wenn Sie ihn einbringen. Aber wir zögern, mit Ihnen auf die Barrikaden zu steigen."* BAR, E 2001(E) 1982/58, 291, EPD, Politische Direktion: Besuch des österreichischen Aussenministers Kirchschläger in Bern, 27-29 January 1972.

59. In the same speech, Kirchschläger explained that his government was very skeptical about the idea of a new system of collective security on a European level and promoted the Austrian proposal for the inclusion of the MBFR talks as the best way of achieving security in Europe. However, he toned down his skepticism by suggesting that it might be best to consider a well concerted co-action of the three initiatives (obligatory system for the peaceful settlement of disputes, European collective security system, mutual balanced force reduction). Speech by the Austrian Foreign Minister Kirchschläger to members of parliament of a number of European states, 27 March 1972, in *Sicherheit und Zusammenarbeit in Europa (KSZE)*, ed. Jacobsen et al., 399f.

60. The Swiss Foreign Ministry repeatedly stated its view that the current military-strategic balance was in the interest of Switzerland and Swiss neutrality and that any force reduction on the Swiss side was out of question since it already operated at "minimum standard." However, by March 1972 it signaled its readiness to participate in control mechanisms established by a possible MBFR agreement and stated the necessity of a close cooperation with all European small states, notably the other neutrals, with regard to the force reduction talks. Breitenmoser, *Sicherheit für Europa*, 110-12.

61. *Le rôle de la Suisse à la CSCE*, témoignage de l'Ambassadeur Edouard Brunner, 4 ; Renk, *Der Weg der Schweiz nach Helsinki*, 31f ; cf. Schmidl, "L'Autriche et le processus d'Helsinki," 94.

62. Renk, *Der Weg der Schweiz nach Helsinki*, 37-43; Cf. Ferraris, *Report on a Negotiation*, 10. The Swiss-Swedish collaboration again proved successful when they accomplished the agreement to a four week Christmas break (from 15 December 1972 to 15 January 1973) in a concerted effort against Soviet resistance. Renk, *Der Weg der Schweiz nach Helsinki*, 50f; Ferraris, *Report on a Negotiation*, 13.

63. Renk, *Der Weg der Schweiz nach Helsinki*, 52.

64. Liedermann, "Die Konferenz über Sicherheit und Zusammenarbeit in Europa aus österreichischer Sicht," 555-77; Liedermann, "Österreichs Rolle beim Zustandekommen der KSZE," 495.

65. Renk, *Der Weg der Schweiz nach Helsinki*, 57f; see also Renk's foreword to Campiche's memoirs in Samuel Campiche, *Marée du soir: carnets*, Préface de Pierre Friederich et Hans-Jörg Renk (Vevey: Editions de l'Aire, Collection Traces de vie, 2001), 10.

66. CSCE Delegation reports no. 25 and 29, 11 and 12 December 1972. Documents cited in Christian Nünlist, "What Role for a Small Neutral State in East-West Détente? New Perspectives on Switzerland's Role in the CSCE, 1969-1975," Paper prepared for the International Conference in Rüschlikon/Zurich, 8-10 September 2005 "At the Roots of the European Security System: Thirty Years Since the Helsinki Final Act," here 22.

67. Ferraris, *Report on a Negotiation*, 13. According to Sizoo and Jurrjens, the Netherlands delegate referred to, the late Jhr. B.E. Quarles van Ufford, later told his friends that he, in fact, had used the word, but in its French form: "He had seen in his mind's eye four baskets standing on the platform and cried out: '*On jette toutes les propositions dans un panier*.' Later on the French word in use became '*corbeille*' instead of '*panier*'." Jan Sizoo and Rudolf Th. Jurrjens, *CSCE Decision-Making: the Madrid Experience* (The Hague: Martinus Nijhoff, 1984), 73, note 2. Ferraris at the CSCE history conference in Zurich in September 2005 gave the name of the Dutch head of delegation van der Valk as the first person to have used the word "basket" in the talks.

68. Minute from Mr. Tickell on CSCE Preparatory Talks (confidential), 25 January 1973, *The Conference on Security and Cooperation in Europe, 1972-1975*, vol. 2 of Documents on British Policy Overseas, Series 3 (London: Stationary Office, 1997), 89, note 7.

69. Ferraris, *Report on a Negotiation*, 16.

70. Ibid.; cf. Renk, *Der Weg der Schweiz nach Helsinki*, 58f.

71. The neutrals were also competitors in the question over where to hold the actual CSCE negotiations. Austria had already indicated its interest in hosting the MPT in their July 1970 memorandum, and the Swiss Foreign Minister Graber at the yearly gathering of the Swiss Ambassadors in Berne in 1970 signaled that the government would like to see Geneva as a future venue for the CSCE talks (BAR, E 2812 1985/204, 4, Handakten Graber: Rede Bundesrat Graber "La situation internationale: La Conférence européenne de sécurité et le Traité allemand-russe" (streng vertraulich), 2 September 1970.) However, neither Austria nor Switzerland was ready to openly challenge Helsinki. Ambassador Campiche, in a report to the internal working group on the CSCE in December 1972, confirmed that the Swiss delegation would officially support Helsinki, while at the same time it was ready to accept a move to Geneva if requested. Austria was obviously applying a similar policy supporting Helsinki and promoting Vienna only if an alternative had to be found (BAR, E 2001(E) 1982/58, 101, EPD, Abteilung für politische Angelegenheiten: Bericht der Arbeitsgruppe zur KSZE (vertraulich), 19 December 1972.) Finally the choice was made to attribute the first and the third stage of the conference to Helsinki, while holding the actual negotiations during stage II in

Geneva. This compromise took into account practical reasons for the dislocation of the negotiations to a more central place with greater facilities, while leaving the prestigious opening and closing of the conference to Finland which deserved the credit for the initial invitation to the talks. Cf. Renk, *Der Weg der Schweiz nach Helsinki*, 68-73; Ferraris, *Report on a Negotiation*, 39f, 70f.

72. According to Renk, the EC Nine began to take over from NATO the leadership in coordinating the activities of the West in the CSCE by January 1973, which in turn forced the neutrals to take a stand and to make their own positions on various matters clear. Renk, *Der Weg der Schweiz nach Helsinki*, 54-56.

73. While the Austrian delegation, in its opening statement to the MPT by Ambassador Heinrich Pfusterschmied-Hardtenstein on 5 December 1972, had already voiced its official support for the Swiss project regarding an obligatory system for the peaceful settlement of disputes, the Swiss so far had never given any clear backing to the demand of the inclusion of the Middle East problem or the link of MBFR and armament control to the Conference.

74. See the National Archives London, FCO 41/1344: Telegram "MIPT: Austrian Proposals" from T.A.K. Elliott to Foreign and Commonwealth Office, 17 January 1973; and Minute from Mr. Tickell on CSCE Preparatory Talks (confidential), 25 January 1973, *The Conference on Security and Cooperation in Europe*, 88; cf. Renk, *Der Weg der Schweiz nach Helsinki*, 56f; Ferraris, *Report on a Negotiation*, 15.

75. At the end of the MPT, however, the Swiss had to settle for the future creation of a "special working body" to treat their proposal on peaceful settlement, and Sweden and Austria were not successful in trying to achieve that matters of security (political and military) should be dealt with in their entirety in the CSCE. The military alliances prevailed in Dipoli with their demand to keep the MBFR and Strategic Arms Limitation Talks (SALT) out of the conference agenda.

76. Breitenmoser, *Sicherheit für Europa*, 120-24.

77. Renk, *Der Weg der Schweiz nach Helsinki*, 60f; Cf. Ferraris, *Report on a Negotiation*, 20-22.

78. According to Brunner, it was the neutrals, which realized at the time that the Soviets were, in fact, ready to pay a price in basket three to achieve a "satisfactory solution" on the question of inviolability of frontiers. *Le rôle de la Suisse à la CSCE*, témoignage de l'Ambassadeur Edouard Brunner, 10f.

79. BAR, E 2001(E) 1987/78, 442, EPD, Politische Direktion: Bericht über die Gespräche zwischen Bundesrat Graber und Aussenminister Kirchschläger in Vienna, 28/29 May 1973.

80. This change, according to British expectations for Stage II, was likely to encourage the formation of a "neutral bloc" keeping some (i.e. more) distance to the West beyond what Austria, Sweden, and Switzerland did during the talks in Helsinki. Steering Brief for the United Kingdom Delegation to Stage II of the CSCE (confidential), 13 September 1973, *The Conference on Security and Cooperation in Europe*, 183.

81. A British brief that had been prepared for bilateral talks with Austria in October 1973 clearly states these differences: "The one area of the agenda where we and the Austrians see things from rather different viewpoints is the military aspects of security. They are not of course involved in the MBFR negotiations and would like the discussion on this point at the CSCE to go further than we would. They tend to be sympathetic to ideas which we and our allies find difficult." National Archives London, FCO 33/1933: Draft Brief, Visit of the Secretary of State to Austria, 16/18 October 1973.

82. Ferraris, *Report on a Negotiation*, 191.

83. Ibid.

84. Renk, *Der Weg der Schweiz nach Helsinki*, 109-12, 185f. Renk gives 25 February 1974 as the date of the presentation of the first common proposal and thus as the "moment of birth" of the N+NA group.

85. *Le rôle de la Suisse à la CSCE*, témoignage de l'Ambassadeur Edouard Brunner, 12, 27f; John J. Maresca, *To Helsinki: Conference on Security and Cooperation in Europe, 1973-1975* (Durham, NC: Duke UP, 1987), 21.

86. Wilhelm Kuntner, "Die Konferenz über Sicherheit in Europa—Militärische Aspekte der Entspannungspolitik," *Österreichische Zeitschrift für Aussenpolitik 16* (1976): 23-34, see p. 28; Cf. Otmar Höll, "Kleinstaaten im Entspannungsprozess: Am Beispiel der neutralen und nichtpaktgebundenen Staaten in der KSZE," *Österreichische Zeitschrift für Politikwissenschaft 15/3* (1986): 294; Zielinski, *Die neutralen und blockfreien Staaten und ihre Rolle im KSZE-Prozess*, 231.

87. See Minute from Mr. Fall to Mr. Tickell, CSCE (confidential), 17 June 1974, *The Conference on Security and Cooperation in Europe*, 206.

88. A British source on 24 June reported, "The neutrals wish to try to negotiate a package fairly soon: the Swiss and the Austrians, who have been keenest to elicit the maximum concessions from the East, took part in a neutral and non-aligned caucus this afternoon attended by the Finns, at which they succeeded in securing agreement to support the package." Telegram, Mr. Hildyard (UKMIS Geneva) to Mr. Callaghan (confidential), 24 June 1974, *The Conference on Security and Cooperation in Europe*, 208.

89. Ferraris, *Report on a Negotiation*, 128-31; Maresca, *To Helsinki*, 126-28.

90. BAR, E 2001(E) 1987/78, 443, EPD, Politische Direktion: Offizieller Besuch des Aussenministers Kirchschläger, Protokoll der bilateralen Gespräche in Bern am 3 May, 2-4 May 1974.

91. Maresca, *To Helsinki*, 126.

92. Cf. Renk, *Der Weg der Schweiz nach Helsinki*, 132-36.

93. Ibid., 135f.

94. Telegram "CSCE: State of Play," Mr. Hildyard (UKMIS Geneva) to Mr. Callaghan (confidential), 20 September 1974, *The Conference on Security and Cooperation in Europe*, 334.

95. Telegram "Basket III Sub-Committees," Mr. Hildyard (UKMIS Geneva) to Mr. Callaghan (confidential), 19 October 1974, *The Conference on Security and Cooperation in Europe*, 344; cf. Maresca, *To Helsinki*, 107.

96. To strengthen their common tactics to bring the CSCE to a successful end, the Austrian Foreign Minister and his Swiss colleague in a bilateral meeting in August 1974 agreed on a meeting of the State Secretaries of all neutral states in December 1974. (BAR, E 2001(E) 1987/78, 443, Politische Direktion: Offizieller Besuch des österreichischen Aussenministers Bielka, Protokoll der Gespräche in Bern, 28-30 August 1974.) According to Brunner, meetings between the four neutrals on the level of State Secretaries were subsequently taking place in Stockholm, Helsinki, and Berne. Meetings between the four neutral Foreign Ministers were to follow later. *Le rôle de la Suisse à la CSCE*, témoignage de l'Ambassadeur Edouard Brunner, 28.

97. Ibid. Brunner noted that the only other forum apart from the CSCE in which the N+NA again acted together as a group was the United Nations Disarmament Conference in New York in 1978.

REVIEW ESSAYS

Refocusing the Critical Gaze from Sixty Years' Distance: Austrians' Experiences of the Nazi Past in Recent Historical Studies

Thomas Albrich, Winfried Garscha, and Martin F. Polaschek, eds., *Holocaust und Kriegsverbrechen vor Gericht*: *Der Fall Österreich* (Innsbruck: Studienverlag, 2006)

Bertrand Perz, *Die KZ-Gedenkstätte Mauthausen 1945 bis zur Gegenwart* (Innsbruck: Studienverlag, 2006)

Margit Reiter, *Die Generation danach: Der Nationalsozialismus im Familiengedächtnis* (Innsbruck: Studienverlag, 2006)

Lisa Rettl, *PartisanInnendenkmäler: Antifaschistische Erinnerungskultur in Kärnten* (Innsbruck: Studienverlag, 2006)

Matthew Paul Berg

Academic historians may shake their heads in frustration or smile patiently at the perception of their discipline in the popular imagination. Expressions such as "the lessons of history show us that ..." reify the discipline into keeper (or embodiment) of eminently practical, perhaps even obvious, wisdom that we ignore at our own peril. Other forms of popular usage consign history-as-academic discipline to the realm of ivory tower isolation, insofar as they relegate a subject or theme decidedly to the past—that is, by suggesting that it is irrelevant or at best a source of trivia. Those who study contemporary history stand in a particularly challenging relationship to both their fields on the one hand (for example, access to significant archival material remains limited in many instances) and perceptions of the phenomena they study in the popular imagination on the other (insofar as some segments of society may have direct experience with the phenomena under study, or the resonance of that experience in what historian Jan Assmann designated "cultural memory[1]). The National Socialist regime represents a particularly striking convergence of academic and popular interest, of course. Those who study it and its consequences are quite aware of the extent to which themes they investigate have, at times, become personal, professional, and political flashpoints. These themes include analyses of the structure of the so-called Third Reich; exploration of the nature of everyday experiences, including questions of active participation, complicity, and resistance; investigation into wide-ranging consequences of the NS regime after 1945—particularly, but not exclusively, in Germany and Austria; the adjudication of those charged with war crimes and crimes against humanity and the integration of a far more numerous group who had thrown in their lot with the regime for various reasons; memory, commemoration, and expanded notions of victim status; and the dynamics of reconciliation and restitution.

I do not claim that the themes noted above are new to historians working in the early twenty-first century. Indeed, Günter Bischof explored them in *Contemporary Austrian Studies* ten years ago when he reviewed a number of studies that continue to exercise an important influence over academic historians.[2] Serious scholars would agree that the attention these themes have received in Germany and Austria remains particularly compelling, precisely because of the range of reception among the broader public in lands with the legacy of (*Mit*)*Täterschaft*, the ways in which memory has been contested over subsequent generations, and the salience of the past in media representations and political debate.[3]

Those interested in Austrian circumstances are well aware of the implications of the *Opfer/Täter* dualism for political culture, memory, and identity since 1945.[4] While the Waldheim Affair and the particular brand of populism through which Jörg Haider has made his career may be the most prominent examples of ambivalent or problematic attitudes towards the Nazi era in recent decades, such phenomena also catalyzed more sustained direct and open discussion of the past than had previously been the case. More recent developments, such as FPÖ *Bundesrat* Siegfried Kampl's 14 April 2005 comments concerning the "vicious persecution of former Nazis"[5] after the war, or the convictions of FPÖ *Bundesrat* John Gudenus and British historian David Irving in 2006 remind us of the persistence of ambivalence among elements of the public, elected officials, or authors.

The Gudenus and Irving cases are particularly interesting, since charges were brought against them under §3 of the *Verbotsgesetz*. The former had engaged in several instances of minimization or denial of Nazi crimes against humanity (most pointedly in connection with the April 2005 commemoration of the sixtieth anniversary of the war's end during the same *Bundesrat* debate at which Kampl spoke, and later during a tour of Mauthausen); the latter had published and lectured widely in a spirit that moved from revision to denial, and he was arrested for statements made in several speeches he had given in Austria during a 1989 book tour. Due to his acknowledgement that he had made a serious mistake, Gudenus received three years' probation rather than the possibility of up to ten years' imprisonment. Irving sat out just over twelve months of a three-year sentence, only to be released by a presiding appeals court judge with known right-wing sympathies days before Christmas 2006 with the understanding that he would serve the remainder of his sentence at home in Britain on probationary status.[6] Irving's experience elicited criticism of *Verbotsgesetz*-mandated punishment from those on the right and left, within and outside Austria, who regarded the law as a limit on the exercise of free speech. The version of the *Verbotsgesetz* currently in effect underwent legislative review in 1992, suggesting that the majority of Austrian politicians deemed the persistence of such legislation valuable for the Second Republic's democratic, republican values.

The fact that denial continues to flourish is troubling, to be sure—and it is not limited to the West, as the December 2006 Tehran gathering dedicated to "reexamining the Holocaust" convened by Iranian President Mahmoud Ahmadinejad and attended by a number of notorious Western deniers demonstrated. As eyewitnesses, including "political" or "racial" victims of Nazi policy pass away and the indifferent or indignant play a potentially larger role in shaping the contours of cultural memory, credible historical research may well assume an even more valuable public/didactic role than it has to date, even as its guild-specific academic contributions remain important for scholars and students. It is in this spirit that the important new works under review here from Studienverlag must be considered. Taken together, they explore Austrians' experiences and memories of the Nazi past at the private, public, and state levels. Each sheds light on themes or topics that have held interest inside the academy and among the public; each suggests new possibilities for additional research by virtue of that which they offer.

Margit Reiter's exploration of the Nazi era through family memory draws on an established body of German literature rooted in psychoanalysis, the cultural dynamics of memory, and oral history, which she applies provocatively to the Austrian experience. The author establishes at the outset that she is *not* interested in the children of the most prominent NS figures, about whom much is already known in popular literature and television talk shows in recent years; instead, she focuses upon the self-perceptions and self-representation of "children of the perpetrators" in a wider sense, namely those whose parents were middle and lower-level Nazi functionaries or SS men. There are two reasons for her focus on this group. First, it is quite larger than the group of *Prominenten* offspring. Second, Austrian society has shown little interest, awareness, or sensitivity to the ways in which such individuals' formative experiences have been remembered.[7] Memory for these NS progeny, Reiter suggests, operates in a field shaped by the parameters of knowledge about the Nazi past and the roles one's mother and/or father played in the regime (*Wissen*), the lack of such knowledge (*Nichtwissen*), and the extent to which members of this generation had a sense of their parents' relationship to the regime and its crimes that was never discussed openly after the war (*ahnen*).[8] Within the parameters formed by these dynamic tensions, Reiter's interview partners—and, by implication, Austrian society at large—manifest the reactions that shape both personal and cultural memory: ignorance (in some cases a form of repression, she contends), indifference, or the impetus to ask difficult and searching questions about their parents and society under the Nazis.

Critics of the Reiter's work will focus on a small survey sample that might seem too limited to permit her to draw meaningful conclusions. This was a function of voluntary participation in her project. In the end, she interviewed eighteen individuals in their fifties or sixties, an equal number of women and men with balanced representation across *Bundesländer*, rural vs. urban upbringings, and a wide range of professional and trade occupations—a representative enough sample to begin drawing the provisional, but highly suggestive conclusions at which she arrives. Moreover, Reiter brings an impressive sophistication to a highly qualitative study that is consistent with the findings of comparable work done in Germany.[9] Indeed, the author is acutely aware of the delicate dynamics of an oral history project. She understands the interviewer's role as facilitator and has constructed a thoughtful catalogue of questions that would satisfy ethical concerns while simultaneously maintaining focus on recollections that could alternately elicit anger at their parents' values under the Nazis (and subsequently) or embarrassment, or provoke complex feelings of victimization (at the hands of parents, society, or the politics of the postwar Austrian republic).

Interviews with project participants reveal five modes for representing experiences of the NS era and its aftermath within the family framework. Each demonstrates itself capable of coexisting with one or more other modes during the complex processes of transmission of parental experience to children and children's memory formation. First, experience could be conveyed in terms of *victimization*—that is, that mother, father, and/or the individual interview partner had been the innocent victim of the Nazi regime itself, partisans, occupation forces, or Second Republic authorities. Reiter observes that in such cases reversals occurred in the perpetrator-victim dynamic (consider Siegfried Kampl's syntactical choice in the *Bundesrat* speech referred to above). The trope of victimization could be all the more easily drawn upon given the notion of Austrian victim status writ large enabled by the institutionalized *Opfermythos*. Participants also commonly engaged in *justification*; they saw themselves as "accused" who because of their parents' experiences had to answer the reproaches of their own children's or grandchildren's generation; they claimed that they knew nothing of Nazi crimes and violence, or that when they later learned about such actions, people (most frequently the father figure in Reiter's case studies) acted under compulsion or were honor-bound to fulfill their duty or simply acted under a *Befehlsnotstand*. *Distancing* provided a mechanism for interviewees to reject any attraction that National Socialism may have had for their parents—or for themselves—and opened up the possibility of solidarity with the younger generation (for example, interviewees poked fun at Nazi leaders and compared them with Second Republic politicians, or remembered their parents doing so). Others exhibited a particular *fascination* with the ostensibly positive features of the Nazi regime ("cleanliness and order, jobs [...] technological innovations and sense of community"), an enthusiasm that they separated from negative features ("persecution of Jews, war"). Finally, the strategy of *overcoming* facilitated recasting the details of one's own past, transforming the world into which interviewees were born and the role of their parents as life-givers into a family/personal history over which one could be proud.

264 The Changing Austrian Voter

In such cases, "overcoming" functioned similarly to "fascination," yet could also manifest itself as fervent rejection of fascism and a steadfast commitment to democratic republican political culture.[10]

These tropes must be understood in relation to family dynamics, Reiter reminds us, if we are to account for the translation of communicative memory into cultural memory. Here she is at her strongest, and her larger interview-driven chapters that form the greater part of the volume (*"Vaterbilder"* and *"Mutterbilder"*) find a foundation in an investigation of the social and institutional processes by which certain perceptions, knowledge, and memory are shaped. Not surprisingly, the nuclear family was the source of most initial memories and the earliest locus for socialization for Reiter's interviewees. They most frequently identified rather closely with their parents when they were children and generally enjoyed hearing stories about the war and their parents' (again, usually fathers') work. However, she found that others claimed to have grown tired of such accounts even as children and reported that they ceased to ask questions; in still other cases, interviewees recalled that it was made clear to them verbally or through parental behavior that questions were unwelcome.[11] As adults, many of the interviewees who represented themselves as critics of the NS era chose to avoid bringing up questions of their parents' activities—or National Socialism altogether—in the interest of good familial relations. These elderly parents, they claimed, would have seen such questions as a form of personal attack.[12]

Reiter acknowledges that sites of socialization outside the nuclear family also exercised important influences on development and memory and contributed to her interviewees' orientation towards conservative or even right-wing milieus, but also into antifascist circles. For example, the presence of other relatives throughout childhood and into adulthood who had not been *Parteigenossen* and who never refrained from making critical comments about the Nazi era could prove an irritant to Nazi parents and provided a model that indicated different ways of thinking and acting were possible. During the later 1940s and 1950s, the years during which interviewees had been children, the NS past remained a taboo theme in most Austrian schools despite Education Ministry directives to address the subject, but extracurricular activities sponsored by organizations such as the *Österreichischer Turnverband* reinforced the right-wing, often extremist sentiments that so many of their parents continued to harbor. Some of the men Reiter interviewed never broke with their parents' NS worldview; they wound up joining *Burschenschaften* during their university years and became FPÖ supporters. Others were influenced by the new climate of the later 1960s and distanced themselves, if they had not reported doing so previously, from their parents' values and became involved in left-wing political and social activism. Finally, while some individuals recalled being horrified by media coverage of legal proceedings against Nazi criminals, others dismissed reports about war crimes or crimes against humanity as fabrications or alternatively were convinced that they shed light on the cruelty—or grim silence—they had experienced in the parental household.[13] Reiter's recognition of the importance of primary socialization within the family and the influence of external factors ("secondary institutions") is a particular strength of her project, and her sensitivity to the delicacy of these processes in the formation and representation of memory provides a firm structural foundation to the more delicate psychoanalytical dimensions of her case study analyses. If one were to quibble with the book in this respect, it would be with the nearly complete absence of important studies directly relevant for elements of her work on popular sentiment, education, anti-Semitism, memory, and postwar treatment of National Socialists published in English. Reiter may have expected an almost exclusively Austrian (perhaps also Germans) readership, but a work as suggestive as this one would naturally attract the attention of a broader international scholarly public. One might have expected her to take into account the work of a broader community of historians working in the field of Austrian *Zeitgeschichte* whose contributions are directly relevant for her study—for example, Evan Bukey, Peter Pulzer, Bruce Pauley, Robert Knight, or Peter Utgaard.

Memory features significantly, too, in Bertrand Perz's history of Mauthausen since 1945. The author's treatment of the evolution of institutionalized memory at a physical site is a thorough one, and he offers an interesting counterpoint to Reiter's exploration of second-generation memory of the Nazi past. The book posits an ambitious agenda. Perz proposes to examine Mauthausen as museum, cemetery, tourist destination, economic institution, and *Gedenkstätte* from 1945 to the present, as well as to compare commonalities between Mauthausen and other concentration camp sites that have become commemorative sites. While he is an undisputed expert on Mauthausen itself and delivers a richly documented and highly detailed study of the central site for remembrance Nazi crimes in Austria, Perz never delivers on his goal of meaningful, sustained comparative analysis—despite occasional references to memory and commemoration associated with former concentration camps in West and East Germany or Poland. Some readers will find this regrettable, and perhaps consider the work as another example of a project geared toward an Austrian readership. Nonetheless, one would be hard-pressed to find a more detailed study of the way in which the physical site of a concentration camp became an object of conflicting economic and cultural interests during the immediate postwar years, or the political wrangling associated with the establishment of a *KZ-Gedenkstätte*.

Perz identifies three distinct stages of development for Mauthausen's transformation into a *Gedenkstätte*. The first—extending from liberation in 1945 to the official designation of the area as a commemorative site in 1949—was characterized by efforts to secure the main and neighboring satellite camps, regulate jurisdiction, and establish memorial status. The author reconstructs these developments in exquisite detail at both the micro and macro levels, drawing on archival sources in Austria (including federal, provincial, and municipal holdings), in Germany (Bundesarchiv Berlin-Lichterfelde), the Czech Republic (Military History Archive, Prague), and from the National Archives in Washington, DC. For the first several months after liberation, the very integrity of the camp itself was in question. Prisoners scavenged raw materials, furniture, and anything else they deemed useful before beginning their migrations home (Czech prisoners were particularly resourceful in this respect); Austrian firms, particularly Viennese enterprises, attempted to leverage their positions prior to and during the Nazi regime to lay claim to raw materials and real estate at Mauthausen and in the satellite camps. *Gemeinde* administrations in towns such as Mauthausen and St. Georgen lay claim to former SS living quarters to alleviate housing shortages. At the macro level, Perz's narrative traces negotiations between the U.S. occupation authorities and the Upper Austrian *Landesregierung* and relevant *Gemeindeverwaltungen*, the transfer of authority over the territory on which the camp sat to the Soviet occupation authority in 1947, and Soviet interactions with provincial and local authorities into the year 1949—at which point the KPÖ-dominated *KZ Verband* succeeded in working with the *Landesregierung* and a somewhat reluctant federal government to secure *Gedenkstätte* status.

The years between the creation of the *Gedenkstätte* and debate over the establishment of a permanent historical exhibit on the main camp's grounds (from 1949 into the 1970s) form the second phase of Perz's narrative. Questions concerning the politics of memory had surfaced in 1947 when Austrian authorities assumed responsibility for the site; over the next two decades, debate on *what form* commemoration would assume (chapels, plaques)—and for whom (political prisoners vs. "racial" prisoners, different national groups)—only intensified. Perz reminds us that the debate transcended state borders and political boundaries from the start; different national concentration camp prisoner associations formed shortly after the Nazi regime fell, and in Austria, the umbrella *KZ-Verband* operated under a majority communist leadership. Moreover, leading KPÖ figures associated with the *KZ-Verband* such as Heinrich Dürmayer also played prominent roles in the founding of the International Mauthausen Committee (IMK) in 1953. Perz's second phase is of great importance for issues of memory and commemoration for several reasons, two of which warrant particular emphasis. First, although the federal government had approved the general concept for a Mauthausen *Gedenkstätte*, the terms of the *Kriegsgräberfürsorgegesetz* (July 1948) and the burial of Allied soldiers on the camp's grounds brought administration of the site under the competence of the Interior Minister Oskar Helmer. One may speculate as to whether Helmer's suspicion of the *KZ-Verband* had something to do with its members' bona fides as resistors to National Socialism, whereas Helmer had not experienced such rough treatment. Helmer's anti-communism cannot be disputed, however. When the *Gedenkstätte* opened officially on 8 May 1949, Helmer refused to recognize it with an Interior Ministry presence, arguing that the matter was "not an official celebration, but one of the federal association of *KZler*."[14] Second, Perz notes that Dürmayer's success in forming the IMK marked the only formal international recognition of an NS victims' association in Austria—not insignificant at a time when less-implicated Nazis (*Minderbelastete*) were on the verge of reintegration into political life and Austrians were more interested in reconstruction and the Cold War than soul-searching over their involvement in the NS regime.[15]

The KPÖ's position of prominence in framing resistance and victimhood for so-called political inmates involved not only a willingness to challenge a dominant desire to concentrate more on the present and future after 1949 than on the silent or active complicity in a system that made the Mauthausen camp system possible on Austrian soil. Perz cites a number of editorials in primarily Catholic, conservative Austrian newspapers (for example, *die Furche* and Graz's *Kleine Zeitung*) which stressed, as he puts it "that survivors had the right to forget" and that, in effect, "victims of National Socialism should be able to commemorate, but with as little disturbance as possible. This opinion was joined with the perception that coming to terms with National Socialism had been concluded and now [in 1949 – MPB] it was a matter of criticizing other political systems." So, under these circumstances, what was the purpose of devoting hundreds of thousands of Schillings to the preservation of gallows, prison blocks, barracks, and other features of the Mauthausen camps?[16] The ÖVP-led Upper Austrian *Landesregierung* under Heinrich Gleißner supported the creation of the *Gedenkstätte*, admittedly out of cultural/historical tourism considerations, but also as an acknowledgment of the importance of commemoration and out of sensitivity to *KZ-Verband* lobbying efforts. However, the SPÖ affiliated *Linzer Tagblatt* alleged that those who had been behind the authoritarian Fatherland Front [VF] between 1934 and 1938 "had become democrats in the meantime, and established a giant monument to the inhumanity of others in order to wipe clean their own past."[17] In short, among Austrians it was not unequivocally clear which oppressive regime should be held responsible as the source of Austrian misfortune and which victims deserved greatest recognition (Social Democrats at the hands of the VF or political prisoners regardless of their *Lager* allegiance, as opposed to Jews and other "racial" prisoners). To further complicate matters, Mauthausen was a "green" camp—that is, it was run primarily by criminals—so that efforts by the Communist-dominated *KZ-Verband* to emphasize pride-of-place for political prisoners was something of an exercise in myth-making. This assumed absurd proportions in the 1950 account of Mauthausen's last days authored by Hans Marsalek—a long-serving inmate who had functioned as camp scribe, worked closely with Dürmayer in the *KZ-Verband*, and served *as Obmann der österreichischen Lagermeinschaft Mauthausen*—which attributed the camp's liberation to an uprising of communist prisoners shouting slogans in praise of the Red Army, rather than to the appearance of U.S. tanks.[18] For a cold warrior such as Helmer, such representations merely confirmed his suspicion that the *KZ-Verband* stood closer to the Soviet Union than it represented Austrian interests. If there was a point of commonality among supporters of the three original postwar political parties, it was the firm conviction, consistent with the *Opfermythos*, that Mauthausen was a categorically alien, un-Austrian phenomenon. This conviction dominated the official narrative represented at the *Gedenkstätte* into the 1970s.

Perz's third phase, ca. 1970 to the present, corresponds to initial Kreisky-era emphases on historical and political education and the establishment of the historical exhibit at Mauthausen that—side by side with the commemoration of international victims achieved through fixed memorial installations—ushered in a more systematic effort to move beyond rhetoric and myth to a significant extent. Developments in the direction of *Vergangenheitsbewältigung*, beginning in earnest with the

Waldheim controversy in the mid 1980s and then continuing into the 1990s revealed an intensification of this trend, culminating in the creation of the new visitors' center with its oral history exhibit in 2003.

A counterpart to Perz's thorough, albeit somewhat conventional, narrative study of a "national" site of remembrance, Lisa Rettl's vigorous investigation into monuments to fallen partisans in mixed German-Slovene speaking regions of southern Carinthia brings a particularly compelling theoretical approach to bear on *local* sites. Although she focuses primarily on the case of a monument installed in Völkermarkt/ Velikovec in October 1947, detonated by ultra-right wing German nationalists in September 1953, and newly erected in a much more modest form in September 1962, she also offers brief examinations of memorials in other towns within the region. Rettl's point of departure is her observation that monuments to antifascist resistance fighters remain contested—at least in southern Carinthia—whereas the commemoration of soldiers who fell "in defense of the fatherland" in both world wars and in the *Abwehr* along the Carinthian-Yugoslav border after World War I have long remained the normative discourse in postwar memory. Further, she posits what she calls a consensual division in collective memory of the Nazi era and its immediate aftermath in which the majority of the German-speaking Carinthian *Volk* remember their experience of the war as one as a defensive action against Slovene Communists (those who refused to be—or were not selected for—"Germanization") and the officially sanctioned memory of a mixed-language, antifascist resistance tradition that was not inconsistent with the notion of Austrians-as-victims of the Nazi regime.[19]

There is much to commend in Rettl's approach. One of its most significant strengths is her sophisticated understanding of how commemorative events contribute to the shaping of communal memory and identity. Significant influences on her conceptualization of the project include, among others, Jan and Aleida Assmann, Benedict Anderson, Ruth Wodak, and Heidemarie Uhl's pioneering work on Austrian monuments commemorating fallen soldiers. She synthesizes the work of these scholars with a reliance on discourse theory derived from Michel Foucault and applied to sources such as newspaper accounts, church records, local police and governmental reports, and documentation from the Archivbestände des Verbandes der Kärtner Partisanen as well as from various political parties in the Kärtner Landesarchiv and in the Österreichisches Staatsarchiv/Archiv der Republik.

Monuments to fallen "Austrian German" soldiers on the one hand and fallen partisans on the other have served to create "an illusion of the eternal," Rettl argues.[20] Elaborate installations or simple commemorative plaques have not merely lionized duty and sacrifice; Rettl reminds us that they also promote ongoing identification of communities—sometimes defined as much by their opponents' perception as by their members' own self-conception—with past, present, even future collective aspirations. Rettl's focus on three prevailing discourses, each of which became "institutionalized" in the calculus of southern Carinthia's social/cultural/political dynamic is the book's other principal strength. The first discursive element is the partisans' representation of themselves and their critics. The second is right-wing pro-German Carinthians' (many of whom were former Nazis) representation of themselves, of acceptable, assimilated ("Germanized") Slovenes, and of Slovene partisans (depicted as Yugoslav agents, Communists, a corrosive element in southern Carinthia). The third is an official state representation that stressed an Austrian identity that (a) has been divorced from the German identity championed by many among the Carinthian majority; (b) has sought to recognize the contributions of resistance fighters against the *Wehrmacht*; (c) has emphasized Austrians' victim status; and (4) has remained determined to safeguard Carinthia's territorial integrity while maintaining positive relations with Yugoslavia. Close analysis of these competing discourses, as applied to the contested histories of the *PartisanInnendenkmäler* in Völkermarkt/Velikovec and in Peršmanhof, makes for what is arguably the most sophisticated and elegantly presented study among the four volumes under review here. Yet as strong as Rettl's work is, the abrupt end to her study and complete absence of any sort of conclusion—whether it might have been suggestions for further research, or the applicability of her approach to case studies such as South Tyrol, or even a mere *Zusammenfassung*—leaves the reader unsatisfied. This is all the more surprising and disappointing given the purposefulness with which Rettl establishes the grounds for her case study and her bold methodological approach.

The only work of essays under review here, the volume assembled by Thomas Albrich, Winfried Garscha, and Martin Polaschek, offers a consistency of thematic integrity not often found in edited collections. Eleven topical case studies among a total of thirteen chapters focus on various dimensions of Nazi war crimes and crimes against humanity committed by Austrians and/or on Austrian soil, as delineated in the *Kriegsverbrechergesetz* (KVG) promulgated by the Provisional Government on 26 June 1945 with Allied approval. These essays are richly based in primary sources (for example, *Gerichtsurteile*, *Tagebücher* generated by the State's Attorneys, protocols of hearings housed in the AdR, DöW, and provincial archives) from cases brought before the *Volksgerichte* up to 1955, then before special *Geschworenengerichte* and other judicial bodies after the 1957 amnesty. All of them provide ample detail from the testimony of defendants and witnesses. Each after its own fashion remains true to the questions established in the editors' introduction that form the leitmotif of the volume: what role did the Austrian judiciary actually play in the prosecution of Nazi perpetrators and in the expiation of war criminals, particularly given the high percentage of prominent and lesser administrators of ghettos, organizers of major deportations, and death camp personnel identified by Simon Wiesenthal and others as Austrians?[21] Were the death sentences of the 1940s or the lenient sentences and spectacular acquittals of the 1960s and 1970s typical of an Austrian way of dealing with war crimes and crimes against humanity? What was the legal basis for the creation of *Volksgerichte* in 1945 and what sorts of political, structural, or legal difficulties limited their ability to adjudicate and punish? Did the Austrian postwar judicial system fail with respect to adjudication and punishment of such perpetrators?[22] Individual essays take up these questions through their foci on particular categories of crimes, for example, participants in the *Reichskristallnachtpogrom*, the "euthanasia" program, mass shootings and crimes committed in ghettos in Eastern Europe, deportations, activities in the Auschwitz and Mauthausen camp systems, denunciations, and death marches during the war's closing weeks.

Winfried Garscha and Claudia Kuretsidis-Haider argue that the great majority of cases brought before the *Volksgerichte* involved suspicion of illegal membership in the NSDAP between 1933 and 1938. Such cases were tantamount to treason, given the Austrian Nazi Party's emphasis on the integration of Austria into the Third Reich. Consistent with the Moscow Declaration, Austria could, thus, position itself among the "liberated nations" through adjudication of traitors, collaborators, and others who had "sullied the honor of the nation."[23] The KVG did not take the "racial" component of Nazi criminality into consideration, however—a phenomenon that changed only with the Eichmann Trial and broader public awareness of the genocidal dimensions of Nazi violence at a more abstracted macro level[24]—which contributed to the perception that juridical considerations (and, for that matter, *popular* concern) did not acknowledge victims of National Socialist criminality on the basis of their ethnic or religious heritage.

It would not come as a surprise then, as Thomas Albrich and Michael Guggenberger point out, that despite a strong evidentiary basis detailing chains of command and a wide range of perpetrators, not a single murder case was adjudicated in association with crimes that claimed the lives of twenty-two Viennese Jews on *Reichskristallnacht*,[25] or that throughout Austria over ninety percent of alleged pogrom perpetrators never found themselves in a courtroom.[26] The number of individuals arrested in connection to mass shootings associated with "liquidation" of ghettos was quite minimal, and the percentage of those brought to trial and convicted of murder under the KVG was low and lower still, respectively. Structural factors may have played a contributing factor here, according to Eva Holpfer and Sabine Loitfellner. In a climate shaped by the 1957 amnesty and the Eichmann arrest, Justice Minister Christian Broda urged in the early 1960s that Austria authorities be quick to pursue remaining Nazis, or the Republic would risk losing its good name in international circles as more information became available about NS crimes against humanity in the East. Consequently, the Interior Ministry created a special section, Abt. 2c/18, to engage in the hunt for Nazi war criminals, and the SPÖ and ÖVP agreed to extend the statute of limitations on murder committed under cover of the NS regime. Holpfer and Loitfellner note that Abt. 2c/18 was not particularly vigilant, not least because a number of rehabilitated former Nazis had entered the federal police ranks (including this special section) and were largely uninterested in further investigations into NS-related crimes. Nonetheless, the names of some 5,500 Austrian suspects came to light—in most instances through the efforts of Dutch, Israeli, or West German authorities.[27] In the end, only forty-three individuals were tried for murder/crimes against humanity. Twenty received guilty verdicts, and twenty-three were acquitted. In addition to the lack of consistent, inspired work by members of Abt. 2c/18, lackluster prosecution and adjudication may also have been a product of two other factors: the structure and internal dynamics of *Geschworenengerichte* arrangements and a largely indifferent population who had come to accept integration of former Nazis into Austrian private and public life and whose attention had focused on more prominent cases, such as the Eichmann trial.[28]

While each of the eleven categories of cases presented in *Holocaust und Kriegsverbrechen vor Gericht* is compelling in its own right, many readers will be interested in two particular contributions. Heimo Hailbrainer's essay on denunciation takes up the adjudication of this widespread practice in Nazi-dominated Austria in cases where the consequences were deadly for those denounced. Most of these denunciations targeted those allegedly critical of the regime or who were said to have uttered defeatist remarks ("*'heimtückische' und 'wehrkraftzersetzende' Äußerungen*").[29] Of the 10,015 cases prosecuted on KVG-related charges, a whopping 61.5 percent of them involved denunciation—a statistic that stands in marked contrast to the Garscha/Kuretsidis-Haider assertion, cited above, that most cases brought before *Volksgerichte* involved illegal membership in the NSDAP, and which provides juridical insight and complimentary findings to studies such as those of Herbert Dohmen and Nina Scholz that study denunciation from the perspective of social history.[30] Perhaps the most intriguing essay in terms of its implications for further research is Susanne Uslu-Pauer's study of cases related to death marches during the winter of 1944/45. The murder and ill treatment committed during the closing weeks of the war did not take place in the relative isolation of death or concentration camps, but increasingly out in the open before the eyes of the civilian population of Austria and Germany. In fact, there proved to be no shortage of willing helpers who acted with or without orders.[31] Uslu-Pauer notes that cases adjudicated in 1945/46 met with stricter punishment on the whole than those taken up after the initial amnesties of 1948 and reintegration of most *Minderbelastete* by 1949—a political consideration given that a number of SS men who had been responsible had since found their way into the SPÖ or the ÖVP. Readers will find interesting that it appears a higher percentage of convictions in relation to arrests was meted out for crimes associated with *Todesmärsche* than with any other category of crimes besides denunciation (125 criminal cases involving 265 accused, with twenty-six of twenty-nine death penalty cases enforced and twenty-one life sentences handed down).[32] The fact that so many witnesses were able to provide testimony to provide convictions and that Uslu-Pauer identified such a wealth of archival material, promises the possibility for fresh insights into these aspects of the final weeks of the war on Austrian soil.

Minor idiosyncrasies notwithstanding, the four works reviewed here make a strong case that study of the contested place of the Nazi past in both Austrian communicative and cultural memory has broken new ground. For Austrians themselves, the events of recent years underscore the importance of innovative, careful, source-based inquiry into Austrian experiences between 1938 and 1945, with implications for ways in which the Nazi era is remembered at the private, communal, and federal levels. Moreover, these studies contribute to an important ongoing civic pedagogic project that must not be undervalued. Recent work produced by Austria specialists within or outside the Second Republic on the

274   The Changing Austrian Voter

dynamics of postwar memory in a European context and in the field of Austrian *Zeitgeschichte* more specifically suggests that a still more purposeful internationalization of contemporary Austrian studies will advance scholarship in an even more meaningful, cooperative fashion. The implications for academic work and public didactic possibilities in Europe and elsewhere require nothing less.

Notes

1. On cultural memory, see Jan Assmann, *Das kulturelle Gedächtnis: Schrift, Erinnerung und politische Identität in frühen Hochkulturen*, 2nd. ed. (Munich: C.H. Beck, 1997), 48ff.

2. Günter Bischof, "Founding Myths and Compartmentalized Past: New Literature on the Construction, Hibernation, and Deconstruction of World War II Memory in Postwar Austria," *Contemporary Austrian Studies*, vol. 5, *Austrian Historical Memory and National Identity*, eds. Günter Bischof and Anton Pelinka (New Brunswick, NJ: Transaction, 1997): 302-42. Of particular relevance in Bischof's essay, given the foci of the books under review here, are Meinrad Ziegler and Waltraud Kannonier-Finster, *Österreichisches Gedächtnis: Über Erinnern und Vergessen der NS-Vergangenheit* (Vienna: Böhlau, 1993); Peter Bettelheim and Robert Streibel, eds., *Tabu und Geschichte: Zur Kultur des kollektiven Erinnerns* (Vienna: Picus Verlag, 1994); Werner Bergmann, Rainer Erb, and Albert Lichtblau eds., *Schwieriges Erbe: Der Umgang mit dem Nationalsozialismus und Antisemitismus in Österreich, der DDR und der Bundesrepublik Deutschland* (Frankfurt: Campus, 1995).

3. For Austrian circumstances, consider the following studies of media and political treatment vis-à-vis *Vergangenheitsbewältigung*: Heidemarie Uhl, *Zwischen Versöhnung und Verstörung: Eine Kontroverse um Österreichs historische Identität fünfzig Jahre nach dem "Anschluß"* (Vienna: Böhlau Verlag, 1992); Gerhard Botz and Gerald Sprengnagel, eds., *Kontroversen um Österreichs Zeitgeschichte: verdrängte Vergangenheit, Österreich-Identität, Waldheim und die Historiker* (Frankfurt am Main: Campus Verlag, 1994); Heinz P. Wassermann, *"Zuviel Vergangenheit tut nicht gut!" Nationalsozialismus im Spiegel der Tagespresse der Zweiten Republik* (Innsbruck: Studienverlag, 2000); Helene Maimann, *Was bleibt. Schreiben im Gedenkjahr* (Vienna: Czernin Verlag, 2005); Matthew Paul Berg, "Commemoration vs. Vergangenheitsbewältigung: Contextualizing Austria's Gedenkjahr 2005," *German History* 2008 (January) 26:1, forthcoming. See also media coverage of Wolfgang Neugebauer and Peter Schwarz, *Der Wille zum Aufrechten Gang: zur Rolle des BSA bei der gesellschaftlichen Integration ehemaliger Nationalsozialisten* (Vienna: Czernin Verlag, 2005) and Maria Mesner, ed., *Entnazifizierung zwischen politischem Anspruch, Parteienkonkurrenz und Kaltem Krieg: Das Beispiel SPÖ* (Vienna: Oldenbourg, 2005), Kurt Scholz, "Was macht das B vor dem SA?" *Die Presse*, 11 Jan. 2005; "Zeitgeschichte: Die rote Nazi-Waschmaschine," *Profil* Nr. 3, 17 Jan. 2005: 12-16; Hans Rauscher, "Rot-Braun, Schwarz-Braun: Die SPÖ hat ihre Vergangenheit untersuchen lassen, die ÖVP noch nicht," *Der Standard*, 15 Jan. 2005; Eva Blimlinger, "Der Mut zum Fleck," *Falter* Nr. 27, 8-14 July 2005: 8-10 and Maria Mesner's response ,"Das Dilemma der Polemik," *Falter* Nr. 28, 15-21 July 2005: 18.

4. This literature is an extensive one, of course. As representative examples of the ways in which this dualism has been framed, see Günter Bischof, "Die Instrumentalisierung der Moskauer Erklärung nach dem zweiten Weltkrieg," *Zeitgeschichte* 20

(1993): 34566; Anton Pelinka and Erika Weinzierl, eds., *Das große Tabu: Österreichs Umgang mit seiner Vergangenheit*, 2. Auflage (Vienna: Österreichische Staatsdruckerei, 1997); Anton Pelinka, "Von der Funktionalität von Tabus: zu den 'Lebenslügen' der Zweiten Republik," Gerhard Botz, "Geschichte und kollektives Gedächtnis in der Zweiten Republik: 'Opferthese,' 'Lebenslüge' und Geschichtstabu in der Zeitgeschichtsschreibung," and Brigitte Bailer, "Alle waren Opfer: der selektive Umgang mit den Folgen des Nationalsozialismus" in *Inventur 1945/55: Österreich im ersten Jahrzehnt der Zweiten Republik*, ed. Wolfgang Kos and Georg Rigele (Vienna: Sonderzahl Verlagsgesellschaft, 1996), 23-32, 51-85, and 181-200, respectively; Ziegler and Kannonier-Finster, *Österreichisches Gedächtnis*.

5. *Stenographisches Protokoll der 720. Sitzung des Bundesrates der Republik Österreich vom 14. April 2005*, 125.

6. For Gudenus' *Bundesrat* comments, see *Stenographisches Protokoll der 720. Sitzung des Bundesrates der Republik Österreich vom 14. April 2005*, 117 and 119-20. On his remarks at Mauthausen, consult "Gudenus wird Immunität erneut aberkannt: Landtag erneut mit einstimmigem Auslieferungsbeschluss—Aussagen zu Häftlingsfotos im KZ-Mauthausen werden untersucht," *Der Standard* 15 Sept. 2005 <http://derStandard. at>; "Gudenus wird der Prozess gemacht," *Kurier* 27 Jan. 2006 <http://kurier.at/oesterreich/ 1259495.php>; "Ex-FP Abgeordneter wegen Wiederbetätigung zu einem Jahr bedingt verurteilt," 26 April 2006 <http://derStandard.at/>. See also Richard Bernstein, "Austria Refuses Bail to Briton Accused of Denying the Holocaust," *The New York Times*, 26 Nov. 2005; "Austria Imposes 3-Year Sentence on Notorious Holocaust Denier," *The New York Times*, 21 Feb. 2006; "Drei Jahre Haft für David Irving," *OÖ Nachrichten*, 21 Feb. 2006 <http://www.nachrichten.at/politik/innenpolitik/424435>; Mark Landler, "Austria Frees Holocaust Denier from Jail," *The New York Times*, 21 Dec. 2006 <http://www. nytimes.com/> (archive).

7. Margit Reiter, *Die Generation danach*, 11.

8. Ibid., 14. Put differently, Reiter is interested in the "floating gap" between parents (the *Erlebnisgeneration*) and subsequent generations who serve as carriers of (cultural) memory. See also ibid., 18.

9. See, for example, Harald Welzer, Sabine Moller and Karoline Tschuggnall, *"Opa war kein Nazi". Nationalsozialismus und Holocaust im deutschen Familiengedächtnis* (Frankfurt am Main: Fischer Taschenbuchverlag, 2002); Aleida Assmann and Ute Frevert, *Geschichtsvergessenheit –Geschichtsversessenheit: Vom Umgang mit deutschem Vergangenheiten nach 1945* (Stuttgart: Deutsche Verlags-Anstalt, 1999), particularly 19147; and Harald Welzer, Robert Montau and Christine Plaß, *"Was wir für böse Menschen sind!". Der nationalsozialismus im Gespräch zwischen den Generationen* (Tübingen: Edition Diskord, 1997).

10. Reiter, 48f.

11. Ibid., 68-69.

12. Ibid., 70-71.

13. Ibid., 74-82.

14. Perz, *Die KZ-Gedenstätte Mauthausen*, 109.

15. Ibid., 109ff.

16. Ibid., 113.

17. Ibid., 115. From *Linzer Tagblatt*, 7 May 1949. On memory with respect to the Austrian civil war of 1934 and the authoritarian regime of 1934-1938, see Elisabeth

Klamper, "'Ein einig Volk von Brüdern': Vergessen und Erinnern im Zeichen des Burgfriedens" in *Zeitgeschichte* 24 Heft 5/6 (1997): 170-85.

18. Perz, 127-28. Marsalek distanced himself from this fabrication in the 1970s.

19. Rettl, *PartisanInnendenkmäler*, 12.

20. Ibid., 15.

21. Albrich et al., eds., *Holocaust und Kriegsverbrechen vor Gericht*, 7.

22. Ibid., 8.

23. Garscha and Kuretsidis-Haider, "Die straftrechtliche Verfolgung nationalsozialistischer Verbrechen—eine Einführung" in *Holocaust und Kriegsverbrechen*, 17.

24. Ibid., 18.

25. Albrich and Guggenberger, "'Nur selten steht einer dieser Novemberverbrecher vor Gericht': Die straftrechtliche Verfolgung der Täter der so genannten 'Reichskristallnacht' in Österreich" in *Holocaust und Kriegsverbrechen*, 31.

26. Ibid., 52.

27. Holpfer and Loitfellner, "Holocaust Prozesse wegen Massenerschießungen und Verbrechen in Lagern im Osten vor Geschworenengerichten: Annäherung an ein unerforschtes Thema" in *Holocaust und Kriegsverbrechen*, 88-91.

28. Ibid., 119-22.

29. Heimo Hailbrainer, "'Der Angeber musste vorhersehen, dass die Denunziation eine Gefahr für das Leben des Betroffenen nach sich ziehen werde': Volksgerichtsverfahren wegen Denunziation mit Todesfolge in Österreich" in *Holocaust und Kriegsverbrechen vor Gericht*, 245.

30. Herbert Dohmen and Nina Scholz, *Denunziert: Jeder tut mit—Jeder denkt nach—Jeder Meldet* (Vienna: Czernin Verlag, 2003).

31. Susanne Uslu-Pauer, "'Vernichtungswut und Kadavergehorsam': Straftrechtliche Verfolgung von Endphaseverbrechen am Beispiel der so genannten Todesmärsche" in *Holocaust und Kriegsverbrechen vor Gericht*, 279.

32. Ibid., 280.

György's Machine Gun, Ildikós New Car: The Controversial Hungarian Revolution of 1956 Revisited

Peter Berger

My earliest memories connected with the 1956 Hungarian uprising go back to the time when I was just four years old. Some of my parents' acquaintances from Budapest had decided to leave the Hungarian capital during the massive Russian onslaught that killed the revolution. They found temporary domicile in a refugee camp near the small Austrian town of Stockerau, some fifteen miles away from Vienna. In my father's car we drove to this camp, a row of dilapidated barracks of the old Habsburg Empire's army, striking the visitor by their gray dullness. I cannot recall any faces of the people we met there, but I remember their gratitude at my father's handing them a small sum of money. Within a few weeks or months of our visit, most of them received affidavits from friends or relatives in the United States and were, thus, legally entitled to settle down in the New World. An overwhelming majority of the estimated 180,000 Hungarian refugees who in late 1956, from fear of political repression after the revolution's defeat, crossed the border into Austria, opted for a life in North America, Australia, or Western Europe. Approximately 10,000 chose to stay in Austria and became perfectly assimilated citizens of the Alpine Republic, whose miraculous rise to prosperity was just about to begin.

Twenty years later, I received an invitation to dinner by one of my grandmother's cousins who lived in Budapest's Kerepesi Street. House fronts in this section of the town still showed traces of the fighting in 1956. Hungarian people had long learned to avoid asking critical questions about their country's recent past. Communist party boss János Kádár, whom everyone considered a betrayer of the revolutionary cause in the immediate aftermath of 1956, had meanwhile earned himself a reputation as guarantor of the average Hungarian's high living standard, certainly high if one compared it with the rest of the Soviet Bloc. Also, Kádár was given credit for the fact that a small group of Hungarian dissident intellectuals enjoyed limited freedom of expression. My host, an affable, retired high functionary of Hungary's police corps, had been a member of the Hungarian Socialist Workers' Party (MSZMP) since the days of his adolescence. When Hungary fell under German occupation in 1944, he threw a Molotov cocktail into an office of the GESTAPO and subsequently managed to escape the wrath of German SS and Hungarian Arrow Cross men. Being a hero of the resistance most certainly did boost his postwar career under communist auspices. However, in October 1956 both the career and life of "Uncle Feri," who happened to be not only a Communist but also a Jew, threatened to come to a premature ending. Hungary's revolt against Stalinism and the Soviet military presence was barely three days old when a band of street fighters appeared at his apartment door to inform him that those "Jewish Bolshevik parasites" who, despite earlier efforts at their extermination, still sucked the blood of true Hungarians, would now definitely be put to death. Crammed into the loading space of a truck, Uncle Feri and a dozen other men were moved to a bare plot of land beyond Budapest's city limits where obvious preparations for a mass execution were occurring. It was pure chance that a convoy of Russian tanks retreating from the capital appeared on the scene, causing the rebels to turn tail and leave their near-victims to themselves. Uncle Feri died from a stroke in the 1980s. I doubt that he could have agreed with Austrian journalist and author Paul Lendvai, whose recently published history of the Hungarian revolution mentions the fears shared by many Jewish Hungarians in the fall of 1956, that violent outbursts of anti-Semitic hatred might be imminent. But, says Lendvai, "No such thing occurred in reality."[1]

Of the impressive range of books published in 2006 to commemorate the Hungarian revolution's fiftieth anniversary, a volume dedicated to the work of the Austrian magnum-photographer Erich Lessing deserves special mention. Its title is *Budapest 1956*,[2] and it contains an array of portraits of revolutionaries—men, women, and near-children—who faced Lessing's camera during occasional breaks in the street fighting. Do they look pleased by the opportunity to hunt down enemies of the people? It seems so in the case of a man, presumably in his late twenties, casually leaning against an armored car which carries five other fighters and pointing his gun into the foggy Budapest sky. But maybe his martial pose is nothing but masquerade to impress two pretty young nurses, skeptically surveying the scene from the side of the road. Then there is the picture of János Mész, nicknamed John with the wooden leg, a member of the notorious group of freedom fighters who made the Corvin movie theatre their headquarters. Mész has an automatic rifle girded around his waist, his hands clasp another gun, and his body is covered with ammunition belts. With lips tightly pressed together, he seems the embodiment of a warrior—or rather a sophisticated joker? Among Lessing's best known photos of the revolution is that of a Russian truck seized by the rebels and decorated with the Kossuth coat-of-arms, one of the state symbols of Hungary's short-lived democratic republic of 1945-1947. Young men carrying guns surround the vehicle, leaving the impression of students of philosophy somehow embarrassed by the sudden advent of war. The revolution featured more than a few armed philosophers. One was György Konrád, whose essay "Budapest Promenades, 1956" has been included in the Lessing volume to complement its photographic section.[3] When, on the fourth day of the Budapest street fighting, Konrád volunteered for the Hungarian Revolutionary National Guard's student corps, his fellow students handed him a machine pistol. "I carried it with me like distinguished gentlemen sport an umbrella," writes Konrád, "Who knows, it might be needed some time, better to be on the safe side."[4]

Readers interested in the origins of the Hungarian uprising will be pleased with Francis Fejtö's concise historical introduction to *Budapest 1956*. Fejtö tells us, among other things, that in post-1947 Hungary permission to study at a university was usually made contingent on an applicant's proletarian or rural extraction. Anyone who like György Konrád had an urban middle-class family background was, at best, reluctantly tolerated on Hungarian campuses. At enrollment, the student cards of such "capitalists" were marked with an X, a letter reserved for aliens to the working class and, thus, unreliable elements. It must have been a harsh disappointment for the Stalinists at the helm of Hungary's Socialist Workers' Party to see how a proletarian majority among academic recruits, instead of being eternally grateful to Communism for having cleansed the university from feudalistic and bourgeois elements, cheered the Polish events of mid-October 1956 which carried the Communist reformer Wladislaw Gomulka to power in Warsaw. At the same time, Budapest's students demanded the return to a democratic multiparty system, withdrawal of the "friendly" Russian troops from Hungarian soil, and an increase of the minimum wage in Hungary's nationalized industries. Of course, as the Hungarian revolution progressed, the part played in it by dissenting young intellectuals became rather ephemeral.

While students were conspicuously absent, "juvenile workers, rowdies and vandals, rough guys from poor neighborhoods"[5] resisted the Red Army in the streets of Budapest. What caused these foot-soldiers of the revolution to risk their lives still remains a moot question.

Historians who in the post-revolutionary Kádár era represented the officially authorized view of 1956 used to label the insurgents of that year, men and women, as criminals or "hooligans." Like most exaggerations designed to serve a political purpose, the Hungarian communist propaganda of the late 1950s and 1960s held a grain of truth. I quote from György Dalos, whose book about the Budapest uprising, together with Paul Lendvai's work, tops the list of remarkable German-language accounts of the revolution published to commemorate its fiftieth anniversary.[6] As a genuine popular revolt, the Hungarian events of 1956 surely attracted lawbreakers and rowdies of all kinds, says Dalos. But the leaders of the rebellion, as a rule, were from a different mold. One could find among them innocent idealists like János Szabó ("Uncle Szabó") who professed his belief in socialism with a human face, but also men like Jószef Dudas. He was the self-proclaimed chairman of a fictitious National Revolutionary Committee and editor of a pamphlet called Independence, which he and his friends produced in the seized editorial offices of the Communist daily paper *Szabad Nép* (*The Free People*). Dudas had the reputation of an unrestrained nationalistic demagogue. Another revolutionary eccentric, Gergely Pongrácz, considered himself a military genius. On several occasions, he boasted that his militia of volunteers could defeat any Russian expeditionary force operating on Hungarian soil, no matter how powerful it was. In fact, it took but a few days for the Red Army to rout the Hungarian revolutionaries who were inadequately armed and lacked coordinated command. Hungary's regular army could not provide the rebels much help. However, the Soviet victory did not come without losses. The Russians, together with allied Hungarian state security units and troops subordinated to the interior ministry, suffered 350 casualties in the fighting. Another thirty-seven Hungarian secret police and army personnel were shot or lynched by the revolutionary mob.[7] Expressing one's displeasure with lynching scenes involved the risk of being killed on the spot. György Konrád witnessed an elderly man dressed in a luxurious winter coat who hurled a loud "shame on you" towards a group of rebels about to hang several AVH-men (secret police) on alley trees. Minutes later, his own dead body dangled from a branch. In the years following 1956, communists "from Moscow to Beijing"[8] used the documented evidence of such instances of lynch law to bolster their claim that Hungary's revolution was synonymous with reactionary fascist terror. Against this, Hungarian intellectuals in exile such as Agnes Heller and Ferenc Farkas tried to defend the rebels' honor by pointing to their overall discipline and firm commitment to avoid spontaneous acts of brutality.[9]

In the 1950s, the Hungarian Socialist Workers' Party resided in a building at Budapest's Republic Square, just steps away from the "Erkel" music theatre and Rákosi Street, a boulevard running from what the war had left of Elizabeth Bridge to Pest's Eastern Railway Station. On 30 October 1956, one of the most brutal killings of policemen and communist functionaries took place right in front of the party headquarters. With János Kádár firmly installed as their leader, the communists later moved their main offices into a huge edifice on the Eastern bank of the Danube, facing Margaret Bridge. Until after the end of World War II, the site was occupied by a residential building in Art Deco style, one floor of which had been leased by my maternal ancestors. Thus one could say that the oppressors of Hungarian freedom in 1956 were subsequent tenants of my grandparents. I doubt this was the reason why First Secretary Kádár, the dominant figure in Hungarian politics from 1957 to 1988, enjoyed a surprising amount of esteem in our family circle—the kind of esteem one has for a personality of undeniable stature.

Kádár launched his political career in the 1930s, when Hungary was ruled in a semi-authoritarian fashion by the last commander-in-chief of the Habsburg navy, Miklós Horthy. The prototype of a Bolshevik party soldier, Kádár spent three and a half years behind prison bars. Upon his release, he played a somewhat dubious part in the 1943 decision of the underground Communist party to disband its cadres. Shortly after Hungary became a people's republic in 1948, Kádár rose to the rank of interior minister. In this function he served as a pliant tool in the hands of the Hungarian Stalin, Mátyás Rákosi, preparing the show trial against László Rajk, a former cabinet member accused of "Titoist" sympathies. Two years after Rajk was sentenced to death, Kádár himself fell victim to a Stalinist purge. According to Paul Lendvai, fear may have been the reason why Kádár, following his political rehabilitation in the wake of Nikita Khrushchev's rise to power in Moscow, refrained from open criticism of the by now defunct Rákosi regime. When in November 1956 the Kremlin bosses—convinced of the need to crush the Budapest revolution and to remove its figurehead, Prime Minister Imre Nagy—offered Kádár the post of First Secretary of the Communist Party, his acceptance might again have been due to feelings of terror.

Throughout the early stages of Kádár's reign, the state used all its available power to indiscriminately persecute those who took part in the revolution, "sparing neither the former head of government nor the underage apprentice."[10] We know today that Kádár's personal efforts led to the trial and execution of Imre Nagy in June 1958. Between 250 and 300 revolutionaries of varying prominence were put to death by Hungarian courts by 1961. In addition, 20,000 men and women served a term of imprisonment, and up to 100,000 were subjected to a wide range of discriminatory measures including expulsion from the workplace and denial of access to higher education. It seems unwarranted, though, to go as far as Paul Lendvai did in calling the Kádárist purges the worst act of revenge in modern Hungarian history. A more appropriate judgment is delivered by the authors of a "black book on Communism,"[11] in whose opinion the early Kádár years were "a period of ambivalence," given that ongoing repression against perceived enemies of the state was accompanied by first reluctant steps towards a general amnesty that was finally proclaimed in 1963.

The next two decades or so witnessed Hungary's astonishing transformation from poor Cinderella to wealthy princess of the communist world, thanks to an unprecedented mixture of government-promoted historical amnesia, cautious decentralization of the state-planned economy, and an equally circumspect foreign policy of reconciliation with the West (which involved certain opportunities for Hungarians to travel abroad, and later amounted to the gradual liberalization of goods and capital imports). In the eyes of many of his fellow countrymen, and even more so of benevolent commentators outside Hungary, Kádár the former bloodhound became Kádár the wise elder statesman—somehow reminiscent of Emperor-King Francis Joseph of Austria-Hungary whose reign began with the bloody suppression of a revolution in 1848-1849, but whom the revolutionaries' children and grandchildren learned to revere as a kind-hearted father of the people.[12]

In 1981, János Kádár, with his international reputation standing at an all-time peak, granted an exclusive interview to Austrian television journalist (and Hungarian-in-exile) Paul Lendvai. The relaxed conversation of the politician and the news correspondent mirrored the friendly relationship between official Hungary and Austria. One of Lendvai's fellow journalists from Budapest referred to Kádár and Kreisky (the Austrian chancellor) as K&K, a witty allusion to the times of Habsburg rule, when the twin K's were used to label common (Austro-Hungarian) institutions as "*kaiserlich und königlich*," imperial and royal. During the reign of Francis Joseph, a treaty concluded in 1867 between the Austrian and Hungarian halves of the Empire, known as "the compromise," allowed both the Magyar landowning nobility and Austrian industrial capital to co-exist on mutually profitable terms. Throughout the 1980s, Austria's construction and oil refining industries profited from large Hungarian orders. At the same time, the communist government in Budapest, by pointing at its special relationship with Austria, made the rest of the world believe in its seemingly unwavering commitment to human rights, democracy, and market reform.[13] Neither party was interested in burdening an obviously harmonious relationship with discussions of the tragic events of 1956. Most Hungarians timidly avoided talking about the revolution, just like most Austrians wished to avoid an honest confrontation with their country's Nazi past. Their tacit agreement to let the sleeping dogs of history lie once again made the Hungarian and Austrian nations look like two sides of the same coin, K&K.

Once a month, the cozy Viennese suburban home of E.S., a Budapest-born orthopedist, hosts between thirty and forty guests, all of Hungarian origin, who enjoy a drink and a snack with friends, and listen to someone delivering a short talk. Usually these talks explore the realm of culture and the arts. But sometimes it happens that their subject is politically controversial, as in early January 2007 when E.S. invited photographer Erich Lessing, an octogenarian, to share his personal memories of the 1956 Hungarian uprising. To the bewilderment of many of his listeners, Lessing, instead of confining himself to an anecdotal narrative, presented an historical analysis of the events of 1956 and explained what he thought were the reasons for the freedom fighters' ultimate failure. "He should have stuck to his camera business," complained one of the attendees of the meeting after Lessing had left, "Let our professional historians, if anyone, judge on the merits and shortcomings of the revolution." Statements like this reflect the traditional Magyar attitude of suspecting every foreigner who deals with Hungarian history to harbor prejudices. But assuming that Hungary's traumatic experience in 1956 could be dealt with by Hungarians alone, a huge problem would still remain unsolved. "The 1956 revolution," wrote Miklós Krassó, a philosopher and disciple of the great György Lukács, "from its beginning was condemned to vindicate the thought and deeds of each and every political faction in Hungary: socialists, anarchists, liberals, fascists, and conservatives."[14]

Which group, then, can justifiably claim authorship of Hungary's revolt against Stalinism and foreign occupation? As long as interpreting Magyar history for domestic use remained an exclusive domain of the Hungarian Communist party, 1956 was seen as a counter-revolution launched by supporters of "Horthyite fascism" and backed by foreign imperialists. While it was admitted that political crimes of former dictator Mátyás Rákosi contributed to the outbreak of the rebellion, reform-minded communists like Imre Nagy who had criticized Rákosi from within the party were accused of ignorance of the danger of imminent anarchy. In 1972, János Kádár surprised friends and foes alike when he cautiously questioned the counter-revolutionary dogma by admitting that 1956 had been, "among other things," a national tragedy. Shortly before the demise of Communism in 1989, a panel of historians charged by state minister Imre Pozsgay with reassessing the events of 1956 proposed to call these events a "popular uprising." Pozsgay himself was honest enough to confess that his party feared nothing more than official authorization of the term "revolution," since such a step would have destroyed the foundations of communist self-esteem. Everything changed with Hungary's adoption of democracy and political pluralism. After almost forty-five years of single party rule, a freshly elected National Assembly gathered in Budapest on 23 October 1989 to pass a new Western-style constitution and to commemorate the students' and workers' demonstrations of that same day in 1956, when Hungary's struggle for freedom began. From then on, 23 October would be a public holiday. József Antall, the conservative prime minister and a historian by profession, underscored the importance of acknowledging that 1956 had always been a controversial issue both within Hungary and among emigrants. He then called upon the advocates of mutually exclusive views of 1956 to practice tolerance. Representatives of the democratic left used to see the revolution as a courageous attempt at defending undeniable achievements of Hungarian postwar social reform against the cynicism and lust for power of Stalin's disciples. In contrast, Hungarians leaning towards the political right refuted the notion of 1956 as a "social" movement. In their eyes, the rebels' sole motivation consisted in breaking the chains of Soviet tyranny. Until 1992, a fragile peace prevailed between the two opposed camps. But in October of that year, Árpád Göncz, president of Hungary and a liberal veteran of the revolution, was shouted down and insulted by extremists of the nationalist right when addressing a non-partisan commemorative meeting. At present, self-styled guardians of the heritage of 1956 on the left and the right treat each other with open contempt or even hatred, much to the detriment of Hungary's domestic political culture and international standing, a point justly emphasized by Paul Lendvai as well as György Dalos.

Recently, I browsed the bookshelves of the museum shop at Vienna's historical museum on Karlsplatz, host to a highly acclaimed exhibition[15] about Hungarian refugees stranded in Austria in 1956. Besides the exhibition catalogue, I acquired a slender volume written by Marta S. Halpert. She investigates the 1956 revolution not from the angle of big politics, but concentrates on the lives of ordinary men and women who were driven into exile—or decided to stay in Hungary, despite what had already happened or would happen in the future. My own parents left Budapest in 1948, eight years before the tragedy of 1956. Their fellow emigrants' stories would not be included in Marta Halpert's book, and I did not expect to find them there. I also expected no familiar faces appearing on the photos in the catalogue of the Vienna museum. But then the picture of an elegant lady in her thirties by the name of Ildikó Völker, her arm resting on the door of an impressive U.S.-built limousine, stirred up memories. On the page of the catalogue with Ildikós photo one finds a quote by Austria's Interior Minister of 1956, Oskar Helmer, who wished to assure his countrymen that most Hungarian refugees would be gotten rid of as quickly as possible. The woman leaning against her car seems to provide a case in point. My father and mother in 1948 certainly harbored no plans to remain in Vienna, and neither did the majority of their generation of exiles. Instead, they found asylum in the Netherlands. Ownership of a 1959 Chevrolet Impala (license number: AD-48-95) with tail wings of perfect beauty reflected the Bergers' gradual social ascent. Today, members of our family once again reside in Budapest.

Hungary's accession to the European Union in 2004 caused a considerable number of descendants of emigrants of 1948 and 1956 to return. They complain about the pitfalls of living amidst a process of transition from state socialism to capitalism, they curse endemic corruption and excessive bureaucracy, and they are concerned about the vitriolic tone in Hungary's domestic politics, the rising tide of racism, and ubiquitous anti-Semitism. Despite all this, no one seems to seriously contemplate leaving the country.

Notes

1. Paul Lendvai, Der Ungarn-Aufstand 1956: Eine Revolution und ihre Folgen (Munich: C. Bertelsmann, 2006), 147.

2. Eric Lessing, *Budapest 1956: Die ungarische Revolution* (Vienna: Christian Brandstätter, 2006).

3. György Konrád, "Spaziergänge in Budapest, 1956," in Lessing, *Budapest 1956*, 112-29.

4. Ibid., 115.

5. Geert Mak, *In Europa, Eine Reise durch das 20. Jahrhundert* (Munich: Pantheon, 2007), 665.

6. György Dalos, *1956: Der Aufstand in Ungarn* (Munich: C.H. Beck, 2006).

7. Stéphane Courtois et al., *Das Schwarzbuch des Kommunismus* (Munich: Piper, 1998), 483.

8. Lendvai, *Der Ungarn-Aufstand 1956*, 122.

9. Vera Sophie Ahamer, "Ungarn 1956—Ein historisches Ereignis als politisches Legitimationsinstrument," *Zeitgeschichte* 3. 33 Jahrgang (2006): 115-134.

10. Dalos, *1956*, 213.

11. *Schwarzbuch des Kommunismus*, 485.

12. László Kontler, *A History of Hungary* (Basingstoke: Palgrave Macmillan, 2002), 430.

13. Béla Rásky, "Title of Article," in *Außenansichten. Europäische (Be-)Wertungen zur Geschichte Österreichs im 20. Jahrhundert*, ed. Oliver Rathkolb (Innsbruck: Studien Verlag, 2003), 296 f.

14. Quoted in Ahamer, "Ungarn 1956," 115.

15. October-November 2006.

New Scholarship on Austria, Germany, and Italy in the International Arena during the 1930s

Gerald Steinacher, ed. *Zwischen Duce und Negus: Südtirol und der Abessinienkrieg 1935-1941*
(Bozen: Verlagsanstalt Athesia, 2006)

Manfred Scheuch, *Der Weg zum Heldenplatz: Eine Geschichte der österreichischen Diktatur 1933-1938*
(Vienna: Buchverlag Kremayr & Scheriau/Orac, 2005)

Gabriele Volsansky, *Pakt auf Zeit: Das Deutsch-Österreichische Juli-Abkommen 1936*
(Vienna: Böhlau Verlag, 2001)

Alexander Lassner

A well-known Austrian historian once remarked to me in conversation that *"alles was man über den Anschluß schreiben kann, ist schon geschrieben worden."* The three books *Zwischen Duce und Negus: Südtirol und der Abessinienkrieg 1935-1941*, *Der Weg zum Heldenplatz: Eine Geschichte der österreichischen Diktatur 1933-1938*, and *Pakt auf Zeit: Das Deutsch-Österreichische Juli-Abkommen 1936* both support and disprove that assertion. Some of these works—either as a whole or partially—continue to echo established historical myth while failing to engage sufficiently proper methods of historical inquiry. Others do add substantially to our knowledge, thus showing that there indeed remains much to be written when it comes to studies that deal with Austria and its neighbors in the period of the 1930s.

Of the three works, *Zwischen Duce und Negus: Südtirol und der Abessinienkrieg 1935-1941*, edited by Gerald Steinacher, is the least directly related to issues of Austria in the interwar period. It focuses, rather, on a part of the former Austro-Hungarian Empire, the South Tyrol, that was ceded to Italy in the aftermath of World War I, and which was, during the interwar period, an area of contention. Fascist Italy sought to colonize and absorb the South Tyrol; Nazi Germany sought to bide its time for the moment and to seize South Tyrol at a later time when Italian weakness permitted it, and Austria under the authoritarian leaders Engelbert Dollfuss and Kurt Schuschnigg sought to persuade Benito Mussolini to return South Tyrol to Austria, or at least to stop some of the worst Italian excesses against the Tyrolese population. This book is not a single work, but, rather, a series of essays written by a somewhat diverse group of scholars, both amateur and professional. Their stated aim is to place the South Tyrolean experience of the war in Abyssinia into the broad context of European history during the 1930s, as well as to examine the regional cultural memory of that war.

The first essay by Gerald Steinacher provides a brief overview of the terrain that is covered in the remaining essays. Here the author discusses such basic issues as the kind of war that Italy prosecuted in Africa (total), the number of south Tyroleans that fought in the Italian army, the great unpopularity of the war in the South Tyrol, and the efforts directed by Rome at Italianizing the former Austrian province. One of the most interesting points that Steinacher makes here is the manner in which the Italian government attempted to use the war in Africa as a means of seducing Tyroleans into accepting their place within a greater emerging Roman Empire—an empire that would span the shores of the Mediterranean. Overall, he writes, these efforts failed spectacularly, and as late as the 1970s, southern Tyroleans were still bent on destroying Italian monuments in the region, which reminded them of Italian rule.

Nicola Labanca continues some of the themes introduced by Steinacher, for example, the grand, imperial aims of Mussolini, while focusing his essay on the war in Abyssinia. Mussolini was determined to correct the *"vittoria mutilata"* (mutilated victory) that Italy had suffered at the Versailles peace conference, and to that end he and his collaborators demanded a "new empire" for Italy. The author then details the international situation in the early 1930s with a particular focus on what he argues were the different imperial goals that Italy had for its conquered territories as opposed to the goals that Italy's competitors had for their own imperial possessions. This difference was driven in part by the fact that Italy was unable, in the final analysis, to pacify and to exploit its imperial possessions. In the meantime, he believes, such institutions as the League of Nations were fatally weakened by Italian aggression, despite the fact that France and Britain might have stopped Italy through concerted action; how this might have been accomplished given the desire of key British and French statesmen to retain Italian friendship so as to support central European allies and as a counterweight to Nazi Germany is left unanswered. Labanca concludes with a section on historical writing and memory in Italy in which he highlights and laments that Italians have done little to recognize the essentially racist and murderous nature of Italy's wars of expansion in the 1930s and 1940s.

The article by Ulrich Beuttler deals with Italian foreign policy from the early 1920s until 1935. While following the general lines of all of the articles in this volume with respect to Mussolini's desire to build a new Roman empire, Beuttler concentrates on Italy's strong relationship with the United States in the 1920s and up until the crisis of 1935—a relationship in which the United States became Italy's most important trade partner by 1929 (though the United States lost this standing to Germany in 1932). Perhaps the most significant conclusion to which Beuttler comes is that, according to him, Mussolini's foreign policy showed little pro-German attitude prior to 1935; the Italo-German relationship based in part upon common ideology was not, therefore, a foregone conclusion. Ultimately, the author notes, Great Britain was unable to manipulate the League of Nations into bringing effective sanctions against Italy in order to stop its aggression in Africa, and Great Britain and the United States instead embarked upon courses of appeasement with Italy, an appeasement that would soon be extended to Germany.

Certainly one of the most interesting portions of the book is the photographic collection put together by Gerald Steinacher and Ulrich Beuttler. Here the two authors have collected a series of photographs from five South Tyrolean soldiers who served in a variety of roles from combat soldier to medic. The accompanying written observations and commentaries from the soldiers themselves are variously banal, profound, and humorous. In the case of the latter, in a letter form Alfred König to his brother, König observed that "*du kannst dir gar nicht vorstellen, wie viele Tauben hier sind, es genügt ein Luftdruckgewehr für die Jagd, da man ganz nahe herankommt*" (p. 94). By the autumn of 1936, most of the South Tyrolean soldiers had returned to Italy with their Italian counterparts, though a small group remained for some time thereafter. The soldiers' photographs are divided into eight subject areas covering the crossing to Africa, the people of Abyssinia, the countryside, the native fauna, war, everyday life for the troops, the practice of religion, and the memory of the war in South Tyrol.

Leopold Steurer reviews the manner in which the war played out in South Tyrol and among the German speaking population. After the Saarland voted for reunion with Germany, many in South Tyrol became more assertive *vis-à-vis* the Italian government in Rome while, at the same time, looking more to Germany, and less to Austria, for their salvation from Italian dominion. In the meantime, Mussolini's regime took stronger and stronger measures to Italianize the region—measures that were ultimately unsuccessful. Although the author refused to use a standard scholarly footnote/endnote approach to citations over the course of his article, it is clear that he is utilizing letters from native South Tyroleans, among other sources from the *Archivio Centrale dello Stato* (Rome) and the *Tiroler Landesarchiv* (Innsbruck), and these letters are very good at revealing the atmosphere of resentment and disobedience in South Tyrol towards the government in Rome. Tyroleans generally felt less loyalty to Italy than did newly acquired (after World War I) Slovenian and Croatian population; a significant number of Tyroleans deserted their units or avoided service altogether by crossing the border into Austria and Germany. Moreover, Tyroleans showed a marked lack of enthusiasm for the war in general. Here Steurer provides the scholar one of the more interesting discoveries of his research, namely a ratings system created by the Italian Ministry for the Interior that categorized the degree of loyalty of Tyroleans (p. 201). Ultimately, the author correctly notes that the Italians were unable to defend their acquisition of South Tyrol against a ruthless and increasingly powerful Nazi Germany.[1]

Essays by Martin Hanni and Thomas Ohnewein focus on South Tyrolean soldiers' memory of the war in Abyssinia and on the statistics regarding how many South Tyroleans were drafted, deserted, and fought and died during the war in Abyssinia. Hanni's work reveals the complexity of views held by those Tyroleans that were drafted and fought in Africa as to what they were doing: while some Tyroleans actually viewed the Ethiopians as allies against the Italians, others felt themselves sympathetic to the Italian cause and hoped the end result would be improved opportunities for the common man. Hanni has done the historical profession a further service by making detailed interviews of seventeen Tyrolean veterans, which are available in the archives in Bozen (Bolzano). Ohnewein, for his part, has compiled a truly fascinating set of statistics on the subject of South Tyrol and its peoples' participation in the Italian war in Abyssinia; this set of statistics should be consulted by any historian writing on the subject.

Finally, the essay by Aram Mattioli seeks to place the conflict in Abyssinia in perspective as regards the brutality of the Italian conquest and the losses suffered by the momentarily conquered Ethiopians. The population of Abyssinia suffered immensely as the result of ruthless Italian aggression in pursuit of imperial dreams. If the author's statistical research and deductions are correct, the Ethiopians endured casualties of approximately 380,000 killed from a population of 10 million. In his essay, the author continues the theme introduced by Labanca, that Italy's pursuit of empire under the fascists was of an essentially more brutal and terroristic nature (one that was not above mass murder) than that practiced by Great Britain, France, or the other imperial powers. Mattioli subscribes to Eric Hobsbawm's view of the war in Abyssinia as the real beginning of the "disaster age" which would soon lead to the Second World War.

Overall, *Zwischen Duce und Negus* is a worthwhile, but uneven, effort. While the essays are of interest, many beg larger unanswered questions, exhibit errors, or are misleading. To start with, it is clear that in taking the stance that Mussolini was a bent on an expansive empire which was to rival that of ancient Rome, the authors (without acknowledging it) have sided with those scholars who fall *between* the schools of G. Salvemini, Denis Mack Smith, MacGregor Knox, and Brian Sullivan on the one hand, and Renzo De Felice, Rosaria Quartararo, and Donatella Bolech Cecchi on the other. Yet the authors fail to situate their work within this broader historiography.

Smith, Knox, and Sullivan have argued that an aggressive and thoroughly Fascist Mussolini determined no later than 1924 that Italy would ally itself with Germany. Such a coalition could "correct" by force the *vittoria mutilata* imposed on Italy by Britain and France after World War I and build a world class empire.[2] On the other side of this debate is the school articulated in four volumes on Mussolini by Renzo De Felice and generally supported in the works of his protégées Donatella Bolech Cecchi and Rosaria Quartararo. De Felice and his supporters argue that Mussolini was not bent upon grand imperial conquest and that he could still have favored the West as late as 1939-1940.[3] Between these two schools, but not equidistant, there have been historians who chart more moderate courses. They variously argue that between 19351938 Mussolini became firmly, if not irrevocably, tied to aggressive German foreign policy.[4]

But although the authors of *Zwischen Duce und Negus* may be said to fall between these two schools, this detracts rather than adds to the worth of their effort. If they are, in fact, convinced that Mussolini's fascist regime was bent on creating a Mediterranean empire to rival that of ancient Rome—an empire in which mass murder and brutality of any sort were justified—how do Steinacher, Labanca, Beuttler, Steurer, Hanni, and Mattioli answer the evidence presented by Smith, Knox, and Sullivan? This has a direct impact on whether we should view the war in Abyssinia as the beginning of the "disaster age," as Mattioli argues and with which his fellow scholars seem to concur. If one is marking the start of any twentieth century disaster age, Japan's vicious machinations in the Far East from 1932 onward would seem a far better choice.

This leads to another oversight on the part of the authors. Steinacher, Labanca, Beuttler, Steurer, Hanni, and Mattioli seem oblivious to the fact that their agreed upon interpretation of Italian imperial goals under Mussolini (that of a Mediterranean empire to be obtained at all costs) does not follow recent Italian- or German-language scholarship, but that of the Italian and English language scholars Salvemini, Mack Smith, Knox, Sullivan, and their protégées. Nowhere in the book is this debt acknowledged. Yet this oversight is hardly surprising given the dearth of English language sources cited by the authors in either the footnotes or in the select bibliography. One wonders especially how scholars can write on the subject of interwar Italian foreign policy, military policy, and the war in Abyssinia and not include numerous seminal works in the English language on the subject.

From a structural standpoint, the book tends to lead to repetition throughout, as the authors continually have to set the scene for their own particular discussion. This is by no means a major problem, but it does lead to the work becoming somewhat tedious at times. More serious is the failure of the book's editor to maintain scholarly standards in citing evidence. While some of the authors (Steinacher, Beuttler, Hanni, Mattiolo) use footnotes correctly, the other authors use few and/or partial references, thus undermining the value of their work. It hardly needs to be stated that scholars are not free to write numerous pages of text without citations, or to make up forms of citation that suit them, but which do not correspond to standards.

Other problems with the book exist on an essay to essay basis, some of which are interpretive and some of which are factual. On the interpretive side, for example, the authors claim that Italy waged a "total war" in Africa against the Ethiopians, but the term "total war" is never qualified. The war may well have approached total for Ethiopians, but, given Italian mobilization efforts in World War II, the war can hardly be said to have been total for Italy. Rather, the term seems to be used by the authors as a way of differentiating Italian colonial aggression from that of the traditional Western colonial powers, which they argue was more benign. Yet any link between Italian ruthlessness against the Ethiopians as a product of an imperial fascist ideology is problematic at best. One might also argue, with just as much validity, that—as Italian military forces ran into tough resistance and as Italian military incompetence came perilously close to losing the war against its Ethiopian foe—Italian desperation and brutality increased. Similar dynamics are evident in both the Spanish and French decisions to use quantities of mustard gas against the peoples of the Rif during the Rif Rebellion in Morocco (1920-1926). Without using gas, the British were murderously brutal against the Boers (1899-1902) and the Mau-Mau (1954-1960). Moreover, Italian documents, reports, and diaries display a racist contempt for their African adversaries that can also be found in sources from their fellow Europeans.[5] Unfortunately, the idea that poison gas was a legitimate weapon was commonplace in political and military circles in the interwar period; no less a personage than Winston Churchill advocated its use during his tenure as War and Air Minister. In the final analysis, the authors' research is insufficient to sustain their argument.

More serious examples of factual errors within the book are claims that Mussolini mobilized Italian troops on the Brenner after the assassination of Dollfuss (p. 63), and assertions that legalized Nazi activities in Austria with the *Deutsch-Österreichische Juli-Abkommen* of 11 July 1936 (p. 213). It is unclear as to whether or not Mussolini would have directed a partial mobilization of Italian troops in response to the July 1934 putsch attempt; what he did do, however, was to redirect to the Austro-Italian border *already mobilized* troops which were on maneuvers in Alto Adige. As regards the *Abkommen* of 11 July 1936, despite the various interpretations that may be given to the contents of the document and its signing, one issue is indisputable: the *Abkommen* did not make Nazi activities in Austria legal. Such errors of fact are perhaps the most inexcusable problems with the book, though, thankfully, they are rare. Overall, this book is a worthwhile addition to the literature of the 1930s in central Europe, though it is, admittedly, a niche title.

The same favorable words cannot be used to describe *Der Weg zum Heldenplatz: Eine Geschichte der österreichischen Diktatur 1933-1938*. Manfred Scheuch, born in 1928, is a socialist journalist who came of age during the Kreisky era, the former chief editor of the *Arbeiter-Zeitung*, and a deeply involved member in the *Sozialdemokratischen Partei Österreichs* (hereafter SPÖ). He has also authored numerous books on Austria and Europe. In writing *Der Weg zum Heldenplatz*, Scheuch raises the question of whether Austria's path towards becoming a part of Nazi Germany was unavoidable. Unfortunately, in seeking the answer to this question Scheuch neither breaks new ground nor brings us new interpretations, but, rather, treads the same worn ground of leftist interpretations of the *Christlichsoziale Partei Österreichs* (hereafter CPÖ), *Heimwehr*, and the Dollfuss and Schuschnigg governments' errors and the path to the Anschluß.[6]

Scheuch's work can be divided into three basic sections. The first and largest of these deals with the birth of the Austrian Republic and the contest that developed thereafter between the forces of the right and left; the next begins with the suppression of the socialists by Dollfuss and ends with his murder by the Nazis; and the final—and shortest—section concerns Austria under Schuschnigg and the road to the Anschluß. The author's polemics and agenda make themselves visible quickly in the first pages: the socialists were the true creators and supporters of the first Austrian Republic which was the grantor of freedom and equality. Therefore, the socialists will not admit to any "*geteilte Schuld*" for the ultimate destruction of that state at the hands of the right (read: CPÖ, *Großdeutsche Volkspartei, Landbund, Heimwehr, Vaterländische Front*) (p. 14). Conveniently forgotten by the author is that fact that many in the SPÖ were in favor of an Anschluß with a socialist Weimar Germany immediately after World War I.

Scheuch holds the Austrian governments of Dollfuss and Schuschnigg as "Austro-fascist" since he has discovered the list of common traits that conclusively demonstrate whether a government may be said to have been fascist (pp. 8-9). The author's contentions show a disinterest for the last sixty years of scholarship that is quite remarkable. In taking these views, Scheuch shows no acknowledgement—or even knowledge of—the wider scholarship on the issue of whether or not the governments of Dollfuss and Schuschnigg were, in fact, fascist. Here the author, at a minimum, should have cited the works by Timothy Kirk and Robert Paxton as to where, exactly, "Austro-Fascism" is to be placed on the axis of fascisms in Europe during the 1930s.[7]

The author goes on to downplay to the point of dismissal any notion of a "red danger" from the socialists and their communist allies. This is a curious interpretation to say the least. In Austria, the members of the two largest political parties—the SPÖ and the CPÖ—were actively suspicious and hostile towards one another; this much is true.[8] But this was not simply due to the CPÖ and the *Heimwehr's* intense clericalism and anti-Marxist stance, as Scheuch portrays the matter (see, for example, pp. 29, 31, 34, 52, 123); the SPÖ and its allies embraced Marxist rhetoric and anti-clericalism, even if a majority of them (though by no means all of them) ultimately remained more moderate in action. Given the numerous, violent communist uprisings (successful and unsuccessful) throughout Central and Eastern Europe in the wake of World War I and the difficulties of discerning that Austrian socialism proved to be less radical than its advocates claimed it to be, it is hard to see that the Austrian left was without blame in alienating potential partners.

Scheuch spends considerable time and effort cataloguing the errors of the CPÖ, the *Heimwehr*, and the *Vaterländische Front* in the radicalization of Austrian politics and suppression of parliamentary democracy, but he neglects any sustained discussion of intransigence in and the agenda of the SPÖ or its paramilitary *Republikanischer Schutzbund* in the process. The result is an extremely one-sided and distorted picture, even if it can be argued that the right bore a great degree of responsibility in the ultimate abandonment of Austrian democracy and embrace of authoritarianism. For example, the split in the socialists themselves between the moderate Karl Renner and the radical (Austro-Marxist) Otto Bauer is never mentioned—a split that led to great instability in the SPÖ and, therefore, within the republic. Nor does the author bother to mention that it was the SPÖ that refused to participate in a national government after 1920 precisely *because* the CPÖ won a majority of votes, and which forced the CPÖ to govern in unstable coalitions. With respect to the *Heimwehr*, it is true that its origins may be traced to 1919 and that it was associated with right-wing politics (p. 24). But Scheuch neglects to mention the fact that armed "worker guards" and "factory guards" were created contemporaneously in Austria's large towns by the left, and which the SPÖ largely controlled.[9] Instead, Scheuch attempts to make it seem as though the socialists *only* resorted to arms and paramilitary formations defensively and at the provocation of the right (p.

296   The Changing Austrian Voter

26). Such slight of hand is unworthy of the author, but it is unfortunately all too frequent throughout the book.

Thereafter the author chronicles the growing and sometimes violent confrontations between the *Schutzbund* and the *Heimwehr*, the malfunctioning of the Austrian parliament, Dollfuss's circumvention and ending of parliamentary democracy, the assassination of Dollfuss, and Schuschnigg's unsuccessful attempts to prevent an Anschluß with Nazi Germany (the later summary in only forty-two pages). When Scheuch is at his best here he is simply re-treading the ground of such authors as Adam Wandruszka, Ludwig Jedlicka, Norbert Schausberger, Manfried Rauchensteiner, Bruce Pauley, R.G. Ardelt, Walter Wiltschegg and others; there is nothing new or particularly interesting in the author's interpretation. What continues to be noticeable, however, is his lack of expertise on the subject matter and the way in which he manipulates evidence to support his views.

At his worst, Scheuch goes about selecting that evidence which is helpful to making the categorical argument he seeks to make, while suppressing that evidence which is inconvenient and which would force nuance and subtlety upon him. An egregious example of this is his chapter titled *"Aufrüstung—aber gegen wen?"* In it, Scheuch emphasizes that the *Bundesheer* was politicized into a force for the internal defense of "fascist" Austria, instead of one geared to external defense (pp. 220, 222), while further noting that the Schuschnigg government was less concerned with the coercive power of Hitler's Germany than it was with restoring the Habsburgs and purchasing a guarantee of Austria from Italy at the cost of the Little Entente and Yugoslavia (p. 223). The author attempts to make it look as though, in the wake of the *Deutsch-Österreichische Juli-Abkommen* of 11 July 1936, Austria developed a working relationship with the German *Wehrmacht*, while permitting the *Bundesheer* to be penetrated by the Nazis (p. 224). The assumptions and errors by the author here are rife.

To begin with, it is unclear why the SPÖ and its allies' initial politicizing of the *Bundesheer* in 1919-1921 is considered by the author inherently legitimate, while the desire by the CPÖ and its allies to return to imperial traditions is inherently illegitimate. More to the point, practically every one of Scheuch's points hereafter is either wrong or a distortion. The *Bundesheer* may well have turned towards internal defense at a time when the state was under siege by the (suppressed) socialists and (illegal) Nazis, but it was most certainly also maintained and developed from 1934 to 1938 as a *defensive* instrument of the state *against external aggression*, especially from Nazi Germany. As then State Secretary for Defense General Wilhelm Zehner remarked in March 1935:

[I]t is impossible that from now on Austria remains behind [in der Hinterhand bleibe] while the whole world is rearming. It is, therefore, absolutely necessary to rearm and later—in one and one half or two years—to introduce compulsory military service. At present there is a shortage of everything, and especially also ammunition. If something doesn't happen it would inspire neighbor states [to believe] that they would have the possibility to roll right over Austria. If, however, Austria was in possession of a well equipped army with which one would have to reckon in a serious case, this [army] would represent a hindrance.[10]

The term "neighboring states" included, first and foremost, Nazi Germany and Yugoslavia. Any basic reading of the literature on this matter should have pointed this out to Scheuch.[11]

The author's understanding of Schuschnigg's stance *vis-à-vis* Nazi Germany is equally far off base, as is his belief that Austria was trying to obtain a guarantee of Austrian from Italy at the cost of the Little Entente and Yugoslavia. In fact, the Schuschnigg government repeatedly rejected attempts by the Italians and Hungarians to guarantee Austria at the cost of Austria's neighbors.[12] Further, the Austrian government cleverly evaded every attempt by the German government to bring about closer political and military relations even as late as the beginning of 1938. As Otto Stein (a convinced Nazi and henchman of the philo-Nazi Franz Papen at the German embassy in Vienna) put the matter in October 1937:

[Schuschnigg] has recognized National Socialists as the real, indeed as the only dangerous enemy of these plans [to strengthen Austria]. [...] In this obstinate struggle all the means of enforcement are at the disposition of the government, and experience teaches that, in case of necessity, the Federal Chancellor is willing to employ them ruthlessly. In the hands of the National Socialists there are no other means of enforcement than that backing of the Reich and the will to hold out in spite of every hardship. In the age of machine guns and light armored cars, which make it possible for relatively small detachments to make short work of large but not equally armed masses of people, the NSDAP must reject the idea of an armed uprising.[13]

Indeed. Schuschnigg, Zehner, and Austrian Chief of Staff Alfred Jansa actually went so far as to start officer exchanges with the French army in late 1937 (though these were cancelled as German pressure increased). Thereafter, the Schuschnigg government rejected a Hungarian demand to attach Czechoslovakia—a demand that the Hungarian government claimed had German sanction.[14] All the while the Schuschnigg government successfully purged the *Bundesheer* of Nazi elements, leaving a *Bundesheer* that was, in fact, a reliable instrument for the defense of Austria, if it were called upon to fight.[15]

298   The Changing Austrian Voter

Another serious problem with *Der Weg zum Heldenplatz* is Scheuch's singular focus on domestic politics in Austria as the real key to Austria having some sort of chance to have avoided the Anschluß. By focusing on domestic politics and the socialists' dissatisfaction with the Dollfuss and Schuschnigg governments (which led to their alienation from the regime), the author fails to see the greater importance of the external, foreign-political, and security situation. He does not understand that from 1934 to 1938 the Schuschnigg government resolutely and repeatedly attempted to obtain and Austrian Pact of security with Italy, France, and Great Britain (which amounted to a defensive military alliance); he does not understand that these attempts failed as late as early 1938; he does not understand that Italy, France, and Great Britain all believed, by late 1937, that the Nazis were a minority in Austria and could not obtain power unless the Nazi German government coerced the Austrian government with the threat of military invasion; and he does not seem to understand that Italy, France, and Great Britain all explicitly abandoned Austria to Nazi Germany in February 1938 since they were unprepared to go to war for reasons that had nothing to do with the issue of democracy or its absence in Austria, but everything to do with their own security goals and the perceived balance of power in Europe.

Finally, *Der Weg zum Heldenplatz* does not meet scholarly standards for an historical work; it is, in short, a journalist's polemic masquerading as a history. Evidently Scheuch has received special dispensation to make assertion after assertion without regard to footnotes or even a complete bibliography. It is clear that he does takes quotes from sources that are not in the bibliography at all and refuses to cite the source, mentioning only the author (see, for example, p. 222 and pp. 249, 250). This is simply unacceptable, but obscuring one's sources may help explain why Scheuch believes that he can get away with the distortions and misinformation so characteristic of his book. The work also discredits itself for relying on a very narrow group of (mostly dated) German-language secondary sources and entirely ignoring all scholarship on the subject in English, French, and Italian (to say nothing of Czech and Hungarian).

Gabriele Volsanky's *Pakt auf Zeit: Das Deutsch-Österreichische Juli-Abkommen 1936*, the last of the books under examination, is, overall, a flawed work of merit, based upon the author's dissertation. In contrast to *Der Weg zum Heldenplatz*, Volsansky's work, despite its problems, helps to advance our understanding of the dark times that befell the Austrian state in the mid- to late 1930s. The author begins her work with a short chapter in three sections on Austria's international situation in central Europe in the period 1933-1936, although portions of the discussion continue through the fourth chapter. This section of the book begins as a thoroughly synthetic affair, but by the second through fourth chapters (pp. 22-70) it begins to incorporate primary source material. These four chapters are an important part of Volsansky's work as they set the interpretive stage for crucial pieces of what is to follow, and it is due to shortcomings here that the work as a whole is less compelling than it could be.

The problems in the first four chapters are twofold. First, Volsansky's secondary sources are dated, and second, the author's primary *and* secondary sources are entirely from German-language sources (the former from German and Austrian archives). This is the case, despite the fact that there is essential evidence about the Dollfuss and Schuschnigg governments' actions and motivations scattered about numerous archives in Europe and the United State, and extensive and essential secondary works on this period written in English, French, and Italian. Had the author consulted some of these sources, her understanding of the rationales of these two Austrian governments may have been different. Unfortunately, Volsansky's limited sources immediately cause her to hew too closely and too readily to outdated interpretations from the 1970s (see pp. 228-29, 276-82) and *ex post facto* works that are highly unreliable and filled with lies and distortions (for example, the memoirs of Schuschnigg and, as well, *Der Hochverratsprozess gegen Dr. Guido Schmidt vor dem Wiener Volksgericht*). Moreover, she ignores recent works.

As a consequence, in the first fifty pages of the book, the reader is subjected to numerous historical distortions. While it is true, for instance, that Dollfuss tended to avoid dealing with the League of Nations, it is not true that he preferred Austria's relationship to fascist Italy to such an extent that he leaned away from any "Western" (that is, British, French, and Italian) help (p. 12). The Dollfuss government repeatedly, openly, and internationally accused the Nazi German government of supporting terrorism and sedition, and Dollfuss asked for *Western* help to stop those activities in June 1933, January/February 1934 (going so far in February as to submit a 168 page dossier to London, Paris, and Rome detailing German subversion in Austria), and June 1934 (six weeks before Dollfuss was murdered).[16] The reasons as to why the Austrian government was never able to obtain a satisfactory result from its actions had little if anything to do with its authoritarian form of government and much to do with Britain, France, and Italy's perceived vital interests.[17]

Volsansky goes on to repeat the line of argument that the Nazi assassination of Dollfuss (briefly) spurred the Western powers into action. According to her, the measures taken by Britain, France, and Italy now included more substantive declarations on Austria's independence, numerous additional agreements, and, ultimately, a sharp reprimand of Germany at the Stresa Conference in April 1935 and a joint declaration on the independence of Austria (p. 13). Unfortunately, the author misses completely the role of the Schuschnigg regime in initiating and advancing most of this action. The author is blind to the Schuschnigg government's work in trying to develop and obtain an Austrian Pact with the Western powers from 1934 to 1937 and Britain's adamant refusal—even as a part of the Stresa Conference in April 1935—to do anything other than to "consult" about Austria; a British standpoint that reflected its unwillingness to offer guarantees to *any* country on the continent, even to such strategically vital countries as (democratic) France and Belgium, to say nothing of countries like Czechoslovakia or Romania. Unsurprisingly, the author shares the view of the Schuschnigg government as one that isolated itself through its pro-Italian policies 1934-1936, leaving it little choice but to conclude an agreement with Nazi Germany when the international situation degenerated over the course of 1935-1936 (pp. 46-47, 223).

Yet despite these and other missteps, Volsansky correctly recognizes that the Schuschnigg government did not conceive of the *Abkommen* as a lasting solution, but as an expedient meant to buy time for an improvement in the international situation. German agents, for their part, sought to use the *Abkommen* as a wedge from which to derive greater and greater advantages for subverting the Austrian state, either through interpretation of existing points or through demands for additional concessions (pp. 32-35, 46-47).

Here it is that we come to the core of Volsansky's argument: that the official and unofficial parts of the *Abkommen* were partly contradictory, while the *Abkommen* as a whole suffered from inexact language that was subject to widely disparate interpretations. In the final chapter of her book, which accounts for over two-thirds of the book's length (pp. 71-227), the author systematically attempts to deconstruct the *Abkommen*, emphasizing these issues of disharmony and vague wording that made up the body of the agreement (see, for example, pp. 71-72, 185-99, 223-24).

Volsansky is correct to point out these differences, and she does an admirable job of showing how many of the disagreements between

Austrian and German statesmen and diplomats played out, especially the legalistic wrangling that took place between the two states. In doing so, the author proves that neither government actually abided by the *Abkommen*, but, rather used that agreement to try to maneuver the other side into making concessions that would undermine that side's agenda: Austria's agenda being that of resisting Germany, and Germany's agenda being that of conquering Austria.

What Volsansky fails to discuss satisfactorily (and here she is the victim of her limited sources and, more significantly, the limited scope of her work) is *why* the *Abkommen* ended up taking the contradictory and ambiguous form that it did. The majority of the participants in drafting the *Abkommen* were diplomats and lawyers, so there was hardly a lack of understanding on the drafters' part about the meaning of the words that they chose to use, or which phrases were unclear and which phrases were exact. Indeed, the endless bickering and wordsmithing that went into the actual creation of the agreement—which Volsansky herself portrays—shows that these men were quite aware of each distinction and/or ambiguity that they included. Moreover, Schuschnigg understood what liars he was dealing with in the likes of Adolf Hitler, Hermann Göring, Papen and others, and he hardly became their dupe by permitting them to include wording that he, Schuschnigg, did not recognize as being subject to wide interpretation.

The key to understanding the contradiction and ambiguity purposefully built into the *Abkommen* lies in the Schuschnigg government's understanding the international strategic situation. The senior members of that regime understood early on that Nazi Germany would eventually use force to seize and digest portions of central Europe in particular as a preliminary to a major war, and Schuschnigg and his closest collaborators understood that Austria was first on the German menu after the remilitarization of the Rhineland.

Thus the *Abkommen* was created with purposeful ambiguity and contradiction by both sides. On the Austrian side this was because Schuschnigg and his collaborators believed that they could mire the Nazis in endless legal arguments and maneuvers in interpreting the *Abkommen* and thereby win time for international matters to tilt back into a more pro-Austrian path, or at the very least, to avoid Nazi German military aggression when it came, as Schuschnigg believed that it ultimately would. On the German side, this was because Hitler and his cronies believed that they could attain their ends through pro-German interpretations and purposeful subversion of the *Abkommen* backed by the coercive might of the *Wehrmacht*.[18] While it is questionable as to whether or not the conclusion of the *Abkommen* ultimately delayed Austria's demise, it is equally true that Austria's national strategic situation was not going to improve over the course of 1936-1938 given the differing vital interests, power calculations, and ideological views between the European great powers, most especially Britain, France, and Italy. Thus, as long as Nazi Germany desired Austria and was willing to risk war to conquer it, the small Danubian state was almost certainly lost no matter what course of action it took.

There is a harmful theme that is apparent in all three of these volumes which deserves close attention, namely the fact that in all three books, though to varying degrees, the authors show themselves thoroughly unfamiliar with the international literature and historiography on the subjects about which they are writing. Without engaging this literature or even recognizing its existence, the authors implicitly concede the limited value of their works, and they write as provincial scholars for a provincial audience. *Zwischen Duce und Negus* is the least egregious example of this, as it does engage some of the recent German and Italian literature on the subject. Nevertheless, even at their best, the authors represented in *Zwischen Duce und Negus* fail repeatedly to position their work within the larger debates. Volsansky, too, is guilty of over-reliance on dated German-language secondary sources and *ex post facto* accounts. While she nevertheless does contribute to furthering our understanding of events leading to the Anschluß, she has limited the contributions of her own work through her narrow and one-sided source material. Finally, at the other end of the spectrum is Scheuch's book: the author's partisan socialist *"Scheuch"-klappen* are in evidence from the first page of the book, as he ignores virtually all of the international literature and much of the Austrian literature on fascism, the Anschluß, and international diplomatic and military events in Europe during the 1930s. If his book may be said to do anything, it is chiefly to set back the state of scholarship on the Anschluß.

Authors writing in the field of the international history of the 1930s must remember that their works, once published and a part of the scholarly arena, will be assessed insofar as they help to further scholarship and to advance the goal of building a more complex truth about what happened in the past, even if it is with the knowledge that an absolute truth is beyond our attainment.

Notes

1. After Mussolini was deposed by the Fascist council in 1943, German leaders under the direction of the Gauleiter of Tyrol-Voralberg, Franz Hofer, quickly occupied South Tyrol. Thereafter, they replaced Italian communal, administrative, and state authorities with Germans, took over Italian businesses, dissolved Italian police forces, and once again made German the official language. See, Dennison I. Rusinow, *Italy's Austrian Heritage 1919-1946* (Oxford: Oxford UP, 1969), 310-22, 323. Hitler was only too happy to permit this activity.

2. See especially Gaetano, Salvemini, *Prelude to World War II* (London: Doubleday, 1953); Alan Cassels, *Mussolini's Early Diplomacy* (Princeton , NJ: Princeton UP, 1970); D. Mack Smith, *Mussolini's Roman Empire* (London: Longman, 1976); D. Mack Smith, *Mussolini* (London: Weidenfeld and Nicolson, 1981); H. MacGregor Knox, *Mussolini Unleashed: Politics and Strategy in Italy's Last War* (Cambridge: Cambridge UP, 1982); Enzo Santarelli, "Mussolini e l'imperialismo" in his *Ricerche sul fascismo* (Urbino: Argali!a, 1971); Brian R. Sullivan, "The Italian Armed Forces, 1918-1940," *Military Effectiveness* 2: 179-81; Brian R. Sullivan, "From Little Brother to Senior Partner: Fascist Italian Perceptions of the Nazis and of Hitler's Regime 1930-1936," in *Knowing your Friends: Intelligence inside Alliances and Coalitions from 1914 to the Cold War*, Ed. Martin S. A. Alexander (London: Frank Cass, 1995), 86-88; Brian R. Sullivan, "More than Meets the Eye: The Ethiopian War and the Origins of the Second World War," in *The Origins of the Second World War Reconsidered*, Ed. Gorden Martel (London: Routledge, 1999), 193-98.

3. Renzo De Felice, *Mussolini il Duce: Lo Stato totalitario 1936-1940*, vol. 2 (Turin, 1981), 307, 310, 329; Donatella Bolech Cecchi, *Non bruciare i ponti con Roma: le relazioni fra l'Italia, la Gran Bretagna e la Francia dall'accordo di Monaco allo scoppio della seconda guerra mondiale* (Milan : A. Giuffre!, 1986), 513-14; Rosaria Quartararo, *Roma tra Londra e Berlino: La politica estera fascista dal 1930 al 1940* (Rome: Bonacci, 1980), 624.

4. For example, Robert Mallett dates Mussolini's commitment to war against France and England to 1933. Ludwig Jedlicka shows a Mussolini who was already showing great signs of disinterest in Austrian independence as early as 1935 while leaning toward the Reich, while R. M. Salerno believes that "in 1936 Italy's die [to go along with Germany no matter what the cost] had been cast." Fulvio D'Amoja views the year 1937 as the pivotal year, for at the end of it, Mussolini was ready to concede Austria to Germany. H. James Burgwyn follows the general lines set by De Felice, but argues that the "sea change" in Mussolini's foreign policy occurred in September 1937, at which time "whatever residual neutrality had existed in Mussolini's mind vanished [during his visit] in Berlin." The author further contends that Mussolini might have continued to harbor ideas about reconstructing the Stresa Front as late as the Anschluß, but that after that event the Duce was squarely within the "'iron cage' of Germany's military might." Burgwyn concludes by stating that as late as 1940, "[h]ad Germany not invaded France, Italy's nonbelligerency might have gone on indefinitely." Robert Mallett, *The Italian Navy and Fascist Expansionism* (London: Frank Cass, 1998), 2, 8; Ludwig Jedlicka, *Ein Heer im Shatten der Parteien* (Graz: H. Böhlaus Nachf., 1955), 136-37; Fulvio D'Amoja, *La politica estera dell'impero: storia della politica estera fascista dalla conquista dell'Ethopia all'Anschluss* (Padova, 1967), 104-06; R. M. Salerno, "The Mediterranean Triangle: Britain, France, Italy and the Origins of the Second World War, 1935-1940," Ph.D. diss., Yale University, 1997, p. 99; H. James Burgwyn, *Italian Foreign Policy in the Interwar Period 1918-1940* (Westport, CT: Praeger, 1997), 224, 227-28.

304   The Changing Austrian Voter

5. See, for example, William T Dean III, "The Colonial Armies of the French Third Republic: Overseas Formation and Continental Deployment," Ph.D. diss., University of Chicago, 1999. One might add that the democratic libertarian British could be murderously ruthless as well. During the Boer War (1899-1902), they had set up concentration camps in which 28,000 Boers and no less than 14,000 black Africans died of starvation and disease (Boer casualties represent 50 percent of the Boer child population). Some casualty estimates run as high as 620,000 for the black African casualties. Thereafter, during the 1954-1960 Mau-Mau uprising in Kenya, the British established camps to hold suspected rebels; somewhere between 130,000 and 300,000 rebels are thought to have perished. See Caroline Elkins, *Imperial Reckoning: The Untold Story of Britain's Gulag in Kenya* (New York: Henry Holt, 2005).

6. See the introduction in Günter Bischof, Anton Pelinka, and Alexander Lassner eds., *The Dollfuss/Schuschnigg Era in Austria: A Reassessment*, vol. 11, Contemporary Austrian Studies (New Brunswick, NJ: Transaction, 2003), 1-9.

7. Ibid., 10-31; Robert Paxton, *The Anatomy of Fascism* (New York: Knopf, 2004).

8. Other parties at the time included the *Großdeutsche Volkspartei* (Greater German People's Party of Austria, [hereafter GVP], and which appeared in September 1920 from the merging of seventeen national and provincial groups), *Landbund* (an agricultural league of peasants), the Communist Party of Austria [hereafter KDP], and the *Deutsche Nationalsozialistische Arbeiterpartei* (German National Socialist Workers Party, or DNSAP [hereafter Nazi]).

9. Ludwig Jedlicka, "The Austrian Heimwehr" *Journal of Contemporary History* 1.1 (1966): 127-44.

10. Protokolle des Ministerrates der Ersten Republik [hereafter, PMER]/2, 988, 3. [international situation], 22 March 1935. See also, *I Documenti Diplomatici Italiani* [hereafter, DDI], 7, XVI, 755, Preziosi to Mussolini, 18 March 1935; DDI, 7, XVI, 771, Preziosi to Mussolini, 20 March 1935; DDI, 8, I, 180, conversation Mussolini and Schuschnigg, 11 May 1935; *Österreichisches Staatsarchiv/Archiv der Republik, Bundesministerium für Landesverteidigung/Allgemeine Reihe*, 27 2/3 28 2/2 1935, 27 3/3 7040, "Absichten für den Ausbau des BH," Jansa to various military attachés, 27 May 1935. See also the May comments by Schuschnigg to Puaux. *Documents Diplomatiques Français*, 1, X, 464, Puaux to Laval, 27 May 1935. The internal evidence of the BMfLV harmonizes with Zehner's expressions at the cabinet meeting: at the 20 November 1934 rearmament conference, Austria's demands for defensive equality of armaments were ignored. In the meantime, Germany and Hungary were rearming, and Austria was at a greater and greater disadvantage. ÖStA/AdR, BMfLV/AR, 18-1935, 18-12/1, 1768, "Abrüstungskonferenz ... " [Zehner ?] to Foreign Office, 5 March 1935. On the cabinet's preparatory measures for Universal Military Service in May, see PMER/2, 995, 17. "Vorbereitende Maßnahmen zur Einführung einer Dienstpflicht," 2 May 1935.

11. See Alexander N. Lassner, "Peace at Hitler's Price: Austria, the Great Powers and the Anschluß, 1932-1938," Ph.D. diss., Ohio State University, 2001, pp. 159-63, 202-14, 296-314. Scheuch's starting point on this matter should have been, at a minimum, the following two works: H. Lerider, "Die operativen Maßnahmen gegen die Nachfolgerstaaten der Monarchie von 1918-1938 unter besonderer Berücksichtigung der Ära Jansa," *Militärwissenschaftlichehausarbeit* (Vienna, 1975); H. Trauttenberg, "Die Abwehrvorbereitungen gegen einen deutschen Angriff im Bereich der 4 Div. in Jahren 1936-1938." *Militärwissenschaftlichehausarbeit* (Linz-Ebelsberg, 1972). It is worth mentioning that even these two works are now superseded in many respects, though they are a required start to the issue.

12. Lassner, "Peace at Hitler's Price," 67, 117-18, 296-314.

13. Akten zur Deutschen Auswärtigen Politik 1918-1945 [hereafter, ADAP], D, I, 263, Stein to Foreign Ministry, 14 October 1937. See Stein's evaluation of 23 October: "Taken as a whole, [Schuschnigg's] policy was therefore designed to maintain the present situation in Austria, and any improvement for the benefit of the National Opposition [i.e., covert Nazis] would be wrested from him only with the strongest kind of pressure." ADAP, D, I, 266, Stein to Foreign Ministry, 23 October 1937. See also Goebbels' realization that Schuschnigg was not going to permit the subversion of Austria. Fröhlich, ed., *Die Tagebücher von Joseph Goebbels*, vol. 5, 27 December 1937. Opinion in the German Foreign Office was similar. *Diplomáciai Irtok Magyarország Külpolitikájához*, I, 311. Sztójay to Kánya, 13 November 1937.

14. The best scholarly research—which reflected contemporary Austrian evaluations—indicates that Nazi infiltration into the *Bundesheer* by early 1938 amounted to scarcely 5 percent, a rather good showing considering the strenuous efforts made by the Nazis in Austria and Germany. Erwin A. Schmidl, *Der "Anschluß" Österreichs: Der Deutsche Einmarsch im März 1938* (Bonn: Bernard & Graefe, 1994), 56. The figure of 5 percent corresponds to the *Bundesheer*'s own evaluations from 1936-1937, namely, that there was no extensive penetration by the Nazis into the *Bundesheer*, and that such infiltration as had taken place was poorly organized. ÖStA/AdR, ÖVB/Budapest, #6, Zl. 96.889-13, "Gerücht über die ns. Einstellung der ... ," Schmidt to all ambassadors, 22 December 1937; ÖStA/AdR, BMfLV/AR, 15 5/2 Sektion III 1937, 144.205, 25.463 – MA/1937, [Nazi activities in the 4th Division], 4th Division to BMfLV, 1 December 1937; ÖStA/AdR, BMfLV/AR, 15 5/2, Sektion III 1937, Zl. 25.265-MA/37, [Nazi activities in the 4th Division], Infantry Regiment 14 to 4th Division, 5 November 1937; ÖStA/AdR, BMfLV/AR, 15 5/2, Sektion III 1937, 25.265-MA/37, [Nazi activities in the 4th Division], Infantry Regiment 14 to 4th Division, 5 November 1937; ÖStA/AdR, BmfLV/ AR, 15 5/2, Sektion III 1937, Zl. 25.184-MA/37, Artillery Regiment 4 to 4th Division, 4 November 1937; ÖStA/AdR, BMfLV/AR, 15 5/10 Sektion III 1937, 15 5/10, "Bericht über die innerpolitische Lage ... ," 7th Division to BMfLV, 3 March 1937; ÖStA/AdR, BMfLV/AR, 15 5/10 Sektion III 1937, 15 5/10 104246, "Lagebericht June 1937," note by director of public security, June 1937; ÖStA/AdR, BMfLV/AR, 15 5/10 Sektion III 1937, 15 5/10 104262, "Monatsbericht Juli 1937," 1st Division to BMfLV, 4 August 1937; ÖStA/AdR, BMfLV/AR, 15 5/10 Sektion III 1937, 15 5/10 103624, "Monatsbericht July 1937," 8th Brigade to BMfLV, 9 July 1937; ÖStA/AdR, BMfLV/AR, 15 5/10 Sektion III 1937, 15 5/10 104555, "5 Div. Innerpolitischer Lageericht Aug. 1937," 5th Division to BMfLV, 9 September 1937; ÖStA/AdR, BMfLV/AR, 15 5/10 Sektion III 1937, 15 5/10 105990, "Illegale Einflüsse ... ," 4th Division to BMfLV, 8 November 1937; ÖStA/AdR, BMfLV/AR, 15 5/10 Sektion III 1937, 15 5/10 106497, "Politische Bericht für den Monat ... ," 4th Division to BMfLV, 9 December 1937; ÖStA/AdR, BMfLV/AR, 15 5/10 Sektion III 1937, 15 5/10 106497, "Monatsbericht für den ... " 3rd Division to BMfLV, 13 December 1937; ÖStA/AdR, BMfLV/ AR, 15 5/10 Sektion III 1937, 15 5/10 106710, "Illegale Einflüsse ... " 4th Division to BMfLV, 8 November 1937; ÖStA/AdR, BMfLV/AR, 15 5/10 Sektion III 1936, 15 5/10 100.005, "Lagebericht über den Monat Mai 1936," Allgayer to BMfLV Na, 25 June 1936; ÖStA/AdR, BMfLV/AR, 15-18 Sektion III 1936, 15 5/10 100834, "Monatsbericht II/1936," 2nd Division to BMfLV, 3 March 1936; ÖStA/AdR, BMfLV/AR, 15-18 Sektion III 1936, 15 5/10 104.774, "Monatsbericht Oktober 1936," 6th Division to BMfLV, [no date]; ÖStA/AdR, BMfLV/AR, 15-18 Sektion III 1936, 15 5/10 104.025, "Monatsbericht über den ... ," 3rd Division to BMfLV, 3 September 1936; ÖStA/AdR, BMfLV/AR, 15-18 Sektion III 1936, 15 5/10 104.356, "Monatsbericht über den ... ," 3rd Division to BMfLV, 2 October 1936; ÖStA/AdR, BMfLV/AR, 15-18 Sektion III

1936, 15 5/10 104.774, Stümpfl to BMfLV, 6 November 1936. Box 15-18 Sektion III 1936 contains numerous additional reports.

15. National Archives and Records Services [hereafter, NARS], T120/2838/E453708E453714, "Im Auftrag des Baron von Neurath ... ," German Embassy London to Bülow, 16 June 1933; NARS, T120/2838, E45370, minute for the German Secretary of State, 31 July 1933; NARS, T120/2838/E453718, German Foreign Office to London, Paris, Rome, 26 July 1933; NARS, T120/2838/E453721, memorandum by German Foreign Office, 2 August 1933; NARS, T120/2838/E453770, Reuters's Report, 3 August 1933; ADAP, C, I, 383, memorandum Bülow, 31 July 1933; Documents on British Foreign Policy [hereafter DBFP], 2, V, 270, Vansittart to Harvey, 25 July 1933; *Documents Diplomatiques Français* [hereafter, DDF], 1, V, 275, Corbin to Paul-Boncour, 26 January 1934; DBFP, 2, VI, 201, Simon to Selby, 23 January 1934; DBFP, 2, VI, Appendix I to 201, [Austrian] *aide-mémoire*, 23 January 1934; DBFP, 2, VI, Appendix II to 201, [Austrian] résumé, 23 January 1934; DBFP, 2, VI, 202, Selby to Simon, 25 January 1934; DDF, 1, V, 313, François-Poncet to Daladier, 2 February 1934; NARS, M1209/2/0634-0639, #73, Kliefoth to Hull, 14 February 1934; ADAP, C, II, 501, Rieth to Bülow, 12 June 1934.

16. Lassner, "Peace at Hitler's Price," Chapters 2 and 3.

17. Ibid., Chapters 6 and 7.

18. Ibid., Chapters 6 and 7.

BOOK REVIEWS

Michael Gehler, *Österreichs Aussenpolitik der*
Zweiten Republik—von der alliierten Besatzung
bis zum Europa des 21. Jahrhunderts, **2 vols.**
(Innsbruck: Studienverlag, 2005)

Thomas Nowotny

For all nations, even the most powerful ones, a foreign policy agenda is largely set by external circumstances, by history or geography, by global trends, and by the actions of other agents in the international scene. That imposes severe limits to free decision making in the realm of foreign affairs. These restraints are, of course, more stringent the smaller a country is. While the foreign policy choices available to a smaller country are not diverse, options do exist; different decisions with different consequences can be made. The foreign policy of even a smaller country is, therefore, not just dictated by external circumstances, by the nature of the global system. Individual actors are important as well.

Who are those acting for their respective states? During 1995-2006, the United States' conservative Republicans have consolidated their power. In this period, they controlled not just the Congress, but also gained control of the executive branch. They also have a large say in setting the agenda of the judiciary, and—most importantly—they have succeeded in shaping the public political discourse. Nonetheless, the U.S. political system is still multifaceted and certainly more multipolar than political systems in Europe. While in this respect, too, the two sides of the Atlantic have tended to converge, the position of the executive in European countries is still more powerful than it is in the United States.

308   The Changing Austrian Voter

In most European countries, the main political functions—agenda setting, consensus building, actual decision making—are vested not with the so called "sovereign"—the elected representatives—but with the government.

That also holds true for Austria and for the realm of Austria's foreign policy. In describing Austria's postwar foreign policy, Michael Gehler is, thus, justified in focusing on the decisions and the decision makers in this small group of foreign policy mandarins: a few select politicians and a few select diplomats. Until quite recently, the dawn of what Gehler describes as the "Short Eighties," they were, in most instances, given free reign to focus attention on relations with their counterparts in other countries. With a few—but important—exceptions, they were free to ignore the impact of their actions upon internal politics. In most cases, they did not incur major risks when ignoring Austrian public opinion, the parliament, the media, or non-governmental organizations.

As mentioned, even before the end of the Kreisky era in the early 1980s, exceptions to this pattern existed. Internal Austrian politics, for example, were very much a factor in shaping decisions on issues like the political autonomy of the ethnic Austrians in South Tyrol and the drive for fuller participation in the economic integration of Western Europe which took place since the 1960s. In dealing with these issues, diplomats and politicians thus felt compelled to also seek understanding, legitimacy, and consent from the Austrian parliament, media, and public. But even then, those questions were being dealt with under the auspices of a "primacy of foreign policy." It was understood that one should aim to anchor in internal Austrian politics those decisions that had been shaped by the dynamics of international politics. It was not the other way round. Things were not done so as to support, via international actions or postures, some merely internal Austrian politicking.

The "Waldheim Affair" became a symbol and marker for this turn of the tide from the "primacy of foreign policy" towards the "primacy of internal politicking." When the issue of his service in the *Deutsche Wehrmacht* on the Balkans was brought up, Waldheim's first—and fateful—retort of "just having done his duty" might have been unreflective and somehow accidental. The international furor caused by these remarks led to an emotional, nationalistic, "circling of the wagons" counter-reaction of the Austrian electorate. It very much boosted Waldheim's position in the electoral campaign for the Austrian presidency. With new relish, Waldheim thus repeated his "just having done my duty" explanations, and he did so in full disregard of the further damage this did to Austria's international position.

That was the first major example of such self-inflicted damage. Others would follow, equally motivated by the "priority of internal Austrian politicking":

- the disregard for the intent of the international community to make the recognition of the independence of Slovenia and Croatia contingent upon some attempts to dampen the ethnic conflicts that would inevitably result from the dismemberment of Yugoslavia;
- the agitation around the nuclear power station Temelin in the Czech Republic and similar campaigns to impede the EU accession of the Czech Republic;
- the dysfunctional, counter-productive positions and tactics in the negotiations to limit the north-south truck traffic over the Alps; and finally but not least;
- the style of dealing with international—specifically EU—objections to a government that would include the right-wing populist "Freedom Party" of Jörg Haider.

Michael Gehler is good in describing this interplay between domestic and foreign politics. It was and is, of course, most pronounced in the three fields that are being dealt with most extensively in this two volume, 1,292 page work; namely (1) the efforts that led up to the State Treaty of 1955 and to the reestablishment of Austria's full sovereignty, (2) the question of "South Tyrol"[1]; and (3) participation in European integration.

Other issues are well covered too, such as the long struggle for the full and decent restitution and compensation for the victims of the Nazi era, the discussions on Austria's security status and security options (between neutrality and NATO membership), and the reactions to the Soviet invasions of Hungary (1956) and Czechoslovakia (1968).

Michael Gehler gives lengthy attention to the descriptions of the impact such activities had on Austria's domestic politics. He does so to the extent that in some places the book becomes as much a work on domestic politics as it is on foreign policy.[2]

But even in so broad a picture, some important fields are less well painted, and some spaces are even left blank. Development assistance is an example of an area less well covered. In a book published in 2005, the statistics (pp. 434f) and descriptions on Austria's development assistance only led up to the year 1983. A description of the developments thereafter would not have changed very much the conclusion that the volume of Austria's development assistance does not compare well with efforts of "like minded" European countries such as Norway, Sweden, Denmark, or the Netherlands. But it would have at least brightened[3] and detailed the picture a bit.

Austria's policy in the United Nations is also insufficiently covered[4]; even in this very sketchy picture, some patches are simply left void. Regrettably, this is the case for Austrian efforts at the United Nations that were—and still are—central to its multilateral diplomacy there. Austrian efforts have generally been recognized as a significant contribution to international/global governance, that is, efforts to shape the legal regime dealing with global issues, and extend to efforts such as that of the Austrian diplomat Winfried Lang who had been central to the successful international move to limit emissions that destroy the ozone layer of the upper atmosphere (Montreal Protocol). Austria had a leading role, too, in defining the legal regime for outer space. It was the driving force behind UN efforts to impede the proliferation of small arms.[5] It was one of the main backers of the landmine treaty; and it had, of course, contributed significantly to the codification of international law in the succeeding "Vienna conferences" (on the law of treaties, on the status of diplomats, and so forth). There is no mention of these efforts and of such significant contributions to global governance. Instead, the book somehow conveys the impression that Austrian actions at the United Nations were just a "default setting" during a time when Austria was still prevented from becoming fully active in the realm of inter-European politics and European integration.

This lack of attention to issues of global governance is symptomatic of a tendency toward an unbalanced coverage of events that permeates the whole book. While Austrian internal politics receive fairly broad attention, while they are described as having shaped many foreign policy decisions, unequal attention is given to the outside forces that had at least as strong an impact upon those decisions. The policies of other countries, the evolution of international relations, and so forth are mentioned only in some of the cases where they had been decisive. In other instances, they are ignored. In the very extensive chapters on Austria's participation in European integration, for example, the certainly crucial positions of the Soviet Union, France, and Italy are being given their proper place. Not so the positions and actions of other players that were relevant, too, such as the European neutrals, Great Britain, or the United States.

Short shrift is also given to some emerging global issues that also determine policy choices, including, for example, global economic trends such as the economic rise of East Asia, the steep economic decline and deep socio-political crisis in the formerly Communist countries, the globalization of investment and trade, and the transition to an information-based economy.

Understandably, in a book that covers a long stretch of a half-century and numerous subjects, not all of them can be given the attention they would merit. Inevitably, too, many of the descriptions and explanations thus reflect commonly and widely held peremptory judgments. Notoriously though, these frequently have been shaped and colored by the need of politicians to make a point, or by the tendency of the media to simplify and to remain on the surface of issues. One accepts them at the risk of failing to obtain a more complete and accurate picture.

This reliance on popular interpretations of events shows, for instance, in Gehler's dealing with Austria's policy of military security in the era of Chancellor Bruno Kreisky. I chose this example because this is an issue I know quite well, for in the early 1970s I served as private secretary to the chancellor and had been charged specifically with maintaining relations with the defense and security establishment. This era saw the politically controversial shortening of obligatory military service from nine to six months, the drafting of a new security doctrine, and the subsequent reorganization of military defense.

On these issues, Gehler pictures Kreisky as a sort of pacifist, with little respect for and trust in the military, and with a strong preference to secure Austrian's security by way of political instead of military means. This is a view still widely held, not least among Austrian conservatives who—like conservatives around the world—wish to paint their liberal opponents as being "soft" on security issues and unappreciative of military power.

This rough portrait does not reflect reality. In fact, Bruno Kreisky was supremely aware of military reality. Probably his view of the global order even accorded it too prominent a place. For Kreisky, the military East-West standoff was the element that more than anything else defined and shaped the post-World War II global order.[6] Taking seriously issues of military strategy, he was, thus, extremely uneasy with what he found when he became chancellor in 1970. He encountered a stark dichotomy between the geopolitical situation of the country and its security being anchored in neutrality on the one hand, and a military establishment that ignored these realities and acted as a kind of not so secret NATO ally in the fields of strategy, tactics, and logistics on the other hand.

The Western military establishment had not been happy about Austria becoming a neutral country, since the Western part of neutral Austria blocked vital connections between the southern and northern NATO flanks. This impaired NATO military efforts. Therefore, it is not surprising that military leaders in the West, especially in the United States and

France, originally opposed the "Neutrality and State Treaty Package" that released Austria into its full independence and that preserved the unity of its territory. French and American diplomats with a wider interpretation of security finally prevailed over these narrow-minded military leaders. Later, these military leaders basically returned to the position they held before the State Treaty. This becomes evident in their impact upon the nascent Austrian defense forces. They did not treat them as defense forces of a neutral country.

Austria's post-1955 military planning, as a part of the NATO planning, was geared to the eventuality of a full scale East-West conflict. In this context and according to the NATO script, Austria's military forces were assigned the task of retarding—to the greatest extent possible—the Soviet/Warsaw Pact advance towards the west, and while retreating, conceding this eastern (larger and more populous) part of Austria to the Soviet/Warsaw Pact forces. At that stage and after having retreated to western Austria, the Austrian military forces would have become integrated into NATO efforts to secure the north-south connection over the (smaller and less populous) Western part of the territory.

Kreisky objected to this strategy for two reasons mainly. First, in line with many military thinkers,[7] he believed military defense to be ineffective if not supported by the population. The larger part of the Austrian population that lives in the eastern part of the country would have been abandoned to the Soviet/Warsaw Pact forces early on (with the Austrian government decamping to the west, too). How could this larger part of the population support a military that had already decided not to shield them from Soviet occupation? Second, these plans of the Austrian military were widely known. They signaled that in event of an East-West war, or even in the event of a very serious East-West crisis, Austria would be resigned to accept a division of the country that it had successfully avoided in the period of Allied occupation from 1945 to 1955. Both East and West were thus enticed to include the western and the eastern part of the country respectively in "their" theater of operations.[8] This strategy was hardly a contribution to Austria's security; moreover, it cast its shadow over the foreign and security policy even in times when East-West tensions were less acute.

Kreisky thus charged the military with developing a better plan for providing security to *all* of the Austrian territory, one which would not rely on the support the country might receive from NATO. In addition, the military strategists should plan also for threats below the level of a full blown East-West war, when in a serious crisis, the option of reoccupying

313

the western or eastern part of the country might seem an enticing and prudent option[9] to the two mutually hostile military alliances.

In response to these guidelines, *Generaltruppeninspektor* General Emil Spannochi came up with a new plan (*Landesverteidigungsplan*) based on the concept of non-linear, "territorial" defense[10] with small military units operating in guerilla-like fashion and with the support of the population, often behind the front lines of an advancing enemy. This concept was better suited to the military capacities of Austria, to its geography, to the lessons taught by history, and, finally, to its security status as a neutral country positioned between two powerful military blocks.

That being said, it remains true that, as Gehler maintains, Austria spent relatively little on its military and substantially less than equally neutral Switzerland and Sweden. It also is evident that this under-investment in the military created problems with some neighboring countries and with leading NATO countries that feared that an enemy might advance into their flanks over the thinly defended Austrian territory. But there can be no doubt that any more effective and better financed defense would have to be based on the concepts of Spannochi and Kreisky, and not on the older dysfunctional concepts that had been replaced by these newer ones.

In a similar vein, there is too ready an acceptance of the usual stereotypes concerning the priorities in the foreign policy of Bruno Kreisky. Michael Gehler buys into the widely held view—reinforced by the political opposition[11]—that Kreisky devoted little attention to (Western) European affairs in general and to Western European economic integration in particular, concentrating instead on the countries of the "Third World."

Surprisingly, this claim is followed—on the very same page—by an extensive quote from a meeting of Kreisky with Roy Jenkins disproving the prior claim of Gehler and demonstrating both the nearly prophetic realism of the chancellor, as well as his strong devotion to the idea of European integration.[12] Kreisky predicted the step by step approach of Austria toward the (then) European Economic Union up to the formation of a joint EFTA-EEC economic space. He claimed, furthermore, that a membership of the neutrals in the EEC would become possible provided that there would be a change in the geopolitical configuration, defined at that time and in Kreisky's view mainly by the East-West polarity.

Its was this view of the centrality of the East-West conflict that motivated Kreisky's engagement with the "Third World" issues and not, as Gehler claims, undiluted leftist idealism and youthful sympathies for liberation movements. As mentioned, in Kreisky's view it was the struggle between East and West, between the U.S. and Soviet led alliances that defined and shaped the world order. The two alliances blocked each other on the central fronts in Europe and in East Asia. In these regions, "deterrence" proved effective. The two camps thus sought to advance their cause in the world's "soft underbelly," namely, the poor countries of the Third World. Yet the West frequently opposed attempts of these countries to rid themselves of the vestiges of colonialism, to advance their status in the world, and to seek a better base for their economic development. The West thus courted the danger of seeing these countries turn towards the Soviet camp, providing that camp with a solid advantage, especially when successful in securing the sympathies of states in strategic regions such as the Middle East or the southern rim of the Mediterranean.

It was to thwart this danger that Kreisky chose to strengthen a nonaligned "third camp," safe in its own identity, independent of both East and West, and with understanding and helpful friends in Western Europe.[13] It was this view, too, that inspired his Middle East policies and that led him to postulate the inclusion of the southern rim of the Mediterranean into the so-called Helsinki Process (the CSCE, later the OSCE).

One more example involving Kreisky's foreign policy and its misinterpretation by Gehler occurs when Gehler peremptorily defines it as being shaped by "anti-Atlantic posturing" (*"anti-Atlantische Attitüden"*) (p. 554). It is true that Kreisky took seriously the obligations of permanent neutrality. But he fully appreciated that the Western Alliance was the necessary bridgehead of this neutrality. As reflected in many of his speeches, he saw in the Western deterrent the necessary counterpart to Soviet power and, thus, as a necessary prerequisite for stability in Europe. Resulting from this view was his reluctance to join European leftists in their condemnation of the U.S. intervention in Vietnam and their opposition to the stationing of medium-range U.S. missiles on European soil.[14] It is worth mentioning, too, that in the study of his private home, the sole photos were those of U.S. presidents, hardly a sign of emotional anti-Americanism or anti-Atlanticism.

A perhaps inevitable lack of depth and comprehensiveness is also evident in some parts of the book that deal with later phases of Austria's foreign policy. For example, with the crucial decisions before during and after the breakup of Yugoslavia, Gehler claims that Western chancelleries could not have foreseen that large scale violence would result from such a breakup (p. 690). Yet both breakup and violence were widely predicted.[15] It was in order to thwart both effects that Austria took the initiative in establishing an EFTA Industrial Assistance Fund for Yugoslavia, then in the throes of a deepening economic crisis. Since 1989, too, Chancellor Vranitzky used his international contacts to alert other countries to the danger looming in Yugoslavia. The decision when to recognize the independence of Slovenia and Croatia was colored and shaped by an emotionally charged domestic debate heated up by the tabloid *Kronen Zeitung* and Austrian television ORF. Both were partial to an early recognition of the Slovenia and Croatia's independence, which other European countries and the United States wanted to forestall.[16] Gehler's rendering of these events thus should have been complemented by a description of prior activities to support Yugoslavia. A more detailed account of the domestic political discussion and strife surrounding the decision to recognize the independence of Croatia and Slovenia would have been helpful here.

Some of these gaps and misinterpretations might be explained by the choice of persons whom Gehler interviewed for the book. Doubtless, these interviews added new insights and information that had not previously been available. But the choice of interviewees seems not just eclectic, but arbitrary. Just one of the Secretary Generals of the Ministry of Foreign Affairs—Ambassador Reichmann—had been interviewed, and this in 1992. None of the diplomatic advisors of the chancellors were interviewed, and only a few of the "political directors" of the Foreign Ministry were. The only chancellor interviewed was Josef Klaus. If a book relies on such testimony about events long in the past, one has to make sure that all relevant players have been given a chance to present their story. Should this prove impossible because of the large number of persons that would have to be interviewed, it becomes even more relevant to ensure that the selection of interviewees is representative of the whole. This has not been the case.

The main deficiency of the book, though, is sloppy editing. One even could wonder whether any editing has been done at all. Least damaging are factual errors that could have been avoided (such as on page 713, where Alija Izetbegovic is identified as the leader of the Croats in this part of former Yugoslavia, while in fact being the political leader of the Bosnian part of the population which was involved in fighting both the Serbs and the Croats). More serious, vexing, and ultimately enervating are the countless overlaps and the incessant repetitions in the book.

316 The Changing Austrian Voter

Sometimes the same issue is dealt with three times, and the chronological order is reversed again and again. While in a book of this complexity and size some repetitions and some factual errors might be unavoidable, there clearly would have been room for tightening up. There is much fluff in the 1,292 pages of this book.

That being said, one has to acknowledge the contribution made by this book. Every person dealing academically with Austria's foreign policy will have to consult it. The information provided is certainly broad and valuable. But the book is not and cannot be the final authority on all of the many questions it addresses. This is impossible in view of the complexity and number of decisions that have been made in Austria's foreign policy over the sixty years covered in the text.

Notes

1. Perhaps given too prominent a place in Gehler's work, for after the signing of the "*Packet*" and the "*Operations - Kalender*" in 1969, it very much ceased to rank amidst the two or three top priorities in Austrian foreign policy, with Austria mainly monitoring the implementation of the concessions made to South Tyrol by the Italian government.

2. Of course, the two realms never have been separate. In recent years, they have become more closely intertwined all over the world. The process is most advanced in EU Europe where the foreign policy of one member country might be considered EU internal politics and vice versa.

3. This is especially true if one includes the quite substantial assistance provided by Austria after 1989 to the ex-Communist countries in general and in particular to its eastern neighbors and to the successor countries of Yugoslavia.

4. Some Austrian ambassadors to the United Nations are not among the many persons that Gehler interviewed for this book.

5. As reflected in the number of casualties they cause, these small weapons are the true weapons of mass destruction. Their proliferation was an essential prerequisite for the escalation of violence and civil war in Africa, for example.

6. In retrospect, it is evident that he accorded too small a role to the economic, social, and cultural developments that also define this world order.

7. Prominent among them is former general and Federal President Theodor Körner, for whom Kreisky had worked as secretary in the early 1950s.

8. In fact, as documents retrieved after 1989 show, this was indeed the case. In their scenarios of a central war, both the Warsaw Pact and the NATO forces envisioned the use of Austrian territory.

9. This was an eventuality which colored the reactions of at least some Austrian politicians and military members at the time of the Soviet invasion of Czechoslovakia in 1968.

10. This was his principal contribution to the new order of military defense and not, as Gehler claims, his organization of the small, highly mechanized *Bereitschaftstruppe*.

11. For example, former State Secretary and ÖVP parliamentarian Rudolf Steiner notes: "[O]ne kiss less for Arafat and one more trip to Brussels would have been useful [. . .]."

12. In his youth when still attending the Gymnasium, Kreisky had become member of the "Pan European Movement" of Coudenhove Kalergi. But there is a similar signal at the opposing stretch of his life, after the disintegration of the Soviet empire when, in an uneasy and somewhat resentful retirement, he bemoaned his having become powerless at this historic juncture, "Ah—to be younger and to be in politics again with the chance to become engaged in this vast project of building a truly united and integrated Europe [...]."

13. At that time, such a concept seemed conclusive. Today and in retrospect, it is clear that it relied too heavily on traditional strategic concepts, severely underestimating nonmilitary factors such as social and cultural developments or the impediments to such developments. This is a failure reflected, too, in the simplistic notion that it would just take the addition of money through a new "Marshall Plan" to advance the economic development of Third World countries. Yet if one holds this criticism against Kreisky, one would have to hold it even more strongly against American neo-conservatives and their naïve belief in the reach and effects of military power. Kreisky was aware, at least and forty years before them, that next to military power, economic power was important, too.

14. Thus also supporting the German Social Democratic Chancellor Helmut Schmid with whom otherwise relations were not as cordial as with his predecessor Willy Brandt.

15. They were foreseen, for example, by the group of European "foreign policy planners" in conferences in which I participated. As mentioned elsewhere (p. 694), Austrian military planners had also predicted them. This is one of the rather frequent contradictions in the book.

16. With such support from the leading media, Foreign Minister Alois Mock very consciously made this "wedge issue" in one of his repeated attempts first to weaken and then to dissolve the coalition with the Social Democrats for which he wanted to substitute a coalition with the FPÖ (an aim later realized by his successor, Wolfgang Schüssel).

Fritz Fellner and Doris A. Corradini, eds., *Österreichische Geschichtswissenschaft im 20. Jahrhundert: Ein biographisch-bibliographisches Lexikon* (Vienna: Böhlau, 2006)

Günter Bischof

It behooves a profession to be self-reflective, to take stock of its practitioners and leaders, and to produce historical perspectives on itself; this is especially true for the historical profession that usually presents its views on everybody else. This is generally done in the form of dictionaries of national biographies, *Gelehrtenlexika*, *Who's Who*, and so forth. Fritz Fellner, one of the "grand old men" of the Austrian historical profession in post-World War II Austria and long-time professor of modern history at the University of Salzburg, notes that he has had a life-long interest in the biographies of historians and issues of Austrian historiography,[1] ever since he edited the diaries of the historian and politician Josef Redlich as a young scholar. So the idea of a biographic dictionary simmered in his mind for much of his professional life. In retirement, he finally had time on his hands; with Doris Corradini he found a collaborator to begin systematizing and archiving a massive set of biographical data of Austrian historians in the twentieth century.

As Fellner explains in an exceptionally lucid introduction (pp. 7-15), the challenge was who goes in and who stays out. The criteria he adopted was to concentrate on professional historians who have been teaching at the university level (*Dozenten* and chairs, associate and full professors), archivists and museum professionals, as well as historians with no jobs in academia, and professional writers and journalists who produced multiple volumes of histories. Friedrich Heer (pp. 173f), a giant among twentieth-century Austrian historians, as well as the Austrian "Barbara Tuchman" Brigitte Hamann (p. 163), and universalist cultural historians Egon Friedell (pp. 131f) and Erik Kuehnelt-Leddihn (p. 245) are good examples of the latter. Archeologists with their close association to ancient and medieval history, as well as political scientists producing contemporary and intellectual history such as Anton Pelinka (pp. 311f) and Norbert Leser (p. 255) were included. Scholars of literary, linguistic, and music histories, however, were excluded. Legal and art historians, especially if their careers were launched by attending the rigorous training of the *Institut für österreichische Geschichtsforschung* (IÖG), show up in this dictionary, too. A line had to be drawn somewhere, so the small army of gifted historians writing local, regional, national, and international history were not included. In the past, they may have been amateurish "*Heimatforscher*," but no more.

Today some of the most talented university-trained historians of the younger generation in Austria are not directly affiliated with universities or archives and are, thus, no-shows in this dictionary. Austrian universities (and the Federal Ministry of Research) for the past generation have miserably failed to offer jobs to an entire generation of historians that they trained; many of them survive on grants to pursue their professional interests as historians. Among them are top-notch researchers working for Boltzmann Institutes, like the one in Graz for the study of the consequences of war ("*Kriegsfolgenforschung*"). While its prolific director Stefan Karner, who is also a professor at the University of Graz, is listed (p. 212f), his talented team and publication collaborators Barbara Stelz-Marx, Peter Ruggenthaler, and Harald Knoll are not. Neither is the terrific Graz historian Johannes Feichtinger, who is affiliated with important projects, but not the university there. Martin Kofler is the most prolific historian on East Tyrolese history in particular and a frequent contributor to Austrian Cold War history in general, as well as one of the great champions of recent Austrian history as the editor of contemporary history at the *StudienVerlag* in Innsbruck. Gerald Steinacher is one of the most distinguished historians of World War II and Cold War intelligence history in Central Europe, as well as an internationalist-minded historian of the South Tyrolese region and a non-IÖG trained archivist in Bozen. Meinrad Pichler, Harald Walser, and Eugen Dreier are high school teachers and founders of the "Malin Society" in Vorarlberg, a highly active group in regional contemporary history of the entire transnational Lake Constance area. Werner Koroschitz and Lisa Rettl do not shy away from engaging reluctant Carinthians in controversial World War II discourses via exhibits in the Villach City Museum. Georg Rigele is one of the top environmental and technology historians

320   **The Changing Austrian Voter**

in Austria and a frequent producer of important and popular historical exhibitions in Vienna and Lower Austria. Erwin Schmidl did not fill out his questionnaire. But his prolific collaborators in the historical section of the Austrian Ministry of Defense Walter Blasi and Felix Schneider were apparently not asked to fill one out. Wilfried Garscha from the *Dokumentationsarchiv des Österreichischen Widerstandes* in Vienna is listed (p. 137); Claudia Kuretsidis-Haider his outstanding collaborator and co-founder of the research group on postwar judicial history is not. These and many other university-trained younger historians are missing in this dictionary. They are dedicated to the profession, and some are more productive than those included. However, they were unlucky in being born into a time when fewer university positions became available. By excluding them from this dictionary, an elitist university-centered profession is ignoring them twice.

Numerous biographies in this volume make it clear that attending and passing the vaunted three-year course of the IÖG—the Austrian Institute of Historical Research—affiliated with the History Department of the University of Vienna has acted as the principal gatekeeper of access to top university or archival careers in Austria for much of the twentieth century. I cannot think of similar institutions anywhere in the Western world that play this unique mediating role in the profession. The biographies of many historians are included whose careers began to prosper early in the twentieth century at universities and archives in present day Austria who were born in the nineteenth century throughout the vast domains of the Habsburg Monarchy. This seems to have given Austrian universities access to a much larger—today we would say multicultural—talent pool all the way into the interwar period than was the case after 1945 in the small monolithic and homogenous Austria created in 1918. Historians born between 1840 and 1970 thus made it into this dictionary. Fellner and Corradini have been collecting data on some 3,000 historians, among them some 460 questionnaires collected from currently active historians (this one included, pp. 58f); they promise that these data will eventually become available online as well. They are clearly disappointed that 240 of 700 questionnaires sent out were not returned despite multiple invitations. One wonders why colleagues refused to cooperate. Did they consider it an exercise in vanity rather than professional stock-taking? Whatever the case, in the end 1,040 biographies are published in this valuable dictionary.

As a prosopography of the Austrian historical profession, these bios make for fascinating reading; in fact, for a dictionary, this is book is hard to put down once you begin perusing it. What ends up in these biographies is as absorbing as what is missing. Without doing hard data analysis, much of what one learns about the historical profession in Austria remains impressionistic. As in the rest of the world, the historical profession seems to have been largely a male domain in the first half of the twentieth century. It began opening up to women after World War II when higher education became more accessible to all segments of the Austrian population and growing numbers of women entered all professions. It would be interesting to analyze how much the rigorous demands of the historical profession (like careerism in other professions) hindered women from starting families too.[2] One of the strengths of this dictionary is its presentation of personal data on family and social background. One might be surprised how many aristocrats entered the profession in the nineteenth century.

Was there more professional mobility prior to World War I? Across borders, cross-hiring between the lands of the Habsburg Monarchy and Wilhelmine Germany was more apparent in this era than after World War II (the interwar years are a transition period in more ways than one). This might have been due to the fact that in the bourgeois Central Europe of the late Monarchy the tradition of continuing the old "gentleman's tour" and studying at a number of the great universities in German-speaking lands was still alive and well. More historians, such as Josef Redlich or Robert Heine-Geldern, studied for a few semesters at German universities than seems to be the case today. In post-World War II Austria, talented young historians like Grete Klingenstein or Gerald Stourzh tended to study on Fulbright scholarships or other programs in the United States rather than in the Federal Republic. One is also left with the impression that the younger generations of Austrian postwar historians are not more mobile than their predecessors despite many more opportunities to study abroad. Most of them end up working at the university from which they received their doctoral degrees.

The biggest mystery in these biographies are the war years of the historians born in the 1910s and 1920s when careers were being interrupted (how many were ended we will never know). Fritz Fellner's own entry is representative of this cohort (pp. 119f). Born in 1922, he began his studies in history at the University of Vienna in 1940, which were suspended by service in Hitler's *Wehrmacht*. These years tersely appear as "*[1941-1946 Kriegsdienst u. -gefangenschaft]*." One is left wondering in which theaters of war he and the many other historians who are listed served. In the collection of his historiographical essays, we learn in the introduction that he fought on the Eastern front (reading notes on Srbik's lectures sent by a friend to the frontline!). Ever since the *"Wehrmachtsaustellung"* traveling through Austria and Germany in the later 1990s, all kinds of problematical issues have been raised about *Wehrmacht* war crimes on this front.[3] I remember him telling me years ago about being a prisoner of war in an open-field American cage in Italy at the end of the war. The same was true of my beloved teacher of ancient history at the University of Innsbruck, Franz Hampl, born in 1910 in Bozen (pp. 164f). This erudite Renaissance man trained at the University of Leipzig and had his first appointment at the University of Giessen before he was drafted into the *Wehrmacht*. Again in his entry is the terse comment *"[1942-1945 Kriegsdienst u. – gefangenschaft]."* I recall him talking glowingly in his fabulous Innsbruck lectures about serving as an officer in the Italian theater and having the opportunity to walk the entire battlefield of Cannae. Clearly, these men would have preferred to study or teach at the university rather than sacrifice the best years of their lives fighting in Hitler's war of expansion and extermination. Yet their generation had been fated to be warriors. Those lucky enough to be "born later" should not be judgmental about their wartime service. Yet we, as historians, are also fated to be curious.

Then there are the ringing silences in some biographies. Ludwig Jedlicka, born in 1916 (p. 205), is known as one of the "fathers" of Austrian *Zeitgeschichte*, being appointed to the first director of contemporary history at the University of Vienna in 1961 (upgraded to chair in 1969). After receiving his doctorate from the University of Vienna in 1939, his entry notes *"1941 "Kustos Heeresgeschichtliches Museum"* and then *"1945-53 Lektor Furche- Verlag."* Oliver Rathkolb has only recently demonstrated that Jedlicka was the proverbial cat with many lives. He was the quintessential Austrian Nazi careerist and survivalist in dramatically changing political worlds. He proudly joined the *Hitler Jugend* in 1930 and the National Socialist Party in Austria in 1935 when it was illegal. When the Nazis took over Austria, he thus could claim to be an *"alter Kämpfer"* and embark on a career as a Nazi and escape the frontlines. He worked for the cultural office of the City of Vienna and then the Military History Museum and ended up as a propagandist for the Nazis. Studying in the mid-1930s with professors of the vaunted *grossdeutsche* "Vienna school," many of whom were close to the Nazis,[4] most embarrassing is the fact that his adviser, Heinrich von Srbik, only reluctantly passed Jedlicka's anemic ninety-five page dissertation in 1939 because he feared repercussions from the Nazi party! All of this was conveniently silenced after the war until Rathkolb brought it back to light.[5] The background of the Nazi careerist Taras Borodajkewycz, one of Jedlicka's wartime mentors, is similarly muted. Forced to retire at the end of the war, he made it back into the profession by 1955. He was a rare case of being forced into early retirement a second time in 1965 for preaching anti-Semitism in his lectures at the *Hochschule für Welthandel* in Vienna in 1965 (p. 63). In Austria, the punishment for these Nazis in academic garb was never too severe as evidence by the fact that they usually collected their full handsome pensions. In the case of Johannes Hollnsteiner (p. 194), who was a friar and left his order in 1941 when he became the historian for the *Gau Oberdonau* in 1941, the incarceration in the American internment camp in Glasenbach (1945-1947) is recorded. A few did pay a higher price for their service to the Nazi state.

While Austrian historians in the twentieth century clearly were swept up in the cauldron of wars and the serendipity of changing regimes, some adapted to the prevailing political winds more keenly than others. Franz Huter, born in 1899 (p. 200), served both in World War I and briefly in World War II. He was appointed to a professorship at the University of Innsbruck in 1941—where he wrote the *grossdeutsche* nationalistic people's history ("*volkstümelende 'Volksgeschichte'*") so prevalent not only in Vienna but in the provinces as well[6]—and was fired in 1945. Reappointed in 1950, his colleagues in Innsbruck did not mind his wartime "service" and elected him dean in 1959/60. Otto Brunner, born in 1898, had climbed to the peak of the historical profession in Austria with his appointment as the director of the *Institut für österreichische Geschichtsforschung* during the war. Fired in 1945,[7] he retired in 1948, only to see his career revived with the appointment to the chair of medieval history at the University of Hamburg, where in 1959/60 his colleagues also voted him in as *Rektor* (p. 70). These 1934, 1938, and 1945 purges in the historical profession are subtexts in this dictionary, too, but less easily discernible than other stations on the career track.[8]

Not only are the Nazi years muted in many bios; other political activities are glossed over as well. Reinhard Farkas, born in 1954 (p. 118), a high school classmate of mine in Bregenz, worked for the Austrian Communist Party after his graduation, before he embarked on his career as a historian at the University of Graz in the 1980s. His years as a communist *appartschik* are recorded tongue-in-cheek as having spent time in "private business" ("*1974-80 privatwirtschaftl. Tätigkeit Wien u. Bregenz*"); his training as a communist in Moscow is swept under the carpet.

Emigration and exile is another prominent theme discernible in these biographies. In the cohort of historians coming of age in the interwar years, some served the Nazis more or less reluctantly, many were persecuted for political (cf. Joseph Buttinger, pp. 75f) or "racial" reasons; they lost their jobs and were forced to flee their native country in order to save their lives. The distinguished list of Viennese Jews forced to flee Austria and embarking on splendid careers in Great Britain and the United States after World War II is long. Ernst Badian, born in 1925, survived the war in New Zealand, received his degrees in ancient history at Oxford, and ended his career as the John Moors Cabot Professor at Harvard (p. 46). (Sir) Ernst Gombrich, born in 1909, received his doctorate in art history from Vienna and immigrated to London in 1936, where he became director of the prestigious Warburg Institute. Robert Kann, born in 1906, received his doctorate in law from the University of Vienna and his doctorate in history from Columbia University to embark on a stellar career as a historian of the Habsburg Empire at Rutgers University (p. 210). Friedrich Katz, born in 1927, spent the war years in Mexico and returned to Vienna for his doctorate. His career as one of the most distinguished scholars of Mexico alive led him via Berlin to the University of Chicago where he retired as the Morton D. Hull Distinguished Service Professor (p. 215). Peter Pulzer, born 1929, studied at the London School of Economics and Cambridge and taught at Oxford, and was appointed Gladstone Professor of Government, one of the most elevated chairs in British academia (p. 330). Eric Voegelin, born in 1901 in Cologne, was a law student and assistant of Hans Kelsen's in Vienna in the early 1920s. Being fired from the staff of the University of Vienna in 1938, he spent the war years as an itinerant instructor at various American universities and ended up teaching political theory at Louisiana State University in Baton Rouge. He was appointed a Boyd Professor, the rare and highest honor the LSU system had to offer to its faculty. He returned to teach at the University of Munich in 1958 and ended his career as a fellow of the Hoover Institution at Stanford (p. 431). Heinrich Benedikt, born 1886, emigrated to the United Kingdom during the war and returned to the University of Vienna to receive one of the rare appointments in 1947 for an émigré scholar (p. 54), just like Friedrich Engel-Janossi (pp. 113f) who survived the war at American University and returned to Vienna in 1959 as an honorary professor.[9] Frederick Engelmann made his career at the University of Alberta in Canada (pp. 114f), George Kent at the University of Maryland (p. 217), Siegfried Pollak/Sidney Pollard at Bielefeld in Germany (pp. 323f), and Albert Hollaender at the Guildhall Library in London (pp. 193f). This cohort is proof of the egregious losses of top talent Austria suffered as a result of both the Nazi madness and the failure by the often narrow-minded political and academic postwar elite to invite these scholars back to teach and research in Austria. This dictionary carefully read thus adds to the growing literature on Austria's partially self-inflicted "brain drain": the wholesale loss of a generation of intellectual elites.[10]

Can one discern any methodological trends and/or creative innovations to the historical sciences in the tribe of Austrian twentieth-century historians?[11] The distinguished school of "historical social sciences" initiated by Michael Mitterauer (pp. 286f) at the University of Vienna comes to mind (also a graduate of the *Institut für österreichische Geschichtsforschung,* or IÖG). The Gombrichs and Katzs initiated their creative scholarship in their American and British exiles. Inspirational trendsetters such as Michel Foucault, Fernand Braudel, Edward Thompson, and Joan Scott do not seem to have sprung from the womb of the Austrian historical profession. Why not? Was it that the *Institut für österreichische Geschichtsforschung* mentioned above has been proliferating a hidebound positivistic paradigm of close textual reading of documents rather than the study of subtexts? Fellner himself makes this point in another of his publications.[12] Rather than exiting its students with the fashions of poststructuralist, linguistic, gender, and cultural studies "turns," the IÖG gave a premium to initiating its students into the editing and interpretation of imperial edicts and papal bulls. (I, too, sat in a medieval history seminar by an IÖG graduate in Innsbruck were students were terrorized with exact translations and textual interpretations of obscure heretical texts from medieval Latin). Familiarizing students with creative new historical methodologies was not given a high premium. Is it the IÖG's goal in punching the admissions tickets to the profession to squash the thrill of innovative methodologies in the historical profession in Austria? There are, of course, young historians who eagerly absorb the new methodologies far removed from the IÖG, but they usually are not appointed to university chairs to help spread these new ideas. Much of the excitement about new approaches to history comes from new non-university affiliated, internationally recognized institutions such as the *Institut für Kulturwissenschaften* and the *Institut für die Wissenschaften vom Menschen* in Vienna. The prestigious chairs have for a long time come from the tightly-knit fraternity of IÖG graduates; this is one of the subtexts of this dictionary as well.

In spite of the drawbacks mentioned above, the historical profession owes Fritz Fellner and Doris Corradini (incidentally both graduates of the IÖG) a debt of gratitude for their "grunt work" in compiling this dictionary of the historical profession in Austria—and the *Kommmission für Neuere Geschichte Österreichs* for publishing this volume in its publications series. It will be a key reference work for a long time to come, especially if these biographies will be updated online, and every self-respecting library and member of the Austrian fraternity of historians should own a copy.

Notes

1. Fritz Fellner recently published his many path-breaking essays on Austrian historiography in his volume *Geschichtsschreibung und nationale Identität: Probleme und Leistungen der österreichischen Geschichtswissenschaft* (Vienna: Böhlau, 2002). In fact, these erudite and, at times, opinionated essays can be read as complimentary texts, elucidating many of the issues implicit in the individual biographies of the dictionary. Corradini also served as an editorial assistance for this book (see p. 12). For a spirited recent broadside against a key essay in Fellner's book and his failure to critically investigate the Nazi affiliations and intellectual affinities of Austrian historians with Nazi *völkisch* history, see Alexander Pinwinkler, "Österreichs Historiker im Nationalsozialismus und in der frühen Zweiten Republik—eine ausgbliebene Debatte? Kritische Überlegungen zu Fritz Fellner's Essay 'Der Beitrag Österreichs zu Theorie, Methodik und Themen der Geschichte der Neuzeit," *Zeitgeschichte* 32 (January/February 2005): 35-46.

2. To his credit, Fellner was a postwar leader in Austrian academe in training and welcoming women to the profession; see his pioneering essay with valuable statistical annexes, "Frauen in der österreichischen Geschichtswissenschaft," in: idem, *Geschichtsschreibung und nationale Identität*, 92-128.

3. Ibid., 9. On the heated and polemical debates about the exhibition on *Wehrmacht* crimes committed on the Southeastern and Eastern European fronts in World War II, see Helga Embacher, Albert Lichtblau, and Günther Sander, eds., *Umkämpfte Erinnerung: Die Wehrmachtsausstellung in Salzburg* (Salzburg: Residenz Verlag, 1999).

4. For a competent survey of this group, see Gernot Heiss, "Von Österreichs deutscher Vergangenheit und Aufgabe: Die Wiener Schule der Geschichtswissenschaft und der Nationalsozialismus," in *Willfährige Wissenschaft: Die Universität Wien 1938 bis 1945*, ed. Gernot Heiss et al. (Vienna: Verlag für Gesellschaftskritik, 1989), 39-76. Fritz Fellner defends their scholarly contributions to German history and chides the younger generation of contemporary historians for ignoring their work and being obsessed with their "brown past," "Geschichte als Wissenschaft," 87ff.

5. Oliver Rathkolb, "Ludwig Jedlicka: Vier Leben und ein typischer Österreicher. Biographische Skizze zu einem Mitbegründer der Zeitgeschichteforschung," *Zeitgeschichte* 32 (November/December 2005): 351-70 (esp. 352-57). Rathkolb's sleuthing to discover Jedlicka's past may be a response to Fellner's attack against the entire generation of younger "self-righteous" contemporary historians for having ignored Jedlicka's Nazi past and for failing to be embarrassed about having been "proud recipients of a research prize named after this illegal National Socialist," "Geschichte als Wissenschaft," 88. I was a recipient of the Jedlicka Dissertation Prize in 1990.

6. Pinwinkler, "Österreichische Historiker im Nationalsozialismus," 39.

7. Next to Brunner, Wilhelm Bauer and Heinrich Srbik lost their chairs at the University of Vienna; Leo Santifaller, the fourth chair, also got into trouble for National Socialist content in one of his publications; see Heiss, "Von Österreichs deutscher Vergangenheit und Aufgabe," pp. 39ff.

8. Fellner oddly thinks that the purge of the conservative *grossdeutsche* historians in 1945 was more severe than the purge of the Jewish historians in 1938, "Geschichte als Wissenschaft," 80. Pinwinkler rightly takes him to task for it, noting that some historians may have lost their jobs but not their pensions, let alone their lives, in the purges after 1945; the purges of 1938 resulted both in the loss of jobs and *Heimat* and may also have resulted in state-sanctioned murder, see "Österreichische Historiker im Nationalsozialismus," 41.

9. See also Fellner's admirable portrait "Friedrich Engel-Janosi – 'un divin piacere', Ein Lebensbild," in *Geschichtsschreibung und nationale Identität*, 346-59.

10. For a more comprehensive survey of émigrés from all professions, see the massive volumes of Friedrich Stadler, ed., *Vertriebene Vernunft: Emigration und Exil österreichischer Wissenschaft*, 2 vols. (Vienna: Jugend und Volk, 1988); the historical profession's losses and portraits of émigré historians are in volume 2, pages 474-518; see also Johannes Feichtinger, *Wissenschaft zwischen den Kulturen: Österreichische Hochschullehrer in der Emigration 1933-1945* (Frankfurt am Main: Campus, 2001).

11. For further background on this very issue, see Fellner's comprehensive, "Geschichte als Wissenschaft," 36-91.

12. Ibid., 62.

ANNUAL REVIEW

Austria 2006

The BAWAG-ÖGB Disaster
The 2006 General Elections and the 2007 SPÖ-ÖVP Coalition Government
EU Presidency, January 2006
Topography in Carinthia: A Never-ending Story
Economic Data and Statistical Data
Final Note

Reinhold Gärtner

The BAWAG-ÖGB Disaster

The year 2006 seemed to be a good year for the SPÖ. In all the polls, the SPÖ had a comfortable lead over the ÖVP. In addition, the coalition partner FPÖ/BZÖ was completely preoccupied with internal disturbances, especially after the foundation of the BZÖ in April 2005. So the SPÖ's leadership could relax and wait for the 2006 State Diet Elections.

But something unexpected happened. In October 2005, the *Bank für Arbeit und Wirtschaft* (BAWAG) had given a loan to REFCO of some €425 million. The owner of BAWAG was the Austrian Trade Union, the *Österreichischer Gewerkschaftsbund* (ÖGB). Though the ÖGB is not a political party's union, it is clear that the ÖGB is dominated by the SPÖ. Thus what would become the most serious financial scandal in the Second Republic was immediately connected to the SPÖ.

BAWAG, the fourth largest Austrian bank, was founded in 1922 as the *Arbeiterbank* and was liquidated in 1934 for political reasons. In 1947 it was reopened and in 1963 renamed BAWAG. At the end of the 1980s, BAWAG managers began to perform controversial financial transactions, especially in the Caribbean. These transactions were stopped in 1994, but reinstated in 1995. The then-director general, Helmut Elsner, was responsible for this coup. In 2001, BAWAG bought *Postsparkasse* (P.S.K.), and in the same year, BAWAG's losses amounted some €1 billion. The ÖGB—still the owner of BAWAG—gave a guarantee for this loss, so BAWAG was able to continue to operate. In 1999 BAWAG had invested in REFCO with 10 percent stake; then it sold its REFCO stake in 2004 to the investment company Thomas Lee Partners. In August 2005, REFCO became a publicly traded company on the stock market and performed quite successfully during the first weeks. However, on 10 October 2005, Philip Bennett, head of the REFCO board, was released and the share price of REFCO started to sink. On 13 October, REFCO transactions were stopped, but on 16 October 2005, BAWAG gave this €425 million loan to REFCO. Soon after that, REFCO was insolvent. The finance control authority in Austria instituted official proceedings against BAWAG and its management, and in January 2006 Ewald Nowotny, professor for financial systems at the University of Linz, was appointed head of the board of directors of BAWAG. It was mainly due to Nowotny's knowledge and management that BAWAG was able to survive at all and could finally be sold at the end of 2006.

In April 2006, a warrant for Bennett's arrest was issued. In April, the Vienna criminal court began proceedings against Fritz Verzetnitsch, former head of the ÖGP and chairman of the board of BAWAG, and Günter Weninger, the head of ÖGB's finances. Also in April 2006, the ÖGB finally decided to sell BAWAG, and Morgan Stanley was engaged to carry out this sale. In the same month, REFCO creditors called in some €1 billion from BAWAG, and the new chairman of the ÖGB, Rudolf Hundsdorfer, called the ÖGB's present situation "dire." Nowotny asked for a settlement between the ÖGB and REFCO creditors, but REFCO creditors did not accept this proposal.

To avoid legal procedures against him, Helmut Elsner fled to his domicile in southern France. Until February 2007, he avoided extradition to Austria, but now he is back and in detention awaiting trial.

Interestingly, the ÖGB had close connections to REFCO. An ÖGB foundation, DESANA, held a 27 percent share of REFCO stock. In May 2006, REFCO creditors agreed to a provisional settlement: BAWAG's $1 billion in U.S. accounts were frozen. In June 2006, the media pointed out that the ÖGB's debts amounted some €2.4 billion. Finally, at the end of December 2006 BAWAG was sold to CERBERUS Capital Management.

What was criticized by many was the carelessness (or ignorance) of the ÖGB regarding financial management. The ÖBG's strike funds had been one of the bargaining chips of the ÖGB, and the actual amount of this fund has never been made public. The same ÖGB representatives who on many occasions criticized the dangers of neoliberal financial policies had participated in these transactions and, thus, gambled away billions of Euros. It was not really surprising, then, that the credibility of the ÖGB elites was seriously damaged after the publication of the extent of these crimes.

Contrary to the trade unions in the First Republic, since its foundation in 1945, the ÖGB has been a corporative trade union; thus all political parties can have their representatives in the executive bodies of the ÖGB. Despite its supraparty character, though, the public mainly considers the ÖGB to be a social democratic union. The reason for this is that the *Fraktion sozialdemokratischer Gewerkschafter* (FSG—SPÖ) is the most powerful group within the ÖGB both on a regional and on the national level. The *Fraktion christlicher Gewerkschafter* (FCG—ÖVP) is second and the strongest party in only one member union, the *Gewerkschaft der Privatangestellten* (GPA).

The head of the ÖGB has always been a member of the FSG. So it was not really surprising that the ÖVP tried to stoke the fire and make the BAWAG disaster an important topic in the election campaign. But the ÖVP had to be careful not to harp on this debacle lest it stir the electorate's feelings of mercy for the SPÖ.

So the election campaign had already begun long before it was officially announced (and even before the concrete date for the election was agreed upon).

Until the beginning of 2006, the SPÖ was—according to polls—more or less ahead of the ÖVP. With the publication of more and more pieces of information about the BAWAG debacle, though, the ÖVP was able to gain ground continuously and soon was first. Under these circumstances, it was not really surprising that almost no one in Austria thought that the SPÖ could finish first in the elections. The discussion was about the size of the gap between the ÖVP and SPÖ and about the very important question regarding whether the BZÖ would get at least 4 percent of the votes cast (or a seat in one of the regional electoral districts of Carinthia) and, thus, manage to get seats in the Diet.

But as is sometimes the case, things went differently than expected. The ÖVP election campaign was concentrated on the fact that very many things had been improved in the recent six years of the ÖVP/FPÖ

(ÖVP/BZÖ) government. But at least some voters didn't feel this to be true in their everyday lives, and the SPÖ concentrated more on social equality, on eradicating tuition fees at universities (which are quite moderate at approximately €730 per year), and on a retreat from the purchase of Eurofighters.

The BZÖ and the FPÖ were fighting for the same clientele with very strong xenophobic arguments (like the BZÖ's proposal to expel 300,000 foreigners, or the FPÖ's fierce attacks against Islam).

The 2006 General Election and the SPÖ-ÖVP Coalition Government, 2007

The result of the 2006 State Diet Elections was not really expected by very many: it was not the ÖVP which finished first, but the SPÖ.

Another interesting point was whether or not the BZÖ would manage to be represented in the new State Diet. The election in Austria is based on proportional vote, with a 4 percent hurdle, and most polls had the BZÖ unable to reach this percentage. The second possibility is to get a seat in one of the forty-three regional electoral districts, but it was very unlikely that the BZÖ would manage to get one. The only realistic chance was the district Carinthia East, in which the FPÖ had been relatively strong in the 2002 general elections. Ultimately, the BZÖ was successful: it got 4.1 per cent of the votes cast, but this was due to its strength in Carinthia (25.4 percent, with Governor Jörg Haider). In all of the other eight counties, the BZÖ was an almost negligible political party (netting between 1.7 and 3.3 percent of the vote). If the BZÖ had not managed to get seats in the State Diet, a SPÖ-Grüne coalition would have been possible (and very likely).

There was another political party of some interest: Hans Peter Martin's "Liste Matin." But Martin could get only 2.8 percent of the vote. Martin had been very successful in the European Parliamentary Elections in 2004, where he collected 14 percent of the vote (and came in third). In 2004, though, the populist arguments of Martin were successful because of the weakness of the FPÖ (which had gotten only 6.3 percent, in comparison to more than 23 percent in the 1999 European Parliamentary Elections). In 2004, Martin's only issue was misuse of privileges, but this was not enough to help him in the State Diet elections.

So the result of the elections was a five party parliament, and all of a sudden, Alfred Gusenbauer's SPÖ had the chance to nominate the new chancellor. Before that, though, it was necessary to find a coalition

Table 1
Election Results in Votes and Comparison of Votes Per Party in 2002 and 2006 in Percentage and Seats Won

Party	2006	2006		2002	
		Percentage	Seats	Percentage	Seats
SPÖ	1,663,986	35.3	68	36.5	69
ÖVP	1,616,493	34.3	66	42.3	79
FPÖ	519,598	11.04	21	10.0	18
Grüne	520,130	11.05	21	9.5	17
BZÖ	193,539	4.1	7	no candidacy	
Liste Matin	131,688	2.8	0	no candidacy	

Source: Ministry of the Interior; voter turnout was 78.5 percent.

partner. Theoretically, there were many possibilities for forming a new government; realistically, all options except an SPÖ-ÖVP coalition were very unlikely. The ÖVP could have formed a coalition with two of the smaller parties (Grüne, FPÖ, BZÖ). However, the Grüne Party was not willing to cooperate with either the FPÖ or BZÖ, and both the FPÖ and BZÖ had said on many occasions that neither of them would cooperate with a traitor. An SPÖ minority government would have needed the support of two smaller parties, too, and the SPÖ saw itself confronted with the same dilemma as the ÖVP. President Heinz Fischer (SPÖ) also favored an SPÖ-ÖVP coalition. According to the constitution, the Austrian president has the right to appoint a government; in practice, though, he does not insist on this right but appoints the chairman of the political party which has gained the majority of the seats in the State Diet to form a government which then is formally introduced by the president (the so-called *Rollenverzicht*—abandonment of role—of the president).

One obstacle for a new SPÖ-ÖVP coalition was the frozen atmosphere between these to parties which began after the coalition negotiations of 1999/2000. In 1999, the SPÖ finished first, but the third ranking ÖVP had formed a coalition with the second ranking FPÖ. Thus the SPÖ was still licking its wounds from 2000.

So Alfred Gusenbauer was in a position in which his election campaign promises were unlikely to be fulfilled. Moreover, the ÖVP was seemingly offended about the fact that the majority of the votes went to the SPÖ.

As a first step of the newly created *Nationalrat*, the SPÖ, together with the FPÖ and Grüne, planned to introduce an investigative committee to look into purchase of Eurofighter jets, a measure which the ÖVP did not see as constructive in establishing confidence between the two possible partners. On 30 October, this investigative committee was introduced, together with a second one which would examine the role of state financial observers in the BAWAG disaster and the role of other banks in East European transactions. The ÖVP said that it would not take part in further negotiations to form a new government until these two committees had finished their investigations. November went by, and so did December, but in December President Heinz Fischer invited Gusenbauer and still-Chancellor Schüssel (ÖVP) to open talks in his office, and the result was that Fischer was willing to appoint a now government on 11 January, which he did.

The negotiations brought some interesting results although SPÖ supporters in particular criticized them severely. Many could not understand why most of the important ministries (Interior, Foreign Affairs, Finance, Economics and Labor) were given to the ÖVP. In addition, the coalition agreement was criticized, too. Two of the SPÖ's main points in the election campaign were the removal of tuition fees at universities and the retreat from the purchase of Eurofighter jets, and in both cases, the SPÖ couldn't successfully achieve its goals. The final proposal was that tuition fees should be compensated by certain kinds of social work (comparable to Israel's Perah program), and the retreat from the Euro-fighter purchase seems at the moment to be very unlikely, too. Protests came from the socialist youth and the socialist students' organization.

EU Presidency, January 2006

From 1 January until 30 June 2006, Austria held the EU presidency for the second time (after the second half of 1998). One effort was to discuss the further proceedings in the appropriation of the EU constitution (which was not really successful; there are still no promising results to be seen among the EU member states). Another effort was to fix the details of the next budget of the European Union which was successful when a compromise among the member states was found (period 20072013). An outstanding result was the European Union–Latin America Summit which was held in Vienna.

Topography in Carinthia: A Never-ending Story

In Austria, there are six autochthonous minorities. According to *Volksgruppengesetz* (1976), these six minorities are recognized as *Volks-*

Table 2
Distribution of Cabinet Posts in the SPÖ-ÖVP Coalition Government

Position	Politician	Party
Federal Chancellor	Alfred Gusenbauer	SPÖ
Vice Chancellor	Wilhelm Molterer	ÖVP
Federal Minister of Finance	Wilhelm Molterer	ÖVP
Federal Minister of the Interior	Günther Platter	ÖVP
Federal Minister for European and International Affairs	Ursula Plassnik	ÖVP
Federal Minister for Economics and Labor	Martin Bartenstein	ÖVP
Federal Minister of Justice	Maria Berger	SPÖ
Federal Minister for Defense	Norbert Darabos	SPÖ
Federal Minister for Transport, Innovation, and Technology	Werner Faymann	SPÖ
Federal Minister for Science and Research	Johannes Hahn	ÖVP
Federal Minister for Education, Arts and Culture	Claudia Schmied	SPÖ
Federal Minister for Social Affairs and Consumer Protection	Erwin Buchinger	SPÖ
Federal Minister for Women, Media and Civil Service	Doris Bures	SPÖ
Federal Minister for Health, Family and Youth	Andrea Kdolsky	ÖVP
Federal Minister for Agriculture, Forestry, Environment, and Water Management	Josef Pröll	ÖVP
Secretary in the Federal Chancellery	Reinhold Lopatka	ÖVP
Secretary in the Federal Ministry of Finance	Christoph Maznetter	SPÖ
Secretary in the Federal Chancellery	Heidrun Silhavy	SPÖ
Secretary in the Federal Ministry for European and International Affairs	Hans Winkler	ÖVP
Secretary in the Federal Ministry for Transportation, Innovation, and Technology	Christa Kranzl	SPÖ
Secretary in the Federal Ministry for Economics and Labor	Christine Marek	ÖVP

Source: Bundeskanzleramt Österreich <http://www.austria.gv.at>.

gruppen. They are Slovenes (especially in Carinthia), Croatians and Hungarians in Burgenland, Slovaks and Czechs (especially in Vienna), and the group of Roma and Sinti.

In the State Treaty of Vienna (1955), the status of the minorities (especially Slovenes and Croatians) was explicitly mentioned (Art. 7). Above all, their right to have bilingual topographical signs was protected.

But nothing happened. A first attempt to introduce these bilingual signs (October 1972) was followed by attacks perpetrated by Carinthian nationalists who irrationally feared a "Slovenization" of Carinthia (the bilingual sings were removed immediately after being erected). Again, not much happened. A few bilingual signs were erected, but there were still very many villages housing a considerable Slovenian population which had only German names on its topographical signs.

In December 2001, the Supreme Court (*Verfassungsgerichtshof*) decided that in villages with a Slovene population of more than 10 percent topographical signs had to be bilingual. But Jörg Haider insisted on German place name signs, saying that bilingual signs would not be erected as long as he was governor of Carinthia. In 2005, the year celebrating the fiftieth anniversary of the State Treaty of Vienna, new attempts were made to erect bilingual signs, but they are still not present in a widespread and thorough way.

The conflict (and the irrational fears of parts of the German-speaking majority of Carinthia) goes back to the years after World War I. In those days, fights occurred at the border between Carinthia and Slovenia, and in a referendum in October 1920, the people were asked to decide whether they would prefer to stay with Austria or become part of Slovenia. The vast majority voted for Austria, but it is often forgotten that the vast majority of Slovenes in Carinthia voted for Austria, too.

The tensions between Slovenian- and German-speaking Carinthians also go back to the Second World War. During the Second World War, many massacres were committed, especially among the Slovenian population. In April 1942, the mass expulsion of Slovenian Carinthians began; they were forced to leave their homes and were deported to the "*Altreich.*"

Though many Slovenian Carinthians were soldiers of the *Deutsche Wehrmacht*, they and their families began to fight for the resistance when they heard about the crimes being committed in Carinthia. But after the liberation from National Socialism, this resistance was often seen (especially by *Kärntner Heimatdienst*, a German nationalist organization in Carinthia) as anti-Austrian, although, in fact, it worked for the country's liberation from National Socialism.

Economic and Statistical Data

Inflation was at 1.5 percent in 2006 (compared to 2.3 percent in 2005); HVPI was at 1.7 percent (it was at 2.1 percent in 2005, while the

EU average for 2006 was 2.2 percent). The public deficit amounted 1.5 percent in 2005 (€3.709 billion; 1.2 percent in 2004), and public debts amounted to 63.3 percent (€155 billion; 63.8 percent in 2004).

In 2005, GNP was €29.800 per capita (compared to €28.900 in 2004). In 2005, imports amounted to €96.499 million (€72.397 for the EU 25) and exports amounted to €94.705 million (€67.414 for the EU 25; €91.094 million and €89.848 million in 2004, respectively). Imports from NAFTA were €3.729 million; exports to NAFTA amounted to €6.384 million.

In 2006, 3,280,000 people in Austria were employed (compared to 3,228,000 in 2005), among them were some 390,000 foreigners (compared to 373,700 in 2005). The rate of unemployment was lower at 6.8 percent (compared to 7.3 percent in 2005). According to the International Labour Organization, the rate of unemployment was at 4.8 percent in 2006 versus 5.2 percent in 2005. The EU average in 2006 was 7.3 percent for the EU Fifteen, and 7.9 percent for the EU Twenty-Five). Among foreigners, the rate of unemployment was at 9.8 percent, compared to 10.6 percent in 2005.

At the end of 2005, 8,265,900 people were living in Austria. Among them were 7,451,900 Austrians and 814,100 foreigners, including 308,900 from the former Yugoslavia and 113,600 Turks.

In 2005, 78,190 children were born in Austria, and 75,189 people died. Those born in Austria, though, are not automatically Austrian citizens because Austria's citizenship law is based on *ius sanquinis* (in contrast to *ius soli* which is the case, for example, in the United States), which means that children being born in Austria do not automatically get Austrian citizenship, but the same citizenship as their parents. According to the 2001 census, some 120,000 people being born in Austria did not have Austrian citizenship. Life expectancy is at 76.65 years for men and 82.24 years for women.

Final Note

The year 2006 saw a large change in the community of political scientists in Austria. In September 2006, Anton Pelinka left the University of Innsbruck. From 1975 to 2006, Pelinka, a long-time co-editor of *Contemporary Austrian Studies*, had been professor of Political Science at the University of Innsbruck, and he certainly is Austria's most well-known political scientist. Pelinka has been a visiting professor at many universities, among them New Delhi, Michigan, Harvard, and Stanford, and he is now teaching at the Central European University in Budapest.

List of Authors

Matthew Paul Berg is an associate professor of history, John Carroll University in Cleveland, Ohio.

Peter Berger is a professor of history at the Institute of Social and Economic History, University of Economics and Business Administration, Vienna, Austria

Günter Bischof is the chair and Marshall Plan Professor of History and the director of CenterAustria, University of New Orleans

Rudolf Bretschneider is the managing director of GfK Austria (Institute for Market and Opinion Research) and lecturer, University of Vienna, Austria.

Herbert Dachs is a professor of political science, University of Salzburg, Austria.

Thomas Fischer is a research affiliate with the Austrian Institute for International Affairs (ÖIIP) and visiting lecturer, University of Vienna, Austria.

Reinhold Gärtner is a professor of political science, University of Innsbruck, Austria.

Peter Gerlich is a professor of political science, University of Vienna, Austria.

Christoph Hofinger is the co-founder and scientific director of the Institute for Social Research and Analysis (SORA), Vienna, Austria.

Alexander Lassner is an assistant professor of strategy at the Air War College, Maxwell AFB, Montgomery, Alabama.

Günther Lengauer is the head of the research department of Media Watch, Institute for Media Analysis, Innsbruck, Austria.

Kurt Richard Luther is a senior lecturer in politics at the Keele University and convenor of the Keele European Parties Research Unit (KEPRU), United Kingdom.

Thomas Nowotny is a retired Austrian diplomat and lecturer at the Institute for Political Science, University of Vienna, Austria, and senior consultant at the Austrian *Wirtschaftsservice* (AWS).

Günther Ogris is the co-founder and scientific director of the Institute for Social Research and Analysis (SORA), Vienna, Austria.

Imma Palme is the executive director of the Institute of Empirical Social Research (*Institut für Empirische Sozialforschung – IFES*) in Vienna, Austria

Anton Pelinka is professor of political science emeritus, University of Innsbruck, Austria, and professor of political science at the Central European University of Budapest, Hungary

Fritz Plasser is professor of political science and dean of the faculty of political science and sociology, University of Innsbruck, Austria.

Manfred Prisching is professor of sociology at the University of Graz, Austria, and a member of the Austrian Academy of Sciences.

Oliver Rathkolb is the director of the Ludwig Bolzmann Institute for European History and Public Spheres in Vienna, Austria, and lecturer at the Institute for Contemporary History, University of Vienna, Austria.

Peter Ruggenthaler is a senior researcher at the Ludwig Boltzmann Institut für Kriegsfolgen-Forschung, Graz, Austria

Gilg Seeber is a professor in the department of political science, University of Innsbruck, Austria.

Peter A. Ulram is a research manager at GfK-Austria (Institute for Market and Opinion Research) and professor of political science, University of Vienna, Austria.

Eva Zeglovits is the head of the Elections & Politics research department at the Institute for Social Research ant Analysis (SORA), Vienna, Austria.

Contemporary Austrian Studies

Günter Bischof and Fritz Plasser, Editors
Transaction Publishers, New Brunswick (N.J.) and London (U.K)

Volume 1 (1993)
Austria in the New Europe

Volume 2 (1994)
The Kreisky Era in Austria
Oliver Rathkolb, Guest Editor

Volume 3 (1995)
Austria in the Nineteen Fifties
Rolf Steininger, Guest Editor

Volume 4 (1996)
*Austro-Corporatism: Past –
Present – Future*

Volume 5 (1997)
*Austrian Historical Memory &
National Identity*

Volume 6 (1998)
Women in Austria
Erika Thurner, Guest Editor

Volume 7 (1999)
The Vranitzky Era in Austria
Ferdinand Karlhofer, Guest Editor

Volume 8 (2000)
The Marshall Plan in Austria
Dieter Stiefel, Guest Editor

Volume 9 (2001)
Neutrality in Austria
Ruth Wodak, Guest Editor

Volume 10 (2002)
Austria and the EU
Michael Gehler, Guest Editor

Volume 11 (2003)
*The Dollfuss/Schuschnigg Era in
Austria. A Reassessment*
Alexander Lassner, Guest Editor

Volume 12 (2004)
*The Americanization/
Westernization of Austria*

Volume 13 (2005)
Religion in Austria
Hermann Denz, Guest Editor

Volume 14 (2006)
*Austrian Foreign Policy in
Historical Perspective*
Michael Gehler, Guest Editor

Volume 15 (2007)
Sexuality in Austria
Dagmar Herzog, Guest Editor